Getting Things Done in Washington

Getting Things Done in Washington

Lessons for Progressives from Landmark Legislation

Joseph H. Boyett, Ph.D.

Author of *Won't Get Fooled Again: A Voters Guide to Seeing Through the Lies, Getting Past the Propaganda, and Choosing the BEST LEADERS*

ASJA Press
Bloomington

Getting Things Done in Washington
Lessons for Progressives from Landmark Legislation

ASJA Press
an imprint of iUniverse, Inc.

iUniverse books may be ordered through booksellers or by contacting:

iUniverse
1663 Liberty Drive
Bloomington, IN 47403
www.iuniverse.com
1-800-Authors (1-800-288-4677)

ISBN: 978-1-4502-9472-0 (sc)
ISBN: 978-1-4620-0064-7 (dj)
ISBN: 978-1-4502-9650-2 (ebk)

Library of Congress Control Number: 2011902456

Printed in the United States of America

iUniverse rev. date: 03/23/2011

CONTENTS

Introduction

This book is for liberals, progressives, and social democrats—all those who believe we can and should use the power of government to improve the lives of all Americans and who are disappointed that so often, particularly recently, government has not achieved that most important of missions. I want to accomplish three things with this book. First, I want through the stories that follow to inspire you as a fellow progressive or just someone who wants to get things done in Washington. Progressives and Americans in general everywhere are feeling somewhat disheartened today after the struggles over the last few years. I know I am. We expected so much from the audacity of hope and got so little. We expected the fight for change to be hard but we did not expect it to be this hard. I want to lift your spirit by revisiting hard fought legislative battles in the past that we won. I want to renew your faith in the possibilities of change by reminding you that our fathers, mothers, grandfathers and grandmothers who shared our desire to use the power of government to make the lives of their fellow Americans better won great victories. If they did it, we can too. I want to inspire you to commit to the struggle for what is right, not just for this year or this political season but also for your lifetime. I want you to commit to our country's future. I want to inspire you to do so by telling you the stories of your parents, grandparents and great grandparents that did just such a thing. There is a way forward if we are prepared to take it.

Second with this book, I want to derive lessons from these historic legislative accomplishments. I want to give you a set of actionable steps, things you can start doing to win current and future legislative battles. I want to give you a manual for getting things done in Washington.

Finally, I want to remind you of what this country was like before the legislation I discuss in this book was passed. Conservatives always engage in nostalgia about returning to the good old days of small government and limited, or no, federal regulation. I want to remind you of what it was really like to live in our country when the federal government was weak and the states were strong. I want to remind you what it was like when there was no federal oversight of the food and drug industry. I want to remind you what it was like when elderly people had no access to affordable health insurance. I want to remind you what it was like when labor had no rights to organize or fight for decent wages and working conditions. I want to remind you what it was like when there were no limits on big business and when minorities had no civil rights. I intend this book to be a history lesson and wake-up call. Conservatives say they want to take back the country. What they really want to do is send the country back, send it back to some very dark days. They will accomplish that goal if we let them. We must not.

Take heart. There have been moments in America's political history when the nation might never have progressed or would have taken a decidedly different course except for the political acumen and personal sacrifice of certain individuals who against great odds got things done in Washington. In each case, success was by no means certain and often was in doubt until virtually the last moment when a few individuals were able to persuade others of the wisdom of one direction for the country rather than another. There have been times in our history during which Americans just like you made impossible legislative action not just possible but reality. Legislation that no one thought could pass did and the country was fundamentally changed. This is the story of those times and more.

I have chosen the legislative achievements covered in this book for several reasons. First, of course, I chose them because they were great legislative achievements that literally changed the lives of all Americans. Second, they contain powerful lessons concerning the way our government works and often fails to work. Third, they involved social and political topics that we struggle with as a country even today such as access to healthcare, the right of labor to organize, the regulation of big business, protecting the safety of our food supply and, of course, civil rights. Finally, I chose these accomplishments because sufficient time has passed so that the historical record of what happened and why is more complete than it is for more recent legislative achievements.

This is not just a book about glorious moments in our history or near super-human achievement, although it certainly discusses such things. It is a story about lessons we can learn in a free society about what it takes to right wrongs, move forward, and make this country a better nation. It is about sacrifice, compromise, faith, struggle, confidence, hard work, political smarts, and, most importantly, perseverance—not giving up. These are the stories of men and women who triumphed over inertia, who found a way to achieve the common good through the elevation of common purpose and desire. These are the stories of men and women who took us forward when we could have stood still or skidded backward. These are the stories of men and women who seized the moment and in the face of disaster when we could have fallen apart as a nation or sunk into the meaningless pursuit of selfishness showed us how we could achieve. This book examines the lessons that we can learn from these remarkable moments in American history. This is the story of men and women who rose above the pressures of their day to find pathways to take them, their followers and their country into a new world. A nation that forgets these people and their lessons of political and legislative accomplishment is a nation that will not reward or attract the quality of men and women we need to legislate in the future. We remember the fruits of their labors— the protections of the food and drug administration, anti-trust laws, the right of labor to organize, the Civil Rights Acts, Medicare, and so on—but we forget the struggle and the men and women who fought to make these protections and freedoms a reality. We appreciate their accomplishments but forget just how miraculous their accomplishments were. We have not learned from their experiences.

Today the challenge of legislative accomplishment looms larger than ever. Factions proliferate. The corrupting force of money for influence is stronger than ever. The manipulation of the media is pervasive and more sophisticated. The use of known psychology of influence is more problematic. Propaganda artfully disguised as truth is more widespread. All sides on every issue use these weapons of persuasion resulting in every side persuading just enough of those in the middle to keep the other side from winning. No side wins and we all lose. We cannot go forward, not because we have no forward path, but because we have multitudes of paths all blocked by one interest or another. We are at stalemate. Has it always been that way? No. In fact, this nation exists and much of the protections and freedoms we enjoy rest on a foundation of great legislative accomplishment, not legislative gridlock.

LESSONS ABOUT GETTING THINGS DONE

Given all of the institutional and societal barriers to getting anything of substance done in Washington, it is amazing that anything truly important has ever gotten done. However, major change has occurred, not often and not without tremendous effort, but it has occurred. That is what this book is about. It is the story of men and women who found a way to accomplish meaningful change in public policy against great odds and the lessons they can teach us.

If you are interested in politics, particularly if you are a progressive interested in harnessing the power of government for the common good then you should find this book very interesting and informative. Even if you are not interested in politics that much, I think you will find value in what follows. Most of us go through life trying to accomplish something of value. After all, what is the point of life without accomplishment? Washington is one of the most difficult places in the world to accomplish anything so any accomplishment there contains lessons that have a broader implication.

As we examine their accomplishments, we will discover a number of important lessons these stories teach us about what achieving real change in public policy demands. For example,

1. Grassroots organizing—One of the key lessons we'll learn from the stories in this book is that real change never starts getting done in

Washington. In fact, if you leave getting things done to Washington, nothing will ever get done. Contrary to what they might say, most people do not run for office to get things done. They run for office to fulfill their own personal need for power, prestige, position, and so on. They run for office and run for office and run for office to get the office, not to get things done. Those things of substance that get done are started in most cases by ordinary citizens in ordinary towns far away from Washington most often by people with little, if any experience, in politics but with a simple conviction and determination to right a wrong. In short, an important lesson to learn from the heroes in this book is that if you think something is wrong with this country do not wait for your president, congressman or senator to do something about it. They will not. Look in the mirror if you want to know where change has to start. That is a political lesson. It is a life lesson also.

2. Patience and perseverance—In the pages that follow, we'll learn the uncomfortable fact that real change takes time, often a lot of time. It never comes instantly or easily. This book is not about policy victories won in a single legislative session or two or five for that matter. These victories often took decades. This is not a book for those who are faint of heart or who want instant legislative gratification. If your purpose for reading this book is to find a way to change the world, or at least those parts of the world that you do not like, without exerting too much effort or having your efforts take too much time, look elsewhere. If you think 70 years is just too much time to spend to accomplish something, if you shutter at the thought of setting out on a journey that you may not complete in your lifetime, then this book is not for you. However, if you want to learn how real people undertook the challenge of addressing real social problems and got breakthrough legislation passed, this book is for you. It will show you how they achieved the legislatively impossible and teach you the lessons to help you do the same. These are stories of people who never gave up, who never lost sight of their goal, and who never gave in. Here you will learn that the power of NO is ultimately no match for the politics of YES, WE CAN.

3. Confrontation—Those who would change the world in a major way must confront the world in a major way. They must be willing and able to stage image events to garner attention and raise the consciousness of average voters often at the real risk of physical harm. Often the confrontation necessary to spur change is led by a polarizing figure who becomes a liability to the cause once the stage is set for actual legislation.
4. Knowledge-Base—Someone or some group must take responsibility for amassing the evidence for the need for change and developing the reasoning to counter the arguments of the opposition. This usually requires someone who is not only adept at doing the research and uncovering the facts but who can present these facts in a persuasive way.
5. Compromise and Coalition Building—The change leadership must stay focused on the main objective and make compromises to expand the base of support without alienating those who are truly committed to the cause in order to get anything done. This requires leaders who can see the big picture and have the ability to tap into the needs of widely diverse interest groups to find common advantage in moving ahead by marshaling the facts and structuring the argument for change to appeal to the greatest number while not alienating those in the change movement that are most devoted to change.
6. Vote Buying—Change requires legislative expertise, the knowledge and power to negotiate, trade votes and exchange favors with Senators and Congressmen who are neutral or only weakly opposed in order to build a sufficient majority to secure passage of the legislation. Politics is a dirty business where shady backroom deals are required to construct good legislation.
7. Pivotal Image Event—Real change frequently requires a catastrophe, crisis or shocking expose either real or manufactured to spur the general population to demand action.
8. Piecemeal Legislation—A single piece of legislation is rarely enough to accomplish real change. As hard as it is to pass a much-needed law, the first success usually falls short of the goal. Additionally legislation is usually required.

9. Threat from the Courts—Opponents of change never accept defeat gracefully. Beaten in the halls of Congress, they inevitably turn to the courts seeing to have the entire law or major features declared unconstitutional. Frequently they succeed, either significantly weakening the legislation or forcing proponents of change to launch efforts to enact new legislation to undo the damage.
10. Threat from Public Apathy—Finally, there is the threat of time. Aroused to demand change, the public can gradually lose interest over time. Opponents take advantage of the ebb in public concern to pass new legislation stripping the original legislation of much of its power or cutting funding for enforcement.

These are just a few of the lessons I will elaborate upon in much greater depth as I tell the stories of the genuine heroes profiled in this book. We will begin more than 200 years ago. Fifty-five men met in Philadelphia over one hot summer in 1787. They sought to fix a constitution that was preventing anything from getting done in Washington. Their struggle and the compromises they made to get their constitution adopted contains important lessons concerning what it takes to get things done in Washington and why it is frequently so hard for progressives to get anything done.

1

THE STRUGGLE FOR THE CONSTITUTION

We begin our search for the secrets of legislative accomplishment with undoubtedly the greatest political achievement in American history, perhaps the greatest political achievement in all history—the drafting and ratification of the U.S. Constitution and Bill of Rights. Fifty-five men, possibly acting illegally, drafted a document in 1787 laying out a new form of government for the country, a form of government that most Americans at that time did not want. With the help of a few other like-minded citizens, these men got their constitution ratified and fundamentally and forever changed the direction of the country. They achieved an extraordinary political accomplishment at a deeply troubled time in the country's history.

THE TIME AND PLACE

Let me take you back to that time and place. It is 1786--five years after the British surrender at Yorktown, three years after the signing of a treaty between Great Britain and the newly created United States. The new country is vast, stretching all the way from the Canadian border to just above the Gulf of Mexico, from the Atlantic Ocean to the Mississippi

River. In land mass, the United States' 890,000 or so square miles is larger than France, Italy, Spain, Germany, Britain and Ireland combined. Yet, most of this territory is still untamed wilderness. As Clinton Rossiter, author of *1787: The Grand Convention*, says "except in the eastern parts of the Middle States and the southern part of New England, the forest, not the clearing, [is] the dominant feature of the landscape."[1]

The country has less than 4 million inhabitants (not counting native Americans who went, as Rossiter says "uncounted and unloved") including some 680,000 African-American slaves 90 percent of whom live in five states where they make up more than one-third of the population. Compared to the populations of Spain (10 million), Germany (20 million), France (25 million) and Britain (15 million) America is inconsequential. It has only 24 cities with more than 2,500 inhabitants and only 5 cities with more than 10,000 compared to Amsterdam with 200,000, Paris with 600,000 and London with 950,000.

For most Americans, travel is problematic at best. As Rossiter says, "roads [are] bad, bridges few, ferries leaky, rivers whimsical, stagecoaches cranky, and inns ill-kept."[2] The traveler who ventures out finds "roads that [are] frequently nothing more than mile upon mile of mud wallow, cut by hundreds of streams, creeks, and rivers, most of which [are] unbridged, so that they [must] be forded or crossed by ferry."[3] Not infrequently, travelers die when their stagecoach tips over while fording a river. They are just washed away never to be seen again. At best, a traveler can expect to advance 50 miles in a day but more typically, he is lucky if he makes twenty. A determined man can make it if he is sufficiently determined. Most are not so determined. Most people do not travel very far from home very often.

Most Americans stay at home and work the land. Ninety percent are involved in agriculture or a related industry such as fishing or lumbering. Only one in ten is a merchant, lawyer, or a member of some other profession. Manufacturing is still largely restricted to small shops operated by families who farm in their off hours.

Much of the farming is for subsistence or barter particularly beyond the few heavily settled regions near the Atlantic coast. At the same time, the soil is good so many families, at least in the more settled areas, can produce surplus crops for export. Wheat, corn, tobacco, rice, indigo, meat, fish, furs, naval stores, hides, and lumber are all regularly shipped from American shores to the West Indies and Europe in return for manufactured goods. Land ownership, particular ownership of land that yields surplus product for export, is the fastest way to wealth for most people.

While Americans work largely with their hands, they are surprisingly literate. The country has more than eighty, largely weekly newspapers. Few schools exist, so the extended family shoulders the primary responsibility for teaching the young to read, write and cipher. European visitors are typically surprised to find that the young nation is "full of men who had never seen the inside of a schoolhouse and yet [are] extremely well educated for the responsibilities of their stations in life."[4] In turn, Americans are proud of their colleges. Harvard, William and Mary, Yale, Princeton, Columbia, Brown, Rutgers, Dartmouth, and others already exist and states are creating the first state universities. The University of Georgia was the first, chartered in 1785.

There are no privilege-ridden classes in America as in Europe but there are class distinctions. About three percent of the population—primarily wealthy landowners—form a uniquely American aristocracy. About twenty percent of the population consists of the "meaner sorts"—laborers, servants, and hardscrabble farmers—who are "mired in a swamp of much poverty and little hope, and [are] victims of a depressing political apathy."[5] Most Americans fall in the middle, sturdy farmers, hardy shopkeepers, and independent artisans for which the dividing line between them and their betters is decidedly fuzzy. And, then there are the African-American slaves who are simultaneously vital to the American economy and "a challenge to the American conscience."[6] Only a handful of slaves are ever set free and those that are find few white men who will accept them even as second-class citizens. Slavery is an embarrassing contradiction to the equality and natural rights of all men, ideals that drove the revolution. Few Americans are prepared to address or even consider that contradiction.

A TROUBLED NATION

For all its promise, the nation is troubled and its troubles are not just about slavery. The problems are many and growing. Many are economic. Although some areas are prospering, much of the country is enduring a postwar depression. The national government, which had sold war bonds and borrowed heavily to finance the war, is struggling to find a way to pay off its debts and, indeed, even to find the money to pay what it owes to revolutionary war soldiers. The states are increasing taxes to pay their own war debts. Most poor farmers believe that the taxes they are required to pay are unfair. Merchants in seaports are under pressure from foreign creditors to pay for goods they have imported. They in turn are putting pressure on country storekeepers to pay their debts who in turn are putting additional pressure on cash strapped farmers. Hard money—gold and silver—is scarce and getting scarcer. Many farmers who are in danger of losing their farms because they cannot pay their debts are seeking relief from their state legislatures. The state legislatures are responding to the political pressure. Some states, in an effort to help those in debt, are going so far as to suspend the collection of debts for a number of years. Other states such as Rhode Island, New York, New Jersey, Pennsylvania, the Carolinas, and Georgia are responding by printing paper money and insisting that creditors take the near worthless script in payment of all debts. The lack of a standard currency makes trade across state boundaries increasingly problematic.

Frustrated farmers in New Hampshire, Vermont, and Connecticut resort to violent protests when their state legislatures do not provide similar relief for debtors. The most chilling of these protests begins in Massachusetts in 1786.[7] There a former revolutionary officer by the name of Daniel Shays leads a group of some 2,000 debt-ridden farmers in a six-month armed uprising against the state protesting taxes and preventing the hated debtor courts from operating. Finally, in January 1787, Shays' rebels march on an arsenal at Springfield defended by 1,200 state troops. There is canon fire. Four rebels die. State troops wound many more. Ten years after the Declaration of Independence and less than four years since signing a peace treaty with the British, Americans are in open rebellion again. Neighbors are fighting neighbors. George Washington expresses what many are feeling. He writes, "I am mortified beyond expression…when I view the clouds that have spread over the brightest morn that ever dawned upon a country… Without some alteration in our political creed, the superstructure we have been seven years raising at the expense of so much blood and treasure, must fall. We are fast verging to anarchy and confusion!"[8]

Added to the country's troubles are lingering interstate and regional rivalries. New England states fight over rights to codfish markets. South Carolina is offended every time someone in a Yankee state broaches the subject of slavery. States argue over boundaries and navigation rights. Vermont has fought a brief war with New York over a border dispute.

As Fred Barbash, author of *The Founding* put it, "America [in 1786 is] thirteen small democratic republics, with their own interests, their own currencies, their own little armies and even their own foreign policies. When [Thomas] Jefferson [speaks] of 'my country,' he [means] the commonwealth of Virginia, not the United States."[9] The country is not a country so much as "a collection of regions, which differ considerably in economics, religion, attitudes, customs, ethnic mix, and even in some cases language."[10]

Only a few years into their grand experiment the American people have lost their way. Many of the politically astute are confident they know why. The country's constitution is not working. George Washington writes to a friend that conditions are so bad that something has to be done "to avert the humiliating and contemptible figure we are about to make on the annals of mankind."[11] William Grayson, a Congressman from Virginia writes that the country is in danger of becoming "one of the most contemptible nations on the face of the Earth" if things did not change.[12] John Hancock, then Governor of Massachusetts, tells his legislature that strengthening the union requires the immediate attention of all of the states and that the very existence of the nation depends upon it.

THE ARTICLES OF CONFEDERATION

Of course the constitution that is not working is America's first constitution—the Articles of Confederation. "Anticipated in 1774, mulled over in 1776, proposed in 1777, and finally ratified in 1781," the Articles created nothing more than a loose confederation of independent states.[13] It was probably as much as the country was prepared for at the time. Having just fought a war to free themselves from the control of a far away central government, Americans were not prepared to grant central power to another closer but still far away government. Framers of the Articles made the federal government weak on purpose

A major weakness was that Congress had no power to tax. It could "requisition" funds from the states but had no way to force the states to comply. The states decided if and when and to what extent they would honor the requisitions. Some were more responsive than others were. For example, Virginia generally tried to meet its obligations but Massachusetts rarely bothered and New Hampshire usually pleaded poverty. Between 1781 and 1784, the states paid only a little more than 20% of money requisitioned by the national government ($1.4 million of $6.5)[14] As a result, the country could not pay its bills. Catherine Drinker Bowen in her book *Miracle in Philadelphia* says that the Continental Congress was so short of cash that when a messenger arrived to bring the news of the country's victory over the British at Yorktown members had to contribute money from their own pockets to pay the man's expenses.[15] Congress could and did continue to send Benjamin Franklin to France to beg for loans, but France was already finding the loans burdensome and anyway many Americans were beginning to have doubts about financing their government through increasing dependency on the generosity of a foreign country who would undoubtedly want an increased influence on the nation's public affairs in return.[16]

A second key weakness of the Articles had to do with the requirements to get anything done. There was only a one-house Congress and each state had one vote. Amendments to the Articles required unanimous consent. Matters dealing with major issues such as questions of war, peace, international relations and finance required the approval of at least nine of the thirteen states. And, while lesser matters could be decided by the assent of the "votes of a majority of the United States, in Congress assembled," that phrase was interpreted as the absolute majority of seven not just the majority of states present and voting. The Rule of Seven interpretation meant that if a few states were absent, sent only one delegate (each state was required to have two delegates present), or if the delegation of a few states was split, then nothing could be done. "In short, to get seven affirmative votes in the face of absent, undermanned, or split delegations [was] exceedingly difficult."[17] Delegates from two, three, or sometimes even one state could prevent Congress from taking any action.

Finally, the Congress had no power to regulate commerce or mediate the interstate squabbling and sectional rivalry that plagued the nation. Often these disputes had to do with the use of navigable waterways that were critical for the movement of commercial goods. A few people might travel overland by stage but if you wanted to ship large quantities of tobacco or rice or whiskey or most other commercial products you did it over the nation's great rivers. The dispute between Maryland and Virginia in 1784 over the use of the Potomac is a good example. In order to get its tobacco and grain to market, Maryland had to ship its product through a section of the Chesapeake Bay that Virginia controlled. Commerce intended for residents of Northern Virginia and the Shenandoah Valley had to pass over a stretch of the Potomac River controlled by Maryland. When Maryland raised taxes on goods shipped via the Potomac, Virginia countered with a threat to tax Maryland ships using the Chesapeake Bay. The Maryland/Virginia dispute was the type of interstate squabble that Congress under the Articles had no power to mediate. It was up to the states themselves to resolve such issues. Consequently, representatives of Maryland and Virginia held a meeting to discuss the issue. Ultimately, this meeting led to the Constitutional Convention. I will get to that in a moment. However, first I want to introduce a key player in the drama that follows—James Madison. Some historians have called Madison the "father of the U.S. Constitution," although he rejected that title. He may not be the "father" but he was, without a doubt, the Constitution's chief philosophical architect and its most knowledgeable and effective proponent during the ratification process. We will look to Madison for many of this chapter's "getting things done" lessons.

> **LESSON: Get the timing right.** Timing may not be everything, but it is extremely important. The Articles were weak, but they were probably all that the country was ready for in 1781. The country had to experience the defects of the Articles before it was prepared to adopt a stronger form of government. It took something like Shay's Rebellion to jolt people into action. By 1787, the country was ready to consider something more than a weak confederation. As Rossiter says: "Most of the ingredients of American nationalism were in the place by 1787: common language, common origin and outlook, common legal and political institutions, common culture, common enemies, and common memories of a successful drive toward independence. There lacked, indeed, only that condition of political unity and sense of emotional unity which would follow on the creation of a central government with dignity and authority."[18]

JAMES MADISON

James Madison was born on March 16, 1751 on a plantation in Virginia, the oldest son of James Madison, Sr. a wealthy landowner. He attended the College of New Jersey (now Princeton) where he earned his degree in just two years. Born into the Virginia landed aristocracy, he enjoyed a life of privilege. First elected to the Virginia Convention and the General Assembly in 1776, Madison spent a lifetime in politics. He served as one of Virginia's delegates to the Constitutional Convention and was one of the major contributors to *The Federalist Papers* interpreting and justifying the Constitution. He served in the U. S. House of Representatives. He worked with Thomas Jefferson to found the Democratic Republican Party (ancestor of the current Democratic Party). He served as Secretary of State under Thomas Jefferson and served two terms as President. Undoubtedly, Madison's most important political contribution was his critical role in the drafting and ratification of the U.S. Constitution.

Madison was an unlikely candidate for political fame.[19] He was not charismatic. He was small, five feet four and one hundred pounds. Washington Irving described him as "withered." A British minister said he was "meager," and a critic referred to him, as a "pigmy." Someone else said he was "no bigger than a half piece of soap." He had "pale skin like parchment" and spoke so softly in a little "squeaky" voice that people often had to strain to hear him. He was "bookish" and shy. In his youth, instead of riding, hunting, fishing, and drinking like his peers, he spent his time reading books. Supposedly he slept only three or four hours each night and kept a candle lit and paper and pen handy so that he could more easily jot down thoughts that came to him during the night, which they often did. Madison was so shy, he did not rise to speak for the first six months of his service in the Continental Congress as a delegate from Virginia. While in Williamsburg on a trip, someone stole his hat. Madison stayed inside for two days until he could purchase another one from a passing peddler because he was embarrassed to have anyone see him without his hat.

Madison thought of himself as "feeble," "pale," and "sickly" all his life although he lived to be eighty-five years old and never really suffered from any identifiable disease or chronic illness,. Because of what he described as his "bad health," he expected a short life. "When he was twenty-one, he told his Princeton friend that he could not make plans for the future since 'my sensations of many months past have intimated to me not to expect a long or healthy life."[20] When asked later to travel abroad on political assignments, he said that his nerves were not up to it—he wrote Jefferson in 1785 that "crossing the sea would be unfriendly to a singular disease of my constitution."[21] While never truly ill, he frequently suffered from strange attacks that some of his biographers have called "epileptoid hysteria—that is to say, an emotional illness with symptoms resembling epilepsy."[22]

Finally, Madison exhibited "a certain provincialism with regard to the rest of the world and a certain naiveté with regard to his fellow human beings."[23] Alexander Hamilton told a British minister that Madison was "very little acquainted with the world."[24] George Clinton, who was Madison's as well as Jefferson's vice president, said that Madison had "too little practical knowledge."[25] Madison sponsored provisions at the Constitutional Convention such as a national veto of state laws that the more worldly wise tried to tell him the delegates would never adopt. Running for office for the Virginia House of Delegates Madison refused to engage in the standard practice of wooing voters by offering them kegs of free whiskey. As a result, he lost the election.

Although provincial and naïve, Madison had a towering political intellect and giant legislative talent. He did his best work at conventions and in congresses. "He was what the eighteenth century called a man of the cabinet, not of the field. He was a prodigious worker at his desk, an omnivorous reader."[26] Those who worked with Madison at the Constitutional convention rated him highly. William Pierce, a Georgia delegate described Madison this way:

> Mr. Maddison is a character who has long been in public life; and what is very remarkable every Person seems to acknowledge his greatness. He blends together the profound politician, with the Scholar. In the management of every great question he evidently took the lead in the Convention, and tho' he cannot be called an Orator, he is a most agreable, eloquent, and convincing Speaker. From a spirit of industry and application which he possesses in a most eminent degree, he always comes forward the best informed Man of any point in debate. The affairs of the United States, he perhaps, has the most correct knowledge of, of any Man in the Union. He has been tWice a Member of Congress, and was always thought one of the ablest Members that ever sat in that Council. Mr. Maddison is about 37 years of age, a Gentleman of great Modesty-with a remarkable sweet temper. He is easy and unreserved among his acquaintance, and has a most agreable style of conversation.[27]

This shy, soft spoken but highly intelligent man was to play a leading role in recreating the nation. His involvement in this extraordinary undertaking begins in earnest in 1785 as Maryland and Virginia started to work out their waterway dispute.

THE ROAD TO PHILADELPHIA

That year representatives of Maryland and Virginia met at George Washington's home at Mount Vernon to discuss the "Potomac problem" I mentioned earlier. The results of the four-day meeting were encouraging.

The two states agreed to declare the Potomac a "common highway" for the use of their citizens. Maryland and Virginia would share in any taxes or other revenue from use of the Potomac and would split the cost of lighthouses. In turn, Virginia agreed not to tax Maryland's ships passing through the Chesapeake Bay.

When George Mason, who had been one of Virginia's representatives to the Mount Vernon conference, submitted his report to the Virginia Assembly, he included a recommendation that Virginia and Maryland meet annually to continue their discussions and that the discussions be expanded to include taxes and other issues affecting commerce. The Virginia Assembly referred Mason's report to a committee headed by James Madison who had sponsored the original resolution calling for the Mount Vernon conference. Madison, who like Washington and Mason was convinced that the Articles needed strengthening, saw the results of the Mount Vernon Conference as a real opportunity. With the support of Washington, Mason and others, Madison proposed that Virginia issue a call to all the states to meet in Annapolis in September to consider "a uniform system in their commercial relations." In January 1786, Virginia issued the call and appointed Madison as one of the state's five delegates.

> **LESSON: Take advantage of any opportunities to move your proposal forward.** Mason saw the meeting between Maryland and Virginia to discuss navigation rights on the Potomac and Chesapeake as an opportunity to call for another conference with a wider agenda. The Maryland/Virginia discussions led to the Annapolis Convention that led to Philadelphia.

MADISON'S PREPARATION

In the spring and summer of 1786, in what may have been the greatest one-man "skull session" in history, Madison retired to his study in his beloved home Montpelier armed with a number of books he had collected (many sent from Paris by his friend Tom Jefferson) dealing with governments of the past. There are scholars and then there are scholars. Few can plow through the strengths and weaknesses of the Amphyctionic Confederacy of early 16th century Greece, the Helvitic Confederacy of 14th century Switzerland or the Belgic and Germanic confederacies of the mid-1600s. Few of us could have waded through Fortune Barthelemy de Felice's, *Code de l'Humanite, ou La Legislation Universelle, Naturelle, Civile et Politque (13 volumes)* or Diderot's *Encyclopedie Methodique*, Abbe Millot's *£lements d'Histoire Generale (11 volumes)*, Abbe de Mably's *De l'Etude de l'Histoire*, Jacques-Auguste de Thou's *Histoire Universelle*, as well as such traditional works as *Plutarch's Lives*, the orations of Demosthenes, and the histories of Polybius.[28] Madison devoured all of these and more. He compiled lists of the good and bad features of governments of the past in a lengthy paper entitled "Of Ancient and Modern Confederacies," in which he outlined the history of the Lycian, Amphictyonic, and Achaean confederacies of ancient Greece, and of the Holy Roman Empire, the Swiss Confederation, and the United Provinces of the Netherlands. He recorded how those confederacies had succeed or failed at dealing with many of the matters that troubled the United States under the Articles such as financial support, diplomatic representation, cooperation in time of war, regulation of commerce, coercion of members who disobeyed confederacy orders, and so on. "He sought especially to identify the constitutional bonds of union, the way these bonds worked or failed to work in practice, and the particular causes of the demise or enfeeblement of the confederation."[29] Madison recorded the facts and lessons he learned from his prodigious research in a booklet of forty-one pocket-sized pages, easy to use in debate or writing. He mastered the lessons of history. Madison's preparation for the convention, particularly his scholarly research on the problem with confederate forms of government was "probably the most fruitful piece of scholarly research ever carried out by an American."[30] The little scholar was ready to create a new constitution. But, it wasn't to be; not yet.

THE ANNAPOLIS CONVENTION—SEPTEMBER 1786

When Madison arrived at the Annapolis Conference in September, he was disappointed to see that only five states sent delegates. Luckily, Alexander

Hamilton of New York, a long time advocate of replacing the Articles with a new constitution was one of them. The Annapolis delegates were mostly nationalists who were in favor of replacing the Articles but they recognized that they were too few to proceed. The Annapolis delegates decided to ask Congress to call another conference. This one had to have authority to deal with all the problems with the Articles, not just the issue of interstate commerce. They latched on to a phrase New Jersey had included in its instructions to its Annapolis delegates to address not just commerce but "other important matters." With the approval of others in attendance, Hamilton and Madison drafted a resolution for presentation to the states assemblies calling for a convention in Philadelphia to "devise such further provisions that appear to them necessary to render the constitution of the Federal Government adequate to the exigencies of the Union."[31]

It was a bold move. The chance of a sufficient number of states agreeing to send delegates to Madison and Hamilton's Philadelphia Convention were uncertain even with Washington's blessing and support. Washington would have to agree to attend and, ideally, lead the conference if it was to have legitimacy. In addition, they needed something more to spur the states to action. They got it with Shay's Rebellion. The news of the conflict in Massachusetts was a wakeup call. In February, Congress endorsed the idea of a convention in Philadelphia. America had finally started down the road to a new form of government.

THE CONSTITUTIONAL CONVENTION

Congress had approved the Philadelphia convention but only for proposing amendments to the Articles that would require ratification by all of the states. That was not at all what Madison and many of the other delegates to the Philadelphia convention had in mind. As Gary Wills points out, while we call the 1787 convention the Constitutional Convention no delegate to that convention would have dared to use such terms for to do so would have been considered a violation of their oath of allegiance to the Articles of Confederation and possibly even treason.[32] Indeed as Wills notes, the Constitutional Convention was in fact an Anti-Constitutional Convention. At the time, the Articles of Confederation was the constitution. In Philadelphia in 1787, a core of convention delegates were determined not to amend the Articles but to scrap them entirely. It was not what Congress sent them to do but it was what they planned to do from the beginning. Edmund Randolph presented the "Virginia Plan" at the opening session. It called for:

- abolishing the Articles of Confederation, not amending them,
- having the new Constitution ratified by special conventions and not by the state legislatures, as the Articles required, and
- empowering the federal government to veto laws passed by the state legislatures thus abandoning the concept of state sovereignty that had been central to the Articles.[33]

These were radical proposals that went far beyond anything Congress had intended when it called for the convention. Patrick Henry, the great orator from Virginia, had been suspicious from the beginning. Appointed as a delegate to the convention, he refused to attend saying he "smelt a rat."[34] Henry had been right. The "rats" were about to abandon the Articles ship for a new one.

Due to the subversive nature of the endeavor the Philadelphia delegates were undertaking, and that is in fact what it was, the convention met in secret session.

> It even had to move to the second floor of the State House, so no one could overhear what they were doing…[For] if the state legislatures that had sent these delegates found out what was going on, they would have recalled them for breaking their instructions…. Against a drumbeat of criticism directed at 'the dark conclave,' Washington himself, as presiding officer, strictly monitored the secrecy provision until the final document was released, and the delegates scuttled nervously away from the scene of the crime.[35]

It was very likely that the delegates to the Philadelphia Convention would have been accused of treason accept for one thing. Benjamin

Franklin and George Washington attended and gave the convention cover. No one in the country was about to call these men, particularly Washington, traitors. Madison was largely responsible for convincing a first reluctant Washington to attend and serve as the presiding officer. Without Washington, there probably would have been no convention or, at least, no acceptance of its legitimacy.

> The delegates to the convention were decidedly young at least by the standards of our time given the enormous task they were undertaking which was to do nothing short of achieve a miracle and save a nation. Jonathan Dayton, one of the delegates from New Jersey was just twenty-six. Alexander Hamilton, James Madison and Gouverneur Morris were all in their thirties. The average age of the delegates was just forty-three but then only because a few elder statesmen such as Benjamin Franklin at 81 skewed the average.[36]

Their relative youth belied their experience. Most had served in the Continental Congress and many had been state legislators and/or helped write the constitutions for their states. They were respected men of political experience. Richard Henry Lee of Virginia praised them as "gentlemen of competent years." Thomas Jefferson went further. These were, he said, "an assembly of demi-gods."[37]

Meeting from May to September, often in sweltering heat, fifty-five men constructed the U.S. Constitution. It was a remarkable achievement with many sticking points where a failure to compromise would likely have resulted in a failure to produce a document at all. I will not go into the details of the debates, arguments and deal making that went on in Philadelphia during that summer.

Virginia had taken the lead in promoting the Philadelphia Convention and now as the Convention opened it took the lead in proposing the first plan for a new constitution authored primarily by James Madison—the Virginia Plan. Madison and his Virginia colleagues were politically astute enough to know that the first plan presented would have advantages over any other because it would dictate the discussion.[38]

The Virginia Plan as presented by the head of the Virginia delegation, Edmund Randolph consisted of fifteen resolutions with the following key features:

The plan proposed a legislature of two houses, an executive and a judiciary.

Voters would elect the members of the first branch of the legislature (later called the House of Representatives) with the number of seats in the legislature proportional to the wealth of each state as gauged by the taxes paid or based upon the number of free inhabitants plus 3/5ths of slaves.

The first branch would choose the members of the second branch of the legislature (later called the Senate) which would also have proportional representation and together the two houses would select the president and appoint judges.

The national government would have the power to veto state laws.

Finally, special assemblies chosen directly by the people would ratify the Constitution not the state legislatures.[39]

> **LESSON: Dictate the discussion; make your opponents work from your proposal.** At both the Philadelphia Convention and, as we shall see later, prior to the debate over the Bill of Rights, Madison developed and offered a proposal that formed the basis of debate. The question was not "What kind of new government should we create?" or "How should the Constitution be amended?" The question put before the delegates and Congress was "What parts of the proposal put forward by Virginia should we accept and what parts need revision or modification." In both cases, while Madison lost on several major points, he got most of what he wanted largely because the debate started from a discussion of what he wanted.

Undoubtedly, the most controversial of the Virginia proposals and one that nearly broke up the convention had to do with proportional representation. The small states were incensed. Under the Articles, all states had an equal vote in Congress. It was a tradition. If membership and voting power in the first house, which had the power to choose the members of the second house, were proportional then small states would suffer. Large states would dominate the government, which everyone knew would have much more power than under the Articles particularly if that power extended to the ability to veto state laws as the Virginians proposed. A Delaware delegate expressed the fears of the small states this way. With their voting strength in the first house and the power to veto state laws, "will not these large states crush the small ones whenever they stand in the way of their ambitions or interested views?"[40] The large states countered that proportional representation was simply in keeping with democratic principles. While the Articles may have granted each state an equal vote, that was wrong. "[A]s all authority was derived from the people, equal numbers of people ought to have an equal number of representatives," argued James Wilson of Pennsylvania. "Are not the citizens of Pennsylvania equal to those of New Jersey? Does it require 150 of the former to balance 50 of the latter? Shall New Jersey have the same right or influence in the councils of the nation with Pennsylvania? I say no. It is unjust."[41]

It took weeks but eventually the delegates reached a compromise. The first branch of the legislature (the House) would have proportional representation chosen by the people with slaves counted as three-fifths of a person. The second branch (the Senate) would have equal representation with its members chosen by the state legislatures. As Ralph Ketchum, one of Madison's biographers says the compromise on proportional representation was critical. Without it the small states might have bolted and there may have been no Constitution. "As long as representation by population seemed likely, the small states resisted every effort to increase the general powers, and the large states on the whole favored such an increase. However, the moment the states were made equal in one branch of the legislature, the small states became by and large supporters of increased national authority."[42]

Madison opposed the compromise but admitted later in life that it was a turning point. He explained to Martin Van Buren that "the threatening contest in the Convention of 1787 did not, as you supposed, turn on the degree of power to be granted to the federal government, but on the rule by which states should be represented and vote in the government." [43]

LESSON: Be willing to compromise. Your purpose is to achieve passage of something that moves your agenda forward even if that means you do not get everything you want. Madison had to back off some of his extreme ideas. He learned to lose. He favored proportional representation for both houses and lost. He favored giving the national legislature the power to negate state laws and lost. He favored the popular election of the executive and lost. One Constitutional scholar has estimated that during the Philadelphia Convention, "of seventy-one specific proposals that Madison moved, seconded, or spoke unequivocally in regard to, he was on the losing side forty times."[44] Still, Madison won in the long term on the major issue. He got a new and much stronger constitution. Madison himself said that the compromise over proportional representation that gave the small states equal representation in the Senate was critical to the success of the convention. The 3/5ths compromise over the counting of slaves was equally important in winning the support of the southern states. The Constitution, as Rossiter says, "was, in truth, a shrew armistice among men who had become convinced that their common interests would never be realized unless their special interests were compromised... [It was] the creation of politicians who had a genius for inventing 'half-way' solutions."[45] He continues: "The Federalists also won because, in most of their decisions and dealings, they showed good judgment in distinguishing the possible from the unacceptable, in knowing when to hold fast and when to give way. By adding anyone of a half-dozen techniques and arrangements to their Constitution [such as] a veto on state laws...the Framers might have tipped the delicately balanced scale of opinion against their cause... But the Framers... had a good collective sense of what the people, if properly instructed, would accept."[46]

THE REMARKABLE DOCUMENT

The Constitution fifty-five men constructed during the hot summer of 1787 in Philadelphia was a remarkable achievement. The document is notable for many reasons. Rossiter argues that perhaps the most impressive feature of the document is the language the framers used.

> It was "plain to the point off severity, frugal to the point of austerity, laconic to the point of aphorism…a statement in 'simple and precise language' of 'essential principles only' that could be 'accommodated to times and events' no living man could foretell… It was "a remarkably indulgent charter, one that invited future generations of Americans to govern themselves both imaginatively and expansively…It was "precise and vague at one and the same time…a bundle of compromise and a mosaic of second choices…a shrewd armistice among men who had become convinced that their common interests would never be realized unless their special interests were compromised; and..the creation of politicians who had a genius for inventing 'half-way' solutions" but never-the-less solutions.[47]

Beyond its simple language, the Constitution these men drafted was a careful working out through discussion and compromise of the essential principles by which the nation would be governed. It was, says Rossiter:

> a kind of registry of critical decisions about the nature and destiny of the United States of America, notable not just for the specific decisions the framers made"—the choice of a single-headed executive, the creation of a two-chambered legislature, the prohibition on titles of nobility--…but the more fateful confirmations of the past and gambles with the future…[It] was an act of confirmation: a solemn pledge…that certain decisions taken by and for the American people were closed forever. The Constitution was designed to be the last formal act of the Revolution, and it put the stamp of irrevocable legitimacy on the three great legacies of 1776: independence, republicanism, and union. From these three commitments there could be no turning back; to these the people of the United States would henceforth be bound so tightly that only another, far bloodier revolution could reopen them for consideration.[48]

In creating this remarkable document, the framers gambled that Americans were disenchanted enough with the Articles of Confederation that they were "ready for a forceful shove toward emotional and political unity." [49] However, the framers were careful not to shove too much. The Constitution delegated "responsibilities of sovereignty" to the Congress and President and the laws and treaties they made would be supreme and binding on the states. However, the federal government would not have the power to negate state laws, as James Madison had proposed. The Constitution would not redraw local and regional boundaries as some had proposed. Finally, while the states would no longer be fully sovereign they would have a kind of "half-sovereignty" with "large responsibilities for the safety and happiness of their citizens...The states would endure as healthy political entities."[50]

As I said, the Constitution these men forged in Philadelphia was a remarkable political achievement but even more remarkable—amazing really—is that these founders were able to sell their new constitution to the country. They were able to secure its ratification. It is to that story that I want to turn next because if what happened during the spring and summer of 1787 in Philadelphia contains lessons for drafting legislation, what happened during the struggle for ratification contains even more lessons on what it takes to get legislation adopted. So, for some more lessons on getting things done in Washington we will turn to what happened during the months following the Philadelphia convention. In particular, we will look at the debates at the Virginia ratification convention in Richmond, Virginia during June of 1788 for it was there that proponents and opponents of the new constitution most fully engaged in a debate over its merits.. Furthermore, the future of the country hung on the results of the Virginia convention. Without Virginia, the new Constitution could not succeed. Indeed, without Virginia's ratification the country itself may not have endured.

FEDERALISTS AND ANTI-FEDERALISTS

Initially Madison was at best only lukewarm in his support of the Constitution produced in Philadelphia. He wrote Jefferson that the document as it emerged from the convention would "neither effectually answer its national object nor prevent the local mischief's which every where excite disgusts against the state governments."[51] However when he saw the opposition, he dropped all reservations and became a passionate advocate convinced that nothing less than the survival of the nation depended upon the ratification of the new constitution.

The framers had done everything they could to encourage Congress to send the proposed new constitution along to the states with a note of confidence and urgency. Washington had signed a covering letter offering a ringing endorsement. Not everyone in Congress was so enthusiastic. Some opponents such as Richard Henry Lee wanted to send the new constitution to the states without a recommendation for adoption or call for action of any kind. Baring that Lee and other opponents sought to send the document along to the states with proposed amendments such as the addition of a bill of rights, the elimination of the vice-presidency, and an increase in the size of the House of Representatives. Madison and the supporters of the constitution were able to defeat these proposals and pushed though a carefully worded resolution that sent the constitution along to the states with "very moderate terms" of approval but endorsement by a majority of the Congress.

Very quickly, the proponents of the new constitution, who called themselves "Federalists," began to call their opponents Anti-Federalists. As Jackson Turner Main notes in his book *The Anti-Federalists: Critics of the Constitution, 1781-1788*, it was a nice piece of misdirection.

> Originally, the word 'federal' meant anyone who supported the Confederation. Several years before the Constitution was promulgated, the men who wanted a strong national government, who might more properly be called 'nationalists,' began to appropriate the term 'federal' for themselves. To them, the man of 'federal principles' approved of 'federal measures,' which meant those that increased the weight and authority or extended the influence of the Confederation Congress. The word 'antifederal' by contrast implied hostility to Congress. According to this definition, the anti-federal man was opposed to any effort to strengthen the government and was therefore unpatriotic.[52]

> **LESSON: Portray the opposition as naysayers who offer no coherent alternative.** The Federalists were able to exploit the fact that the Anti-Federalist had no coherent alternative to offer to the new constitution. Even the name "Anti-Federalist" was a benefit to the Federalist's cause. As we shall see, the Federalists used a similar tactic in the Virginia Ratification Convention when they successful portrayed the choice as one between preserving the union and seeing it dissolve. The new constitution was the only way forward.

People in Boston, New York, Philadelphia, Baltimore, Alexandria, and other seaport towns supported the Constitution as did most people who were property owners, creditors and/or concerned with trade and commerce and therefore needed a stable currency.[53] The Federalists were also strong in many of the small states such as Delaware, New Jersey, Georgia, Connecticut, New Hampshire and Maryland that felt least capable of dealing with their economic and security problems by themselves.

Anti-Federalists were a patchwork or special interests with no unifying theme except their opposition to the new Constitution. They included state-politicians who feared losing political power and influence, debtors, those opposed to taxation and those who felt a strong national government would be a threat to state and regional interests. Anti-Federalists worried that the new Constitution would create a remote and inaccessible all-powerful government controlled largely by the wealthy and culturally refined to the detriment to the common man.

Anti-Federalists argued that the chief goal of government should be to protect individual rights and liberties particularly the freedom of individuals to pursue personal and private happiness through the accumulation of property free from government interference. Politics, they said, was corrupting. Humans by their nature were prone to use any power they obtain to seek more and more power. Consequently, government should be kept small and close enough to the people, so that every citizen could participate by devoting time and energy to public service, meetings, and policy discussions and thereby keep watch over their liberties. The very idea of creating a strong national government was horrifying and, said George Mason "totally subversive of every principle which has hitherto governed us…never was a government over a very extensive country without destroying the liberties of the people… popular governments can only exist in small territories.[54] The proposed Constitution was seriously flawed, said the Anti-Federalists. Congress should call a second convention to correct the excesses. In particular, they argued the people needed a bill of rights to protect them from infringement of their basic rights to trial by jury, freedom of the press, freedom of religion and so on. Seven of the states had bills of rights, so why didn't this federal constitution?

The Federalists responded by pointing to the weaknesses of the Articles of Confederation with regard to foreign policy and national defense.

1. The United States is in violation of its obligations to England under the peace treaty that ended the Revolutionary War, especially its obligations to return or pay for property taken from loyalists during the war.
2. Despite treaties with Spain, Americans are forbidden access to the entire Mississippi River; Spain maintains forts and Indian allies who control much of the territory of Alabama, Mississippi, Tennessee, and Kentucky.
3. The United States can raise no adequate armed forces to defend these borders and have no adequate defense on the seas and coasts, which leaves American shipping unprotected.
4. The United States is unable to pay its debts incurred during the American Revolution.
5. The result of this is that no foreign country will consider entering into negotiations to make additional treaties for the sake of commerce and security.[55]

The Federalist argued that the national government needed to have the power to raise and maintain a professional army, to tax to support that army, and enforce treaty obligations. Those were exactly the powers that the new Constitution provided.

In respect to a bill or rights, the Federalists noted that the delegates to the Constitutional Convention had not included a Bill of Rights because they saw no necessity for doing so. Hamilton explained "Why declare that things shall not be done which there is no power [in Congress] to do?"[56] James Wilson added that drawing up a Bill of Rights would have been impractical anyway. "Enumerate all the rights of men? I am sure that no gentleman in the late Convention would have attempted such a thing."[57] Some delegates made light of the whole notion suggesting that in addition to rights of trial by jury, no taxation without representation and so on that there be added a clause "that everybody shall, in good weather, hunt on his own land, and catch fish in rivers that are public property…and that Congress shall never restrain any inhabitant of America from eating and drinking, at seasonable times, or prevent his lying on his left side, in a long winter's night, or even on his back, when he is fatigued by lying on his right." [58]

> **LESSON: Play offense; not defense.** The Federalists countered the Anti-Federalists by going on the offense, not playing defense. Instead of defending the Constitution against the Anti-Federalists arguments that it gave too much power to the Federal government thereby threatening individual rights and freedoms, the Federalists changed the base of the argument and counter attacked on a new flank—national defense and foreign policy. Later when the Ant-federalists argued that prior amendments were necessary to correct deficiencies in the Constitution, Madison and the Federalists countered by shifting the debate to the continuation of the union, a debate they knew they would win.

The Federalist "began their campaign to win ratification in a "one-up" position: They had a program—the Constitution—for the reform of a sick system, and their opponents, many of whom agreed that something must be done to strengthen the common government, had none."[59] The Anti-Federalists had no positive plan to offer, they were united only in opposition, in the negative. Thus, the Federalist could and did put forward the argument that the document they had produced in Philadelphia, while imperfect, was the best hope for the nation. The alternatives offered by the Anti-Federalist—tinker with the Articles, let the Union dissolve into three or four regional confederacies, or call a new convention to amend the Philadelphia document and add a bill of rights—were not tenable. The choice as Madison put it was "the simple one whether the Union shall or shall not be continued."[60]

Ratification required the approval of nine states but not just any nine states would do. At least four states—Massachusetts, New York, Pennsylvania, and particularly Virginia were critical. Without them, the new government could not succeed.

The Federalists won early and relatively easy victories in five states. Delaware was first to approve the Constitution. Pennsylvania, New Jersey, Georgia, and Connecticut soon followed. Massachusetts, a key state, ratified on February 6, 1788, but only after the Federalists gave in and agreed to demands to attach recommendations that Congress approve a series of amendments including a bill of rights after ratification. Then, the ratification process slowed. New Hampshire met but Federalists voted to adjourn when they decided they did not have the votes. New Jersey first rejected the Constitution and then rescinded its rejection and itself adjourned. In March, Rhode Island rejected the Constitution by a 10 to 1 vote in a popular referendum. However, victories in Maryland in April and South Carolina in May gave the Federalists some hope. By June, eight states had ratified. The Federalists were just one state short but Virginia and New York had not yet ratified and they were critical, none more so than Virginia. Virginia was both the largest state and the most influential. If Virginia rejected the proposed new constitution, New York would likely also reject and without New York and Virginia, the union would undoubtedly fail.

FEDERALIST #10

Since the convention in Philadelphia, James Madison had been busy in New York helping Alexander Hamilton write a series of articles called *The Federalist Papers* explaining and defending the constitution to doubtful

New Yorkers. In those papers, particularly Federalist #10, he had outlined a defense of the constitution and the larger republic it created that he was to return to repeatedly.

A principal argument of the Anti-Federalists against the establishment of a strong national government was that a majority faction such as the large states would dominate the government and repress minority factions such as the smaller states. Madison admitted that factions existed and that by their very nature they would seek to pursue their own interest at the expense of the rights of other citizens and even the interests of the community as a whole. How then to control these factions? The framers, said Madison, had carefully designed the Constitution to use the very existence of factions to fight the evils of factions. Rather than seeking to abolish factions by retaining a confederacy of small homogeneous communities or regions of like opinions, passions and interests, the new American constitution would tolerate, even promote, the clash of interest groups. The Constitution would protect minorities, such as the small states, because it would create one large extended republic with many factions all competing for their own interests.

In effect, Madison turned the Anti-Federalist argument on its head. You are worried about the tyranny of a majority faction. Well, said Madison, so are the Federalists, and we have created a constitution that is carefully designed to prevent that which you and we most fear. Rather than being a threat to the minority, this large and powerful republic that we propose to create will be the minority's friend.

> **LESSON: Turn your opponent's arguments in on themselves.** Find a way to show that what your opponents argue is a vice is in reality a virtue; they can accomplish their goal only by doing that which they argue one must not do. Use a form of logical judo in which the power of your opponents' arguments are leveraged against them such as Madison did with his argument that, contrary to what the Anti-Federalists thought, the best way to preserve individual freedom and liberty was through a strong central government that could prevent the excesses from factions and tyranny of the majority.

ON TO VIRGINIA

In March at the urging of his friends in Virginia, Madison hurried home. There were forces at work determined to prevent Madison from serving as a delegate to Virginia's Constitutional Convention scheduled for June. Madison had to do something he never enjoyed and rarely ever did---campaign for office. Madison won and his victory set up one of the greatest legislative debates in the country's history, a debate upon which the future of the country depended.

By the time that Virginia's convention assembled in June 1788, eight states had already ratified the Constitution but the success of the Federalist effort to create a new form of government was uncertain. If Virginia failed to ratify, then New York would also likely decline to do so and the entire effort would be in jeopardy. The Virginia Anti-Federalists, led by the country's most famous orator Patrick Henry, had a strategy to see the Federalist plan unravel—provoke doubts in the new Constitution, demand amendments and force reformers to call a second general constitutional convention. It would be largely up to Madison to defeat Henry and his fellow Anti-Federalists.

As one historian has noted, the Virginia "state convention brought together nearly every public man of major influence in Virginia for a brilliant and dramatic recapitulation of the larger national debate. With stirring speakers on both sides, the shorthand record of the confrontation is a classic illustration of the way in which Federalists successfully rebutted a persuasive case that constitutional reform might undermine the democratic Revolution."[61]

At the beginning of the Virginia Convention, George Mason proposed to consider the new Constitution clause by clause before a vote on ratification could be taken. Mason reasoned that the Federalists might be slightly ahead in the vote count and he feared that they might push through a quick vote to ratify before the Anti-Federalist could mount their arguments. It was a big mistake. No one was more familiar with the proposed Constitution or its clause-by-clause rationale than James Madison. A clause-by-clause debate would be just the kind of debate that would give Madison the advantage. Patrick Henry, on the other hand, preferred and actually did better in talking about the fundamental thrust of the document and basic principals as he tried to do in the first days of the Convention. As Gary Wills says, "Good as [Patrick] Henry was as an orator and debater, he was not a reflective or studious person, and he was up against a man who had thought and debated and persuaded on this subject through two years that sharpened all of [his] analytical power and parliamentary deftness."[62] The battle lines were drawn. Others would participate but the chief combatants would be Patrick Henry and James Madison. They could not have been more different in style.

Almost immediately, Patrick Henry rose and began hurling his oratorical thunderbolts. Ignoring the clause-by-clause rule he had supported, Henry launched into a generalized attack on the Constitution as a whole. "Whither is the spirit of America gone? Whither is the genius of America fled?" he roared. "We drew the spirit of liberty from our British ancestors. But now, Sir, the American spirit, assisted by the ropes and chains of consolidation, is about to convert this country into a powerful and mighty empire. . . . There will be no checks, no real balances, in this government. What can avail your specious, imaginary balances, your rope-dancing, chain-rattling, ridiculous ideal checks and contrivances?"[63] The rights of the people were endangered. The people of Virginia were faced with the threat of tyranny. "Trial by jury, the cherished right of "our glorious forefathers of Great Britain"...would be forfeited; many other traditional rights of Englishmen would perish; local control of the militia would vanish; and federal tax collectors and sheriffs would infest the land, plundering and oppressing the poor. Worst of all, the new constitution would lead to monarchy."[64] It was a masterful performance and typically of Patrick Henry.

Madison was impressed but hot surprised. He had challenged Patrick Henry before. In 1784, while serving as Governor of Virginia, Henry had promoted an idea to have the people of Virginia "pay a moderate tax or contribution annually for the support of the Christian religion or of some Christian church, denomination, or communion of Christians or of some form of Christian worship."[65] Madison saw the effort as one to create an "established" church and an attack on freedom of thought. Knowing that he was no match for Henry's oratory and being younger and less known, Madison found a way to fight back. He wrote and distributed a petition called "Memorial and Remonstrance Against Religious Assessments" laying out fifteen clear reasons why Henry's proposal would be a violation of the guarantee in the Virginia constitution that every man had the right to exercise religion according to his own conscience. "An avalanche of these petitions soon cascaded back to Richmond, some bearing a hundred signatures."[66] Henry's proposal was dead but his lifelong animosity toward the young, upstart Madison was assured.

Madison rose to offer his reply to Henry. Blair Grigsby, in his account of the Virginia convention described the scene:

> [Madison's] low stature made it difficult for him to be seen from all parts of the house; his voice was rarely loud enough to be heard throughout the hall. He... rose to speak as if with a view of expressing some thoughts that had casually occurred to him, with his hat in his hand and his notes in his hat; and the warmest excitement of debate was visible in him only by a more or less rapid and forward see-saw motion of his body.[67]

Madison was prepared for the debate. No one else understood the Constitution as well. However, he had learned at the convention in Philadelphia that just preparing extensively and reasoning well was not enough. He had to "deal subtly with other men's unreason, to help others see the difference between their phantoms and real fears." [68] Additionally, Madison was not prepared to accept simple statements made without supporting evidence or arguments filled with logical inconsistencies.

Madison began by calling for a calm and rational examination of the Constitution's merits, not arguments based upon emotions. He then turned to dismantling Henry's argument by pointing out his inconsistencies and illogic. Henry had argued that the Constitution endangered public liberty, but said Madison, Henry cannot point to any specific instances or ways that the Constitution does so. Additionally Henry's arguments were illogical said Madison. First, Henry complains that amending the

Constitution requires the consent of three fourths of the states. Then, he turns around and argues more than nine states should be required for approval of the new Constitution. Madison then reminded the delegates that of one of the principal problems with the Articles had been the requirement for unanimous consent for changes, a problem the new Constitution remedied.

> **LESSON: Provide a well-reasoned response to objections from the opposition.** Madison's extensive preparations prior to the Philadelphia convention, particularly his extensive research on the problems with confederate forms of government made him by far the most knowledgeable delegate. He was able to discredit alternative proposals and at the Virginia Convention systematically and persuasively counter the Anti-Federalist arguments.

So went the debates. Over the next twenty-four days, repeatedly Patrick Henry would take to the floor with a passionate improvised assault on one provision or other of the Constitution. Madison would counter with a steady appeal to logic and reason. Typical and perhaps pivotal was Madison's rejoinder to the Anti-Federalist's argument that he offered on June 13, 1788. It had to do with the Mississippi River.

THE MISSISSIPPI RIVER DEBATE

In 1784, Spain closed the port of New Orleans to American commerce. It was a devastating blow to Kentuckians. They needed access to the Mississippi river and to the port of New Orleans to take their whiskey, corn and tobacco to market. In 1785, Congress sent John Jay, America's Secretary of Foreign Affairs, to meet with the Spanish emissary Don Diego de Gardoqui to discuss the New Orleans port closing, navigation of the Mississippi, boundary disputes between Spain and the United States, and American access to Spanish markets. Jay and Gardoqui engaged in discussions for over a year. In May 1786, Jay informed Congress that Spain was willing to open its ports and markets to American commerce thereby providing much needed relief to Northern fishermen and shippers who had suffered from the loss of trade with England. In return, Spain wanted the United States to give up any rights to navigate the Mississippi river for twenty-five or thirty years. Jay argued that by accepting Spain's proposal the United States would gain some "immediate advantages in exchange for a postponement that, given the remoteness of the lands in the Mississippi valley, would not for years have much practical effect."[69] As Ralph Ketchum notes, "Jay's view reflected, ominously, a much keener awareness of the interests of the Eastern, trading portion of the new nation than of the agricultural [southern] regions."[70]

Congress hotly debated the issue and ultimately voted strictly along sectional lines with seven northern states in favor and five southern states opposed. Since under the Articles nine states were required to approve a treaty, the Jay-Gardoqui proposal was defeated. It did not matter. Southerners and Westerners felt betrayed. The northern states had shown that they would willingly sell out other parts of the nation for a temporary economic advantage. The Anti-Federalists raised the subject of the Jay-Gardoqui Treaty at the Virginia ratification convention in June 1788, as a perfect illustration of the dangers they said were implicit in the proposed new Constitution.

James Monroe rose to help make the Anti-Federalist's case. The State of Virginia, he reminded the delegates, had always supported opening the Mississippi to navigation and the "use of the inhabitants whose interest depended on it."[71] In his discussions with Spain, Jay had violated his instructions from Congress that "he enter into no treaty, compact, or convention whatever…which did not stipulate [the United States'] right to the navigation of the Mississippi."[72] The southern states were surprised that the northern states would use navigation of the Mississippi as a "species of barter." But, that is exactly what the northern states were prepared to do. The Articles of Confederation had prevented the northern states from sacrificing the interests of the southern states because it required at least nine states to approve a treaty. Under the new Constitution, two-thirds of a quorum (or as few as seven states) would be sufficient. Given that mankind in general and states in particular were governed by their own interests,

Monroe said he had no doubts that the northern states would "not fail of availing themselves the opportunity...of relinquishing [the Mississippi] in order to depress the western country, and prevent the southern interest from preponderant."[73] It was a powerful and emotionally charged argument. The Federalists were in trouble. Then, Madison took the floor.

Madison said he did not intend to differ from the Anti-Federalists on facts but on principals. First, the people of the eastern states never supported surrendering the Mississippi. Indeed, it was not in their interest to do so. "If the carrying business (shipping) be their natural province," asked Madison, "how can it be so much extended and advanced as by giving encouragement to agriculture in the western country, and having the emolument of carrying their produce to market?"[74] The carrying trade depended upon agriculture to have something to carry and the greatest opportunity for expansion in agriculture lay in the western country whose expansion required access to the river.

Yes, admitted Madison, seven states had agreed to give up navigation of the Mississippi but only temporarily and for a reason, that went beyond purely selfish interests. They were concerned about the possibility of Great Britain and Spain reaching an agreement or coalition that might permanently bar the United States from use of the river. These states believed that relinquishing the right to navigation for twenty-five or thirty years with the stipulation that the United States would have permanent rights to navigation thereafter was an effective way to prevent any British/Spanish agreement from being concluded and to ensure permanent navigation rights. Of course, Madison hastened to say, however plausible the reasons offered by those who supported the treaty, he had uniformly disapproved of it and did now.

In respect to whether the old or new constitution provided greater protection for the southern states, Madison said it was clear that the new constitution was much better.

> Under the new constitution, "two thirds of the senators present, (which will be nine states, if all attend to their duty,) and the President, must concur in every treaty which can be made. Here

> are two distinct and independent branches, which must agree to every treaty. Under the existing system, two thirds of the states must concur to form a treaty. However, it is one body.[75]

Was not it reasonable to conclude, asked Madison, that two independent branches would provide greater protection than just one? Plus, Madison reminded the delegates, it was the defects in the Articles that led to the Jay-Gardoqui Treaty controversy to begin with. The country needed a stronger system of government to prevent just such a thing from happening again.

Madison's reasoning was devastating to the Anti-Federalists. While it is doubtful whether he changed any votes, he effectively undercut the Anti-Federalists arguments and therefore defused the Mississippi issue. The convention could get back to the clause-by-clause consideration of the Constitution.

Madison left the Anti-Federalists with one remaining argument, the need for amendments, including a bill of rights to provide greater protections to the southern states. In particular, the Anti-Federalists were concerned about provisions in the new Constitution such as equal representation of states in the Senate that seemed to give excessive power to the smaller northern states. They argued that the framers should correct the unacceptable *before* Virginia agreed to ratify the document. Patrick Henry made the argument for amendments before ratification this way:

> I should …take that man for a lunatic, who should tell me to run into adoption of a government avowedly defective, in hopes of having it amended afterwards…Do you enter into a compact first, and afterwards settle the terms?[76]

It was a powerful argument but, said Madison and other Federalists, flawed in two respects. First, the framers had carefully designed the new constitution to restrict the powers of the central government to those responsibilities that the states could not effectively exercise on their own. Additionally, the internal checks and balances built into the document together with the almost certain agricultural majority in the House "would all combine to guard against a dangerous consolidation or against misuse of governmental power by the North."[77] Second and perhaps more importantly, said the Federalists, time was running out. The states that had already ratified were not going to reverse their decisions just "to gratify Virginia."[78] Even if they did, there was little prospect that a second convention to consider amendments could ever reach an agreement. This might be the last chance to secure the union that was as important to Virginia and the rest of the south as it was to the north.

Edmund Randolph, the Governor of Virginia who had refused initially to sign the Constitution in Philadelphia had the final word. He warned the delegates that the old confederation was gone whether they liked it or not.

> It is gone, whether this house says so or not. It is gone, sir, by its own weakness...The Confederation is gone; it has no authority. If, in this situation, we reject the Constitution, the Union will be dissolved, the dogs of war will break loose, and anarchy and discord will complete the ruin of this country.[79]

With that the delegates voted, they defeated the question of previous amendments by a vote of 88 to 80. Then Virginia ratified the constitution by a margin of 10 votes 89 to 79. The Anti-Federalists were able to tack on a series of *recommended* amendments that Madison and the Federalists promised the new Congress would consider during its first secession but the Federalists had won. Virginia would be part of the union. New York soon followed.

> **LESSON: Focus on winning the support of key opinion leaders.** If Washington and Franklin were involved in the drafting of the Constitution and supported its ratification, that was enough for many people. At the Virginia Convention, Randolph's change of sides and stirring final argument in favor of ratification undoubtedly had a significant impact on swaying delegates who were still wavering.

THE BILL OF RIGHTS

The federalists had won but they knew that it was likely that the majority of the people in the country were opposed to the new constitution. Unless they could win over popular Anti-Federalist sentiment, the nation would still be in trouble. Madison, in particular, recognized that the Bill of Rights that he had fought hard against and that the Federalists had promised to deliver in the first Congress would now be necessary. But, how could he deliver on the promise without weakening the new constitution that he had struggled so hard to create?

When Congress assembled, Madison was anxious to get on with adopting a Bill of Rights a number of states had demanded as a condition of ratification. Indeed two states Rhode Island and North Carolina were still holdouts refusing to ratify until they saw a Bill of Rights actually in place. Others in Congress were not that interested. They were much more concerned with getting on with the important business of state. William Jackson of Georgia put in it nautical terms: "Our constitution sir, is like a vessel just launched, and lying at the wharf...Let us, gentlemen, fit our vessel, set up her masts, and expand her sails, and be guided by the experiment in our alterations."[80] Of course one can question whether the "important business of state" that Congress wanted to pursue was indeed as important as the Bill of Rights. For example, the delegates were obsessed with the important business of coming up with a title for the President. Many wanted something regal such as—His Highness the President of the United States and Protector of Their Liberties.

Madison persisted. It was important, he argued, to move expeditiously on adopting a Bill of Rights for one simple reason. "If the Federalists could not show that they were as committed to liberty as the Anti-Federalists, they were not going to have power for long, or know how to deal with it while they held it."[81]

Madison recognized that if he was going to get his colleagues to consider seriously a Bill of Rights then he had to offer them some specific proposals. Therefore, he took on the task. He went about the process in the same methodical manner he approached everything. He began collecting every newspaper clipping he could find that discussed a federal bill of rights. He assembled notes on all of the proposed Constitutional amendments that the states had tacked on to their ratifications. There were over 200 including 32 specific proposals from the New York convention alone. The proposed amendments ranged from those to protect freedom of the press to those seeking to restrict the term of the President to two years to those dealing with regulating taxation and elections. Madison extracted the key amendment proposals common to most states and added a few of his own. As Patrick Henry had feared, Madison threw out most of the Anti-Federalists' proposals such as those dealing with reducing the central government's taxation powers, judicial authority, and authority over commercial treaties. Madison explained to Edmund Randolph that he intentionally restricted the amendments he proposed "to points which are important in the eyes of many and can be objectionable in those of none."[82]

The House agreed to take up Madison's proposed amendments but then got sidetracked while it debated how to raise money to fund the new government. In the mean time, Madison's proposals were printed in newspapers arround the country. Overall they were well received. Equally important the Anti-Federalists implicitly demonstrated, if not their approval, at least their acceptance by remaining silent.

Finally, at much nudging and nagging from Madison the House agreed to submit Madison's proposals for amendments to a select committee charged with responsibility to "cull out those of the most material kind without interrupting the principal business of the House."[83] The committee went to work and kept much of Madison's wording except in a few areas. For example, Madison's article on religion provided that there would be "no national religion." The committee changed the wording to read:"No religion shall be established by law, nor shall the equal rights of conscience be infringed." Similar changes were made to Madison's wording about freedom of speech, the press and the right peaceably to assemble. On the whole, however, the committee members reported out a document very similar to that Madison had given them. Madison was pleased.

On August 13, 1789, the Virginia delegation submitted the committee's revised amendments for consideration by the House as a whole. They were met with indifference. The members if the House were preoccupied with a more important matter—their salaries. Would $6.00 per day appear extravagant to their constituents? Again it was only after considerable nagging from Madison that the House agreed to debate the amendments. Almost immediately, Madison encountered a snag.

Madison had sought to incorporate the amendments into the main body of the Constititution rather than tacking them on at the end. Roger Sherman of Connecticut objected. He wanted the amendments added to the Constititution as a kind of appendix. After an all day debate, Madison was able to beat back the change, at least for awhile, and debate on the amendments themselves began.

The representatives began tinkering with Madison's wording. The amendment dealing with religion, said one, shoud be changed to read "Congress shall make no laws touching religion, or infringing the rights of conscience." Another wanted the words "to instruct their representatives" added to the amendment dealing with the right of people to peaceably assemble. Madison pleaded with the members to stop the nickpicking but the debate droned on. He was particularly exasperated when a member from South Carolina proposed dropping what Madison considered the most important of the amendments, those that prevented the states from infinging on the freedom of speech, press and religion. No sooner had Madison rallied support to beat back that motion than he was presented with an even more disasterous one. Elbridge Gerry, perhaps in jest but perhaps not, proposed that the House consider not just the twelve amendments before them, but all 200 or so that the states had tacted on to their ratifications. Again, Madison rallied the opposition and Gerry's proposal was defeated. Then Sherman, recognizing that support had grown for his earlier proposal, renewed his motion that the amendments be added as an appendix. Exhausted from his struggle to preserve his constitution and amendments, Madison this time didn't object. He wrote to a friend, " It became an unavoidable sacrifice to ...the dispatch if not the succcess of the business, to give up the form by which the amendts when ratified would have fallen in the body of the Constitution, in favor of the project of adding them by way of appendix to it."[84] Sherman's proposal was approved by a wide margin.

The House appointed a committee to combine and consolidate the amendments into a final list. The committee reported out a list of seventeen amendments, which the House quickly approved and sent to the Senate.

The Senate debated the amendments for six days. After merging some of the amendments, adding some new ones and dropping others including Madison's favorite that prevented states from violating personal freedoms, the Senate sent twelve amendments back to the House. A conference committee worked out outstanding differences and on September 25, 1789, the Congress sent twelve amendments to the state legislatures for ratification. It took two years, but eventually the states approved ten of the twelve amendments. Rhode Island and North Carolina ratified the Constitution. Thanks to Madison and the Federalists, the country had a new form of government.

> **LESSON: Placate your opposition by carefully constructing a response that appears to meet their objections without actually doing so.** Appear to be accommodating while simultaneously advancing your own position. Consider what Madison did with the Bill of Rights. Madison had been opposed to a Bill of Rights. However, he came to realize that they were necessary to win Anti-Federalist support or at least minimize their opposition to the new form of government. The Anti-Federalists sought much broader amendments to the Constitution than Madison was prepared to accept. His challenge was to design a set of amendments that would reassure his opponents without weakening the new government. Madison omitted most of the changes that the Anti-Federalists wanted. However, he included amendments that offered sufficient assurance to the people that their rights would be respected and protected by the new government. That was enough.

THE IMPOSSIBLE TASK OF GETTING THINGS DONE IN WASHINGTON

As I said earlier, the Constitution fifty-five men constructed during the hot summer of 1787 in Philadelphia was a remarkable achievement. The framers sought to replace a form of government that was dysfunctional because of the barriers it placed in the way of getting anything done. The Constitution these men created and sold to the American people was a substantial improvement over the Articles. There is no doubt about that. However, it was far from perfect at least from the point of view of anyone who wants to get things done in Washington.

The framers intentionally designed the American government to prevent reformers from easily accomplishing anything of consequence. James MacGregor Burns, among others, has argued that James Madison did all he could to see to it that under the new system of government change would come slowly and major change would almost never occur at the whimsy of the majority of the moment. Madison succeeded beyond his wildest imagination.

One has only to consider how the U.S. government works to appreciate the obstacles to major change the founding fathers built into the system of government they devised. Any piece of legislation must be approved by the U.S. Senate and House of Representatives and signed by the President before it can become law. It then must withstand any constitutional challenge before the Supreme Court. Today, Senators are elected statewide and serve the interests of the voters in their states. Representatives are elected in districts and serve the interests of voters in their district. The President is elected nation-wide, not by a majority of the popular vote, but by a majority in an arcane electoral college that allocates votes to states according to their number of Senators and Representatives. Consequently, the President serves the interest of the nation or at least the voters in states with the most electoral votes. Members of the Supreme Court are appointed by the President and confirmed by the Senate often because they share the President's and majority party's ideological and/or policy preferences. Like the President, Supreme Court justices are supposed to serve the national interest but often they serve the ideological/policy preferences of a President and Senate that has long vanished from the national stage.

To make matters even more complicated, the President, Senators and Representatives serve different terms. Representatives must stand for election every two years. Senators are elected for six year terms and every four years we vote for a President. Supreme Court justices serve for life. Senators, Representatives, the President and members of the court thus operate on different time horizons.

Increasingly, voters elect representatives from districts that have been intentionally drawn to the advantage of one party and/or political ideology over another, Democratic or Republican, liberal or conservative. Often the party that controls the House is different from the party that controls the Senate. Even when the same party controls the House and Senate, the president may be from a different party. Because of the way we elect members of Congress and the president and the frequency with which they must stand for reelection there may be and often are sharp ideological differences and policy preferences between the two branches themselves and between the Congress and the president. Additionally, the rules of order in the two houses of Congress differ so that the very path a bill has to negotiate to become law is quite different in the two houses. For example, Senate rules concerning cutting off debate/filibuster, make it impossible to get controversial legislation passed without a super-majority of 60 members voting in the affirmative.

Finally, since different presidents appoint and different Senates confirm the justices on any particular sitting Supreme Court over what may be decades, the court itself may be severely split ideologically making unanimous ruling difficult, if not impossible. Consequently, the Court may uphold laws or declare them unconstitutional by the thinnest majority. Additionally, at any time the court may be and often is significantly out of step with the prevailing political mood and wishes of the president, Congress and American people.

Beyond these institutional barriers there are the barriers caused by individual and collective competing interests of a pluralistic and ever more fragmented society. For all of the people who at any given time are suffering because of the way things are and hoping for change, there are a smaller but often richer and more powerful group who are prospering from the way things are and are determined to see that no change occurs. The closer advocates of change get to making change happen the more determined the opposition becomes. And, since change always involves a certain amount of the unknown which most of us find frightening, those opposed to change usually have an easier time convincing us to do nothing. They have the fear of the unknown on their side. To get things done advocates of change have to overcome all the incentives built into the system to do nothing. Whenever anyone proposes a major change in public policy, they immediately encounter resistance from those who are threatened by and/are frightened by the change. Momentum starts building to oppose change and it gains strength like a ball rolling down a hill gather anti-change speed as it goes.

Getting things done in Washington is difficult but it is not impossible. In the chapters that follow, I will introduce you to some true heroes who got things done in Washington and suggest lessons we can learn from their accomplishments. We will start with the story of a little known bureaucrat from the Department of Agriculture who led a "pure food crusade" to secure the passage of legislation that would revolutionize the quality of drugs and America's food supply.

A SUMMARY OF LESSONS FROM THE STRUGGLE FOR THE CONSTITUTION

Get the timing right. Timing may not be everything, but it is extremely important. The Articles were weak, but they were probably all that the country was ready for in 1781. The country had to experience the defects of the Articles before it was prepared to adopt a stronger form of government. It took something like Shay's Rebellion to jolt people into action. By 1787, the country was ready to consider something more than a weak confederation. As Rossiter says: "Most of the ingredients of American nationalism were in the place by 1787: common language, common origin and outlook, common legal and political institutions, common culture, common enemies, and common memories of a successful drive toward independence. There lacked, indeed, only that condition of political unity and sense of emotional unity which would follow on the creation of a central government with dignity and authority."[85]

Take advantage of any opportunities to move your proposal forward. Mason saw the meeting between Maryland and Virginia to discuss navigation rights on the Potomac and Chesapeake as an opportunity to call for another conference with a wider agenda. The Maryland/Virginia discussions led to the Annapolis Convention that led to Philadelphia.

Dictate the discussion; make your opponents work from your proposal At both the Philadelphia Convention and prior to the debate over the Bill of Rights, Madison developed and offered a proposal that formed the basis of debate. The question was not "What kind of new government should we create?" or "How should the Constitution be amended?" The question put before the delegates and Congress was "What parts of the proposal put forward by Virginia should we accept and what parts need revision or modification." In both cases, while Madison lost on several major points, he got most of what he wanted largely because the debate started from a discussion of what he wanted.

Be willing to compromise. Your purpose is to achieve passage of something that moves your agenda forward even if that means you do not get everything you want. Madison had to back off some of his extreme ideas. He learned to lose. He favored proportional representation for both houses and lost. He favored giving the national legislature the power to negate state laws and lost. He favored the popular election of the executive and lost. One Constitutional scholar has estimated that during the Philadelphia Convention, "of seventy-one specific proposals that Madison moved, seconded, or spoke unequivocally in regard to, he was on the losing side forty times."[86] Moreover, recall that Madison saw his favorite amendment to hold the states accountable for personal freedoms go down to defeat. Still, Madison won in the long term on the major issue. He got a new and much stronger constitution. Madison himself said that the compromise over proportional representation that gave the small states equal representation in the Senate was critical to the success of the convention. The 3/5ths compromise over the counting of slaves was equally important in winning the support of the southern states. The Constitution, as Rossiter says, "was, in truth, a shrew armistice among men who had become convinced that their common interests would never be realized unless their special interests were compromised... [It was] the creation of politicians who had a genius for inventing 'half-way' solutions."[87] He continues: "The Federalists also won because, in most of their decisions and dealings, they showed good judgment in distinguishing the possible from the unacceptable, in knowing when to hold fast and when to give way. By adding anyone of a half-dozen techniques and arrangements to their Constitution [such as] a veto on state laws...the Framers might have tipped the delicately balanced scale of opinion against their cause...But the Framers... had a good collective sense of what the people, if properly instructed, would accept."[88]

Portray the opposition as naysayers who offer no coherent alternative. The Federalists were able to exploit the fact that the Anti-Federalist had no coherent alternative to offer to the new constitution. Even the name "Anti-Federalist" was a benefit to the Federalist's cause. The Federalists used a similar tactic in the Virginia Convention when they successful portrayed the choice as one between preserving the union and seeing it dissolve. The new constitution was the only way forward.

Play offense; not defense. The Federalists countered the Anti-Federalists by going on the offense, not playing defense. Instead of defending the Constitution against the Anti-Federalists arguments that it gave too much power to the Federal government thereby threatening individual rights and freedoms, the Federalists changed the base of the argument and counter attacked on a new flank—national defense and foreign policy. Later when the Ant-federalists argued that prior amendments were necessary to correct deficiencies in the Constitution, Madison and the Federalists countered by shifting the debate to the continuation of the union, a debate they knew they would win.

Turn your opponent's arguments in on themselves. Find a way to show that what your opponents argue is a vice is in reality a virtue; that the opponents can achieve their worthy goal only by doing that which they argue is what one must not do. Use a form of logical judo in which the power of your opponents' arguments are leveraged against them such as Madison did with his argument that contrary to what the Anti-Federalists thought, the best way to preserve individual freedom and liberty was through a strong central government that could prevent the excesses from factions and tyranny of the majority.

Provide a well-reasoned response to objections from the opposition. Madison's extensive preparations prior to the Philadelphia convention, particularly his extensive research on the problems with confederate forms of government made him by far the most knowledgeable delegate. He was able to discredit alternative proposals and at the Virginia Convention systematically and persuasively counter the Anti-Federalist arguments.

Focus on winning the support of key opinion leaders. If Washington and Franklin were involved in the drafting of the Constitution and supported its ratification, that was enough for many people. At the Virginia Convention, Randolph's change of sides and stirring final argument in favor of ratification undoubtedly had a significant impact on swaying delegates who were still wavering.

Placate your opposition by carefully constructing a response that appears to meet their objections without actually doing so. Appear to be accommodating while simultaneously advancing your own position. Consider what Madison did with the Bill of Rights. Madison had been opposed to a Bill of Rights. However, he came to realize that they were necessary to win Anti-Federalist support or at least minimize their opposition to the new form of government. The Anti-Federalists sought much broader amendments to the Constitution than Madison was prepared to accept. His challenge was to design a set of amendments that would reassure his opponents without weakening the new government. Madison omitted most of the changes that the Anti-Federalists wanted. However, he included amendments sufficient to assure the people that their rights would be respected and protected by the new government. That was enough.

2

The Struggle for Pure Food & Drugs

The struggle for pure food and drugs is an inspiring story of progressive accomplishment. Over a 25 year period in the late 1880s and early 1900s, progressives across the country banded together to fight for federal government oversight of the food, drink and drug industries. Their efforts led to the passage of the most important and far-reaching regulatory statutes in U.S. history—the Meat Inspection Act and Pure Food and Drug Act of 1906. The story of what these men and women did and how they ultimately succeeded contains important lessons for anyone who seeks to get things done in Washington.

The first lesson the pure food and drug crusade can teach us is that the road to legislative accomplishment in Washington usually begins far away from Washington with a spontaneous grassroots movement. Proponents add the remaining ingredients necessary for legislative accomplishment later, sometimes years later. It was like that with the drive to enact a pure food and drug law. Consequently, we begin our examination of the struggle for pure foods and drugs not in Washington, but in towns and cities hundreds of miles away in, for example, New York among the gentile ladies of the Beekman Hill neighborhood.

THE LADIES OF BEEKMAN HILL DECIDE TO SOLVE AN ODOR PROBLEM

On December 9, 1884, fifteen women from the Beekman Hill neighborhood of New York City, who had met regularly for some time for tea and conversation, set out on a journey to discover the source of a particularly noxious odor. They quickly discovered that the offending smell originated in a 30-foot high, 200-foot long pile of manure in a vacant lot owned by Michael Kane, a fertilizer dealer. Kane was one of the city's 14 businessmen who collected the estimated 1,100 cartloads of manure produced daily by the city's 38,000 horses that drew the carriages and wagons and provided the major means of transportation for the metropolis. Kane's workers would transport the manure to vacant lots each day where it would be composted for future sale as fertilizer.[89]

The ladies protested that the smell from the fly-infested excrement on Kane's lot was so bad that nearby residents were reluctant to open their windows even in the middle of summer. Additionally, the waste matter, they argued, constituted a health threat. Kane responded that the waste was much too valuable as fertilizer and the location was ideally suited for the collection and storage of the waste and delivery of the resulting fertilizer to eager customers. He explained to the good ladies of Beekman Hill that he was operating a legitimate and useful business and that they should return to their homes and mind their own business.

When the ladies approached city health officials seeking their help in having the offending, unhealthy pile of noxious waste removed, the officials refused to take action citing their long-standing practice of not interfering with local businesses. One member of the board of health suggested that the ladies forget this nonsense and return to what he called "their afternoon tea-cup visitations."

Insulted by their treatment and frustrated by the indifference of local health officials, the ladies took the matter to a local court before a sympathetic judge. They testified to the noxious smells and brought in a doctor to attest to the danger the offending matter presented to public health. Kane vigorously defended his business practices and produced a local dentist who argued that while the smell from the manure pile was not pleasant, neither was it obnoxious. Anyway, said the dentist, the foul odor had medical benefits. For example, he noted, it offered him relief from his persistent sore throat.

After a four day hearing, the judge declared the excrement and waste to be a public nuisance and ordered Kane to have the offending material removed. Kane, confident that he would be protected by his political connections including a brother-in-law in the New York Senate, refused to obey the order just as other businessmen had refused to obey similar court orders in the past. Writing about the incident in 1896, Mary Trautman, President of the Ladies Health Protective Association, recalled that Kane had received several previous orders to remove the material, "which had always been pigeon-holed, and he thought this one would travel the same road. But it was his first experience with women, and he did not realize what that meant." [90] In fact, it meant a great deal.

The ladies would not take no for an answer. They insisted that the court ruling be enforced and badgered the authorities continuously. Reluctantly, the authorities finally yielded to the ladies demands and forced Kane to obey the court order and remove the offending matter from the neighborhood. The ladies had won but were warned by at least one health department official to not attempt to build upon their victory. If they were wise, he said, they would go home and "not meddle any more in matters that did not concern them." However, as Mary Trautman later put it, the women were now "fully aroused to the necessity of action for the benefit of those who were less fortunate in life and unable to help themselves."[91] Instead of going home, they responded by forming The Ladies Health Protective Association. They launched a campaign to improve sanitary conditions in the city. They chose as their first candidate for improvement a string of slaughterhouses in their neighborhood.

The slaughterhouses were really nothing more than fifty-five tiny dirty, blood-soaked pens. Cattle would be herded through the streets daily to be confined in cellars below the pens "the air of which was so stifling and fetid," wrote Trautman, "that the poor creatures could be seen clambering over each other in frantic efforts to reach up to the gratings for a breath of fresh air."[92]

Children watched as butchers dragged the cattle one by one into the pens and slaughtered them. The floors and walls of the pens were soaked in blood. The butchers hung the meat on large hooks. Dirt, grime, and hoards of flies soon coated the meat. Puddles of blood formed in the streets. Additionally, the lard production/bone boiling works associated with the slaughterhouses produced odors even more overpowering and obnoxious than the piles of horse manure the ladies had just caused to be removed. The ladies demanded reforms but the butchers saw no need to change their methods of doing business just because a group of women wanted them to do so.

The ladies were unable to get a court order to stop the offending practices since there was no law against the operation of slaughterhouses and bone boiling works in the neighborhoods and no legal restrictions on how such businesses could be conducted. The ladies' only option was to take their case to the state legislature, which they did. They demanded passage of laws requiring the butchers to adopt more sanitary and less obnoxious methods in the conduct of their businesses. Of course, the ladies' efforts toward obtaining a legislative remedy failed since the butchers had too much political influence. Ultimately, however, the ladies won at least a partial victory.

The butchers decided to settle. They had spent heavily to defeat the legislation. They realized that once mobilized the ladies were not going away. Owners of four of the largest slaughterhouses in the city agreed to represent the butchers in a meeting with representatives of the Ladies Association. That meeting led to a compromise. The ladies agreed to cease their lobbying efforts to secure passage of new legislation in return for the butchers agreeing to adopt many of the reforms the ladies sought.

Over the next two decades, the Ladies Health Protective Association became a major advocate in New York for improvements in sanitary conditions as well as for the passage of pure food and drugs laws. Their association was just one of many throughout the country. The drive for pure food and drugs originated not in the halls of Congress or legislative offices, but in cities and small towns across the country, indeed in the parlors and living rooms of women who saw and felt the impact of impure foods and adulterated drugs most directly. They were the ones who cared for those sickened by the contaminated foods and drugs. They buried the children who died from tainted products.

THE GRASSROOTS MOVEMENT FOR PURE FOOD AND DRUGS IS BORN

Women organized similar groups to the New York Ladies Health Protective Association in Brooklyn, Philadelphia, Chicago, and many smaller cities all across the country in the late 1800s. Many of these groups grew out of women's clubs that were created originally to study literature, art, or history. What began as an effort toward self-improvement led to a sisterhood united to tackle social problems associated with food, drugs, and alcohol addiction. The Shakespeare Club of Clinton, Missouri was typical of these clubs that later became pure food advocates. In December 1901, having finished their discussion of *Henry* VIII, club members set aside some time to discuss current events. By October of the next year the Shakespeare Club was meeting with the local Civic Club to discuss ways to improve public health and by earlier 1904, the ladies of the Shakespeare Club had become a force in the community lobbying for the passage of pure food laws.

On the national level, the National Woman's Christian Temperance Union (NWCTU) was a major player in the late 1800s and early 1900s in creating public awareness of the pure food and drug problem. The NWCTU was founded initially to fight alcohol abuse but expanded its efforts to pure food, drink and drugs arguing that "adulterated food predisposed individuals to alcoholism and vice; doctored soft drinks and proprietary medications addicted individuals to alcohol and opium, and all addictive 'narcotics and stimulants'...belonged in the same category with alcohol."[93]

The General Federation of Women's Clubs (GFWC) was another national organization that played a major role in bringing the food and drug problem to national attention. Leaders of local women's clubs created the Federation in 1890 to promote "cultural, intellectual and philanthropic interests of individual clubs, and also as a national body of social workers to promote the general welfare by assisting the poor, fighting famine and disease, raising the educational and cultural level, and working for reform."[94] It appealed to non-Christians and those who were not primarily interested in prohibition and grew rapidly. The General Federation of Women's clubs had more than 150,000 members in 595 clubs in 30 states in 1900. By 1905, the clubs had more than 300,000 members.

The National Consumers' League was another national organization that played an important role in the drive to pass state and national pure food and drug laws. Activists founded the League in 1899 to rally consumer action against the exploitation of women and children, particularly in garment manufacturing plants. The Leagues involvement in the pure food and drug struggle was a natural extension of those efforts since women and children who worked in food manufacturing plants would benefit from conditions that were more sanitary. The League had worked with unions particularly in the garment industry to get better working conditions for women so it could attract unions to the pure food and drug cause. It had recruited members by organizing girls and women's clubs in high schools, trade schools, and colleges so it could marshal these clubs to further the pure food effort. In addition, the League sought membership from both men and women whereas the women's clubs and temperance clubs restricted membership to women, so the League could seek the support of men. Particularly in the final years of the struggle, the National Consumers' league played an important role in bringing together the various pure, food and drug advocate groups, women's clubs, temperance unions, religious organizations, state and federal chemists, public health workers, medical professionals, and journalists in a united effort to push for pure food and drug legislation. Finally, and importantly, the National Consumers' League had activist orientation and experience in organizing protests, strikes, and boycotts that came in handy in building public support for the cause.

> **LESSON: Progressives ideas for change rarely originate in Washington.** The drive for pure food and drugs did not start in Washington and professional politicians did not take the lead in proposing change, if fact they resisted change. It began when average men and women such as the ladies

> from Beekman hill decided that something was wrong in the country and that the federal government had to play a role in correcting the problem. Over and over throughout this book we will see that progressive ideas for change almost always originate in this way. If you want to know where to look for the next big idea about how to use the power of government to achieve the common good, look to the people not to the politicians.

Of course, nothing much would have come of these organizations on a national level without some coordination. No single group could have made it happen on its own. Fortunately, these different women's groups found a way to work together because leaders of the various groups were members of other groups. The cross over membership between organizations contributed greatly to their effectiveness. Members of one women's organization would often also join or work closely with other women's organizations on related issues. For example, Sarah Platt Decker, president of the GFWC, was a member of the Denver WCTU and the National Consumer's League. Florence Kelley and Maud Nathan, officials of the National Consumers' League, were also members of the GFWC. Marian McBride served as an officer in both the NWCTU Department of Health and Heredity and the GFWC Household Economics Committee.[95] Members of Jewish and Catholic women's leagues and women's business and professional organizations were also members of the federation women's clubs as were members of Black women's organizations. Finally, many of these same women were active in the women's suffrage movement so they would meet while attending the conventions of the National Council of Women. The cross-membership made it easier for these various groups with different primary agendas to find common ground in their support for pure food, drink and drug laws.

> **LESSON: There must be some national coordination of local grassroots efforts**. The pure food and drug cause benefited greatly from the coordinating and organizing efforts of the Women's Christian Temperance Union, National Consumers

> League and National Council of Women. In addition, it helped that many of these organizations had members in common which made communication and coordination easier.

THE NATURE OF THE PURE FOOD AND DRUG PROBLEM

Why were these women's groups so concerned about pure food and drugs? What was the pure food and drug problem anyway? Let us go back in time to see what it was like to live in the late 1800s in the United States.

Today, we go to the grocery or drug store, purchase the items we need or fill our doctor's prescription and rarely question the basic quality or effectiveness of the products we receive. We assume that while the food we purchase for our families to consume may not be the most nutritious, at least it is not harmful. We assume that the labels on the packages provide a reasonably accurate description of their contents. We assume that companies produce the drugs we buy according to strict safety standards, and if the drugs do not necessarily cure us or relieve our symptoms, they will not kill us provided we follow the manufacturer and our doctor/pharmacist's instructions for proper dosage and use. Sometimes we are wrong. Tainted food enters the food chain. Drugs that are supposed to be safe and effective prove to be neither. For the most part, however, we can buy, consume, and use the goods with confidence. None of that was true in the late 1800s and early 1900s. Many products contained questionable and undisclosed contents if they were not addictive or outright hazardous to health.

Americans saw a rapid increase in the quantity and variety of food, drink, and drugs they could purchase coupled with a rapid decline in its quality starting around 1870. Before that time, most Americans lived in small communities. The fruits and vegetables they consumed were available only seasonally and were locally grown. The meat they ate came from animals they raised and slaughtered themselves or from a local butcher who either slaughtered the animals himself or knew the farmer who did. The butcher, the farmer who sold the produce, the dairyman who sold the milk, the baker who made the bread knew their customers personally. They knew they were responsible and that their customers would hold them responsible for the quality of the food products they provided their neighbors.

After the Civil War, Americans eating habits and the sources of their food changed as the country moved rapidly from a largely agricultural to an industrial economy. In the early 1800s, the dominant meal for most Americans was cornbread and salt pork (dipped in molasses when molasses was available.) Fruits and vegetables were largely absent from the dinner table not only because they were expensive and not readily available but also because most Americans of the time believed consuming fruits and vegetables led to cholera, dyspepsia and other gastrointestinal complaints. Most foods were fried. On arriving in America, most working class immigrants rapidly adopted coffee (often mixed with chicory or cereals) as their breakfast drink and increased substantially the amount of sugar and meat in their diet. Sugar was widely considered as a healthy addition to one's diet consequently sweet rolls, doughnuts, ice cream, cakes and so on were popular. In spite of its wider availability, food was still expensive for most working-class Americans amounting to up to one half of the family budget consequently any savings in the food budget from, for example, cheaper meat, bread or drink quickly translated into money available for other purposes such as money for clothing or heat.

The American diet and source of food changed dramatically in the late 1800s. Enterprising businessmen created Pillsbury, H.J. Heinz, Campbell Soup, Borden, Swift, Armour, Coca Cola and many of the other major national food, beverage, and grocery companies during that period. The Great Atlantic and Pacific Tea Company (A&P) built chain grocery stores across the country to compete with local general stores. Bread making moved from home to local and then regional bakeries. Canned goods became available for most Americans, dramatically changing food preparation, and the American diet.

The American canning industry dates from about 1819. It grew slowly until the Civil War, mostly supplying upscale consumers or sea captains and navies that needed a stable food product for long voyages. Most Americans first encountered canned milk, meat, and so on during the Civil War when they became standard army rations. After the war, first canned milk then other canned food became widely available and the returning soldiers began purchasing the product for their families. By 1870, thirty million cans of food were being processed and sold nationally.

Foods that were once available only during specific seasons were now available in canned form year round. Canned milk was one of the first canned food products that became widely available. Gail Borden, a New York inventor, tinkerer, and promoter, reportedly became obsessed with finding a way to preserve and condense food after learning of the tragedy that struck the Donner party, members of a wagon train headed for California who became snowbound in the Sierra Nevada Mountains in the winter of 1846-1847. Starving, they resorted to cannibalism to survive. Borden sought to create a nutritious food product that could be easily transported and would not spoil. His first attempt involved creating a "meat biscuit" by mixing a liquid extract derived from boiled meat with flour and baking it to the consistency and shape of a cracker. Users crumbled the biscuit and mixed it with boiling water to form a soup that retained much of the nutrition of the original meat. Although Borden was able to sell some of his biscuits to arctic explorers and sea captains, the product ultimately failed to catch on. Some argued that the resulting "soup" while nutritious was far from palatable. Borden's second effort to apply his condensation process to milk proved much more successful. He started selling his canned milk in local New York markets. After the Civil War Borden's Canned Milk became one of the first canned goods sold nationally. Soldiers in the war had become familiar with it as part of their ration and now began purchasing it for their families.

Canned goods changed not only what American's ate but also how they prepared their food. Cooks could now prepare an entire meal using only canned goods. They were no longer dependent on what could be grown locally or was in season. Competition between national brands and local brands to satisfy this increasing demand for canned goods and other processed food increased dramatically. Problems arose.

Initially, vegetables, fruit, and meat were so readily available and cheap canners had no financial incentive to add anything but water to their product. Soon, however, reports began to surface of producers canning spoiled fruits and vegetables and adulterating the product. For example, when demand for white sweet canned corn increased, canners began using sodium sulfite as bleach in their competition to supply the whitest canned corn. Canners used copper and zinc salts to preserve the bright green color and fresh appearance of peas, beans, and other vegetables. Advocates of pure food raised concerns about the amount of lead in solder used to seal the cans. They warned that acid in fruits and vegetables could interact with the lead solder causing toxins to leach into the food. Additionally, they questioned the safety of various preservatives that canners used to prevent spoilage such as borax, saltpeter, cooking salt, salicylic acid, benzoic acid, and even formaldehyde.

Ignorance contributed to the problems with canned goods. French confectioner Nicolas Appert developed the process for canning foods in 1810. The French government had offered a prize of 12,000 francs to anyone who could develop a way to preserve food in order to provide a safe food supply for its army and navy. Appert worked fourteen years before devising the basic canning process, which quickly spread throughout the world. Canners learned and improved the process of canning but it was not until the 1870s when Louis Pasteur and other scientists discovered how microorganisms caused food to spoil that anyone truly understood why the canning process worked. Consequently, canners made mistakes. A superintendent of a canning warehouse in Manitowoc, Wisconsin got an abrupt lesson on the consequences of improper canning in 1894. He was sound asleep in the upper floor of the warehouse when he was jolted awake by a loud noise followed by the foulest of odors. Rushing to the floor below, he discovered that an entire shipment of canned peas had exploded. Rotting peas covered the floor and ceiling. Confused about the cause of the pea disaster, the company president sought help from Harry Russell, an assistant professor of bacteriology from the University of Wisconsin. Russell had studied for a time at the Pasteur Institute in Paris and suspected he knew the cause. He examined the remnants of the exploded peas under a microscope. As he suspected, they contained bacteria. Russell inserted some of the pea bacteria into a new can of peas. A few days later, it too exploded. Russell reasoned that the canners had not cooked the peas properly. He recommended a long cooking time under higher pressure.

Russell was just one of a number of scientists who were developing standards for canning in the 1890s. For example, at the Massachusetts Institute of Technology two bacteriologists, Samuel Prescott and W. Lyman Underwood, studied the specific microorganisms that caused spoilage in canned clams, lobsters, and corn. They published articles providing recommendations for cooking times and pressures. Finally, in 1899, the first book detailing what scientists had learned about the bacteriology of canning was published. However, the canning industry was highly fragmented, and canners were not willing to listen and learn. Why should they? There was little requirement that they do so. It was the same with other foods and drugs.

For example, the dairy industry had its own problems. As dairy farms moved further out of the city, increasingly the milk city dwellers could purchase came from cows raised in cramped and unsanitary conditions in pins attached to local distilleries. Dairymen fed the hot waste product of the fermentation process called swill to the cows. The hot swill would scald the mouths of the cows and the cramped conditions led to distemper. The Dairymen continued to milk the sick and sore-covered cows, sometimes supporting them in slings until they died. They sold the dead and diseased cows to butchers who sold the meat to the poor.

In the1840s, 60,000 families in New York City, including 25,000 children under the age of five, used milk from distillery dairies as a staple of their diets.[96] Impure milk was a primary cause of death of young children. Whenever a public outcry would be raised, prompted usually by some grotesque story in the local papers, the authorities would reluctantly agree to inspect the swill milk producers but only after giving them sufficient warning to allow them to clean up their facilities and ship off the sickest cows.

Not only did the milk often come from diseased cows but also milk producers frequently diluted the milk with water and added adulterants such as chalk, magnesia, and plaster of paris to give the milk a creamy white appearance. By the late 1800's, most food and drug manufacturers were adulterating their products. Flour might contain ground rice, plaster of paris, grit, or sand. Bread often contained copper sulfate or ashes from the ovens. It was the same with most other products.

Product	Adulterate or Contaminate
Butter	Lard, copper, vegetable fats, starch, curd
Cheese	Mercury salts
Lard	Caustic lime, alum, starch, cottonseed oil
Cayenne pepper	Red lead, rice flour, salt, Indian meal, iron oxide.
Ginger	Turmeric, cayenne, mustard
Mustard	Led chromate, lime sulfate, turmeric, pepper
Pepper	Flour, mustard, linseed mean, pepper hulls, nut shells
Horseradish	Turnips
Pickles	Alum, apples, flour
Vinegar	Sulfuric, hydrochloric and pyroligeneous acids, burnt sugar
Coffee	Chicory, peas, beans, acorns, shells, burnt sugar
Coca and chocolate	Iron oxide, animal fats, starch, flour
Fruit juices	Salicylic acid
Soft drinks	Cocaine, caffeine
Beer	Tannic, glycerin, and glycolic acids, valerian (a sedative and antispasmodic intended to "stupefy" the drinker and prevent vomiting.
Whiskey	Fusil oil, menthol alcohol. So called "Rectifiers" took pure alcohol, added flavoring and coloring and sold the resulting product as whiskey or rum or brandy.
Tobacco/cigarettes	Opium, bark, tobacco stems, used cigar butts,

Unbeknownst to consumers, many patent medicines sold to cure a wide range of ailments, including those sold to mothers to administer to their babies, often relied upon alcohol, cocaine, and/or opium for their effectiveness. Manufacturers had little legal obligation to make their products safe, effective or, for that matter, even to inform consumers what the foods, drugs, and drink they were purchasing for themselves and their families contained.

> **LESSON: The problem must be severe and national in scope**
> Members of Congress do not enact changes to public policy to address a minor or local problem. The problem must be, or made to appear to be, national in scope, severe, and troublesome to many voters. The latter is most important. Politicians are driven to legislative accomplishment out of fear of defeat at the next election. As we shall see, the food and drug problem was widespread, severe, and at the turn of the century getting worse.

EARLY EFFORTS TO OBTAIN NATIONAL LEGISLATION FAIL

Throughout the 1800's, Congress did little to require manufacturers to make food, drink and drugs safer or to disclose their content. Instead, Congress focused on protecting manufacturers from foreign competition. For example, in 1850 Congress passed a law regulating the importation of tea. Americans were beginning to attempt to grow tea but faced competition from growers benefiting from cheap labor in China and Japan. Some importers artificially colored their product to make it appear like a different classification of tea. The 1850 law called this adulteration and banned the practice not to protect consumers but rather to help growers in the U.S. compete with their foreign competitors. In 1890, Congress enacted a law forbidding the export or import of infected cattle and the export of unwholesome meat. The law provided for "careful inspection" of exports. Congress expanded the law in 1891 to provide for inspection of all live cattle, hogs, and sheep prior to slaughter in order to protect American exports.[97]

Senator A.S. Paddock of Nebraska introduced the first food bill truly designed to protect consumers in 1889. It passed in the Senate but was defeated in the House. Other Congressmen introduced similar bills in every session of Congress from then until the final passage of a pure food and drug bill in 1906. None passed. In fact, members of Congress tended to ridicule any member proposing them. For example, when a food bill known as the Lard Bill was defeated, Senator Zeb Vance of North Carolina rose to the floor and announced to much laughter, "Mr. President, the Conger Lard Bill is dead. 'Tis Grease, but living Grease no more!"[98] As Harvey Wiley, an important figure in the passage of the 1906 act, put it, "pure food measures (at the time) were smugly looked upon (by members of both houses) as the work of cranks and reformers without much business sense."[99]

> **LESSON: Do not expect early victories or become discourage by initial defeat.** Initial defeat and rejection is a necessary and common component of ultimate success. Congressmen, Senators and the public in general rarely react positively to proposals for major social change when such proposals are first presented. They have to have time to get used to the idea. Early efforts to pass legislation are important even when they lead to defeat after defeat. Each subsequent failure to obtain passage is a step forward if for no other reason than that the idea for reform is becoming less strange and less foreign sounding. Opponents may not be swayed to the idea yet, but they are becoming accustomed to it; "Yes, I've heard about that before."

LOCAL AND STATE EFFORTS DO NOT SOLVE THE PROBLEM

In the late 1800s, advocates of pure food and drug laws turned to the states when they could not get any meaningful legislation through Congress. They had only limited success. First, in many states food, alcohol and drug manufactures exercised such strong political influence that state legislators and other public officials were reluctant to anger them by passing strict food and drug laws. Second, even when states passed such laws they frequently failed to enforce them. Only a few states such as Massachusetts, Ohio and North Dakota funded and supported enforcement. Few states employed a state chemist to inspect foods and drugs for misbranding and adulteration. In some cases, food and drug manufacturers bribed officials charged with enforcement of the laws. Finally, enforcement of the laws, even those requiring minimum levels of sanitation in food handling and preparation, was a daunting task. Enforcement officers were usually overwhelmed particularly when it came to inspecting violations of sanitary standards in home-based businesses. The New York City experience was typical.

In the late 1800s in New York, many families operated mini-food manufacturing and packaging companies out of their homes. Families made and sold Macaroni out of apartment houses in every Italian neighborhood. Families picked and packed nuts in their kitchens and made candy and ice cream for sale on the street or to vendors. Reports of unsanitary conditions and unhealthy food preparation practices abounded. Investigators reported observing such practices as the following:

- A father caring for a child with diphtheria went back and forth from holding the child and operating the macaroni machine and never washed his hands in between.
- A child with scarlet fever handled macaroni as it was drying in the yard.
- Girls with dirty hands and running sores packed nuts for sale.
- A family operated a candy factory out of two rooms in a squalid tenement building described as extremely dirty and totally unfit for food manufacturing.

On the basis of such reports and after an intensive campaign, the National Consumers' League was able to get the New York Legislature to pass laws prohibiting the manufacture and packaging of food products in such unsanitary conditions. However, the laws were almost universally ignored and officials who were given enforcement authority rapidly found themselves without adequate resources to investigate all of the suspected violations.

LESSON: Try a state-based approach first. Americans are suspicious of government in general and the national government in particular. Opponents of national progressive legislation can usually score points by playing upon the general fear of "big government." State-based approaches rarely solve the kinds of problems we are talking about in this book, problems that are severe, national in scope, and not subject to easy fixes. However, it is important to try state-based remedies if for no other reason than to be able to show that states and/or local governments have tried to address the issue but have been unsuccessful in doing so. You must be able to make the case that a federal solution is required.

AN INDIFFERENT PUBLIC

By the end of the century, proponents of pure food, drink and drugs were extremely frustrated. They had made little progress at the national level and the states would not or could not enforce the few laws state legislators grudgingly agreed to pass. It was apparent that Congress and the state legislatures were not going to take any meaningful action until forced to do so by sufficient numbers of angry voters. However, ordinary Americans did not seem to care. After yet another pure food and drug bill law was defeated, one pure food advocate expressed the sentiment of many of his fellow pure food advocates. He said in frustration, "To be cheated, fooled, bamboozled, cajoled, deceived, pettifogged, demagogued, hypnotized, manicured and chiropodized...are privileges dear to us all. Woe be the paternalism in government which shall attempt to deprive us of these inalienable rights." He went on to note, that it appeared the great huckster P.T. Barnum had been right when he said, "Americans like to be humbugged."[100] It was true that working class people were not joining the crusade. As Clayton Copin and Jack High, authors of *The Politics of Purity: Harvey Washington Wiley and the Origins of Federal Food Policy* note, "the impetus for pure food and drugs came largely from the professionals and middle class not the working class. "The movement for a national food law came from food commissioners, agricultural chemists, manufacturers of expensive foods, representatives from rural agricultural states, and ...

middle class women."[101] But is that surprising? Working class men and women did not have the education or access to information to allow them to understand the pure food problem or the time or resources to do something about it. That was about to change. The pure food and drug advocates found a spokesperson that could and would make the scientific case for pure food and drugs, raise the consciousness of average Americans about the need for action, and negotiate the path through confrontation and compromise that would finally lead to passage of a comprehensive pure food and drug law. His name was Harvey Washington Wiley and, more than perhaps anyone else, he was responsible for the passage of the 1906 law. We know the latter because Wiley said so.

GEORGE WASHINGTON WILEY—THE SPOKESPERSON

George Washington Wiley was born to a strictly religious, abolitionist family in Southern Indiana in 1844. He attended Hanover College where he was educated in the classics and learned public speaking as a member of the literary society. He taught public school, apprenticed as a doctor, and eventually attended Indiana Medical College where he received an M.D. Deciding not to practice medicine, Wiley returned to teaching where he developed an interest in analytical chemistry and especially the emerging science of food chemistry. After getting a BS in chemistry from Harvard, Wiley took a position teaching chemistry at Purdue and while there began writing scientific articles on the adulteration of food. These papers led to his appointment to the position of state chemist. As state chemist, he wrote an article detailing the results of research he had conducted for the state board of health on the amount of glucose in sugars and syrups. Wiley gained a reputation as a "sugar" chemist and opponent of the adulteration of foods based upon this and other research. His growing reputation caught the eye of George Loring, the U.S. Commissioner of Agriculture who was looking for a replacement for the department's chief chemist. Loring was particularly impressed with research Wiley had conducted on the production of sugar from sorghum cane. The department was actively working with farmers in the hope of finding a way to produce enough sugar from sorghum to drastically reduce, if not eliminate, the need for sugar imports. Loring saw Wiley's stance on the sugar-from-sorghum issue as more realistic than the extreme views of the existing chief chemist whom Loring disliked and wanted to replace.

Wiley was just thirty-nine years old when he arrived in Washington. He was "tall, stocky, and striking in appearance. He had a rough-hewn oval face, with a prominent nose and slanting black eyes remarkable for their penetrating glance. His short but ample beard, his mustache, and his hair, already beginning to recede on top, were jet black."[102] A highly sociable bachelor with a gift for entertaining conversation and colorful expression, Wiley made friends easily. He was dedicated to his profession, hard working, and very ambitious.

For the next ten years, Wiley spent most of his time working on the sugar-sorghum issue. He learned how to navigate through the Washington bureaucracy, rally interest groups in support of appropriations, and sway congressional committees to his point of view. However, his efforts met with little success. In spite of a number of promising experiments, the department made little progress in reducing sugar imports. Perhaps more troubling for Wiley, his Division of Chemistry was losing ground to the Bureau of Animal Industry and other parts of the Department of Agriculture that were developing their own capabilities in chemistry. Wiley needed to find another mission for his division, one that could garner more funding and expand his personal influence. He considered several options such as having his division develop an expertise on soil analysis. He decided that the drive for passage of a pure food and drug act was something better suited to his technical abilities and recently acquired political expertise. Wiley set out to become the nation's spokesperson for pure food and drugs. Simultaneously, he began campaigning to get Congress to designate the Department of Agriculture and his Division of Chemistry, in particular, as the chief food and drug enforcement agency.

Wiley's decision to have the Division of Chemistry become involved in the debate over food and drug purity and, in particular the adulteration of foods, was not a true break with the past. The Division of Chemistry's had been studying the adulteration of food products since before Wiley became chief chemist. Indeed, the first annual report the division issued after Wiley's appointment contained information on the addition of cheaper corn, beet, and cane syrup to what producers sold as "pure" maple syrup. However, by the mid-1880s, the Commissioner of Agriculture was giving the matter higher priority. Wiley took advantage of this increased interest from his boss. In 1889, Wiley was able to get Congress to include funds in the appropriation bill specifically designated toward his division's research into adulteration. In subsequent years, Congress increased these funds annually.

Since 1887, the Division of Chemistry had been publishing bulletins on food adulterants but these were highly technical treatise on "the best methods of detecting" adulteration. The Division wrote them for professionals in state experiment stations and boards of health. Wiley now decided to use the funding from the 1889 appropriation to, as he put it, "[give] the people and Congress…at least a general view of the evil."[103] The next year the division issued a bulletin aimed at the lay public. The publication, entitled *A Popular Treatise on the Extent and Character of Food Adulteration* presented a compilation of research findings along with the opinions of scientists and businessmen. It declared that the evidence demonstrated in the strongest manner that the adulteration of food was widespread and increasing. Even when the adulteration was not harmful, said the report, it was still fraud that hurt everyone, particularly the uneducated and the poor. Additionally, some of the adulterants were poisonous. They sickened consumers and frequently caused death. It was clear, said the report, that the country needed national legislation to outlaw or at least regulate such practices.

Wiley was not a zealot. He favored labeling over stringent government control. He argued that it was sufficient to require manufactures to list on the label any substance added and leave it to the consumer and consumer's physician to decide about use of the food or drug. However, when it came to preservatives, he had a different opinion. Wiley felt preservatives constituted the greatest hazard. Manufacturers used them in such small dosages that they were largely undetectable by the consumer. He thought that the burden of proof of safety should be borne by the advocates of preservatives. Wiley thought Congress should outlaw some altogether. In 1902, during a trip to Europe, Wiley came up with an idea of how to make his case against preservatives in food in a more forceful and dramatic fashion.

> **LESSON: You need a leader/spokesperson who can gain national attention and lend credibility to your cause.** George Washington Wiley was an ideal spokesperson for the pure food and drug movement. His background as a chemist and his position as the head of the Department of Agriculture's Bureau of Chemistry gave him credibility but that was not all. Wiley not only had obvious expertise in the subject matter but also could communicate as effectively with politicians and ordinary Americans as he did with other experts in his field. In addition, it helped greatly that he was outgoing, sociable, and ambitious to make a name for himself as the leader of the pure food and drug cause. You need someone like Wiley.

WILEY'S POISON SQUAD—THE PUBLICITY STUNT

The idea was simple. Wiley recruited twelve healthy young men who agreed to eat all of their meals in a dining room in the basement of the chemistry building of the Department of Agriculture. Their meals were prepared containing different levels of varying types of preservatives that producers commonly added to manufactured foods such as borax, salicylic, sulfurous and benzoic acid, formaldehyde and alum. Wiley weighed the men before and after consumption of the preservatives and analyzed their body waste in order to detect both how much of the preservatives their bodies retained and the effect of the preservatives on their health.

When word got out about the experiments most of the media ran stories about volunteers who got free board and meals for doing nothing but eating food with common preservatives. However, reader interest caught on after George Brown, a reporter for the *Washington Post*, began referring to the preservatives as poisons and the volunteers as Wiley's Poison Squad. Wiley became a celebrity.

Manufacturers criticized Wiley's experiments for the methods he used and his interpretation of the data was suspect. Additionally, Wiley eventually concluded that the real problem with the preservatives was not their harmful impact on human health but that the food manufacturers were being deceptive and committing fraud on an unsuspecting public. He wrote, "I am not one of the people who think there is a very great increase in the attendance at the graveyard due to the practice of food adulteration. In other words, the injury to public health, in my opinion, is the least important question in the subject of food adulteration, and it is one which should be considered last of all. The real evil of food adulteration is deception of the consumer."[104]

Advocates of a strong national pure food, drink and drug act were not always happy with Wiley. First, he seemed to have more interest in food adulteration than adulteration of drink and drugs. In fact, the Bureau of Chemistry did not set up a lab to test drugs until March of 1903. Additionally, many pure food, drink and drug advocates were unhappy with Wiley's flamboyant bid for recognition and seeming determination to take all of the credit for the passage of the pure food and drug act while ignoring the efforts of women activists long before he took an interest in the cause. Still, Wiley was important to the cause if for no other reason than that his flamboyant bids for recognition such as his poison squad garnered press attention which was badly needed.

An additional unexpected boost for passage of a comprehensive pure food and drug law came in 1904 during the Louisiana Purchase Exposition in St. Louis. Congress had established the exposition to celebrate the 100th anniversary of the Louisiana Purchase and the fair's commissioners invited numerous national organizations to hold their conventions at the fair and exhibit. One of these was the National Association of State Diary and Food Commissioners. It set up a major exhibit covering two-acres. The exhibit displayed food value charts and examples of food preservation techniques. Chemists demonstrated simple tests housewives could use to determine the presence of harmful substances in food they were serving their families. Robert Allen, secretary of the association wrote "state legislatures, delegations from women's clubs, newspapers and magazine writers and editors flocked to the exhibit."[105] Initially, food manufactures threatened to seek injunctions to stop the exhibit but eventually decided against such action fearing that it would only result in more public attention. Indeed, after seeing their products displayed as examples of adulterated goods, several manufacturers agreed to stop adding artificial coloring and to replace false labels on their products.

> **LESSON: Do not be reluctant to use publicity stunts to get attention.** Do not expect the media or public in general to pay attention to your cause just because your cause is right. You have to attract their attention. Often that means that you have to stage a dramatic publicity stunt to arouse media and public interest. Wiley's poison squad attracted the interest of reporters looking for a good story. Their stories about young men consuming 'poison' in a scientific experiment grabbed public attention, as did the displays of adulterated foods at the Louisiana Purchase Exposition.

THE PRESS FINALLY GETS INVOLVED

Major legislation rarely gets passed in Washington until the national press gets behind the effort. That did not happen with regard to the pure food and drug law in any substantial way until the early 1900s. The Hearst papers ran a series of articles as early as 1899 on the danger of "embalmed meat" when soldiers in the Spanish-American war became sick and died after eating canned meat preserved with formaldehyde. However, these stories were the exception. Most American newspapers and magazines avoided the issue of pure food and drugs often out of fear that food and drug advertisers would boycott them. It was a typical press response. Most members of the press do not get involved in getting things done in Washington until advocacy groups stage publicity stunts like Wiley's Poison Squad that are so outlandish no self-serving reporter or editor can resist covering them. Some reporters and editors develop an interest in and begin investigating and writing about the wider story once they cover the events proponents stage. Gradually competition to get a good story sets in and interest spreads throughout much of the fourth estate as it did in the case of the drive for pure food and drug legislation.

As I said, up to the early 1900s most newspapers and magazines avoided the issue of pure food and drugs. The press began paying more attention to the issue after the publicity generated by Wiley's Poison Squad. Typical were a series of articles appearing in several magazines starting in late 1902 dealing with the issue of addictive substances in popular patent medicines.

In the November 1902 issue of *American Medicine* the editor wrote an article discussing a paper that had been presented at a meeting of the Colorado Medical Society on the amount of alcohol found in many patent medicines. He wondered why the Women's Christian Temperance Union (WCTU) had not raised concerns about patent medicines since they often contained more alcohol by volume than the beer that the WCTU had attacked. After reading the article, Martha Allen, the head of the Department of Medical Temperance of the WCTU, responded to *American Medicine* pointing out that the WCTU had indeed opposed the use of alcohol and other addictive substances in patent medicines for over twenty years. *American Medicine* printed a retraction of sorts in its next issue in addition to praising the WCTU for its work and recommending that every citizen in the country read a WCTU pamphlet on patent medicines.

Maud Banfield, a nurse who wrote a health column for the *Ladies' Home Journal* was one of the people following this exchange between the *American Medicine* editor and Allen. Noticing the original *American Medicine* article, Banfield wrote an article for her magazine asking, "Why does not the WCTU oppose alcoholic patent medicines?" Allen immediately responded pointing out that the WCTU had indeed opposed such medicine and to support her argument supplied *The Ladies Home Journal* with much of the material she had sent to *American Medicine*. This time, however, there was no retraction.

Edward Bok, the editor of *The Ladies Home Journal* had decided that he had the makings of an expose and began running a series of articles attacking the makers of patent medicines in addition to falsely criticizing the WCTU for failing to do the same. Bok printed lists of patent medicines that contained large amounts of alcohol, accused physicians who condoned the use of such products of violating medical ethics, and accused the patent medicine manufactures of engaging in fraudulent advertising seeking to convince people that were perfectly healthy they had all manner of diseases their nostrums could cure. Mark Sullivan, one of his investigative reporters, wrote an article providing evidence that patent medicine advertisers had threatened to cancel advertising with magazines and newspapers that did not oppose state and local pure food and drug legislation. When Bok rejected the article, *Collier's Weekly* agreed to publish it under the title "The Patent Medicine Conspiracy Against Freedom of the Press."[106] After that, numerous articles and stories about patent medicines and the pure food and drug cause began to appear in national publications such as *The Women's Home Companion*, *Popular Science Monthly*, *Nation*, *Outlook*, and *The New York Times. The Times* became a major advocate starting in 1903 covering most of the major developments in the pure food crusade and criticizing Congress, and in particular the Republican members of the House of Representatives for lack of progress. In a June issue, the *Times* editor wrote, "What is the matter with this Republican House of Representatives? Do they on the whole believe it to be good party policy to leave the cheats and swindlers, the prisoners and the adulterators unmolested?"[107]

> **LESSON: You must get the attention of the media. They can be your best ally or your worst enemy. Make them your best ally.** Pure food and drug advocates got a significant boost when respected publications like the *Ladies Home Journal*, *Collier's Weekly*, *Women's Home Companion*, *Popular Science Monthly*, and others began covering the pure food and drug cause.

CONGRESS BECOMES INTERESTED

Pure food and drug advocates got an unexpected boost in 1903 when Weldon Heyburn, a freshman senator from Idaho, was made chairman of the Senate Committee on Manufacturers. The previous chairman,

Porter McCumber, had long been successful in preventing pure food, drink and drug laws from getting to the floor of the Senate. No one expected Hayburn to be any different. After all, he had opposed most Progressive efforts from conservation to direct election of senators to child labor laws to woman suffrage. To everyone's surprise, Heyburn became a staunch and "rarely conciliatory" ally to the cause. [108] Perhaps Heyburn was simply seeking to protect his job. Idaho women's clubs had warned they would work to defeat any candidate that did not support pure food and drug legislation. Although Heyburn was criticized for being "egotistical, opinionated, pompous, abrasive, temperamental, 'utterly without a sense of humor', unyielding and unable to take criticism," he was "applauded for his courage, patience, and tenacity in resisting the pressure tactics of opponents of pure food, drink, and drug regulation and in creating opportunities to bring [such bills] before the Senate." [109]

> **LESSON: You must push Congressmen and Senators into joining the fight. They need a personal reason to join your cause such as it will help them get re-elected.** Washington rarely leads reform efforts. Congress waits until the efforts are well underway and generating widespread support. Then, a Senator here and a Congressman there will discover the cause and rush to become one of its leaders. After working for years, advocates of change are often astounded to find support for their cause is suddenly coming from the most unexpected places. Senator Weldon Heyburn of Idaho became interested in and a supporter of the pure food and drug cause only after women's groups in Idaho announced that they would work to defeat any candidate who did not support pure food and drug legislation.

THE PRESIDENT JOINS THE CAUSE

President Theodore Roosevelt should have been an early and forceful advocate for pure food and drugs. First, he was angry at the meat packers for, as he put it, "poisoning" his Rough Ryders in Cuba with their tainted canned meat. Additionally, the meatpackers Armour and Swift were perfect examples of the giant trusts his administration was fighting. Yet, when Wiley and other pure food and drug advocates sought Roosevelt's help, he demurred. Of course, he said, he supported their cause and appreciated the need to address the problem but he preferred, he said, to deal with the problem under existing law before "throwing himself on the mercy of Congress for additional legislation."[110] Anyway, he continued, there was considerable and powerful opposition to the ideas of those whom many considered to be radical reformers pursuing a totally impossible, impractical, and politically unattainable ideal.

Part of Roosevelt's reluctance to support the pure food and drug cause was personal. Wiley had gained considerable notoriety as the national spokesperson for the cause. Roosevelt was jealous of the attention the bureaucrat was getting. It did not help that the President had a beef with the publicity hungry chemist. The House Ways and Means Committee called Wiley to testify shortly after Roosevelt became President. The Committee was discussing legislation intended to reduce the tariff on sugar imported from Cuba that the Roosevelt administration supported. Wiley bitterly opposed it fearing that any reduction in the tariff would undercut progress toward developing a domestic sugar supply. He was certain he would be asked his opinion about the legislation and incur the wrath of the new President when he expressed his opposition. Wiley begged the Secretary of Agriculture to get him excused from testifying but to no avail. He showed up to testify with tables, charts and diagrams and the determination to present just the facts about sugar production without expressing his own opinion on the Cuban tariff issue. He testified for two days and, to his great relief, members of the committee never asked Wiley his personal opinion about the Cuban tariff issue. Excused, Wiley was preparing to leave when a member of the Committee interrupted. "Excuse me, Mr. Chairman. I want to ask Doctor Wiley a question." Wiley returned to his seat and received the question he had been dreading. "Doctor Wiley," the Committee member asked, "what do you think of the desirability of passing this pending legislation respecting a rebate of part of the duty on Cuban Sugar?" Wiley replied, "I consider to a very unwise piece of legislation and one which will damage, to a very serious extent, our domestic sugar industry."[111] The headlines next day screamed the news. A member of the new President's own administration was in direct rebellion to administration policy. Roosevelt was furious. He called the Secretary of Agriculture to the White House and demand that he fire Wiley. The Secretary defended Wiley explaining that Wiley had not wanted to testify and had no choice but to answer the Congressman truthfully. Eventually, the President calmed down, admonishing the Secretary never to let such a thing happen again. The President never forgot the incident. It was just another reason not to like the dapper, ambitious, publicity-seeking chemist.

In spite of his reservations and dislike of Wiley, the pure food and drug proponents would not give up. Eventually they were able to convince the President to take a first tentative step in support of their cause. He agreed to insert a brief recommendation for a new pure food and drug law in his State of the Union address in December 2005.

> I recommend...that a law be enacted to regulate interstate commerce in misbranded and adulterated foods, drinks, and drugs. Such law would protect legitimate manufacture and commerce, and would tend to secure the health and welfare of the consuming public. Traffic in foodstufs which have been debased or adulterated so as to injure health or to deceive purchasers should be forbidden. [112]

THE OPPONENTS CHANGE THEIR MINDS—OR APPEAR TO

As Roosevelt had said, there was strong opposition in Congress to any comprehensive pure food and drug law. Powerful Republicans in the Senate such as Henry Cabot Lodge, of Massachusetts, Nelson W. Aldrich and Thomas Platt of New York, Orville Platt of Connecticut and Hernando Desoto of Mississippi represented the business interests of their states. They adamantly opposed a pure food and drug law. The Speaker of the House, Joseph Cannon, was equally determined that no pure food and drug bill would reach the floor for a vote.

The arguments of the opponents of pure food and drug laws were the same arguments Conservatives always make to stymie progress. "It's unconstitutional." "It's un-American." "It's anti-business." "It will destroy the American way of life." "It's over-reaching." "It's evil (or Communist or Socialist or liberal.)" "It's unworkable." "It's just plain wrong."

Then, a turning point occurred. Opponents of change began to realize that thanks to the work of advocates, the press, and the support of a few influential political leaders such as the President, change was becoming inevitable. At that point, the opposition switched tactics. They no longer opposed legislation outright. Instead, they began to offer their support. "We aren't opposed to all legislation, "they said, "just to the particular legislation being offered." They sought to mold and shape the legislation since they could not defeat it. They wanted to compromise it, to weaken it, and to make it ineffectual without appearing to do so. In the case of the pure food and drug law, food manufacturers actually formed an association, the National Food Manufacturer's Association, for the sole purpose of insuring that Congress enact what they called a "proper" law. The real purpose of the association was to insure that Congress would not designate Wiley as the enforcer of the law because of his strong opposition to preservatives and that any regulations enacted into law would be all but impossible to enforce.

Many advocates of a pure food and drug law felt Wiley was too willing to compromise with business interests in order to get some law passed even if it was less than consumer advocates wanted. For example, he reached a compromise with "Rectifiers." Rectifiers mixed pure alcohol, coloring and flavoring to create artificial whiskey, brandy or rum that they then sold to unsuspecting customers as the real think. Wiley agreed to exempt the rectifiers from listing all of their product's ingredients and manufacturing processes on labels as long as they distinguished the blended whiskey they sold from straight whiskey. Staunch consumer advocates felt such a compromise was selling out. Never the less such compromise is usually necessary.

Some opposition groups got behind the legislation not because they sought to water it down, but because they began to see how they could actually benefit from its passage. In the case of the pure food and drug law, some business groups began to support the legislation because they decided that such a law would hurt their competitors. For example, the whiskey producers favored labeling because it would hurt the rectifiers. Other business interests supported a pure food and drug law because of the crippling effect that conflicting state pure food and drug laws were having on their interstate business. States were passing food and drug laws with varying provisions that made it difficult for food and drug companies to package uniform products for distribution throughout the country. Some researchers go so far as to argue that the Meat Inspection Act of 1906 and to a lesser extent the Pure Food and Drug Act resulted from the effort of major meat packers to eliminate competition from smaller competitors and to protect their industry from foreign competition.[113]

> **LESSON: A critical and dangerous turning point occurs when the opposition appears to switch sides.** It was a clear sign that some type of comprehensive pure food and drug legislation was inevitable when conservative Congressmen and Senators who previously had opposed any food and drug legislation suddenly began to voice their support. The danger for pure food and drug advocates was that their former opponents would gain control and produce legislation that sounded good but accomplished little, as in the case of the Wadsworth bill. As opponents of the legislation change their tactics, advocates of change face a dilemma. Finally, they have the opportunity to pass legislation provided they are willing to compromise. Isn't something better than nothing? Isn't a partial victory better than the status quo? Indeed some compromise is reasonable and usually necessary. However, how far can the advocates of change go in making concessions without going too far?

MOMENTUM BUILDS FOR PASSAGE

Momentum for passage of a pure food and drug law began to build once the opposition switched sides. For example, a comprehensive bill supported by women's groups passed the House in 1903 but never reached the floor in the Senate. The next year, Senator Heyburn offered a substitute bill. He was never able to bring the bill to the floor because opponents quibbled over the wording of various provisions. In 1905, Heyburn tried again this time tinkering with the wording to make it more acceptable. For example, Heyburn agreed to insert the word "knowingly" in a segment of the bill having to do with penalties for selling adulterated products in order to win support from retailers. By early January, the American Medical Association had offered its endorsement.

However, there was still considerable opposition. For example, the National Association of Manufacturers proposed a substitute bill and various industry groups offered additional amendments designed to weaken the legislation. In spite of this last minute maneuvering, the Senate finally passed comprehensive legislation in February 1906.

The elation of pure food and drug advocates was short lived. They had won in the Senate but faced unexpectedly stiff opposition in the House where liquor, food processors and drug companies mounted a major last minute effort to defeat or at least significantly weaken the legislation. The bill was delayed in the House then delayed again as other legislation was considered. February passed. April passed. There was no progress. The last minute opposition was working. For all of the progress the advocates of change had made, they were stilling falling short of their goal. One final push was needed. It came from an unexpected source.

A PIVOTAL EVENT—UPTON SINCLAIR PUBLISHES *THE JUNGLE*

At some point on the road to most great legislative accomplishments, there comes a pivotal event so shocking to the public consciousness that it galvanizes support for change. It suddenly intensifies and focuses all previous arguments for action like sunlight through a magnifying glass. The public heat for legislative action turns into a raging fire that threatens to consume political careers. Shays rebellion provided the shock that convinced a core group of prominent Americans that major changes in the Articles of Confederation were required. The event that set the popular mood on fire in support of pure food and drugs was the publication of a single book, *The Jungle*. Its author was a self-described "penniless rat" by the name of Upton Sinclair. He was just 26 years old when *The Jungle* was published but everything in his life had prepared him for the role he was about to play in the passage of one of the greatest pieces of legislation in American history.

Upton Sinclair was born on September 20, 1878, in Baltimore. His mother was Priscilla Harden, daughter of John S. Harden, a wealthy businessman and secretary-treasurer of Western Maryland Railroad. Priscilla was a puritanical woman with aristocratic pretensions who opposed the consumption of tea, coffee and particularly alcohol. Upton's father was Upton Beall Sinclair, a "natty" dressing, amiable, ingratiating salesman who was frequently unemployed because of an addiction to alcohol.

Eventually, the Sinclairs drifted to New York City. There lack of money reduced them to living in a single room of a cheap boarding house. At the age of 10, young Sinclair's mother would often send him out at night to roam the dingy bars in search of his father who would tearfully lament to his young son about the "terror and grief of a defeated life." [114]

Sinclair had no formal education until the age of ten but he was an early and voracious reader. In spite of starting his formal education late, he quickly caught up and passed his peers qualifying to enter high school when he was just twelve. In high school, Sinclair found that he enjoyed writing and telling stories and sold his first magazine article before he was fifteen. At 15, he entered the City College of New York as one of the youngest entering freshman in the school's history. He was an indifferent student but passed his courses with ease while continuing to contribute articles and jokes to a range of newspapers and magazines.

Sinclair graduated from City College in 1897 and using the money he had earned from his free lance writing enrolled in Columbia University graduate school, initially planning to pursue a career in law. He quickly abandoned that goal and devoted himself to exploiting Columbia's lenient drop/add policy in order sample a wide range of courses. Sinclair was said to attend a class just long enough to get the course syllabus and reading list before moving on to sample another offering. He read continually, developing a fondness for Shelly, Emerson, Sir Walter Scott and other Romantics. Wanting to read European writers in their native language,

Sinclair taught himself French, Italian, and German. His ability, according to his son, "to look at a word only once and fix it into his memory" aided his mastery of languages. [115]

Sinclair came to think of himself as someone with a superior intellect and special gifts who could accomplish almost anything. As proof, he would point to his already exceptional accomplishment. For example, how many others, even among the well read, he would point out, could legitimately say they had read all of the most important books in their original language. Sinclair was not modest, but he was not disliked. In fact, most people found him charming.

By the age of 17, Sinclair was not only supporting himself through his writing but making enough to support his father and mother. He kept two stenographers busy churning out as many as 8,000 words per day, seven days a week. At the age of 18, a publisher commissioned him to write a series of short novels about the U.S. Military Academy at West Point. Securing permission from the commanding officers who thought the novels might be good for West Point's image, Sinclair spent several days wandering the grounds and interviewing the cadets about life at the academy. A congenial and avid listener, Sinclair found it easy to get people to talk at length and revealingly about their lives. He found it equally easy to translate the information he gathered into compelling stories. Sinclair quickly produced a thirty-thousand-word novel about "heroic" life at the academy. That novel became a series and the series led to another series, this time based upon life at the Annapolis naval academy.

By the age of 22, Sinclair was a successful but unhappy and unfulfilled writer of pulp fiction. He wanted to become a 'serious' writer and had an idea for a novel about "a woman's soul redeemed by high and noble love."[116] Mimicking one of his favorite writers, Henry David Thoreau, Sinclair abandoned the city for a log cabin in the woods near Lake Massawippi, Quebec, about 30 miles north of the Vermont border. There, he planned to spend the mornings walking among the pine forests working out scenes and dialogue. The afternoons he would spend in his tiny cabin writing his great novel. Writing about himself in third person Sinclair described this period of his life immodestly as follows:

> Last spring, because his heart was shaken with the beauty of it, he went away to wrestle with his vision. Because he knew he had to give all his soul to the labor, he cut himself off absolutely from the world—found a little cabin in the wilds of Quebec where for five months he lived entirely alone, doing a work so fearful that now, as he looks back upon it, it makes him tremble. Each day, as he wrought at his story, the wonder of it took hold of him more and more, until it took the form of a vey demon of beauty that was lashing him and would not let him rest.[117]

The writing did not go well. Sinclair was writing about a woman's moral choices, a topic he knew little about. Then, he found a real woman who could serve as the model for his subject. She arrived during the summer. Her name was Meta Fuller, the daughter of a close friend of Sinclair's mother. Meta and her mother had joined Sinclair's mother for a trip to see her son. Sinclair was stricken and a full-blown romance blossomed.

Upton and Meta walked and talked of love. He read her poetry and warned her he would make a poor husband since he was too devoted to his art. Uneducated and without a career of sense of direction, Meta was fascinated. Upton, she told him, was her "only reason for breathing" and was sent to her "direct from God."[118] They were married in October 1900 and rented a tiny one-room apartment in the city.

With Meta's help, Sinclair finished his novel and shipped it off to Macmillan confident that it would be immediately accepted and that a large check would soon follow. He was wrong. Macmillan rejected his masterpiece, as did a score of other publishers. Editors wrote back with their criticisms—unconvincing characters, cluttered plot, stilted writing. They could not use it. In desperation, Sinclair borrowed $200 and printed a thousand copies of *Springtime and Harvest.* He sent copies to every reviewer he could find hoping that one might write favorably about it. Nothing happened. The book languished earning barely enough to enable Sinclair to repay the $200 loan. He was broke and disheartened. Worse, Meta was now pregnant. What were they to do? All seemed lost until one day Sinclair received word from Funk & Wagnall's offering to republish

Springtime and Harvest under a new title, *King Midas.* Sinclair quick agreed and received a small advance. The republish novel sold poorly but Funk and Wagnall's' interest in his work rekindled Sinclair's confidence. He set off once again to the woods to write a new novel, *Prince Hagen.* Like his first novel, publishers roundly rejected *Prince Hagen.*

Meta gave birth to a son, David in December 1901. Her father insisted it was time for Sinclair to give up his fantasy about writing and get a regular job now that he had a family to raise. Sinclair refused. Soon, Meta left taking the baby to live with her parents. By the fall of 1902, Sinclair was broke and alone, playing poker for money and living in a rundown boarding house in Harlem. Then, by accident, Sinclair met another young writer by the name of Leonard Abbott.

An Englishman, Abbott was an active socialists. Sinclair knew nothing about socialism but at Abbott's insistence began reading pamphlets Abbott provide him on social issues. One was by a prominent socialist, George Herron. Impressed by Herron's ideas, Sinclair wrote him expressing his admiration. In early November, the two met. Through Herron, Sinclair met other prominent socialists and expanded his reading. His growing fascination with socialism led to a new novel, *The Captain of Industry.* It was a dark story about a ruthless capitalist who seduces his own daughter and eventually falls in the ocean where crabs devour him alive. Not surprisingly, Sinclair's new novel was an even greater failure than his first two. Angry at the continued rejection, Sinclair wrote and published a letter to the world proclaiming that he might be nothing more than a penniless rat but that he would not be defeated. He would found his own Sinclair Press, write a trilogy of novels on the Civil War, create a foundation to support young writers and "free them from the slavery of writing for money."[119] Feeling sorry for Sinclair and sympathetic to the plight of writers, George Heron offered to loan Sinclair the equivalent of $16,000 in today's dollars so that he could get to work on his Civil War trilogy. Sinclair accepted and immediately moved himself, Meta and David to a farm near Princeton, N.J. in the summer of 1904.

For the next year, Sinclair devoured the vast resources on the Civil War housed at the Princeton University library. By the end of the year, he had finished his research and had worked out the story line for the first novel that he decided to call *Manassas.* Sinclair was completely absorbed with his novel, sleeping only a few hours at night before resuming his writing. Meta was left alone much of the time. The weather was cold. The cabin was dark and uncomfortable. David was often sick. Meta became increasingly depressed. Then, early one morning in March, Sinclair awoke to find Meta sitting in chair by the window holding something in her hand. He saw a flash of light off metal from the early morning sun and the sound of a click. Jumping out of bed, he raced to Meta and grabbed the gun she had cocked and pressed against her temple. She collapsed in his arms. Later he was to learn that this had not been the first time Meta had considered suicide.

Relief for the couple came in May. Macmillan offered to publish *Manassas.* The weather improved and the money from the advance lifted the Sinclair's out of total poverty. Meta's mood brightened. With little to do but proof galleys, Sinclair took the spring and summer to immerse himself in socialist philosophy. In the course of his reading, Sinclair came across articles in the socialist weekly newspaper *Appeal to Reason* about an unsuccessful strike by Chicago stockyard workers against the meatpackers. Incensed by what he read about the treatment of the workers, Sinclair wrote an impassioned article calling on the workers not to abandon their struggle and sent it to the *Appeal.* The article was accepted and readers received it well. In the mean time, Macmillan published *Manassas.* Sales were disappointing. Once again, Sinclair had failed.

Responding to the enthusiastic reception from their readers to Sinclair's article and aware of the research he had done for *Manassas*, the editors of *Appeal* approached Sinclair with an offer. Would he be interested in writing a novel about wage slavery that could be serialized in the *Appeal.* They offered a $500 advance and agreed that once they were serialized in the *Appeal,* Sinclair could sell the story elsewhere. Sinclair accepted the offer and suggested that he base the story on the Chicago stockyard strikes. The editors agreed. Sinclair then approached his editor at Macmillan. He told them he was going to write a novel about "the breaking of human hearts by a system which exploits the labor of men and women for profits."[120] A radical publication whose readers were not readers of Macmillan's books would serialize the novel. Would Macmillan be interested in publishing the novel after serialization? Macmillan agreed and offered a $500 advance. Ecstatic at his good fortune, Sinclair kissed Meta and David goodbye and set off to Chicago.

Sinclair was going to write something popular, something that would enlighten readers and, most of all, something that would sell. He took as his model *Uncle Tom's Cabin* by Harriet Beecher Stowe. Sinclair intended to write an Uncle Tom's Cabin of the labor movement condemning what he considered wage slavery. Of course, workers were not really slaves "chained" to their jobs and they wouldn't be shot for quitting. Sinclair's decision to focus on the Food and Meat Packing industry was a calculated move designed to make the novel relevant to a wider audience than those just concerned with worker rights or other socialist issues. He was not trying to expose the meat packing industry for selling rotten meat. He was not advocating pure food and drugs. His concerns were with the exploitation of working men and women. He wanted to expose their horrible working conditions. He was aiming at his readers' hearts. He was surprised when he hit their stomachs.

Sinclair arrived in Chicago on September 20, 1904, his 26th birthday. He checked into the Transit House, a sprawling hotel near the stockyards favored by cowboys, ranchers, cattle dealers and writers covering the labor unrest. Immediately, Sinclair began interviewing everyone he could meet that might give him insight and anecdotes about the labor unrest and working conditions in the meat packing plants. He talked to policemen, bartenders, laborers, plant foremen, even undertakers all the while taking meticulous notes. He found that if he dressed in shabby clothes, which was not a problem since those were the only kind he had, and carried a lunch pale, he could wander unrestricted through the Armour packing plant. He absorbed the sights and sounds then rushed back to his room to commit all that he had learned to paper. His contacts expanded exponentially. Each person he interviewed would suggest two, three, or four others he should meet. As he got to know the workers, many began inviting them into their homes. In the evenings, he would sit with them asking questions and recording their stories. He applied all of the interviewing skills he had polished to near perfection while doing the research for his books on life at West Point and Annapolis.

By mid-November, Sinclair knew that he had more than enough material for his book, with one exception. He intended to write a novel but he had no plot. He was worried. Then, one Sunday afternoon as he walked back to his hotel along the unpaved streets of the depressing slum that housed the factory workers, he found his story. He described the experience as follows, in third person, in the introduction to the 1946 edition of *The Jungle*:

> He saw a bridal couple alight from a hack and enter the rear room of a beer saloon. Other persons followed, and the writer joined them. No one appeared to have any objection to his presence, so he sat on a bench by the wall and watched a Lithuanian wedding supper and dance. Several who spoke English explained to him what was going on, and gradually he realized that this was the family he needed for his story. From four o'clock until nearly midnight he sat, making note of every detail and composing in his mind the opening chapter of a novel. By ten years of practice he had learned to go over a scene and fix it verbatim in his mind. The opening chapter was not put on paper until the following Christmas, but it varied little from the mentally recorded version.[121]

Sinclair rushed back to his Princeton, New Jersey cabin with his plot well in mind and his extensive notes at hand. There over the next few months he wrote about the hardships and suffering of the stockyard workers often, as he said later, blinded by tears. He wrote not just about the stockyard workers he had interviewed but about the physical and mental suffering he had experienced as a struggling writer.

By spring Sinclair's story began appearing in installments in *Appeal to Reason*. Reader response was immediate. One wrote, "I am reading *The Jungle*, and I should be afraid to trust myself to tell you how it affects me. It is so simple, so true, so tragic and so human."[122]

By September 1905, *The Jungle* was finished. Sinclair sent a copy to Macmillan. Macmillan agreed to publish but only if Sinclair agreed to remove certain sections that provided gory details of unsanitary and unsafe working conditions in the packing plants such as the following descriptions of the slaughter of the hogs and sausage making.

Hog Killing:

> "They don't waste anything here," said the guide… "They use everything about the hog except the squeal…"
>
> It was a long, narrow room, with a gallery along it for visitors. At the head there was a great iron, wheel, about twenty feet in circumference, with rings here and there along its edge. Upon both sides of this wheel there was a narrow space, into which came the hogs at the end of their journey; in the midst of them stood a great burly Negro, bare-armed and bare-chested. He was resting for the moment, for the wheel had stopped while men were cleaning up. In a minute or two, however, it began slowly to revolve, and then the men upon each side of it sprang to work. They had chains which they fastened about the leg of the nearest hog, and the other end of the chain they hooked into one of the rings upon the wheel. So, as the wheel turned, a hog was suddenly jerked off his feet and borne aloft.
>
> At the same instant the ear was assailed by a most terrifying shriek; the visitors started in alarm, the women turned pale and shrank back. The shriek was followed by another, louder and yet more agonizing--for once started upon that journey, the hog never came back; at the top of the wheel he was shunted off upon a trolley, and went sailing down the room. And meantime another was swung up, and then another, and another, until there was a double line of them, each dangling by a foot and kicking in frenzy--and squealing. The uproar was appalling, perilous to the eardrums...There were high squeals and low squeals, grunts, and wails of agony; there would come a momentary lull, and then a

fresh outburst, louder than ever, surging up to a deafening climax. It was too much for some of the visitors--the men would look at each other, laughing nervously, and the women would stand with hands clenched, and the blood rushing to their faces, and the tears starting in their eyes.

Meantime, heedless of all these things, the men upon the floor were going about their work. Neither squeals of hogs nor tears of visitors made any difference to them; one by one they hooked up the hogs, and one by one with a swift stroke they slit their throats…another with two swift stokes severed the head, which fell to the floor and vanished through a hole. Another made a slit down the body; a second opened the body wider; a third with a saw cut the breastbone; a fourth loosened the entrails; a fifth pulled them out--and they also slid through a hole in the floor.[123]

Sausage Making:

There was never the least attention paid to what was cut up for sausage; there would come all the way back from Europe old sausage that had been rejected, and that was moldy and white-it would be dosed with borax and glycerin, and dumped into the hoppers, and made over again for home consumption. There would be meat that had tumbled out on the floor, in the dirt and sawdust, where the workers had tramped and spit uncounted billions of consumption germs. There would be meat stored in great piles in rooms; and the water from leaky roofs would drip over it, and thousands of rats would race about on it. It was too dark in these storage places to see well, but a man could run his hand over these piles of meat and sweep off handfuls of the dried dung of rats. These rats were nuisances, and the packers would put poisoned bread out for them; they would die, and then rats, bread, and meat would go into the hoppers together.[124]

Sinclair refused to make the changes Macmillan demand. Instead, he offered the manuscript to several other publishers. The reaction was the same. They would publish the book but only if he agreed to remove the painful details that readers might find offensive. Frustrated, Sinclair published a plea to readers of *Appeal to Reason* asking them to order advance copies of his book so that he could raise enough money to self-publish. More than 12,000 orders poured in and Sinclair set about having the book set in type. At that point, Doubleday, Page and Company made an offer. They would agree to publish the book just as Sinclair had written it provided they could obtain independent verification of the accuracy of Sinclair's reporting. Sinclair agreed to the offer and assumed that all was well. It was not.

Shortly after Thanksgiving, Doubleday called Sinclair to a meeting. Herbert Houston, the company's treasurer, tossed a report across his desk. Doubleday, he explained, had contacted James Keeley, the managing editor of the *Chicago Tribune* and asked for his help in checking out Sinclair's story, particularly the gory descriptions of unsafe and unsanitary working conditions. Sinclair held in his hands Keeley's report. It was a serious indictment. Sinclair's facts, said Keeley, were all wrong. Sinclair countered that the Keeley report was part of a conspiracy to silence him and keep Doubleday from publishing his book. Wasn't Robert McCormick the publisher of the *Tribune,* asked Sinclair? Wasn't he known as a staunch defender of local Chicago business? Doubleday shouldn't take the Keeley report for granted. He begged Houston to send someone to Chicago to check out the report. After some further discussion, Houston agreed. He ordered two of Doubleday's attorneys to go to Chicago and attempt to verify who was telling the truth, Sinclair or Keeley.

Thomas McKee was one of the attorneys. Years later McKee told Sinclair that one of the first people he talked to after arriving in Chicago was a publicist for the meat packers. In their conversation, the publicists who was unaware of McKee's mission, blurted out that he was not only familiar with Sinclair's book but had written a report for the Chicago *Tribune* challenging Sinclair's descriptions of the packing plants. McKee returned to New York with his findings. A disinterested reporter had not prepared the Keeley report as Keeley had claimed. It was no more than industry PR. It was a fraud.

Aware that Congress was actively considering the pure food and drug legislation, Doubleday rushed *The Jungle* into print in order to take advantage of the media interest the pending legislation was generating. It sent page proofs to all the major newspapers. Doubleday publicists set about making the publication of *The Jungle* a media event. An unknown and impoverished young author had written an explosive treatise exposing an entire industry for fostering bad meat on an unsuspecting public. The publicists cast aside Sinclair's idea that *The Jungle* was to be the Uncle Tom's Cabin for the labor movement. Sinclair rapidly became a not-at-all reluctant celebrity sitting for seemingly non-stop media interviews about the meat packing industry and the food and drug bill. Then, the industry counter-attacked.

In early March, Ogden Armour sent one of his attorneys to meet with Sinclair's publisher Frank Doubleday with a proposal. Armour would provide Doubleday with an attractive advertising contract in return for one simple favor. Doubleday would cease its efforts to publicize *The Jungle* and would withdraw it from distribution in Europe where competitors could use the novel to attack American meat packers. The plan backfired. Frank Doubleday was repelled by the offer. He had not shown a lot of interest in Sinclair or *The Jungle* before but now Doubleday took an interest. Doubleday not only continued to promote the book but also increased its efforts not only in the U.S. and Europe but worldwide. Sales exploded. Twenty-five thousand copies of *The Jungle* were sold in the first six weeks after its publication, 7,000 in one day alone.

As soon as review copies of *The Jungle* became available, Doubleday sent one to President Roosevelt. Roosevelt, who was receiving thousands of letters demanding that he do something about the abuses describe in *The Jungle*, not only read the book, he sent a three page letter to Sinclair critiquing the book along with an invitation for Sinclair to visit the White House. The two met on April 4th. During the meeting, Roosevelt not only praised Sinclair for his work but said that he was sending a team to Chicago to investigate Sinclair's charges.

> **LESSON: A shocking pivotal event is usually required during the last moments to galvanize public support for change.** The publication of Upton Sinclair's Jungle aroused the public and was critical to the passage of the Meat Inspection Act and Pure Food and Drug Act. Sinclair's graphic descriptions of unsanitary conditions in the meat packing industry outraged Americans. They turned their fury on their elected representatives.

THE PRESIDENT BECOMES MORE DEEPLY INVOLVED

Roosevelt had already received one report evaluating the accuracy of Sinclair's reporting. The Secretary of Agriculture, James Wilson, had launched an investigation into Sinclair's charges as soon as Doubleday published *The Jungle.* In his report to the President, the Secretary concluded that many if not most of Sinclair's charges were deliberate misrepresentations or exaggerations either by Sinclair or by his sources. For example, Sinclair's reports of insanitary conditions were isolated instances and not representative of the packing plants as a whole. Regardless, the Secretary assured the President that he had taken action to toughen sanitary guidelines. Roosevelt did not believe the report provided clear and definitive answers to the charges Sinclair had raised. He wanted another independent investigation conducted by someone who could be trusted to find the truth. He wrote to Wilson, "I would like a first-class man to be appointed to meet Sinclair...get the names of witnesses...and then go to work in the industry."[125] The name of the person chosen to conduct the investigation, ordered the President, was to be kept absolutely secret. Wilson suggested the commissioner of labor, Charles P. Neill, for the task. Roosevelt agreed and suggested that James Reynolds, a lawyer who Roosevelt trusted and had done investigative work for the President in the past, accompany Neill.

Neill and Reynolds met with the Sinclair to obtain documentation of abuses he had collected and suggestions concerning people they should interview that might substantiate his charges. The two then set of for Chicago to conduct their secret investigation. They did not know that someone had warned the packers who launched a desperate effort to clean up the worst of the unsanitary conditions in the packing plants. Their secret investigation was not a secret at all. It was never clear who tipped off the packers but it probably did not matter. Charles Neill was well known. Given the publicity swirling around Sinclair's book, it would not have taken much to guess that Neil wasn't in Chicago for a vacation. After two weeks of interviewing Sinclair's sources and following up on leads suggested by others, Neill and Reynolds returned to Washington to report to the President. Roosevelt later described the report he received on conditions in the stockyards as revolting. Neill and Reynolds had independently confirmed almost all of Sinclair's accusations. The situation was as bad, reported Neill and Reynolds, or even worse, than Sinclair had described.

Sinclair wanted the Neill/Reynolds report released to the public. Roosevelt refused. He had a different idea. He intended to use the threat of releasing the damning report to the public as leverage to force the meat packers to acquiesce to the passage of pure food and drug legislation. The public was already beginning to boycott meat. Roosevelt knew that word had already leaked out about the contents of the Neill and Reynolds report. The last thing the meat barons wanted was more bad publicity, particularly specific charges documented by the President's own investigators. In fact, Louis Swift of Swift and company had already approached him. Swift promised the President that the packers would voluntarily correct the problems if the President would just NOT issue the full report. The journey to passage of major new legislation had entered its final phase, one of intense political negotiation, tradeoffs and vote buying as proponents of the legislation searched for the votes they needed.

> **LESSON: Presidential support is critical, particularly during the final push for legislation but you should expect the president to come late to the struggle.** President Theodore Roosevelt's support for pure food and drug legislation came late but was critical during the final months of debate. His decision to send Neill and Reynolds to Chicago to investigate Sinclair's charges and his threat to release the Neill/Reynolds report was important during last minute vote buying and negotiations. Like Congressmen and Senators, Presidents

> rarely lead the struggle for great legislative accomplishment. They join the cause late and reluctantly even when they sympathize with the proponents of legislative action and agree that problem warrants major change. Presidents are usually more concerned with their power, prestige and position than the welfare of the country. They set sail on a course of action only after taking careful measure of the direction of the wind. Theodore Roosevelt contribution to the pure food and drug cause was typical. Proponents of change reach a critical turning point when Presidents finally decide to throw their political weight and reputation behind major legislative initiatives. Roosevelt's decision to launch his own investigation into Sinclair's charges against the meat packers marked a major advance for advocates of pure food and drugs.

VOTE BUYING LEADS TO FINAL PASSAGE[126]

By May of 2006, the pure food and drug crusaders were within striking distance of seeing their efforts pay off with the passage of a pure food and drug law. *The Jungle* had aroused the public. Pressure was mounting on Congress and the President to do something. The General Federation of Women's Clubs had launched a highly successful campaign to flood Congress with telegrams demanding action on pure food and drug legislation. The *New York Times* published a series of articles in late May charging that the Speaker of the House, Joseph Cannon, was blocking pure food and drug legislation from getting to the floor of the House over the objections of majority of the House members who wanted to take up such legislation. By June the *Times* was reporting that Cannon's Republican colleagues were expressing concern that Cannon's stand might damage the party significantly in the fall elections. They begged him to reconsider.

Responding to public demands, Senator Albert Beveridge of Indiana introduced a bill to address the meat packing plant issue directly. It required the inspection of all meat sold in interstate or foreign commerce. Manufacturers had to destroy meat found unfit for human consumption.

They had to date canned meat after it was inspected. Product the inspectors found to be "impure, unsound, composed of unhealthful ingredients, or…treated with…dyes or deleterious chemical," had to be destroyed.[127] Meat and meat products crossing state lines would have to carry a federal stamp indicating that government agents had inspected the product and that it had passed inspection. The Department of Agriculture would be given responsibility inspections. Finally, the packers, not Congress, would be responsible for paying for the inspections. The Secretary of Agriculture would levy a fee on packer for every animal inspected.

The meat packers were appalled. This was worse than anything they had expected. Seeking allies, the packers went to the American Livestock Association with a threat. If the Beveridge bill passed, said the packers, they would pass along to livestock raisers the cost of these unnecessary inspections. The bill would saddle Livestock Association members with additional costs at a time when they were already struggling. The Association mounted an aggressive campaign sending thousands of letters and telegrams to the White House opposing both the Beveridge bill and the release of the Neill/Reynolds report. Leaders of the Livestock Association requested a meeting with Roosevelt to argue their case. Roosevelt sympathized but restated his conviction that legislation was necessary. He repeated his threat to release the Neill/Reynolds report if the packers and livestock raisers continued to oppose legislation and even had Neill summarize his findings to emphasize how damaging the report would be to the meat packing industry if released.

Beveridge pushed his bill to a vote in the Senate. Afraid the Roosevelt might carry through with his threat and thinking they might have a better chance in the House, the meat packers and livestock raisers panicked and withdrew their opposition. The bill passed the Senate. The battle moved to the House and the packers changed tactics.

The packers reneged on their promise to the President voluntarily to clean up the packinghouses. Now they went public denying that anything was seriously wrong. The country did not need the Beveridge law. Inspections were unnecessary. Cans did not need to be dated since canned meat was safe for years. Preservatives and dyes not only did no harm, they were an enhancement. Requiring packers to pay the cost of inspections would just drive up costs and prices. Finally, the act was unconstitutional. It was an unprecedented and unwarranted intrusion into the conduct of business. If the law passed, the Secretary of Agriculture would be able to shut down any plant he felt was unsanitary with the packers having no avenue of appeal. Businessmen would lose the right to control their own businesses. This would just be the first step. Soon the government would be interfering in the relationship between labor and management. If passed, the bill would destroy a great American industry.

Sinclair appealed to Roosevelt to release the Neill/Reynolds report. Roosevelt refused. The threat of releasing the report, he argued, was enough. Releasing the report would just appeal to sensationalism. It would not add much to what Sinclair had already made public. It would only further depress meat sales and harm "scores of thousands of stock-growers, ranchers, hired men, cowboys, farmers and farm hands all over this country, who have been guilty of no misconduct whatever."[128]

Sinclair decided to take things into his own hands. He did not have a copy of the Neill/Reynolds report but Neil had briefed him on the contents. Moreover, he had his own notes, affidavits and documentation. He went to *The New York Times*, and the *Times* ran with the story. The *Times* revealed the contents of the President's secret report. Surprisingly, Roosevelt was not angry but he chided Sinclair for his reckless behavior. The contents of the report were out but Roosevelt reasoned he could still use the threat of releasing report itself as leverage. He was wrong.

The meat packers and other manufacturing interests prevailed upon two Congressmen, James W. Wadsworth, Chairman of the House Committee on Agriculture and William Lorimer of Chicago, to introduce an alternative to the Beveridge bill that would address the packers' major concerns. Under the Wadsworth bill:

- The cost of inspection would be borne by the government, not the packers,
- Canned meat would not have to be inspected or dated,
- Most preservatives would be allowed,

- There would be no ban on shipment of uninspected meat in interstate commerce, and
- Packers could appeal even the most minor of rulings by the Department of Agriculture to the courts.

As Roosevelt said, the Wadsworth/Lorimer bill was a sham. His threats to release the Neill/Reynolds report had not worked so he released the report.

There was no shockwave of public reaction to the release of the report possibly because the public was already aware of the problems in the packinghouses. The Neill/Reynolds report added little in the way of additional gory details. Indeed, compared to *The Jungle*, the report was mild. However, it did confirm most of Sinclair's charges.

The packers and their congressional supporters attacked the report and the authors personally. Neill and Reynolds were sociologists and theorists, they said, who were seeking to take control of America's meat packing industry from honest and practical businessmen. Congressmen sympathetic to the packers charged the authors with inventing or greatly exaggerating the severity of unsanitary conditions. A description Neill and Reynolds had provided in the report of the carcass of a freshly killed and cleaned hog falling off a conveyor belt and landing in a filthy men's bathroom came under particular scrutiny. Neill and Reynolds had written:

> As an extreme example of the entire disregard on the part of employees of any notion of cleanliness in handling dressed meat, we saw a hog that had just been killed, cleaned, washed and started on its way to the cooling room fall from the sliding rail to a dirty wooden floor and slide part way into the filthy men's privy. Is was picked up by two employees, placed on a truck, carried into the cooling room and hung up with other carcasses, not effort being made to clean it.[129]

Pro-packer Congressmen, particularly Wadsworth and Lorimer, challenged the veracity of the reporting during hearing. They pushed for specifics:

- How much of the hog went into the urinal?
- Which end of the hog entered the privy, head or feet?
- Was it just the nose of the hog or maybe one foot?
- Was Neill sure the hog wasn't cleaned?
- Maybe that was not the proper time to clean the hog. Maybe the workers cleaned the hog later and Neill did not see the cleaning.[130]

Wadsworth offered his opinion that Neill was just a "careless" observer. Lorimer said the report was "filled with generalities" and "lacked specifics except for the report on the poor hog."[131] Neill later said he felt like defense attorneys were examining him and trying everything they could to break him down. Reynolds received similarly treatment. Neill and Reynolds emerged from the hearings with their credibility intact, and their harsh treatment from Wadsworth and Lorimer actually gained them the sympathy of the more moderate members of the committee. However, that was not enough. The committee reported out and the House passed a bill very much like the Wadsworth proposal.

The Senate had passed a bill like Beveridge proposal. The major differences between the House and Senate versions involved the issue of dating of canned meat and the source of funding for the inspections. The Senate version called for the mandatory dating of canned meat and levying fees on packers to cover the cost of inspections. The House bill called for no labeling and funding through government appropriations. Eventually the power of the meat packers and cattle raisers in the House proved too much. Faced with the prospect of getting no bill passed or accepting the House version, the Senate caved.

The major provisions of the Meat Inspection Act were as follows:

- Congress would fund inspections with a permanent appropriation of $3 million per year.
- The Secretary of Agriculture would be responsible for enforcing the law through the Bureau of Animal Industry.
- The Bureau would hire additional inspectors.
- Inspections would be conducted ant-mortem and post-mortem.

- Packers would have to destroy unfit carcasses; fit carcasses would be tagged as inspected and passed.
- Inspectors would have full access to plants.
- The Secretary of Agriculture would specify sanitary standards plants would have to follow to get the government's stamp of approval.
- It would be illegal to ship products in interstate or foreign commerce that had not passed inspection. (Products shipped intrastate were not covered.)

Having passed the Meat Inspection Act, the House began debate on the Pure Food and Drug Act. With the passage of the Meat Inspection Act, the President's support, and public and press demanding action, there was little doubt that a Pure Food and Drug Act would pass. As in the case of the Meat Inspection Act, opponents of the pure food and drug legislation focused on weakening the bill as much as possible and removing what they considered to be the most onerous provisions such as those allowing the Secretary of Agriculture to set food standards and determine the wholesomeness of preservatives. They were largely successful.

- They kept the focus of the law to proper labeling. The law assumed that consumers could protect themselves provided they were properly informed.
- There would be no pre-inspection. Inspectors could detect and cite violations only after the product was on the market.
- There was no provision for the government to inspect manufacturing facilities and/or to issue sanitary requirements.
- Food and drugs were covered.
- Adulteration and misbranding were both violations of the act.
- Drugs were to be considered adulterated if they were sold under a name recognized in the United States Pharmacopoeia or National Formulary and failed to meet the U.S. Pharmacopoeia or National Formulary standards for strength, quality, or purity unless the label listed different standards.

- Food was to be considered adulterated if among other things it contained added poison or other ingredients injurious to health or consisted in whole or in part of filthy, decomposed or putrid animal or vegetable substances unless the harmful substances could be removed prior to consumption. Morphine, opium, cocaine, heroin, chloroform, and a number of other narcotic substances were allowed as long as there quantity and proportion were shown on the label.
- Manufacturers had to list the contents of the products on labels but were not required to disclose their trade formulas.
- Wiley's Bureau of Chemistry would be responsible to testing foods and drugs and reporting violations to the Secretary of Agriculture but the primary remedy the government had to force compliance with the law was to take the offending party to court.

Wiley pronounced himself disappointed with some of the provisions of the act, but in general said he thought it was an important first step.

THE INCOMPLETE VICTORY

So, did the pure food and drug advocates win? Yes and no. The Pure Food and Drug and Meat Inspection Acts represented an historic step forward in government oversight of the food and drug industries and in consumer protection in general, one that has withstood decades of well financed attacks. However, there were major flaws in the legislation. Drugs did not have to work and could still contain addictive ingredients. Food had to meet only minimum standards. Further, there was no provision for the government to test products or take action before adulterated or misbranded drugs and food reached the marketplace.

The Bureau of Chemistry tried to enforce the act but it was small and had limited resources. In the absence of voluntary compliance, the only avenue the Bureau had to enforce its findings was to plea with the Attorney General to take the offending party to court. Enforcement in the courts was always problematic at best. Frequently the Bureau resorted to using the carrot rather than the stick. It offered to certify drug and food manufacturers who agreed to abide by the Bureau's recommendations and accept its advice.

Opponents of the meat inspection and food and drug laws did not give up. In his biography, Wiley tells of several efforts opponents made shortly after the passage of the food and drug and meat inspection acts to limit enforcement. In one instance, the whiskey rectifiers attempted to hire Wiley as a consulting Chemist with the obvious intent of influencing his decisions. Unsuccessful, the rectifiers teamed up with manufacturers of patent medicine to convince the Secretary of Agriculture to appoint a Board of Food and Drug Inspection to review the decisions of the Bureau of Chemistry. Wiley was made chairman of the board which was composed to two other people who were sympathetic to the food, drink and drug manufacturers. Wiley writes that he soon became "a mere figurehead; the two other members voting together overruled [his] decisions constantly."[132] In 1912, Wiley resigned from government. He later accepted an invitation to join *Good Housekeeping* magazine as a contributing editor where he continued to work for the pure food and drug cause.

The Bureau of Chemistry continued playing an important but somewhat diminished role in enforcing the laws until 1927 when Congress created the Food, Drug and Insecticide Administration, later renamed the Food and Drug Administration (FDA).

THE FIGHT MUST CONTINUE, THERE IS NO FINISH LINE

The 1906 acts were the first comprehensive effort by the federal government to regulate food, drink and drugs. Their passage marked the end of a 27-year struggle by pure food, drink and drug advocates to secure some level of meaningful government regulation.

Congress has strengthened the pure food and drug laws three times since 1906. In 1938, Congress passed the Food, Drug and Cosmetics Act in response to a public outcry over a drug called Elixir Sulfanilamide. A Tennessee drug company developed Elixir Sulfanilamide sold it as a sulfa wonder drug for pediatric patients. It contained a solvent that the company had never tested on humans that turned out to have toxic effects similar to antifreeze. Over 100 people, many of them children, died after consuming the drug. The new law gave the FDA oversight of cosmetics and medical devices as well as food and drugs. Most importantly, it required pre-market testing of drugs. Drug manufacturers were required to offer the FDA proof of safety before marketing drugs. The law also prohibited false claims about the effectiveness of drugs and gave the agency power to issue and enforce food standards, conduct inspections of factories and correct abuses in food packaging and quality control.

In 1962, Congress expanded the FDA's powers once again. As in 1938, the new drug law, the Kefauver-Harris Amendments, resulted from a public outcry. This time it had to do with Thalidomide, a sedative that resulted in thousands of grossly deformed newborns. The new law required that drug manufacturers provide evidence that new drugs worked as intended before receiving FDA approval. Additionally, the FDA was given greater control over drug trials, drug manufacturing practices, and drug advertising.

Most recently in 2011, Congress passed the Food Safety Modernization Act. Among other things, the act greatly expanded the authority of the FDA to inspect food production facilities both foreign and domestic, issue mandatory recalls of tainted foods, set nationwide standards for producing and harvesting fresh produce, and create a new method of effectively tracking and tracing fruits and vegetables, to ensure any contaminated produce was located and recalled in a safe and timely manner. Department of Health and Human Services Secretary Kathleen Sebelius called the new law, "the most significant food safety law of the last 100 years."[133] Once again, Congress acted only after a public outcry about repeated instances of contaminated food reaching the marketplace.

WHAT THE PURE FOOD AND DRUG FIGHT CAN TEACH US

If there is one overall lesson we can learn from the fight for pure food and drugs it is that getting things done in Washington is extremely difficult. It takes enormous patience and persistence and typically, advocates of change have to settle for less than they want. Conservatives with a lot more money and a vicious determination to stop progress opposed the food and drug advocates. In the end, both the Meat Inspection Act and Pure Food and Drug act fell short of providing the level of government oversight of the food, drink and drug industries that pure food and drug crusaders wanted. However, these acts were a critical first step.

There is good news and bad news in the pure food and drug story. The good news is that determined progressives can win the battle for change. Victory comes not because progressives are smarter or better funded than their opponents are but because ultimately American voters come to realize that progressives are right. The bad news is that the struggle never ends. Conservatives will always seek to roll back the clock to the 'good old days' which in the case of pure food and drugs meant the days when children died from consuming tainted meat and adulterated drugs so that a few people could get rich.

In the next chapter, I will examine a topic of great interest today, the fight for comprehensive health insurance that resulted in the passage of Medicare and Medicaid. The struggle for health insurance reinforces many of the lessons we have already learned and adds new lessons about what it takes to get things done in Washington.

A SUMMARY LESSONS FROM THE PURE FOOD AND DRUG CRUSADE

Progressives ideas for change rarely originate in Washington. The drive for pure food and drugs did not start in Washington and professional politicians did not take the lead in proposing change, if fact they resisted change. It began when average men and women such as the ladies from Beekman hill decided that something was wrong in the country and that the federal government had to play a role in correcting the problem. Over and over throughout this book we will see that progressive ideas for change almost always originate in this way. If you want to know where to look for the next big idea about how to use the power of government to achieve the common good, look to the people not to the politicians.

There must be some national coordination of local grassroots efforts. The pure food and drug cause benefited greatly from the coordinating and organizing efforts of the Women's Christian Temperance Union, National Consumers League and National Council of Women. In addition, it helped that many of these organizations had members in common which made communication and coordination easier.

The problem must be severe and national in scope Members of Congress do not enact changes to public policy to address a minor or local problem. The problem must be, or made to appear to be, national in scope, severe, and troublesome to many voters. The latter is most important. Politicians are driven to legislative accomplishment out of fear of defeat at the next election.

Initial defeat and rejection is a necessary and common component of ultimate success. Congressmen, Senators and the public in general rarely react positively to proposals for major social change when such proposals are first presented. They have to have time to get used to the idea. Early efforts to pass legislation are important even when they lead to defeat after defeat. Each subsequent failure to obtain passage is a step forward if for no other reason than that the idea for reform is becoming less strange, less foreign sounding. Opponents may not be swayed to the idea yet, but they are becoming accustomed to it; "Yes, I've heard about that before."

Americans are suspicious of government in general and the national government in particular. Consequently, opponents of national progressive legislation can usually score points by playing upon the general fear of "big government." State-based approaches rarely solve the kinds of problems we are talking about in this book, problems that are severe, national in scope, and not subject to easy fixes. However, it is important to try state-based remedies if for no other reason than to be able to show that states and/or local governments have tried to address the issue but have been unsuccessful in doing so. You must be able to make the case that a federal solution is required.

There must be some national coordination of local grassroots efforts. The pure food and drug cause benefited greatly from the coordinating and organizing efforts of the Women's Christian Temperance Union, National Consumers League and National Council of Women.

Every cause needs a leader/spokesperson who can gain national attention and lend credibility to the cause. George Washington Wiley became the spokesperson for the pure food and drug movement. His background as a chemist and his position as the head of the Department of Agriculture's Bureau of Chemistry gave him credibility.

Every movement needs a dramatic publicity stunt to arouse media and public attention. Wiley's poison squad attracted the interest of reporters looking for a good story. Their stories about young men consuming 'poison' in a scientific experiment grabbed public attention, as did the displays of adulterated foods at the Louisiana Purchase Exposition.

The press must join the struggle. Pure food and drug advocates got a significant boost when respected publications like the *Ladies Home Journal, Collier's Weekly, Women's Home Companion, Popular Science Monthly,* and others began covering the pure food and drug cause.

Congressmen and Senators must be pushed into joining the fight. Senator Weldon Heyburn of Idaho became interested in and a supporter of the pure food and drug cause only after women's groups in Idaho announced that they would work to defeat any candidate who did not support pure food and drug legislation.

The President's support is critical, particularly during the final push for legislation. Roosevelt's support for pure food and drug legislation came late but was critical during the final months of debate. His decision to send Neill and Reynolds to Chicago to investigate Sinclair's charges and his threat to release the Neill/Reynolds report was important during last minute vote buying and negotiations.

A critical and dangerous turning point occurs when the opposition appears to switch side. It was a clear sign that some type of comprehensive pure food and drug legislation was inevitable when conservative Congressmen and Senators who previously had opposed any food and drug legislation suddenly began to voice their support. The danger for pure food and drug advocates was that their former opponents would gain control and produce legislation that sounded good but accomplished little, as in the case of the Wadsworth bill.

You need a shocking pivotal event to galvanize public support for change. The publication of Upton Sinclair's *Jungle* aroused the public and was critical to the passage of the Meat Inspection Act and Pure Food and Drug Act. Sinclair's graphic descriptions of unsanitary conditions in the meat packing industry outraged Americans and they turned their fury on their elected representatives.

3

The Struggle for Health Insurance

On July 30, 1965, 47 guests, including the Vice President, members of Congress and other dignitaries, accompanied President Lyndon Johnson to join 200 others including former President Harry S. Truman in the auditorium of the Truman library in Independence, Missouri to witness an historic signing ceremony. The occasion was the signing into law of Medicare. Johnson said, "I'm so proud that this has come to pass in the Johnson Administration…And through this new law…every citizen will be able in his productive years, when he's earning, to insure himself against the ravages of illness in his old age… No longer will old Americans be denied the healing miracle of modern medicine. No longer will illness crush and destroy the savings that they have so carefully put away over a lifetime so that they might enjoy dignity in their later years."[134] With the enactment of Medicare, the United States joined the rest of the industrialized world in providing a guarantee of health insurance to at least some of its citizens. The U.S. was more than 70 years late and chose an approach that no other nation would have considered.

THE LONG ROAD TO MEDICARE

Most Americans do not know that the drive for national health insurance that was so much in the news in 2009 actually began in the early 1900s. Germany had been the first to enact national compulsory health insurance for its workers in 1883. By 1911, England and several other European nations had followed Germany's lead and adopted their own programs.

The push for national health insurance in industrialized nations in the early 20th century was reflective of a significant change in the practice of medicine. In 1912 a Harvard professor, Lawrence Henderson, had this to say about advances in medical treatment at that time: "For the first time in human history, a random patient with a random disease consulting a doctor chosen at random stands a better than 50/50 chance of benefiting from the encounter."[135] Medicine stopped being an art and became a science. However, in the early 1900s, medicine was a science unaffordable to most working men and women in America.

If you worked in America in the late 1800s and early 1900s, you suffered not only from near starvation wages but also from a range of medical ailments, many serious. If you worked for long as a miner, stonecutter, textile worker, furrier, cap maker, baker or hairdresser, you almost certainly would develop bronchitis, asthma and very likely tuberculosis. Regardless of occupation, you worked long hours, with little time to rest or even seek fresh air. You and your family lived in overcrowded and unsanitary tenement housing. You were constantly under stress and exhausted. You likely sought refuge in alcohol that soon ravaged your body. If you were a woman and became pregnant, you worked as long as you could before giving birth and then, assuming you survived the delivery, returned to work as soon as possible since your family depended upon your wages. Your child would very likely never live to reach the age of five. Any bout of sickness for you or a family member had disastrous consequences even if the ill person recovered. Your life would quickly spiral out of control as it did for Emil Bollhausen, a Germany immigrant and cabinetmaker, one of several hundred cases reported in a study of New York City working families in a 1917 study by the Russell Sage Foundation.

Bollhausen had arrived in the United States in 1882. He quickly found work in New York City's furniture industry employing cabinet making skills his father had taught him in Berlin. He married and had a son. His wife worked as a janitress and the family, while not prosperous, could pay the bills. They survived. By 1915, at the age of fifty-four, Bollhausen had found better and higher paying employment working for an antique dealer doing fine finishing and repairs. Then, Bollhausen had heart trouble. He developed pleurisy and pneumonia and was hospitalized. His income naturally stopped since there was no such thing at the time as paid sick leave. Bollhausen and his family entered a downward spiral as described in a report at the time:

> "[H] ospital treatment, then a few day's work, illness again, no money to pay the doctor, the use of patent medicines suggested by neighbors, the hospital again with some improvement followed by four weeks in the country...work again too hard for him, another illness, dispensary treatment...eight months of sickness and treatment and still unable to undertake regular work."[136]

Bollhausen's experience was typical of most workers who were unfortunate enough to become ill. What little assistance workers could obtain for dealing with medical expenses came from fraternal organizations such as the Freemasons or Odd Fellows often in the way of a fraternal or "lodge" doctor who the association paid to treat members. Most good doctors refused to take such patients because the payments were small. Members might also receive a small cash benefit if they could not work because of illness for a length of time, usually a week or more. Such benefits lasted only for a limited time and diminished over time. For example, one association in New York paid $4.00 a week for the first six weeks then $2.00 a week for the next six weeks with nothing thereafter.[137]

In 1916, about one quarter of unionized workers belonged to unions that provided some kind of sickness benefits to their members. This was at a time when only a little over 5 percent of American workers were in labor unions so the coverage was available only to a small segment of the workforce.

Some employers offered health benefits but usually only as a union-avoidance tactic. Employer plans were typically available only to employees over a certain wage level who had been with the company for a certain period and who were under a certain age. All benefits ended when a person left the company regardless of years of service. Most companies would enroll women but most companies in the south restricted health benefits to whites only. Benefits were usually limited to small cash payments to employees who were sick. The payments were usually not sufficient to pay the cost of medical treatment. Other than a few large companies such as Western Union and American Telephone and Telegraph, most companies required employee contributions. Some required employees to cover 100% of the cost through their contributions.

Such "industrial medicine" was better than nothing but not always welcomed by workers. The company nurse that made a free visit to offer you medical care was often required to report your condition to your employer. A physical examination ordered at one company might lead to treatment but at another company, it might lead to immediate dismissal. One could never be sure. Many workers distrusted the company doctors suspecting that they were really just company spies out to eliminate workers found to be poor health risks. Additionally, many companies, particularly Southern timber companies, automatically deducted the cost of paying for company doctors from worker paychecks even if the workers never saw a doctor. Unions consistently denounced "industrial medicine" as coercive and undemocratic.

Most people got the little medical care they received through charities that operated free medical dispensaries (health clinics). These were particularly popular in urban areas with large immigrant populations. Dispensaries served not only the poor and unemployed but the working poor. Many who might have had some limited access to assistance through an association or employer chose to go to a dispensary out of the belief (unfounded) that free care was superior to that they could obtain in doctor's offices. In reality, "dispensaries were not all well equipped, however. In many cases, overcrowding, absentee doctors, haphazard care, and decaying facilities made dispensary treatment a harrowing experience."[138] Additionally, dispensaries were typically open for only a few hours a day or week and usually only during working hours so it was difficult for most working people to visit them without losing perhaps an entire day's pay. Those who did visit found the wait to see a doctor a long one and their visit with the doctor fleeting as he rushed on to another patient. For example, two doctors in one New York dispensary one morning in 1914 reportedly saw 162 patients in just four hours, a rate of more than 40 patients per hour.

Some private physicians were willing to wave their fees for low-income patients. Nurses and midwives, usually female, charged less. Most of these options were available only to whites and only in urban areas. If you were black or lived in a rural area, you had little medical care available either public or private.

Urban or rural the typical experience of the American worker of the time who became seriously ill was similar to that of a cook in New York in 1915. He had held a number of good positions but lost work when he developed a cough because no one wanted to employ a cook with a serious cough. He entered a hospital for treatment but was discharged homeless in a few days. He eventually was able to obtain medication though a dispensary and found lodging at a home for destitute tuberculosis patients run by the Salvation Army. Like most working poor who became seriously ill, the cook soon died. The city buried him in a pauper's grave in potter's field.[139] A person born in 1900 had a life expectancy of just 47 years.

EFFORTS OF THE AMERICAN ASSOCIATION FOR LABOR LEGISLATION

It was not that progressives had not tried to make the benefits of modern medicine available to all Americans. They had. Progressives began pushing for some kind of national compulsory health insurance in the United States at about the same time as in other nations. Theodore Roosevelt made such insurance a major feature of his platform when he ran as the nominee of the Progressive Bull Moose Party against Woodrow Wilson in 1912. When Roosevelt lost, the American Association for Labor Legislation (AALL), a group of progressive social scientists, labor activists, and lawyers, picked up the campaign for national health insurance. The AALL had been successful in getting states to adopt workmen's compensation laws. After Roosevelt's defeat, the AALL turned its attention to national health insurance and introduced a model bill for state-based compulsory health insurance in 1915.

AALL directed its efforts toward the working poor. It excluded higher-income workers and the unemployed. The AALL assumed that higher income workers could better afford to pay for their own care and charity should cover the non-working poor. The AALL's model legislation excluded casual, seasonal and temporary workers (mostly non-whites) also.

Leaders of the AALL expected to have the same success with their model health insurance proposal that they had with their push for workmen's compensation and launched a sophisticated "public education" campaign. Initially, leaders of the American Medical Association (AMA) supported the AALL initiative, reasoning the United States would follow Europe and adopt some kind of compulsory health insurance. Although the AALL was able to get its model bill introduced in the legislatures of 15 states and to get 10 other states to appoint commissions to study the matter, it was unable to secure passage in a single state.

> **LESSON: Gains in one area do not automatically translate into gains in another, even a closely related policy area.** The AALL assumed that its success in pushing states to adopt workman's compensation laws could be transferred relatively easily to success in getting states to pass comprehensive health insurance. It was wrong. The reality is that each new drive for change is a war that you must fight on its own. You can use lessons from previous efforts and you do benefit if you have a track record of success but you still have to fight the current battles just as you fought the battles in the previous war.

THE AMA SWITCHES SIDES

In 1920, the AALL lost AMA support when a group of conservative doctors, fearing that a program of national health insurance would threaten the growing income and prestige of medical professionals, revolted against the AMA leadership in opposition to national health insurance. The AMA announced that it was now opposed to "the institution of any plan embodying the system of compulsory contribution insurance against illness, or any other plan of compulsory insurance which provides for medical service to be rendered contributors or their dependents, provided, controlled or regulated by any state or Federal government."[140] Leaders of the insurance and pharmaceutical industries, large employers and the leadership of the American Federation of Labor joined the conservative AMA doctors in opposing compulsory health insurance.

Doctors were horrified at the prospect of Congress passing some kind of national health insurance. If medical services were free to the insured, the demand would skyrocket. People would expect doctors to treat every little ailment. If access to health care became a right, doctors could no longer deny treatment. Doctors would be at the beck and call of patients with no say so over who they treated or when. Patients, not doctors, would be in control of the relationship. Relief from caring for charity patients would be no relief at all. One doctor wrote; "confiscation by the State of the ancient heritage of the medical professions, the care of the sick poor, is without right, reason, or justification"[141] Another argued that poor people were taken care of and should be taken care of by choice, not compulsion. A law compelling a physician to treat a patient whether poor or rich was "obnoxious to the freedom and democratic spirit of the people of the ...nation." Another wrote, "When a man gives away his services he retains his self –respect; when a man sells them at a ruinous reduction he feels that he has become a bargain counter remnant of his former self." Health insurance would "revolutionize the practice of medicine so that the physician will professionally cease to be an individualist and will be but a cog in a great medical machine." Health insurance would destroy quality. A lowered income would 'limit [a doctor's] training, equipment, and efficiency, and in the end [would] react on the people." Health insurance would "imperil the advancement of medical research...all the great discoveries in medicine have resulted from individual effort. There is no initiative in bureaucratic medicine...Bring your health insurance and what incentive will a young man have to spend his time in research work? You will strike a blow at the very foundation of medicine."

Employers were threatened. A brush manufacturer wrote that he was appalled by the "idea of caring for everybody in this world, whether they have been thrifty or not…No distinction is made in the bill between workmen. The dissolute, lazy and incompetent workman is grouped with the industrious, careful and temperate workman. The latter pays for the vices of the former." A mill owner wrote "This law would [encourage] indifference, lack of initiative and lack of responsibility and loyalty to employer. It would also tend to dishonesty on the part of an employee to obtain coveted benefits…The inevitable tendency of many workers under compulsory health insurance is to feign illness..There is no effective check provided in the measure against malingering." Another wrote that if health insurance were passed, "the public won't buy, the employer won't manufacture, and the man won't have a job."

Private insurers were threatened. "If we have one duty to perform greater than another," wrote one insurance company executive, "it is to turn the tide of public opinion against all kinds of federal and state insurance schemes." Compulsory health insurance would, he said, "bring about the result that all forms of insurance—life, casualty, fire and every other form—shall be carried solely by the government…This is only the entering wedge; if once a foothold is obtained it will mean attempts to have such State Insurance of all kinds.."

As Beatrix Hoffman, author of *The Wages of Sickness: The Politics of Health Insurance in Progressive America*, points out opponents of compulsory health insurance had a common fear that the passage of any such legislation would not only negatively impact their financial interest but would undermine their autonomy and independence.

> All of these groups opposed health insurance on economic grounds. Doctors feared that their incomes would drop if the AALL'S bill became law. Employers denounced the burden of compulsory premium payments. Insurance companies raffled against the threat to their dominance of the life insurance market. The leaders of the American Federation of Labor (AFL) thought social insurance would undermine trade union benefits and forestall labor's

> demands for higher wages. But equally important to opponents was the perception that compulsory health insurance would erode their group's autonomy. For doctors to be free to set their own fees, for employers to limit their responsibility for the health of workers, for insurance companies to sell more policies, and for labor leaders to win the loyalty of workers, each group demanded the ability to operate independently, free from government (and reformer) interference. For these groups, protecting their economic interests was inseparable from defending their autonomy.[142]

In the case of compulsory health insurance, the negative consequences fell especially hard on doctors who would lose autonomy. "Autonomy—the freedom of physicians to choose their own patients, work hours, fields of specialization, courses of treatment, and fee schedules—had long been an essential principle of American medical practice."[143] There could be no reform without some loss of control by physicians on their ability to act independently.

> **Lesson: It is the nature of change that one or more groups, often well financed and influential groups, will be threatened by the change your propose just a doctors in the AMA were.** Reforms inevitably have negative consequences for some groups since there are always groups of people who reap benefits from the status quo. These people will see the change you propose as a threat to their power, position, prestige, and even financial well-being. Your challenge is to identify such individuals and groups early on, understand how your proposed changes affects them, anticipate the form their opposition might take, and prepare to defend your effort. You should try to structure the change you propose to minimize the threat or make it less apparent. Ideally, you should try to co-opt the opposition.

HEALTH INSURANCE IS UNAMERICAN

Critics charged that health insurance was un-American. Compulsory health insurance, opponents argued "is autocratic and not democratic. It strikes at the root and foundation of the fundamental law of our land: life, liberty and the pursuit of happiness."[144] Another wrote, "this legislation is an immediate institution of State socialism, and an abrogation of the rights of the individual to the control of his own life and property." Compulsory health insurance was "Un-American, Un-economic, Unfair, Un-Scientific and Un-scrupulous."

Opponents of AALL's health insurance proposal and those of other progressives in the early 1900s, frequently cited the shortcomings and "horrors" of the European models that progressives relied upon in designing their plans. When statistics on German sickness rates went up slightly after implementation of compulsory health insurance, American opponents of health insurance cited the increase in sick Germans as evidence of a failed system. In fact, German sickness rates went up simply because more Germans were seeing doctors. Similarly, opponents reported that British National Insurance was a "menace to the health of people' because the system of capitation, whereby doctors received payment based upon the number of patients treated, led to hasty and slipshod service."[145] In fact, capitation had almost doubled the average income of British physicians participating in the system, thereby attracting many more doctors to join the system. Additionally, improved access to care had actually raised, rather than lowered, the health of the average working man. When proponents of the British system pointed out that since passage of the health act demands on charities had dramatically decreased, opponents argued that the same statistics simply proved that the British Insurance Act was "drying up the sources of private and voluntary relief."[146]

> **LESSON: Expect opponents to charge that the change you propose is un-American.** You should never make the case for your policy change by citing what other countries have done, particularly European countries, even if these countries have been highly successful and you are basing your proposal on lessons learned from their efforts. Opponents of reform champion the uniqueness of America and the American people that make any system developed and implemented in a foreign country, particular Europe,

> entirely unworkable in the United States. The un-American argument is a standard conservative opposition tactic and one you should be prepared to counter. In particular, they will claim that what you are proposing is European and point to any weakness; failing or flaw in the "European" approach, no matter how minor, as evidence that such a reform is not anything Americans would want for their country. Failure immediately to counter such attacks from the opposition can lead to certain disaster for the reform effort particularly if the opposition is engaging in fear tactics that it usual will be. Show how the change you propose, rather than being un-American, is indeed what America is all about. Turn the un-American argument on its head. Argue that the opponents are the ones who are being un-American since they are setting out to destroy the country by ignoring a wrong and not fixing it, wishing a cancer away rather than treating it aggressively with the healing power of change. Argue that the truly un-American thing to do would be to do nothing. Americans are not "do nothings," they are doers and that is what you are proposing.

THE AALL SERIOUSLY UNDERESTIMATED THE OPPOSITION.

Leaders of the AALL assumed that the need for national health insurance and its benefits were so obvious that their proposal would succeed on its own merits. Consequently, they failed to counter the demagoguery and fiery rhetoric the opposition adopted effectively. By the time the AALL recognized how effective the opposition had been in demonizing national health insurance it was too late.

> **LESSON: You are less likely to persuade Americans with rational thought than passionate presentation**. Expect opponents of change to make loud arguments and lace them with conspiracy theories and predictions of dire consequences should whatever you are advocating be done. Never assume that Americans will recognize the benefits of

> change, even benefits that you think are obvious, unless you point out those benefits to them specifically and repeatedly. Never be seduced by the logic and rightness of your cause. Never assume that what is obvious to you will be obvious to the average American. Never assume that the average American will accept facts more readily, or even as readily, as he will accept arguments based on speculation, superstition or even outright fabrication of data. Do not expect Americans to recognize the difference between the truth and lies unless you specifically point out the difference. As Rashi Fein, author of *Medical Care, Medical Costs: The Search for a Health Insurance Policy*, points out, "It is easy for those who favor particular legislation to be persuaded by the logic of their position, to assume that others will also be persuaded, and.. to believe that logic or a just cause that cannot be denied will translate into votes...[It] is easy to forget that the political arena has its own logic and that legislators have their own ways of analyzing public and private costs and benefits. The desire to be reelected does not influence [proponents of reform]. It does influence legislators."[147]

Another mistake that the AALL made was failing to provide sufficient detail about how their model plan would operate. For example, designers of the AALL model plan left out specifics on how the health insurance would pay doctors. They assumed that administrators could work out the details later. The absence of details made the plan ripe for attack. As soon as a campaign began for health insurance in New York, rumors began to circulate with abandon. Opponents warned medical professionals that doctors would receive as little as twenty-five cents for an office visit and just a dollar for a home visit, exceedingly low sums. The editor of one medical journals declared at a physicians conference that "a report he had in his hand…proved a chilling fact..[that]..medical men of Pennsylvania reaping $5,400 a year [would receive] from health insurance..[would receive] more like $400." [148] Another doctor wrote to his state legislator, "In talking with reputable physicians…I am convinced that the best [physicians] would be driven out of business for they would not submit to the paltry salaries that would be paid physicians [under compulsory heath insurance].[149]

LESSON: Keep it simple but do not leave out too many details. It is critically important to keep your proposed reforms as simple as possible. Americans are uncomfortable with complexity and never understand nuance. At the same time, you must flesh out the details of what the change would mean and how you will accomplish the change. Any absence of detail or confusion about what is being proposed leaves you open to the wildest charges and speculation. The Devil is in the details and when you offer few details or none at all; your opponents will invent lots and lots of Devils. Rumors fill the void and they are usually dire warnings of impending disaster. Once these rumors start circulating it becomes exceedingly difficult to counter them. Proponent's explanations do little good. Voters remember the rumors. So, keep it simple but be ready to supply the details when the opposition challenges you. Most importantly, move to squash rumors right away.

The AALL's battle for health insurance essentially ended with the outbreak of World War I. There were many reasons for the failure of the AALL effort as Harry Millis, a former president of the American Economic Association pointed out in 1938 article:

> The success of the opposition to the proposed legislation was due more to self-interest on the part of many organizations, to fear, to misunderstanding, to willful misrepresentation, to the charge that it was German [a severe indictment in the period around the First World War], and to the fact that the country had not been prepared by investigation and discussion for a system of health insurance than to any of the weaknesses in what was proposed. Instead of such a system being seen as effecting little more than an assembling of existing costs, it was generally regarded as something that would add an enormous and unsupportable burden. It was denounced as unnecessary, socialistic, un-American, a wrong method of attack—sickness prevention was what was needed. [Opponents argued that] it would beget simulation and malingering; it would involve contract medicine, reduce the income of the doctors,

destroy the close personal relationship between doctor and patient, and discourage and undermine medical research. It was not working well in Europe. Such were the more important sources of opposition and the most frequently voiced objection in the absence of a strong, coherent, actively interested group, to an early end the first period in an American health-insurance movement.[150]

NATIONAL HEALTH INSURANCE AND SOCIAL SECURITY

A second opportunity for national health insurance came in 1932 with the election of Franklin Roosevelt, who supported health insurance as part of social insurance legislation. The initial draft of Social Security Legislation however failed to call for a national health insurance program although it did contain a single line calling for a "study of health insurance." That one line received so much opposition from a well-orchestrated campaign launched by the AMA that the administration eventually struck it, fearing that the mere mention of health insurance could doom Social Security.

Although the administration dropped national health insurance from the Social Security bill, its mere mention created alarm in the medical community that some government-sponsored health insurance program might eventually pass as a way, in their opinion, "to get a foot-in-the-door for socialized medicine."[151] This fear led to a shift in the position of the AMA toward health insurance in general. Until then, the AMA had opposed all forms of health insurance, public or private. After 1935, the organization and medical community in general ceased opposing private health insurance. In an effort to ward off government involvement, the medical community began supporting private hospital insurance and began supporting private health insurance plans for surgical and medical expenses like those offered by the non-profit Blue Cross and Blue Shield plans.

EXPANDED ACCESS TO PRIVATE INSURANCE AFTER WWII

Health insurance had been available in at least some parts of the country since the 1930s but it only became widely available after World War II.

During the war, the War Stabilization Board restricted wages and prices so companies and unions turned to providing other non-cash benefits as a way to attract and retain workers. One of these benefits was medical insurance. Once the AMA dropped its opposition to health insurance, American's access to private health insurance began to expand rapidly. In 1940, only about 10 million Americans had hospitalization insurance. By 1964, nearly 150 million did. In 1940, insurance covering major medical expenses such as doctor fees was non-existent. By 1964, over 45 million Americans had such insurance.[152]

In 1939, Senator Robert Wagner of New York introduced a bill for national health insurance but failed to make any progress in even getting it through committee. Four years later two Democratic members of Congress, Senator James Murray of Montana and Representative John Dingell of Michigan joined Wagner and began introducing health insurance legislation for all Americans, not just industrial workers, annually. None of the Wagner-Murray-Dingell proposals made much progress however.

THE TRUMAN ADMINISTRATION

After President Roosevelt died, President Truman endorsed the Wagner-Murray-Dingell bill and became the first sitting American president to offer support formally for national health insurance. Under Truman's proposal:

- insurance benefits would cover all medical, dental, hospital and nursing-home care expenses, sixty days of hospital care per year plus drugs and auxiliary services;
- beneficiaries would include all contributors to the plan and their dependents, and for the medical needs of a destitute minority which would not be reached by the contributory plan, provisions were made for Federal grants to the states;
- the financing mechanism would be a compulsory 3 percent payroll tax divided equally between employee and employer;
- administration would be in the hands of a national health insurance board within the Federal Security Agency which included the

Social Security Board, the U.S. Public Health Service, the Food and Drug Administration, the Civilian Conservation Corps, the Office of Education (later the United States Department of Education), the National Youth Administration and a number of other agencies;

- to minimize the degree of federal control over doctors and patients, doctors and hospitals would be free to choose whether or not to join the plan,
- patients would be free to choose their own doctors, and doctors would reserve the right to reject patients whom they did not want to treat; and
- doctors who agreed to treat patients under the plan would be paid a stated fee, per capita amount or salary for their services by a national health board with the choice of method of payment (fee, per capita, or salary) left to the majority decision of the participating practitioners in each health service area.[153]

After his surprise victory in 1948, Truman pressed Congress to pass his health insurance bill. He met with strong and determined opposition particularly from the American Medical Association.

The AMA launched a $5 million national propaganda campaign professionally designed and directed by a public relations firm, Whitaker and Baxter (W&B.) The campaign played on American's post-war fears of Communism. Americans were told that Truman's proposal was an attempt on the part of the government "to assume control not only of the medical profession, but of hospitals—both public and private—the drug and appliance industries, dentistry, pharmacy, nursing and allied professions."[154] Behind this conspiracy were the Federal Security Administration, the President, Socialists, and the Communist party. The AMA warned Americans that government health insurance "would inevitably erode the quality of medical care by giving the government control over medical services, overcrowding hospitals, and reducing the incentives of physicians to provide quality care." [155]

Whitaker and Baxter solicited local physicians to address meetings of state and county medical societies opposing the Truman plan, planted anti-legislation articles in local papers, and prepared and distributed newspaper editorials and op-ed pieces. Doctors, dentists, druggists, insurance agents and others distributed some 40 to 50 millions pieces of literature attacking the Truman plan. In October of 1950, W&B placed a paid 70-column-inch advertisement in 11,000 newspapers across the country, ran spot ads on over 1,000 radio stations, and mailed letters to 25,000 companies asking for help in opposing the Truman plan.

A key feature of the campaign was a poster showing a doctor sitting at the bedside of a sick child that doctors were encouraged to post in their waiting rooms. The caption read,

> KEEP POLITICS OUT OF THIS PICTURE
>
> When the life—or health of a loved one is at stake, hope lies in the devoted service of your Doctor. Would you change this picture? Compulsory health insurance is political machine. It would bring a third party—a politician—between you and your Doctor. It would bind up your family's health in red tape. It would result in heavy payroll taxes—and inferior medical care for your and your family. Do not let that happen! [156]

It was a clever scare tactic. Allow Truman's proposal to pass and the government will get between you and your doctor. That false charge would be repeated time and time again by opponents to health reform, most recently by those opposed to reforms sought by the Obama administration in 2009.

The AMA was supported by Conservative business groups such as the Chamber of Commerce and insurance industry companies such as Blue Cross, which argued that voluntary, private insurance was the only "American way" to provide health insurance to the country. A conservative coalition in Congress consisting of Republicans and southern Democrats that held a de factor majority weakened Truman's efforts further. This conservative coalition was opposed to Truman's entire Fair Deal political agenda not just national health care.

The campaign worked. In 1950, the strongest supporters of national health care in the Senate were defeated. Truman was to continue to seek compulsory health insurance but the AMA campaign and losses in the 1950 election doomed these later efforts.

> **LESSON: Do not ignore the built in distrust Americans have of power, in particular the power of government.** The failure of Truman's efforts to win government-run universal health insurance, as I said, can be attributed to the AMA's long, intensive and expensive propaganda campaign that played upon American's fears of Communism in the post-war period. However, something else was at work that goes deeper to a core of American belief. Europeans recognize that strong government action is often necessary and frequently desirable to address public issues and serve the common good. Americans hold an opposite belief. Political scientist Samuel Huntington speaks of an American creed whose distinctive feature is a deep-seated distrust of power, particularly government power. "Opposition of power, and suspicion of government as the most dangerous embodiment of power," he writes, "are themes of American political thought." That fact creates an additional, an often insurmountable, hurtle for progressives in the United States. In order to pass comprehensive legislation to address a public need, you must not only convince the public that action is needed and that your proposal is the best approach but you must also overcome the strong and widely held American belief that any expansion of government even for a good cause is inherently dangerous. Those who wish the government to do nothing have a much easier argument to make. Consequently, you should minimize the appearance of expansion of government as much as possible. Create few or no new boards, agencies, or organizations. You want to present your change as a logical and limited expansion of government, not something new but rather just an improvement on an existing government activity and preferably one that is popular. As we shall see, proponents of Medicare sold it not as something new but rather as just an extension of Social Security that was highly popular at the time

By 1952, Truman's drive for universal health insurance was over. He was in his last year in office and the Democratic nominee for president, Adlai Stevenson, was focusing on other issues recognizing that the efforts of the AMA, Republicans and others to label the Democratic health insurance proposals socialism had largely worked. Anyway, American's were losing interest. Many already had health insurance through their employer and more enrolling each year—5 million in 1949, 11 million in 1950, and 9 million in 1951. Middle class workers in particular were benefiting from the post-war economy and job growth, most of which came with employer-sponsored health insurance.

> **LESSON: Keep it simple**. Early I noted that Americans fear complexity. That is why it is extremely important to keep your proposal simple or at least give it the appearance of being simple. The more comprehensive the plan the more difficult it is to get anything passed simply because as you add features, you add to the number of groups and individuals who will feel they have something to lose if your policy change is implemented. Consequently, the more comprehensive your reform, the more enemies you create. Every president who sought comprehensive health reform until the Obama administration failed. Truman failed. Clinton failed. Obama almost failed and Republicans at this writing are threatening to undo most if not all that he accomplished. Your challenge is to construct legislation that is complex enough to address the problem while keeping it simple enough not to frighten your fellow citizens.

THE EISENHOWER ADMINISTRATION

With the election of Dwight David Eisenhower in 1952, the prospects of universal coverage or any expansion of the government's role in health insurance turned dark. Eisenhower had no interest. Indeed Eisenhower campaigned against "socialized medicine." In 1958, he made clear his long time opposition to government health insurance and social security-related programs in general when he said, "If all that Americans want is security, they can go to prison. They'll have enough to eat, a bed, and a roof over their heads." Ironically, as a Army officer for most of his life Eisenhower had been provided free medical care by physicians and dentists working for the government on salary—i.e., socialized medicine. He never liked it when people reminded him of that fact.[157]

It was not only the President. There was little interest in Congress. Members of the Ways and Means Committee in the House and Finance Committee in the Senate were either actively opposed to universal health insurance or showed no interest. There was no real activity toward health care reform until 1958 even though Democrats gained control of Congress in 1954.

THE NEW STRATEGY TO PASS HEALTH INSURANCE LEGISLATION

Various congressmen introduced legislation annually. Proponents of compulsory health insurance switched tactics. Their new strategy had three primary components:

Focus on just covering the elderly, not the entire population. High-risk people always have a problem getting health insurance. It is not just that health insurers consider them to be a bad risk, their fellow citizens actually abandon those at high-risk by refusing to insure with insurers who enroll high-risk people and thus have to charge higher premiums. The problem in the 1950s, as Rashi Fein points out in his book *Medical Cae, Medical Costs,* just continued to worsen as more people enrolled in insurance programs. Those Americans who were a high risk found it even more difficult to find an insurer who would take them. Proponents of mandatory universal health insurance shifted their focus from universal coverage to how to deal with segments of the population—the poor, the unemployed, the retired, those working at low-wage jobs, and those considered high risk—that could not obtain health insurance on their own. The aged became a primary focus for logical reasons. Since World War II, labor unions had made significant gains for their members in the provision of access to health care insurance. However, the elder and retired were left out. If you worked from an employer who offered health insurance, you usually lost that insurance when you retired. Only 22 percent of union contracts provided health insurance for retirees and then only for those who had been with the company for 20 years or more. Additionally, most contracts excluded the worker's spouse from coverage. If by chance you were able to keep your insurance, it was usually not affordable. The average retiree, if he could get coverage, had to spend 15 percent or more of his income on health insurance. Blue Cross and Blue Shield had grown dramatically in the 1940s and 1950s but it was becoming increasingly difficult for workers who had chosen Blue Cross and Blue Shield to keep their coverage after they retired. Premiums for retirees had increased to a point that people living on pensions or Social Security could no longer afford them. Additionally, if you had coverage but missed even a single payment you insurance companies could drop you and you would have little chance of being able to get coverage elsewhere. Consequently, almost no one over the age of 73 in the late 1950s had access to health insurance.[158] In addition, there were still other reasons to focus on the elderly.

- They faced high premiums if they could get insurance at all.
- They did not have an employer to contribute to financing their coverage.
- They had limited resources
- Their medical needs were great.
- They were heavy users of medical care.
- Unlike other groups they could be identified with ease—anyone over 65.
- Unlike a qualification for benefits such as income that might change from year to year, the aged did not suddenly get younger and thus disqualified from coverage.
- A massive social insurance program—Social Security—was already in place to serve the elderly.
- The private insurance market had had its opportunity to cover the elderly and had failed. The only remaining option was a single-payer system of public health insurance guided by the federal government.

- Proponents could sell the health insurance program as just an extension of something that already existed rather than something entirely new.
- There would be no income test so the legislation would not compromise the principle of universal coverage. Indeed the inclusion of everyone regardless of income would set a precedent for universal coverage.
- By agreeing to covering just the aged (who were just 9% of the population), proponents of universal health insurance could portray themselves as reasonable people who were willing to compromise and portray their opponents inflexible and negative.
- In the heterogeneous nation with competing groups—black/white, rich/poor, urban/rural—most people supported the aged if for no other reason than that everyone would someday be in that group. Whites would not become suddenly black. The rich could hardly imagine suddenly becoming poor. People were moving from rural to urban areas not from urban to rural. However, everyone who lived long enough would eventually become old.
- Covering the aged undercut a central argument of opponents to universal health insurance such as the AMA that had argued for nearly a decade that private insurance was continuing to expand and thus a government program was unnecessary. By the late 1950s it was clear that private insurance would never adequately cover the aged.[159]
- Medicare would be just the beginning. The ultimate goal was universal health coverage for the entire population. The expected next step was Kiddicare—federal insurance for America's children.

Build on Social Security. People paid into social security during their working years and then received benefits when they retired. This provided the illusion that Social Security was an insurance program to which people were entitled because of their years of contribution, not a social welfare program. Medicare would be limited to those over 65 and dependents who had contributed to Social Security during working lives. Recipients would have rights to payments because they had contributed to the fund like paying insurance premiums. Medicare would not be a welfare program.

Restrict the scope of benefits. Truman had proposed covering hospital, medical, dental and nursing home costs. Medicare would cover only hospitalization and then only for 60 days per year. In other words, Medicare would be catastrophic insurance. By not covering normal medical expenses, the designers hoped to minimize opposition from Conservatives who were concerned with cost. Doctors and others in the medical profession were concerned about losing income. By focusing on hospitalization advocates sought to change the statement of the problem from one of unequal distribution of medical care services (thus one about the distribution or redistribution of a limited resource) to one of addressing the financial consequences to the aged of using hospital services. Hospital costs were increasing dramatically and the aged were much more likely to be hospitalized and when they were, their hospital stay was twice as long as that for younger patients.

Thodore Marmor, author of *The Politics of* Medicare writes:

> The concentration on the burdens of the aged was a ploy for sympathy. The disavowal of aims to change fundamentally the American medical system was a sop to AMA fears, and the exclusion of physician services benefits was a response to past AMA hysteria. The focus on the financial burdens of receiving hospital care took as given the existing structure of the private medical care world, and stressed the issue of spreading the costs of using available services within that world. The organization of health care, with its inefficiencies and resistance to cost-reduction, was a fundamental but politically sensitive problem which consensus-minded reformers wanted to avoid when they opted for 60 days of hospitalization insurance for the aged…as a promising "small" beginning.[160]

LESSON: Appeal to Americans' self-interest. You must convince the majority of Americans, and preferably a super majority, that the problem or issue your proposed policy change addresses affects them personally. Do not expect Americans to support substantive policy change for altruistic reasons. Americans are selfish when it comes to what their government does. They may contribute to private charities and support government intervention when they see vivid, emotional images of suffering, but their support for such efforts quickly fades. You must construct an emotional argument that the problem affects most Americans lives or potentially could. You must convince the majority of Americans that the problems threatens them and their family' and that they will personally benefit from the policy change you propose even if that is only partially true. Americans only support public policy that will benefit them directly and concretely or at least will not cost them anything. You must make that case for your proposal even if it is largely a false one. That is what proponents of Medicare did. The majority of Americans were not elderly but most had relatives who were and everyone if they lived long enough would become elderly. It was not hard to convince Americans, even young Americans, that they could personally benefit from the government caring for their aging parents or grandparents so they would not have to do so. In addition, it was confronting to know that when one became old, one would have the power of government protecting one from the financial harm that an extended serious illness might cause.

LESSON: Be careful about redistribution issues. Americans accumulate. It is part of the American character to seek out, assemble and hoard possessions either real or imagined. Likewise, Americans live in constant fear of loss of their possessions. Americans are ever watchful that something or someone might come along and take things, physical or emotional, real or imagined, from them. Americans are particularly concerned that the taker might be the government. Conservatives will prey upon American's redistribution fears. They will argue that what you are proposing is an evil

> endeavor to take from the deserving, and give to strangers who are largely undeserving because otherwise they would not be in need of government assistance. You must provide reassurance that no American will lose because of the change you propose. You must project all boats to rise. You must guarantee that all futures will be positive. The final tally must place all above average. There must only be gains. Loses are not allowed.

By the late 1950s, the search was on for a bill that would pass rather than the "best" bill. Medicare proponents were willing to exclude coverage of outpatient care (doctors' bills) even if that meant that under hospital-only Medicare coverage doctors would be encouraged to recommend more and longer hospital treatments, which were considerably more expensive than outpatient care, as a way of both increasing their fees and reducing the patient's cost. This was typical "vote buying," going for the possible rather than the ideal even when the possible would clearly costs the tax payers considerably more in the long run.[161]

Jonathan Oberlander, author of *The Political Life of Medicare,* adds "in sum, the narrowing of the Truman national health insurance proposal into Medicare reflected an incremental strategy of 'consensus mongering.' The aim was to identify less controversial problems and more politically feasible solutions than had previous health insurance proposals. However, despite their carefully crafted strategy, there would be no easy consensus on Medicare."[162]

> **LESSON: Remember politics is the art of the possible.** You have to take what you can get. Progressives do not want to make things just a little bit better. They want to right wrongs. Unfortunately, it is hard to get a lot done in one piece of legislation. The framers did not construct our government that way.

THE FORAND BILL

In August 1957, Congressman Aime Forand of Rhode Island introduced the first legislation to provide health insurance coverage for the aged.

Forand was an unlikely candidate to sponsor what was to lead to the greatest piece of social legislation since the passage of Social Security. He was "a slightly bald, round, cigar-smoking man of medium size and somewhat lackluster manner,"[163] who was nearing retirement, not that committed to health insurance legislation, and thought that there was little chance of passing such legislation for at least ten years. However, Forand had long been interested in helping the "old folks," as he called them and he was on the right committee—Ways and Means. He agreed to sponsor the bill. "He did not spend too much time thinking about the bill. A few days before the close of the 85th session, he quietly dropped the bill into the hopper. It was a shock to all supporters. "They didn't think I was going to do it," Forand later said.[164]

There was little support on the Ways and Means Committee for the Forand Bill. Of the 15 Democrats and 10 Republicans on the committee, only four members, all Democrats, supported the bill. One of the Democrats most opposed to the bill was the chairman, Wilbur Mills who refused to allow the Forand bill to be scheduled even for hearings. Mills had two criteria for what he would allow out of the Ways and Means Committee. First, he was a jealous guardian of Social Security, opposed to anything that might affect its financial soundness or result in the need to increase taxes to keep it viable. Second, Mills refused to allow anything to come to the floor from his committee until he was certain it had majority support in Congress and the nation. The Forand Bill met neither of these criteria. Until it did, Mills would not support it and without Mills' support, it would never get out of committee.

WILBUR D. MILLS—THE ARCHITECT OF MEDICARE AND MEDICAID

Wibur Daigh Mills was born in Kensett, White County Arkansas on May 24, 1909. He graduated as valedictorian of his high school, salutatorian of Hendrix College and studied constitutional law under later Supreme Court Justice Felix Frankfurter at Harvard law school from which he graduated. He was admitted to the bar in 1933 and served as a county and probate judge in Arkansas from 1934 until 1939 when he was elected to Congress. In 1957, Mills became chairman of the powerful House Ways and Means Committee.

People liked Mills. He could speak in the voice of a knowledgeable, Harvard-trained lawyer or in the Southern cracker cadence of an Arkansas man of the people, switching back and forth with ease as the occasion demanded. He believed that "life was based on mutual respect and understanding[and that]...people took care of their own problems and families, including their elderly members."[165] Mills held to traditional values or at least appeared to do so until U.S. Park police stopped him one early morning in the Fall of 1974 driving drunk and accompanied by an Argentine stripper by the name of Fannie Fox. Later that year, reporters sighted Mills performing a drunken dance on stage with Ms. Fox at a burlesque theatre where she was performing. The ensuing scandals led to Mills making the prudent decision not to seek reelection in 1976. However, that was 1976. In 1960, Mills was one of the most power people in Congress.

In 1957, members of Congress respected Mills for his thoroughness and lawyerly attention to detail. As Chairman of the House Ways and Means Committee, he had special responsibility for oversight of Social Security and he had immersed himself in that responsibility. Those who knew him said he had a "complete understanding of the system," and "was the *only* one out of 535 Congressmen who was able to master the actuarial basis of Social Security as well as its financial underpinnings. He was 'completely conversant' with all the factors involved in making actuarial estimates of Social Security payments." [166]

Mills' power stemmed not just from his personal qualities but also from his position. He was the Chairman of the House Ways and Means Committee. All tax, tariff, Social Security, and welfare legislation had to pass this committee on its way to becoming law. This committee made individual committee assignments in the House and the committee Chairman had a big say so in those decisions. House rules and traditions allowed this committee to meet in closed executive sessions to discuss tax and Social Security changes and then bring such legislation to the floor of the House under a "closed rule," meaning that House members could not offer amendments but rather had to vote up or down on the measure as presented by the committee. As Rashi Fein writes:

> Mills's power stemmed from his expertise in tax matters, his control of the professional staff, his political acumen in welding coalitions and doing favors, and his seniority status under the rules of the House then in force. He could call meetings or postpone them, determine the agenda, and orchestrate the debate. In addition, he served as a bridge between the two wings of the Democratic party; the more numerous and liberal Northerners and the more senior, powerful, and conservative Southerners. Finally, there was the fact that a bill that was popular among constituents back home but unpopular among individual Congressmen could be killed in executive session in committee rather than on the floor of the House, where everyone would have to stand up and be counted. Members appreciated Mills's willingness to spare them from the need to cast a public vote.[167]

> **LESSON: Inevitably, the support of a few powerful figures in Congress is critical to success.** You must cater to their needs whatever they are. Each of these figures have their own personal criteria for what they will and will not support and until the proponents of change can craft their legislation to at least appear to meet the requirements of these powerful men and women, no change is possible. No legislation can be passed.

BUILDING A RECORD

Forand was able to get his bill discussed briefly during hearings on extending Social Security benefits in June of 1958. Later that year, six members of the House during a debate on a social security amendment took the opportunity to endorse the Forand bill even though it was not then under consideration. Senator Wayne Morse of Oregon further publicized the

Forand bill by offering it as an amendment to a social security bill under consideration in the Senate. Morse's amendment was defeated on a voice vote but its introduction prompted Senator John Kennedy to include an endorsement of the bill in a speech he gave before the senate the same year outlining what he called a ten-point "bill of rights for our elder citizens." In December of that year, the Democratic Advisory Council, a group of party leaders outside Congress, added its endorsement to the Forand proposal.

> **LESSON: You must build a record.** The discussions on the Forand bill like the discussions surrounding the earlier Wagner-Murray-Dingell proposals were important not because they resulted in any movement on the bill but because they began the process of "building the record," which is a critical step in getting anything done in Washington. You must take testimony from experts and the people. You must accumulate data. You must assemble statistics documenting the nature and extent of the problem. People must get comfortable with the topic and with the people and organizations representing each side of the issue. You must document, define, and plant in the minds of those who can affect change that an issue exists and a remedy is required even if they are unclear about the nature of that remedy. Building a record is a ritual all major legislation must pass through. That is the reason you want to get legislation introduced as early as possible even if you know you have little chance of success. If nothing else, each failure to get legislation through committee or brought to the floor helps to build the record.

THE AMA CAMPAIGN TO KILL MEDICARE

At that point, the AMA made a tactical error. Instead of ignoring a bill that initially had little chance of passing, they countered with a major campaign attacking it. The Forand proposal, said the AMA president, was "at least nine points evil and one part sincerity."[168] If passed, said the AMA, the legislation would undermine voluntary efforts by private organizations including efforts of the medical profession, private voluntary insurance, and public assistance (relief or welfare) to help the aged. If Medicare passed, it would endanger such efforts since a government program would "curb community incentive to support hospitals, nursing homes, health campaigns and health centers. It would discourage communities from experimenting with new techniques, such as home care programs, homemaker services, progressive patient care, and new concepts for treatment through outpatient departments and doctors' offices and the like. It would usurp—albeit inadequately—the magnificent role played by our fraternal, civic, religious, and philanthropic groups in the care of the aged."[169]

Medicare was "socialized medicine and, above all, a dangerous first step toward national health insurance."[170] Dr. Frank Krusen, an AMA spokesperson, denounced everything about the bill in testimony before Congress.

> The government would control the disbursement of funds; the government would determine the benefits to be provided; the government would set the rates of compensation of hospitals, nursing homes, and physicians; the government would audit and control the records of hospitals, nursing homes, and patients; and the government would promulgate and enforce the standards of hospital and medical care. The professional relationship between the doctor and his patient would be hampered. Government regulations would be imposed on patient and physician alike. The bill would lead to 'dangerous overcrowding' of hospitals with 'personal and family financial responsibility eliminated.[171]

Anyway, argued the AMA, government insurance for the elderly was unnecessary since private insurance would cover 90% of the elderly by 1970. [This figure was, of course, from a biased industry-sponsored study.] Regardless of coverage, argued the AMA, the problem was not as severe as advocates of Medicare claimed. The elderly were not going without care. "Medical care is readily available to every citizen of this country, regardless of his age, and regardless of whether he is able to pay for it."[172] If the aged were not using these services it was just because they didn't know they existed.

The AMA hired the master of the bogus argument, Ronald Reagan, to spread its message of fear outlining the "horrors" of the proposed Medicare and its threat to the freedoms that Americans treasured. Reagan warned Americans of the evil Medicare would bring to the country.

> Write those letters now; call your friends and tell them to write them. If you don't, this program, I promise you, will pass just as surely as the sun will come up tomorrow. And behind it will come other federal programs that will invade every area of freedom as we have known it in this country. Until one day. we will awake to find that we have socialism. And If you don't do this, one of these days you and I are going to spend our sunset years telling our children and our children's children what it once was like in America when men were free.[173]

Oh, Medicare was an insidious and dastardly plot, a genuine anti-American conspiracy. James Stuart, an associate of Blue Cross, declared that the Forand Bill was a "frightening nightmare" that would result in families across the country rushing their "aged relatives into nursing homes at the government's expense."[174]

THE AMA ATTACK BACKFIRES

In 1959, the Senate Labor Committee created a Sub-committee on Aging with the encouragement of William Reidy, a staff member of the Labor Committee. Reidy had been on the staff of Dr. Michael Davis, a New York physician, sociologist and expert in medical economics, who had worked on several of the Wagner-Murray-Dingell bills and long supported national health insurance. Reidy thought the Eisenhower administration had made a mistake by ignoring the problems of the aged and Democratic candidates in the upcoming election "needed issues to go against Eisenhower's popularity."[175] He knew that the young Senator John Kennedy had presidential aspirations. Serving as head of a sub-committee on aging would give Kennedy badly needed exposure. Other staff members on the

Labor Committee supported Reidy's idea as did the Chairman Lister Hill, a moderate Democrat from Alabama who was interested in healthcare.

Kennedy was aware of the Forand Bill and had even requested a copy of the bill to review. However, he was tied up with managing a labor reform bill and with work on the McClellan Committee investigating labor racketeering. Reidy approached Kennedy's assistant Theodore Sorensen about the Aging Sub-Committee idea. Sorensen showed no interest. Not giving up, Reidy approached another member of Kennedy's staff, Myer Feldman, who was much more positive and agreed to discuss the idea with Kennedy.

While Reidy was waiting to hear from Kennedy, another member of the Labor Committee, Senator Pat McNamara from Michigan heard about the sub-committee and expressed interest. McNamara was a liberal Democrat who had supported a variety of labor and civil rights issues such as the minimum wage and voting rights for blacks. He was in a tight race for re-election and saw the chairmanship of a sub-committee on aging as way of giving him a good political issue to run on in the 1960 election campaign.

With McNamara expressing interest and Kennedy at least considering the matter, Hill decided to move ahead. Typically, someone wanting to create a new sub-committee would present the idea to the parent committee during a regular session. However, there were no sessions scheduled for the committee in the near future, so Hill decided to move on his own. He requested both the McNamara and Kennedy staffs to draft a resolution creating a Sub-committee on Aging. The McNamara resolution reached Hill's office first. Hill established the sub-committee and appointed McNamara chairman. Joining McNamara were Democrats Kennedy, Joseph Clark of Pennsylvania and Jennings Randolph of West Virginia. The Republican members were Everett Dirksen of Illinois and Barry Goldwater of Arizona.

The movement to pass health insurance legislation had taken one additional step forward. As is typical, progress came when proponents were able to link their legislation to the political ambitions of politicians. Kennedy and McNamara would both benefit politically from the publicity surrounding hearings on health insurance for the aged that the Subcommittee on Aging would hold.

> **LESSSON: Link you legislative proposal to the political ambition of key politicians.** Senators and Congressmen may proclaim that they work for their constituents and "the good of the country," but they actually work for themselves. Show them how they can get personal political mileage out of supporting your proposal and you will get their support. Do not expect them to get behind your cause just because your cause is right and does a lot of good for the country. They could care less. They want to know, "what's in it for me?" You need a good answer to that question. In the case of Kennedy and McNamara, they knew that getting to go around the country holding a lot of hearings on the plight of old people would be good for their political careers. They had a lot to gain and little to lose.

HEARINGS BY THE SUBCOMMITTEE ON AGING IN 1959

During 1959, the Subcommittee on Aging held hearings in Washington, D.C., Boston, Pittsburgh, San Francisco, Charleston, Grand Rapids, Miami and Detroit. The hearings were informal. The Subcommittee invited representatives of the elderly and the elderly themselves to express their opinions and tell their personal stories. Local Congressmen joined in the discussions. The Sub-Committee began incorporating discussion of the Forand bill in these meetings as it took testimony from the elderly and expert witnesses on the problems of older Americans. Wherever the subcommittee held hearings, its staff sought to stimulate interest among local journalists in covering the hearings and reporting on the debate about the Forand bill.

The hearings garnered a great deal of publicity and rejuvenated grass roots interest in the health problems of the aged. Additionally, the hearings boosted morale among proponents of health legislation who came away with heart-rending stories the elderly told about their inability to afford the cost of health care. McNamara said on delivering his final report to the Labor Committee that he came away from the hearing convinced that "there is simply no human justification…for any American to have to suffer unnecessarily a prolonged illness or put off a medical check-up because of his fear of hospital bills and the exorbitant prices of medicines."[176]

As might be expected, the Republicans on the Committee were not impressed with what they heard. The aged, said Dirksen and Goldwater in their minority report, did not have problems much different from other Americans. There was nothing unique about Americans suffering physically and financially from lack of health insurance.

It was a weird and heartless argument. Since suffering was widespread and the proposal was to provide relief to just a segment of the population, the proposal should be abandoned as should the segment of the population whose suffering might be alleviated by action. Of course the reason proponents of the legislation had narrowed its coverage in the first place was repeated Republican opposition to universal coverage.

Throughout 1959 and 1960, supporters of the Forand bill continued to assemble the data, statistics and facts needed to provide a justification for action. However, they recognized that facts alone would not be enough. They had to convince the American people that the elderly were suffering and that legislation was required to alleviate their suffering. They needed an emotional appeal. To that end, the labor movement began organizing rallies and demonstrations in support of the Forand bill. For example, the United Auto Workers (UAW) organized a rally in Detroit where 13,000 attendees heard speeches from the three Democratic candidates for the presidency, John Kennedy, Hubert Humphrey, and Stuart Symington on the problems of the aged including access to health insurance.

THE GRASSROOTS MOVEMENT

The Forand bill had an inauspicious beginning and yet in just three years it became a major issue in a national presidential election. As James Sundquist notes, all this happened without benefit of any of the circumstances that usually thrust a legislative measure into the national spotlight.

> No presidential message or television appeal supported it; no crisis compelled attention to it; it had no status as a party measure in Congress; its sponsor was a little-known congressman who could not bring national attention to it and, indeed, did not try; its

> existence was not reported on the front pages of the newspapers until after it had become a major national political issue. Yet many thousands of people managed to learn of the bill's existence and join[ed] the 'crusade' for its enactment. Support for the Forand bill began as a genuine grass roots movement—surely the most phenomenal such movement of the period."[177]

Ironically, one of the major groups contributing to the growth of the grassroots movement to support the Forand bill and Medicare was the bill's chief opponent, the AMA. Their aggressive, even vicious attack on the Forand bill and its supporters backfired. Indeed, Forand thanked the members of the AMA for their efforts. In a 1960 speech, he said "I want to pay tribute to the AMA for the great assistance they have given me in publicizing this bill of mine...They have done more than I ever could have done [to generate widespread interest in the bill.].[178]

> **Lesson: Turn opposition to your advantage whenever you can.** The AMA made a tactical mistake in launching such a loud and expensive campaign opposing the Forand bill. Proponents of health reform took advantage of the vicious attacks to rally their supports and gain new recruits to the cause. The saying "there is no such thing as bad publicity" fully applies when it comes to getting things done in Washington. Do not be discouraged when opponents attack your proposal. Find a way to turn those attacks to your advantage by using them to stimulate grassroots interest and support.

MOVING THE FORAND BILL THROUGH THE SENATE

Supporters of the Forand Bill had built a record and generated grassroots interest. Now they had to decide upon the best path to follow in bringing the Forand Bill to the floors of the House and Senate for a vote. There was a difference of opinion about how to proceed in the Senate. The two most logical committees to handle a health insurance bill would be the Senate Labor Committee or the Finance Committee. Bill Reidy and others on the Labor Committee staff argued that the Labor Committee had dealt with previous Medicare bills such as the Wagner-Murray-Dingel bills so it had more experience with health insurance legislation. Additional a majority of the members of the Labor Committee already supported Medicare. On the other hand, Wilbur Cohen, who helped write the Social Security Act and was to play a major role in the passage of Medicare, and other Medicare advocates argued that the Finance Committee had much more power and influence in the Senate whose members were mostly conservative. Additionally, since the bill involved Social Security funding, the Finance Committee had to review and approve it at some point. Of course, there was the option of having both committees consider separate bills. However, having two bills under consideration in two different committees would have significantly slowed the process which was exactly what happened in 2008 when two separate Senate committees worked on separate bills for the Obama administrated health reforms. In 1960, supporters of taking the bill through the Finance Committee alone won the argument.

The question then became who would sponsor the Medicare bill in the Finance Committee. There were five possible ranking committee members considered as sponsors on the committee: Chairman Harry Byrd of Virginia, Russell Long of Louisiana, George Smathers of Florida, Robert Kerr of Oklahoma, Paul Douglas of Illinois and Clinton Anderson of New Mexico. Supporters of the bill immediately rejected Byrd, Long, Smathers and Kerr. Byrd and Kerr opposed all forms of national health insurance. Long had made it clear that he disliked the Forand Bill. Smathers was indebted to doctors in his state for supporting him in his win over former Senator Claude Peppers so was not likely to agree to sponsor legislation they vehemently opposed. Douglas would have sponsored the bill but he was a liberal intellectual and well-known supporter of labor causes. His sponsorship, indeed even his active involvement in the Medicare cause, would do more harm than good when it came to winning over a majority of the committee. Consequently, Clinton Anderson got the job by default.[179] It was not a bad choice. Anderson was a close friend of Lyndon Johnson and Robert Kerr; he was popular in the Senate and, perhaps most importantly, no one had accused him of having socialist sympathies and connections although they later would.

Anderson had a daunting task. As hearings began in 1960, he could count only four or five possible favorable votes from the seventeen-committee members. Additionally, a number of bills dealing with health insurance for the aged were now before the committee. Senators Morse, Kennedy and Hart proposed bills that incorporated a payroll tax deduction as the means of financing health insurance for the aged. Senator McNamara, joined by 23 other Democrats, proposed to expand Medicare to cover all those over 65, not just the elderly on Social Security, and to expand benefits.[180] The New Republic declared these competing bills to be "a disorderly collection of jerry –built substitutes and compromises."[181] The Forand bill like all the others seeking a comprehensive approach died in committee.

Never the less, it was clear that, responding to growing public interest in health insurance for aged, Congress had decided that some form of health insurance must at least be considered, if not passed. As *The Nation* put it, "Not in years had Congress be subjected to so much pressure… for and against health insurance for the aged."[182] *The New York Times* added that the "question of medical insurance for persons 65 years of age [had] become one of the hottest political issues in the nation."[183] The Republicans, in particular, were beginning to feel the political heat.

REPUBLICANS DEVELOP THEIR OWN ALTERNATIVE

The sub-committee hearings, union rallies and the AMA's misguided attacks on the Forand bill throughout 1959 and 1960 had gained media attention and the press began asking the Eisenhower Administration and Republicans why they had not developed any alternative legislation. The Administration simply responded that it needed more time to study the problem. Delay is a standard tactic of those who oppose change. If they can stall and delay, request time for studies, and generally argue for slowing the process down, they can increase the chance that those proposing change will become frustrated and exhausted and give up the struggle or that they will gradually lose support as their cause seems increasingly hopeless to their supporters.

That was not happening. Public interest in health care for the elderly was building, not diminishing and advocates of change were anything but frustrated. "Republicans became increasingly grumpy about this demand for health insurance for the aged. Dirksen, in particular, became belligerent during new hearings shouting at witnesses and calling the proposals of Forand supporters "insane" and "stinking."[184]

> **LESSON: Whenever the opposition proposes to study the problem, respond by pushing harder to get something done right away.** An offer to study the problem is a standard delaying tactic opponents will resort to when they discover that public pressure is building to get something done. It is a sign that your efforts to educate the public and garner support from politicians are paying off. It is a signal that you should redouble your efforts to move legislation forward. Do not back off or agree to slow down. Push harder.

The AMA attacks and Aging sub-committee meetings raised public awareness to the point that Vice President Richard Nixon became concerned that opposition from the Eisenhower administration might doom his chances in the 1960 presidential campaign. Attacking socialized medicine was one thing but opposing legislation designed to help the elderly, a growing voter block was another thing. Nixon wanted some kind of Republican plan to put up against the Democratic proposals. However, Eisenhower showed little interest. Eisenhower maintained that action was unnecessary. The problem of health insurance for the aged could be perfectly well handled by individuals themselves or voluntary groups. Passing something like the Forand Bill would, testified Arthur Flemming, Secretary of HEW, just mean that insurance "would become frozen in a vast and unfair government system, foreclosing future opportunity for private groups, non-profit and commercial, to demonstrate their capacity to deal with the problem." [185] Senate Russell Long of Louisiana prophesied that if a national health bill like Forand passed and Congress gave the elderly hospitalization at government expense "many of them would spend their summer vacations in the hospitals" and "the medical resources of the country would become social clubs for the elderly."[186]

THE REPUBLICANS PRESENT A PLAN

Secretary of HEW Arthur Flemming came up with five possible Republican plans but Eisenhower still refused to endorse any option supposedly because he equated any use of tax-derived funds to support health insurance for the aged as socialized medicine. Publicly Nixon announced that he was "searching for an acceptable solution to the [Medicare] problem" and was leaning toward one of Flemming's options that involved having Federal and state governments subsidize the purchase of health insurance by those of the elderly who wished to do so.[187]

Finally, in June of 1960, after much urging by Nixon and other members of his party, President Eisenhower agreed to have one of Flemming's options introduced in the Senate by Senator Levertt Saltonstall (R, MASS). Essentially the plan offered only a modest expansion of existing public assistance programs. Columnist Edward Chase wrote: "It is hard to escape the conclusion that the [Republican] plan is strictly a political gesture, reluctantly taken to ease the politically untenable situation into which sheer negativism had placed the party."[188]

TWO SHARPLY CONTRASTING APPROACHES

By 1960, Congress was considering two sharply contrasting approaches to dealing with the problem of insuring the elderly. First, there was the Social Security-based approach found in the Forand bill and other variations. These bills sought to provide at least some coverage of hospitalization, nursing home care, and cost of surgery financed by an increase in Social Security taxes. The second approach championed by the Eisenhower administration relied upon federal financial assistance to encourage the states to create or expand health insurance coverage for the aged poor. This approach went beyond the Social Security approaches since it covered not only hospitalization, surgery, and nursing home care but also physicians' services. However, the assistance would be limited "to the small minority of old and poor who were very sick for an extended period, lived in states that joined the program, and could meet the burdensome, if not prohibitive, out-of-pocket payments."[189] There was very little possibility of reaching accommodation between supporters of the two approaches. People on both sides were pretty much locked into their positions. Consequently, each side sought to gain support for its approach by courting Senators and Representatives who were still undecided and the largest block of undecided was among Southern Democrats.

THE SOUTHERN DEMOCRATS

Southern Democrats felt the growing public pressure to do something about insuring the elderly but they did not like either the Forand or Eisenhower approach. They were uniformly opposed to any type of federal health insurance but they also knew that their states could not afford the state matching required under the approach championed by the administration. Even if the states could find the funding, few elderly poor in the Southern states would be able to pay the premiums and out-of-pocket costs. They respected Eisenhower and agreed with most of his conservative principals but this was an election year. Supported by House Speaker Sam Rayburn, Senate Majority Leader, Lyndon Johnson of Texas was seeking the presidential nomination and most Southern Democrats wanted to support Johnson and distance themselves from the Republicans. Southern Democrats were in a bind. They did not like the Social Security approach but they could not support the Eisenhower approach either. They wanted a way out. All eyes were on one man who might find a solution—Democratic Representative Wilbur Mills from Arkansas. Southern Democrats were looking to Mills to solution to their problem. He delivered.

THE KERR/MILLS BILL—THE THIRD APPROACH

Mills decided to offer an alternative approach. Together with Senator Robert Kerr of Oklahoma, he introduced a bill to address the problem of health insurance for the aged by providing matching grants to states to expand aid to states providing health care assistance to the elderly poor. The bill would cover 50% to 80% of the cost to provide benefits that actually went beyond those in the Forand bill and other Medicare proposals. Essentially, the Kerr-Mills bill just expanded upon a program that Congress enacted in 1950 to provide federal funds for states to pay for medical care for the aged poor who were welfare recipients by removing the requirement that a person be on welfare to qualify. Participation by states was voluntary and neither Democrats nor Republicans argued that the bill would solve the problem of health insurance for the aged. However, the Kerr-Mills bill was attractive to many Conservatives in the House and Senate because while the bill actually did little or nothing to address the issue it gave Conservatives political cover.

> **LESSON: Conservatives will always argue that the states can do it best.** When pressured by an aroused public to do something about an issue, Conservatives, who are philosophically opposed to ever doing anything, take political cover by arguing that if something must done about a problem the best approach is for the federal government to simply provide funding and let the states actually administer the program. The problem with this approach is that states often fail to enact programs even when substantial funding is provided because the will not or cannot provide the matching funding. However, this approach provides the appearance of actually doing something without doing anything much at all. The best way to counter this argument is to have already tried a state-based approach that you can point to as a example of why state-based remedies won't work.

Mills rapidly pushed the Kerr-Mills bill through the House Ways and Means Committee without debate or even discussion. On June 3, 1960, the Committee passed the bill under closed rule. *The New York Times* described Mills' handling of the bill a "hand washing performance." "Mills had indeed washed his hands, dried them, and walked away from the sink. To his satisfaction he discharged his obligations to the Democratic Party."[190] That was that. The bill went to the Senate.

Robert Kerr of Oklahoma took over the job of pushing the bill through the Senate. Kerr had personal reasons for wanting to get a bill passed as quickly as possible. It had nothing to do with Social Security or Medicare. Kerr was up for reelection. He was certain John Kennedy, the Democratic nominee for president, was going to lose Oklahoma if for no other reason than that, Kennedy was a Catholic and mostly Baptist Oklahomans were never going to vote for a Catholic for president or much of anything else. Kennedy favored the Social Security approach to health insurance for the elderly and planned to make it a issue in his campaign. Kerr needed to separate himself from Kennedy. The Kerr-Mills bill was just the ticket. It was an approach to the elderly insurance problem that would appeal to Oklahomans, especially the powerful Oklahoma medical association.

Progressives were no match for Kerr when the Kerr-Mills bill came to the floor of the Senate. They had pointed and well thought out questions about the implications of the bill but Kerr was ready for them. As one observer said, "there was no match for Kerr, he was the master of 'resounding rebuttal'."[191] House Speaker Sam Rayburn said, "Bob Kerr is the kind of man who would charge hell with a bucket of water and believe he could put it out."[192] Senate Albert Gore of Tennessee said, "The distinguished Senator from Oklahoma can take the least amount of information and look and act more authoritative than any man in the world."[193] Carl Albert, also of Oklahoma who would later become Speaker of the House said Kerr "was like a great engine powered by super fuel."[194] If Progressives had meant to launch a challenge to the Kerr-Mills bill, they had seriously underestimated their opponent when it came to Kerr.

The Senate passed the Kerr-Mills bill. The Conference Committee quickly reached agreement. President Eisenhower signed it into law on September 13th.

At the time Aime Forand said that while the Kerr-Mills bill would "not do any harm, it would not do any good. Personally," he said, "I think it is a shame, I think it's a mirage that we are holding up to the folks to look at and think they are going to get something."[195] Forand was right. "By the time Eisenhower left office, only five states had passed legislation providing for at least some of the benefits under Kerr-Mills: Michigan, Oklahoma, Massachusetts, West Virginia, and Kentucky."[196] In many states, the program covered few new groups of people over 65 since frequently the states just transferred people already covered under older programs to Kerr-Mills in order to get the matching funds.

SALAMI SLICING

It was true that progressives were no match for Mills in the House or Kerr in the Senate. It was also true that they had offered only limited opposition. Wilbur Cohen convinced most of them that Eisenhower was never going to sign a Forand-type Social Security-based bill. Kerr-Mills, he argued, while woefully inadequate, was desirable as a step in the right direction. Cohen recognized that before Medicare legislation could be enacted, the public and Congress had to get used to the idea of public funding of medical care. Once passed Kerr-Mills would establish the precedent of financing medical care for the elderly with public dollars then it would be possible for advocates of Medicare to say "let's get a better way of carrying out the principles [already established by Kerr-Mills.] Some called Cohen's incremental approach to passing legislation "salami slicing"[197] Cohen would get one slice of the political salami then another and another. Eventually he would have enough for an entire policy sandwich. Cohen's true accomplishment was not just his expertise in getting individual slices of political salami but his ability to keep the final sandwich clearly in mind. He never lost sight of his final policy goal.

> **LESSON: You must engage in "salami slicing."** Salami slicing is an important tool for all who want to achieve policy revolutions. Policy revolutions are rarely built all at once but rather slowly, bit-by-bit and step-by-step. The real trick is not to lose sight of the ultimate goal. Each piece of political salami has to add to the ultimate policy sandwich. Cohen knew how to make that happen. Of course, the danger of salami slicing is that opponents of change will use it against those who want meaningful reform. They will argue that the current slice of salami is enough or that at a minimum more time they need more time to see if it is enough. They will suggest that you can add small portions over time if you determine policy sandwich needs more salami. Of course, what they are really saying is that there is no need to slice the entire salami or even build the sandwich.

THE KENNEDY ADMINISTRATION

In the 1960 campaign, Kennedy endorsed Medicare after seeing polls that suggested health care was a wedge issue he could use to gain an advantage over his opponent Richard Nixon. Upon election, President Kennedy launched a campaign to obtain passage of a new Medicare bill sponsored by Senator Clinton Anderson of New Mexico and Representative Cecil King of California. The Anderson/King bill was similar to the Forand bill in that it would provide 90 days of hospitalization, 240 days of home health services and 180 days of nursing home care to the elderly. In spite of holding rallies and making a national televised appeal for support, Kennedy was unsuccessful in moving the legislation forward, proving that even a popular president cannot push major legislation through Congress on his own.

Major opposition came from the Southern Democrat/Republican Conservative coalition. Wilbur Mills remained opposed. He was afraid that the addition of Medicare would threaten the solvency of the Social Security program. Additionally, and perhaps more importantly, due to redistricting, Mills was facing a highly conservative member of the House, Dale Alford, in what was going to a struggle for Mills to maintain his seat in the House. He was in no mood to support legislation that his Little Rock constituents would view as too liberal. Without the support of Mills and his committee, no Medicare legislation could make it to the House floor for a vote.

Kennedy was not prepared to risk all of his political capital on Medicare. He was seeking passage of several other bills on such things as foreign aid, taxes, housing and trade that had a good chance of passing provided the administration did not push to hard on the health insurance bill and alienate Mills as well as others. Regardless, it wasn't clear that Kennedy had the necessary 60 votes to end an almost certain Republican and Southern Democrat filibuster in the Senate even if he could force a House vote in favor. The Anderson/King bill was going nowhere. Medicare was not going to pass in 1961. The timing was not right for Medicare in 1961. However, it was getting right.

> **LESSON: Just because a presidential candidate or a sitting president, even a popular one, expresses support for a change effort do not assume that achieving that change will be easy.** It might be easier to have the president behind your cause but that does not make the passing legislation easy or guaranteed. Progressives often get over confident when they are finally able to elect a popular president who shares their agenda. They expect him to expend his considerable political capital on their behalf. They forget that presidents are not all powerful even if they are extremely popular and they are never pursuing a single agenda item. There are no single-issue presidents. Progressive legislation has to compete with all the other legislation, conservative, moderate, liberal, domestic and foreign that presidents have to juggle. By the early 1960s, at least four presidents or presidential candidates, including Kennedy who was very popular, supported some form of health insurance reform but only one was successful in passing legislation and then, as we will see, it was less than proponents of change had originally sought.

THE PR STRUGGLE

By the end of 1961, proponents and opponents were gearing up for a serious PR fight over Medicare. Proponents created the National Council of Senior Citizens with Aime Forand, who had just retired from Congress, as its chairman. By the end of 1961, the Council was claiming 525,000 members with additional support from 900,000 non-seniors. The council launched a series of massive rallies in major cities, began distributing materials (seven million pieces eventually) and developed alliances with senior citizen clubs and organizations with a collective membership of over two million.

The AMA countered by distributing posters for its members to display in their offices warning of "socialized medicine," and launched an aggressive letter writing campaign targeting congressmen, particularly those on the House Ways and Means Committee. The AMA also launched a campaign to persuade health professionals who had expressed support for senior health insurance through social security such as the American Nurses

Association and American Hospital Association to reverse their decisions and join the AMA in a "united front" of opposition. The nurses association complained of "unethical pressure" but held its ground.

By the summer of 1962, advocates for change seemed to be winning the propaganda war. Gallup reported that 67% of Americans now favored Medicare.[198] That was in spite of the fact that organized medicine had pumped as much as $7 million in just 18 months into the campaigning to defeat Medicare.

The AMA did however have one victory. In May of 1962, President Kennedy gave a major speech in New York City to a massive gather of seniors at Madison Square Garden that was shown to other rallies of seniors across the country via closed-circuit TV and carried on all major TV networks. The AMA demanded equal time from the networks but the networks refused. The organization responded by purchasing time the next night for an address by Dr. Edward Annis of the AMA delivered from the Garden with a symbolic empty arena as a backdrop. Dr. Annis urged viewers to "trust their doctors' judgment on the 'sacred' human relationships involved in the practice of medicine" and ignore the "hippodrome tactics" and "circuses" being orchestrated by the President and Medicare advocates. By most accounts, the proponents "long-planned publicity coup" backfired. Kennedy's address received a loud and enthusiastic reception in Madison Square Garden and around the country at the senior citizen rallies but played less well to the home TV audience. As Fein notes: "the president had forgotten the lesson of his campaign, that arousing a partisan crowd in a vast arena and convincing the skeptical TV viewer at home required wholly different kinds of presentation. He already had support from the senior citizens; he needed more support from the home viewers, and that speech did not induce it."[199] The AMA won the debate that time.

> **LESSON: It is not enough to convince those who are already on your side.** You have to make those who are not yet convinced comfortable with your ideas. It is great to have a charismatic leader who you can put forward to sell your cause. In addition, it feels great to see him enthusiastically

> received by partisan crowds roaring their support. However, do not lose sight of the fact that those adoring fans of your proposed legislation are not the ones you have to convince. The people you need to reach are the show-me skeptics that frown and a twitch as you lay out your ideas. Your task is not to rally the already convinced but to turn the frowns and nervous ticks of the skeptics into relaxed smiles. You have to make those folks comfortable with your ideas.

PROSPECT OF PASSING SOME FORM OF MEDICARE IMPROVE

Prospects for the passage of Medicare improved between 1961 and 1964. The administration focused on increasing the size of the pro-Medicare members of the House Ways and Means Committee by working with House Democratic leadership to extract pledges of support at least for moving a Medicare bill out of the committee from members wishing a Ways and Means committee assignment. By the summer of 1964, pro-Medicare members on the committee were just one vote short of a majority.

Anti-Medicare forces on the committee fought back with a clever legislative trick. Republican John Byrnes of Wisconsin proposed that the five percent increase in Social Security benefits called for in the Anderson bill be increased to six percent. Marmor notes that "this would have raised social security taxes to 10 percent,[200] widely accepted within Congress at that time as the upper social security tax limit, and thus leave no fiscal room for Medicare."[201] Byrnes proposal fell one vote short of approval when ultra-conservative Bruce Alger of Texas, voted no. Alger explained that "'since he opposed the entire Social Security system, consistency would not permit him to expand it even to undermine the chances of Medicare."[202]

THE JOHNSON ADMISTRATION

Senate Democrats attempted to get a Medicare bill passed in the fall of 1964 by attaching it to the Social Security bill for cash increases in benefits that had already passed the House. Mills undermined the effort by promising pro-Medicare Democrats that he would make Medicare the first order of business in the Ways and Means Committee in 1965 if they would reject the rider. Enough agreed with Mills that the rider was defeated and the Senate/House conference committee finally admitted that it was deadlocked. The Social Security measures would have to wait until the next session.

In the 1964 election, Johnson asked Americans to "pass judgment" on Medicare. He asked for a mandate and got it. Johnson got 61% of the popular vote and 90% of the electoral vote crushing his Republican challenger Barry Goldwater. Democrats retained majorities in House and Senate gaining 32 seats in the House and 2 in the Senate. The Democratic landslide brought a surge of new Democratic congressman to the House, all pro-Medicare. The National Council of Senior Citizens claimed a net gain of 44 votes for Medicare in the House.

The political climate changed dramatically. Democrats now controlled the White House and both houses of Congress by considerable majorities, enough to overcome the Southern Democrat/Republican Coalition. With their large majorities in both houses, Democrats could have expanded Medicare coverage. Instead, they stayed with the existing Medicare proposals that provided limited benefits to a limited segment of the population.

> **LESSON: Do not overreach** Once you gain public support for your reform, particularly if it is accompanied by control of both houses of Congress and the presidency, it is tempting to try to set your sights higher, to try to expand your legislative proposal to accomplish more. Do not do it. If you overreach, you give ammunition to your opponents. They will use it to scare the public. Public support for any legislative effort is a fragile thing. Do not abuse it. Take what you can get. You can come back for more at a later day.

Johnson immediately made Medicare his top legislative priority. Perhaps more importantly than the net gain of seats in the House as a whole, the lopsided Democratic majority insured the Democrats of getting two more, badly needed, pro-Medicare seats on the House Ways and Means Committee.

When opinion polls showed overwhelming public support for Medicare, Wilbur Mills, who had blocked previous efforts, switched sides. Republican John Byrnes on the Ways and Means Committee said of Mills late involvement in cobbling together a bill "I assume Wilbur saw the election returns and he could see he was being left behind. The troops were rushing right past him. He figured he'd better give his horse some oats and get up there in front where a leader belonged."[203]

In January of 1965, Anderson and King re-introduced their standard Medicare package covering limited hospital care Social Security beneficiaries and financed through Social Security. The bills were numbered H.R. 1 and S.1 to signify their significance as the highest priority for Johnson's Great Society programs.

ELDERCARE

Recognizing that some form of Medicare was now inevitable and fearing that they could be labeled as obstructionists, Republicans and the AMA changed tactics. They came out with their own "more positive" proposal arguing that the Anderson/King bills would provided inadequate benefits, were too costly, and provided coverage not just to the deserving poor but to the rich who could afford to purchase private insurance. Introduced by Representative Thomas Curtis, Republican of Missouri and Senator Sydney Herlong, Democrat of Florida, the Republican/AMA bill was called "Eldercare."

States would implement Eldercare with federal matching dollars. It would provide a wide spectrum of benefits, including physicians' care, surgical and drug costs, nursing home charges, diagnostic services, x-ray and laboratory fees and other services. Medicare's benefits would be far more limited, covering about one-quarter (25 percent) of the total yearly healthcare costs of the average person. Medicare would not cover physicians' services or surgical charges. Neither would it cover drugs outside the hospital or nursing home, nor x-ray or other laboratory services not connected with hospitalization. Instead of funding the program from Social Security type taxes, the Republicans proposed to pay for the program out of a combination of general revenues (2/3rds) and insurance premiums.[204]

The AMA argued that Eldercare was better than Medicare because it "covered 100 percent of all health expenses including surgery and drugs" which Medicare did not. In fact, Eldercare came nowhere close to covering 100 percent of expenses and was nothing more than an extension of the Kerr-Mills program that was not working. "The AMA was using the literal language of the 1960 Kerr-Mills [bill] to advertise the potential benefits of Eldercare [with full knowledge that only three or four states had come even close to living up to the promises of coverage contained in the Kerr-Mills bill].[205] The language may have been there but the delivery was not. Other Republicans offered similar bills that falsely promised more benefits than Medicare when in reality they offered, if anything, fewer benefits. Representative John Byrnes (R-Wisconsin) offered "Bettercare." As Sheri David, author of *With Dignity: The Search for Medicare and Medicaid*, points out, "the psychological climate of Congress [in 1964] was shifting from why so much? to why so little?"[206]

> **LESSON: Once they realize they are about to lose, opponents will offer a watered-down alternative and/or seek to hijack the change effort.** When the political climate begins to move in the direction of those who have long advocated major change, opponents of change shift tactics and pretend that they have had a change of heart. In fact, nothing has changed but the opposition's strategy. Once they recognize that they cannot stop change, they seek to manipulate it. The manipulation may involve efforts to hijack the change movement and mold it into something more acceptable by watering down elements. Alternatively the manipulation may involve an effort to outdo the proponents of change with false promises of benefits that far exceed what is practical in order to make the proposals of long-term advocates of change seem insufficient.

THE THREE-LAYER CAKE

From January to March, Mills led his committee in deliberations over HR 1—The House Medicare bill. Most members assumed that the bill would be reported out of committee favorably and would pass. When AMA representatives appeared before the committee and argued that H.R. 1 was socialism, the committee dismissed them and Mills from then on refused to consult the AMA.

On March 2, in an effort to reach a compromise with Republicans, Mills invited the ranking Republican on the committee, Representative John Byrnes to present an alternative bill he had been working on since January. The Republicans had decided that their strong identification with the AMA opposition to Medicare may have contributed to their defeat in November and they wanted an alternative Medicare proposal that would not be as closely identified with the AMA as Eldercare was.

Byrnes based his plan on the Aetna Life Insurance Company plan that covered federal government employees. The Byrnes bill would cover hospitalization plus doctor fees and prescription drugs. Individuals over 65 could join but participation was voluntary. Premiums would be "scaled to the amounts of the participants' social security cash benefits," so those receiving higher benefits would pay higher fees. The government would pay for its share out of general revenues.

That same day, Mills met with Wilbur Cohen with a suggestion. Why not combine Medicare, Eldercare and the Byrnes bill? Cohen at first thought Mills was attempting to kill the President's bill but on reflection realized that Mills was suggesting something Cohen himself had proposed. This "three-layer" approach would included

1. Hospitalization Insurance for the aged (Medicare Part A) like the administration proposal [Forand/Anderson bills].
2. A voluntary program of physician coverage (Medicare Part B) like the Republican proposals, and
3. An expanded Kerr-Mills program of assistance to the poor similar to the AMA proposal (Medicaid).

That night Cohen wrote a memo to the President describing Mills proposal and recommending that the administration consider it. [207] Cohen concluded his memo with the observation that "at least nobody will vote against it."[208] He later called Mills solution the "most brilliant move" he had seen in 30 years of legislative experience. He marveled at Mills ability to construct legislation that undercut all of the major opposition. "The doctors couldn't complain because they had been carping about Medicare's shortcomings and about it's being compulsory. In addition, the Republicans couldn't complain, because it was their own idea. In effect, Mills had taken the AMA's ammunition, put it in the Republican's gun, and blown both of them off the map."[209] *Newsweek* said Mills' three-layer approach was "aimed to please all of the people some of the time."[210]

Over the next twenty days, the Ways and Means Committee under Mills' leadership focused on merging the three bills. The committee made a number of changes in the Byrnes bills:

1. Benefits were reduced,
2. Payment for drugs outside of a hospital were dropped, and
3. The program was to be funded in part from premium payments of $3 per month per participant rather than being tied to social security benefits.

The Medicare bill was left largely intact although the length of hospital stays was reduced and the deductibles and co-insurance were increased. The administration had wanted to cover radiology and anesthesiology but Mills insisted that "no physician service, except those of interns and residents under approve teaching programs would be paid.".[211]

Mills served as the chief-negotiator, manager and facilitator. On March 29, the committee reported out its proposed bill (now known as the Mills Bill) as amendments to the Social Security Act: Titles 18 and 19. Title 18, Part A was Medicare offering hospital insurance, Title 18, Part B was the modified Byrnes proposal for voluntary insurance to cover doctor fees. Title 19 was an expanded Kerr-Mills program. The bill was voted out of committee on a straight party line vote with all but two Republicans opposing. It passed the House on April 8, 313 to 115.

THE BILL GOES TO THE SENATE

Having passed the house the three-part Medicare bill went to the Senate for consideration first in the Senate Finance Committee. Immediately, proponents recognized that they were in trouble. The Chairman of the Finance Committee, Harry Byrd of Virginia, was opposed to the bill and in no hurry to get on with Senate hearings. Additionally, Senator Russell Long was concerned, among other things, that the House bill only covered 60 days of hospitalization. He was determined to introduce amendments to change the bill to remove the 60-day limit and provide unlimited catastrophic and long-term care that he thought would make the costs of Medicare skyrocket. Proponents had to neutralize both Byrd and Long if Medicare was to pass the Senate. Byrd came first with the President playing a key role.

Johnson invited Byrd to the White House for a meeting which Byrd thought was to be about Vietnam. Initially Byrd declined saying he had pressing business in Virginia but ultimately agreed when Johnson promised to provide him with transportation back and forth from Virginia so that he could keep his commitments. When Byrd arrived at the oval office, he discovered to his surprise that nine other Democrats including Mills, House Speaker McCormick, and Majority Leaders Carl Albert from the House and Mike Mansfield from the Senate had also been invited to what Byrd thought was to be an informal and private meeting just between him and the president. Byrd was further surprised when Johnson marched his guests into the Cabinet room where TV cameras awaited. Johnson stepped to the podium and delivered a formal statement supporting Medicare. He then called upon his guests to step before the cameras with their comments. As Byrd came forward, Johnson said loudly, "I know that you will take an interest in the orderly scheduling of this matter and give it a thorough hearing."[212] He then asked if Byrd could schedule the hearings promptly. "A red-faced and 'barely audible' Byrd said yes. Johnson banged his fist on the table in front of the Congressman and said 'Good.'[213] The Byrd issue was resolved. That left what to do about Long.

Mills had constructed a bill with a firm eye on costs, thus the limitation to 60 days hospitalization. Long was more concerned about coverage, particularly for the elderly with serious illnesses requiring long-term care. Additionally, proponents of Medicare had long fought to avoid any means testing. Medicare, like Social Security, would be an entitlement that people earned with their contributions and it would treat everyone equally. It would not be a welfare program. Long was proposing that the deductibles and out-of-pocket costs of Medicare recipients would vary by income. That was unacceptable to Medicare advocates since it introduced a welfare-like component.

People questioned Long's motives. "*The New York Times* speculated that Long was either making a graceful retreat from his previous opposition to Medicare, or attempting to sabotage the whole program. *The New Republic* commented that Long couldn't expect to win his amendments, 'but it does his Louisiana heart good to see his friends squirm."[214]

Long was not only willing to cause his friends on the Committee to squirm but was willing to engage in a bit of sleight of hand to get his amendments adopted. On June 17th he went before the Committee with a quick explanation of his amendments, apologizing that he had not been able to bring copies to hand out. However, he assured the Committee that the Johnson administration had approved of the amendments and asked for a quick vote. The vote was called and Long won. The Committee approved his amendments by a vote of 7-6. At that point, Senator Anderson jumped to his feet to announce that he had the proxy vote of Senator Fulbright who was not in attendance and he was casting the proxy vote against Long's amendments. Long objected arguing that he had a more recent proxy from Fulbright. The senators submitted the two proxies to the clerk for review. The clerk ruled that Long's proxy was indeed more recent. Long cast his proxy in favor of his amendments. The vote was now 8 to 6 in favor. Anderson then asked to see Long's proxy. It turned out to deal with different legislation. Long had tricked the Committee. When Fulbright returned, he and Anderson along with Mike Mansfield went to Long to protest the proxy incident. Long said that there must have been some misunderstanding. He agreed to another vote.

There were other "misunderstandings" about the vote on Long's amendments. Senator Douglas said that the vote on Long's amendments had happened so fast that he had voted in error. After considering the implications of the amendments, he now wished to change his vote from "yea" to "nea." Albert Gore, who like Fulbright had missed the meeting, had given his proxy to Senator Ribicoff. Ribicoff had cast Gore's vote in favor of the amendments. Wrong, said Gore, he was opposed to the amendments and had intended Ribicoff to vote in the negative.

Johnson exploded. He called each Democrat on the Committee individually to express his anger. Long's actions were an affront and personal. Long had voted for the Civil Rights Voting Act. Now he was trying to put distance between himself and the President's Great Society agenda just to gain political points in Louisiana. Worse, the vote in favor of Long's amendments, if it held, would kill any chance Johnson had to pass Medicare that year.

The administration went into overdrive. Long's amendments had to be defeated on the next vote or Medicare was dead. Cohen held an emergency strategy session with the White House team. Maybe they could placate Long by extending hospital coverage for an additional 60 days. Anderson objected. On June 23, the Committee took a second vote. Anderson won. The Medicare bill without Long's amendments was voted out of Committee by a margin of 12 to 5. On July 9, the Senate passed its version of Medicare 68 to 21.

The bill went to conference. After a series of amendments, dealing primarily with cost cutting the Conference Committee submitted its report on July 21. The House passed the final bill six days later, followed by the Senate on July 28. On July 30, Johnson signed Medicare into law in front of Truman and the 200 invited guests. The United States joined the rest of the industrialized world in offering a government guarantee of medical insurance to at least a portion its population. We were just 70 years late.

> **Policy change is not something for ideologues.** You must court the powerful even if you find the task distasteful. Most frequently, proposed legislation in the House and Senate moves ahead, is stalled, or disappears because of what a few powerful individuals do or fail to do. You must know who these individuals are. You must know their personal criteria

> for supporting or opposing legislation that usually has nothing whatsoever to do with what is best for the country, their party, or even necessarily their constituents. It frequently has much more to do with personal power, privilege, position and sometimes just the desire for attention. Wilbur Mills shifting role in Medicare had more to do with status and power than it had to do with policy. Similarly, Russell Long's efforts to amend, and perhaps destroy, Medicare during the final debate over its provisions had as much to do with attention-seeking and just play cussedness, as it had to do with concern for the long term care of the elderly. Regardless of why or how you feel about why powerful individuals support policy proposals, you must obtain their support. That means catering to their eccentricity, even those you find unwarranted and/or even distasteful.

A PARTIAL VICTORY BUT A VICTORY NEVER-THE-LESS

Proponents of Medicare won more than they ever expected. As Oberlander notes "The contest over Medicare...ended with a broader government role in health insurance than anyone had anticipated. Not only would the federal government provide hospitalization coverage to the elderly, but it would also operate a program of physicians' insurance and subsidize state medical assistance to the poor. Moreover, the final bill extended Medicare coverage initially to the nearly three million seniors who were not eligible for Social Security."[215] Medicare delivered less than Truman had proposed but much more than proponents of the legislation had considered possible.

Many progressives thought Medicare and Medicaid would be just the beginning. They had carved off a big piece of Cohen's salami with the passage of health insurance coverage for the elderly and poor. They expected to be able to take another slice very soon, this time by extending health insurance to children under a program they were already calling "Kiddiecare." However, more than 30 years would elapse before a program for uninsured children would pass (the State Children's Health Insurance Program or S-CHIP) and then it would cover only children of the working poor and would be a state-based rather than federal program. Several presidents and presidential candidates would propose expanding health insurance coverage—Richard Nixon and Ted Kennedy in 1971, Carter in 1976, and Clinton in 1993. Each would fail largely because they did not know or heed the lessons we have examined so far about what it takes to get things done in Washington. Obama finally succeeded by applying a number of the lessons from this chapter but his reform remains under attack as I write this with Republicans vowing to repeal it as soon as they can.

While progressives were unable to keep slicing the health insurance salami as they hoped, they were able to retain the slices that already had. Progressives have successfully defended Medicare and Medicaid from attacks from the Right for over 40 years. That is not always the case.

In the next chapter, I will examine a time when progressives won a great victory and then lost much of what they had won a little more than a decade later. After a struggle that was even more lengthy and difficult as the struggle for pure food and drugs and health insurance, the American labor movement won the passage of historic legislation guaranteeing workers the right to organize and negotiate with management for better pay and working conditions. In just 12 years, conservatives were able to push legislation through Congress undoing much of the hard won protections. That conservative victory started the U.S. labor movement on a slow process of decline that continues to this day. It is a cautionary lesson about the need for progressives to be vigilant and to work as hard to maintain and preserve gains as they did to win them.

A SUMMARY OF LESSONS FROM THE STRUGGLE FOR HEALTH INSUANCE

Gains in one area do not automatically translate into gains in another, even a closely related policy area. The AALL assumed that its success in pushing states to adopt workman's compensation laws could be transferred relatively easily to success in getting states to pass comprehensive health insurance. It was wrong. The reality is that each new drive for change is a war that you must fight on its own. You can use lessons from previous efforts and you do benefit if you have a track record of success but you still have to fight the current battles just as you fought the battles in the previous war.

Anticipate well-funded opposition and be prepared to counter it. It is the nature of change that one or more groups, often well financed and influential groups, will be threatened by the change you propose just a doctors in the AMA were. Some people and groups will see the change you propose as a threat to their power, position, prestige, and even financial well-being. Your challenge is to identify such individuals and groups early on, understand how your proposed changes affects them, anticipate the form their opposition might take, and prepare to defend your effort. You should try to structure the change you propose to minimize the threat or make it less apparent. Ideally, you should try to co-opt the opposition.

Expect opponents to charge that the change you propose is un-American. You should never make the case for your policy change by citing what other countries have done, particularly European countries, even if these countries have been highly successful and you are basing your proposal on lessons learned from their efforts. The un-American argument is a standard conservative opposition tactic and one you should be prepared to counter. Show how the change you propose, rather than being un-American, is indeed what America is all about. Turn the un-American argument on its head. Argue that the opponents are the ones who are being un-American since they are setting out to destroy the country by ignoring a wrong and not fixing it, wishing a cancer away rather than treating it aggressively with the healing power of change. Argue that the truly un-American thing to do would be to do nothing. Americans are not "do nothings," they are doers and that is what you are proposing. Argue that your approach does not copy any other countries. Your approach is a one-of-a-kind, uniquely American way of solving the problem.

Never be seduced by the logic and rightness of your cause. Never assume that what is obvious to you will be obvious to the average American. Never assume that the average American will accept facts more readily, or even as readily, as he will accept arguments based on speculation, superstition or even outright fabrication of data. Do not expect Americans to recognize the difference between the truth and lies unless you specifically point out the difference. It is okay to use facts and logic but keep in mind that Americans think with their hearts and not their heads.

You must present the change you propose in the simplest of possible terms but do not leave out too many details. Americans are uncomfortable with complexity and never understand nuance. At the same time, do not forget to work out the details or at least most of them before you come forward with your proposal. If you offer few or limited details, your opponents will fill the void with rumors, some involving wild charges and dire warnings of impending disaster should your policy become law. Once such rumors start they are very difficult to counter so you must be prepared to counter them aggressively early on. Do not bore Americans with the details but be prepared to discuss them thoroughly when the occasion demands. Talking to Americans about public policy is like talking to kids about sex. Answer their questions honestly and give them as much detail as they seem to want and are prepared to digest but not more.

Be prepared to counter the argument that the private sector can solve the problem. Initially conservatives will try to convince Americans that no problem exists or that it is a minor problem that will solve itself if only it is left alone. Failing that, your opponents will argue that if something must be done to remedy the problem it is best done by the private sector. Conservatives worship the private sector and the profit motive. Counter the private-sector-can-do-it-best argument by demonstrating that the private sector has had ample opportunity to remedy the problem but has failed to do so. Use the profit motive to your advantage. Demonstrate that because of the nature of the problem and the cost of even the cheapest practical remedy there is simply no profit for private companies in remedying the problem and thus no profit motive to do so. Proponents of Medicare were able to show that private insurance was never going to solve the problem of the elderly's access to health insurance since there was little or no profit for private insurers in doing so. It was easy to demonstrate that by 1960 private insurance providers were covering an increasing number of working Americans but that few strides were being made in expanding that coverage among the aged for the simple reason that the cost of covering them did not yield sufficient profit. Only a non-profit entity such as the federal government could address the issue.

Do not ignore the built in distrust Americans have of power, in particular the power of government. Minimize expansion of government as much as possible. Create few or no new boards, agencies, gurus, czars, or government departments. You want to present your change as a logical and limited expansion of government, not something new but rather just an improvement on an existing government activity and preferably one that is popular. Proponents of Medicare sold it not as something new but rather as just an extension of Social Security that was highly popular at the time.

Appeal to Americans' self-interest. You must convince the majority of Americans, and preferably a super majority, that the problem or issue your proposed policy change addresses affects them personally if you want to win their support. Do not expect Americans to support substantive policy change for altruistic reasons. Americans are selfish when it comes to what their government does. They may contribute to private charities and support limited government intervention in times of disaster or when they are confronted with vivid, emotion arousing images of suffering, but their support for such efforts quickly fades. You must construct a rational or better yet highly emotional argument that the problem impacts or potentially could impact nearly all Americans in some way. You must convince the majority of Americans that the problem threatens them or their family and that they will personally benefit from the policy change you propose even if that is only partially the truth. Americans only support public policy from which they believe they will benefit directly and concretely or which will cost them little or nothing. You must make that case for your proposal even if it is largely a false one. That is what proponents of Medicare did. The majority of Americans were not elderly but most had relatives who were and everyone if they lived long enough would become elderly. It was not hard to convince Americans, even young Americans, that they could personally benefit from the government caring for their aging parents or grandparents so they would not have to do so. In addition, it was confronting to know that when one became old, one would have the power of government protecting one from the financial harm that an extended serious illness might cause.

Be careful about redistribution issues. Americans accumulate. It is part of the American character to seek out, assemble and hoard possessions either real or imagined. Likewise, Americans live in constant fear of loss of their possessions. Americans are ever watchful that something or someone might come along and take things, physical or emotional, real or imagined, from them. Americans are particularly concerned that the taker might be government. Conservatives will prey upon American's redistribution fears. They will argue that what you are proposing is an evil endeavor to take from the deserving, and give to strangers who are largely undeserving because otherwise they would not be in need of government assistance. You must provide reassurance that no American will lose because of the change you propose. You must project all boats to rise. You must guarantee that all futures will be positive. The final tally must place all above average. There must only be gains.

Inevitably, the support of a few powerful figures in Congress is critical to success. You must cater to their needs whatever they are. Each of these figures have their own personal criteria for what they will and will not support and until the proponents of change can craft their legislation to at least appear to meet the requirements of these powerful men and women, no change is possible. No legislation can be passed.

You must build a record. The discussions on the Forand bill like the discussions surrounding the earlier Wagner-Murray-Dingell proposals were important not because they resulted in any movement on the bill but because they began the process of "building the record," which is a critical step in getting anything done in Washington. You must take testimony from experts and the people. You must accumulate data. You must assemble statistics documenting the nature and extent of the problem. People must get comfortable with the topic and with the people and organizations representing each side of the issue. You must document, define, and plant in the minds of those who can affect change that an issue exists and a remedy is required even if they are unclear about the nature of that remedy. Building a record is a ritual all major legislation must pass through. That is the reason you want to get legislation introduced as early as possible even if you know you have little chance of success. If nothing else, each failure to get legislation through committee or brought to the floor helps to build the record.

Link you legislative proposal to the political ambition of key politicians. Senators and Congressmen may proclaim that they work for their constituents and "the good of the country," but they actually work for themselves. Show them how they can get personal political mileage out of supporting your proposal and you will get their support. Do not expect them to get behind your cause just because your cause is right and does a lot of good for the country. They could care less. They want to know, "what's in it for me?" You need a good answer to that question. In the case of Kennedy and McNamara, they knew that getting to go around the country holding a lot of hearings on the plight of old people would be good for their political careers. They had a lot to gain and little to lose.

Turn opposition to your advantage whenever you can. The AMA made a tactical mistake in launching such a loud and expensive campaign opposing the Forand bill. Proponents of health reform took advantage of the vicious attacks to rally their supports and gain new recruits to the cause. The saying "there is no such thing as bad publicity" fully applies when it comes to getting things done in Washington. Do not be discouraged when opponents attack your proposal. Find a way to turn those attacks to your advantage by using them to stimulate grassroots interest and support.

Whenever the opposition proposes to study the problem, respond by pushing harder to get something done right away. An offer to study the problem is a standard delaying tactic opponents will resort to when they discover that public pressure is building to get something done. It is a sign that your efforts to educate the public and garner support from politicians are paying off. It is a signal that you should redouble your efforts to move legislation forward. Do not back off or agree to slow down. Push harder.

Conservatives will always argue that the states can do it best. When pressured by an aroused public to do something about an issue, Conservatives, who are philosophically opposed to ever doing anything, take political cover by arguing that if something must done about a problem the best approach is for the federal government to simply provide funding and let the states actually administer the program. The problem with this approach is that states often fail to enact programs even when substantial funding is provided because they will not or cannot provide the matching funding. However, this approach provides the appearance of actually doing something without doing anything much at all. The best way to counter this argument is to have already tried a state-based approach that you can point to as a example of why state-based remedies won't work.

You must engage in "salami slicing" and be willing to "buy votes." You must seek that which will pass even if what passes will be less, and perhaps much less, than ideal. Proponents of Medicare were willing to exclude coverage of outpatient expenses if that was what it took to placate doctors and other opponents. You must be pragmatic. Remember politics is the art of the possible. You have to take what you can get. Progressives do not want to make things just a little bit better. They want to right wrongs. Unfortunately, it is hard to get a lot done in one piece of legislation. The framers did not construct our government that way.

It is not enough to convince those who are already on your side. You have to make those who are not yet convinced comfortable with your ideas. It is great to have a charismatic leader who you can put forward to sell your cause. In addition, it feels great to see him enthusiastically received by partisan crowds roaring their support. However, do not lose sight of the fact that those adoring fans of your proposed legislation are not the ones you have to convince. The people you need to reach are the show-me skeptics that frown and a twitch as you lay out your ideas. Your task is not to rally the already convinced but to turn the frowns and nervous ticks of the skeptics into relaxed smiles. You have to make those folks comfortable with your ideas.

Just because a presidential candidate or a sitting president, even a popular one, expresses support for a change effort do not assume that achieving that change will be easy. It might be easier to have the president behind your cause but that does not make the passing legislation easy or guaranteed. Progressives often get over confident when they are finally able to elect a popular president who shares their agenda. They expect him to expend his considerable political capital on their behalf. They forget that presidents are not all powerful even if they are extremely popular and they are never pursuing a single agenda item. There are no single-issue presidents. Progressive legislation has to compete with all the other legislation, conservative, moderate, liberal, domestic and foreign that presidents have to juggle. At least four presidents or presidential candidates, including Kennedy who was very popular, had supported some form of health insurance reform by the early 60s, but only one was successful in passing legislation and then, as we will see, it was less than proponents of change had originally sought.

Do not overreach Once you gain public support for your reform, particularly if it is accompanied by control of both houses of Congress and the presidency, it is tempting to try to set your sights higher, to try to expand your legislative proposal to accomplish more. Do not do it. If you overreach, you give ammunition to your opponents. They will use it to scare the public. Public support for any legislative effort is a fragile thing. Do not abuse it. Take what you can get. You can come back for more a later day.

Do not let conservatives hijack the effort. When the political climate begins to move in the direction of those who have long advocated major change, opponents of change shift tactics and pretend that they have had a change of heart. In fact, nothing has changed but the opposition's strategy. Once they recognize that they cannot stop change, they seek to manipulate it. The manipulation may involve efforts to hijack the change movement and mold it into something more acceptable by watering down elements. Alternatively the manipulation may involve an effort to outdo the proponents of change with false promises of benefits that far exceed what is practical in order to make the proposals of long-term advocates of change seem insufficient.

Policy change is not something for ideologues. You must court the powerful even if you find the task distasteful. Most frequently, proposed legislation in the House and Senate moves ahead, is stalled, or disappears because of what a few powerful individuals do or fail to do. You must know who these individuals are. You must know their personal criteria for supporting or opposing legislation that usually has nothing whatsoever to do with what is best for the country, their party, or even necessarily their constituents. It frequently has much more to do with personal power, privilege, position and sometimes just the desire for attention. Wilbur Mills shifting role in Medicare had more to do with status and power than it had to do with policy. Similarly, Russell Long's efforts to amend, and perhaps destroy, Medicare during the final debate over its provisions had as much to do with attention-seeking and just play cussedness, as it had to do with concern for the long term care of the elderly. Regardless of why or how you feel about why powerful individuals support policy proposals, you must obtain their support. That means catering to their eccentricity, even those you find unwarranted and/or even distasteful.

4

The Struggle for the Right of Labor to Organize

On July 5, 1935, President Roosevelt signed into law the National Labor Relations Act, also known as the Wagner Act. In their book, *Labor in America*, Foster Rhea Dulles and Melvyn Dubofsky say this about the importance of the Wagner Act to working Americans. "For the first time in American history, a national administration was to make the welfare of industrial workers a direct concern of government and act on the principle that only organized labor could deal on equal terms with organized capital. Heretofore, America tolerated labor unions; now they were to be encouraged... Age-old traditions were smashed; new and dynamic forces were released. Never before had as much economic and political power seemed within the reach of organized labor. The struggles, hardships, and defeats of a century appeared to have culminated in the possibility of complete attainment of workers' historic objectives."[216] Yet it was not to be.

Within just a dozen years with the passage of the Taft-Hartley Act, anti-labor forces were able to undo practically all that labor had accomplished with the Wagner Act. The journey from the Wagner Act to the Taft-Hartley

Act contains critical lessons about the difficulty of retaining hard-earned gains and the ever-present danger that conservative forces will once again gain the upper hand. This is the story of how pro-labor forces, having won just about everything with the passage of the Wagner Act, lost just about everything with the passage of the Taft-Hartley Act. It is a cautionary tale about the necessity of sustaining hard-earned victories in the face of those who, having lost the battle, refuse to concede the war. In this chapter, we will learn new lessons about why it is important to continue the fight even after you have won a victory and the critical importance of continuing to court the American voter and keep him on your side.

In previous chapters, we learned that for significant legislation to pass it must address a nation-wide issue for which there is no viable state-based solution. The Warner Act and Taft-Hartley Act met that requirement and for exactly the same reason although the designers of these two pieces of legislation were diametrically opposed in their intent. We also learned that the passage of all great legislation required the significant involvement and creativity of one or more leaders, George Wiley when it came to pure food and drugs and Wilbur Cohen when it came to Medicare, among others. The Warner and Taft-Hartley acts had their own leaders. We will get to that in a moment. For now, let us look at a little of the history of the labor movement in American. One cannot fully appreciate the significance of the passage of the Wagner Act in 1935 and Taft-Hartley Act a few years later without knowing something about the history of the labor movement in America, so we will begin there. Conservatives hate unions and rejoice at their decline. Americans overall have become disenchanted. They should not be. We forget just what the world was like when workers had no right to organize. Let me help you remember.

LABOR IN COLONIAL AMERICA

When the nation was settled, the colonists shared the old world belief that the best way to ensure that common working people worked hard was to pay them the absolute minimum necessary for subsistence. Most upper class people assumed that when it came to the lower classes, high wages would lead to indolence. Colony after colony established laws that limited wages. For example, in 1630 Massachusetts set a maximum wage of two shillings a day for skilled workers such as carpenters and bricklayers and eighteen pence for unskilled day laborers provided, of course, that these workers worked "the whole day, allowing convenient tyme for food and rest."[217] Ten hours were the minimum to constitute a "whole day." Additionally, employers could not offer their employees liquor or wine as a supplement to their income. Long hours and low wages were considered to be just the thing "to reduce idleness and protect workers from the temptations of tavern, cockpit, and playing field."[218]

The workers objected. In 1636, a group of fisherman in Maine mutinied when they were not paid their wages. In 1676, licensed cartman in New York City refused to remove dirt from the streets for the threepence per load they were offered. In 1768, twenty tailors in New York struck their employer when he cut their wages. In November 1778, printers in New York demanded and got a pay increase from their employer. Seaman in Philadelphia in 1770, shoemakers in New York in 1785, and printers in Philadelphia in 1786 made similar successful demands for pay increases. However, none of these protests and strikes involved a formal organization. They were just the spontaneous response of workers who came together temporarily to address a labor issue.

> **LESSON: Grassroots organizing is essential.** Again, we see that the effort to right a wrong, in this case the exploitation of workers, begins far away from Washington.

THE FIRST TRUE UNION

The first true union in the U.S. was created in 1794 when shoemakers in Philadelphia established the Federal Society of Journeymen Cordwainers (shoemakers). However, the real growth in unions came in the early nineteenth century as small craft/artisan manufacturing gave way to more large scale manufacturing owned and operate by early capitalists who began hiring workers to manufacture goods to be sold in a wider market thanks to the rapid expansion of transportation systems via canals, turnpikes and steam boats. These early capitalists sought to reduce costs by cutting wages, lengthening the workday, and hiring women, children and prisoners to work in "sweatshops." Journeymen, artisans, and the early unions like the Philadelphia Society of Journeymen Cordwainers fought back with strikes and protests that frequently turned violent.

Employers responded by taking organizers to court where judges applied English common law principals that worker efforts to band together to improve wages and/or working conditions was a criminal conspiracy to restrain trade. Most often, courts ruled in favor of the employers reasoning as one judge put it in his decision that "competition is the life of trade." If the defendant workers were unwilling to work for the wages their employers offered then they were free to do so, but they had no right to directly or indirectly attempt to prohibit someone else from taking the jobs at a lower rate of pay. Such interference was unlawful and an act of individual oppression. It led also to "public inconvenience and embarrassment" which, of course, could not be allowed. [219] In other words, it was illegal. As late as the 1830s, courts were fining and/or imprisoning workers for engaging in such "conspiracies."[220]

> **LESSSON: Do not expect the courts to be on your side.** Regardless of level—state, local federal or even the Supreme Court—courts rarely lead or are even on the side of reform. Voters do not elect nor do politicians appoint people to the bench for challenging conservative keep-things-as-they-are doctrine. Judges are supposed to follow precedent and do nothing to change things. Courts are typically the enemy of progress.

Throughout much of the 1800s, the economy dictated union fortunes. In good times, the unions were generally successful in holding out for better wages and working conditions. However, each downturn in the economy resulted in significant setbacks with the early unions losing membership. Many went out of existence. New unions replaced them when economic conditions once again improved.

UNIONS IN THE 1800S

During the 1830s, the wages of workers rose but not enough to keep up with inflation. The workday was as long as 15 hours sometimes, often more than 12. Not surprisingly, one of the major grievances of labor during the mid-1830s had to do with the length of the workday. Workers wanted a 10-hour workday (6AM to 6PM with an hour off for lunch and hour off for dinner) instead of the traditional one of sun-up-to-sun-down. Employers objected because, they said, a shortened workday "would surely lead to intemperance and ruin" and promote "habits likely to be generated by the indulgence of idleness."[221] Of course, the real reason business owners objected to a shorter workday was the impact shorter hours would have on their profits but the moral argument sounded better.

If the company a person worked for failed, the worker was not paid and had no way of getting what he was owed since the courts and government were on the side of the businessmen. When these abandoned workers could not pay their bills, courts imprisoned them for debt. Increasingly two classes were developing, a working class and a capitalist aristocracy. The government was on the side of the aristocracy as were both major political parties. The men who ran the government were almost all part of the capitalist aristocracy.

In response, unions began expanding their focus from just wages and working conditions to wider and more political goals such as arguing for the value and protection of the working classes in the face of increased capitalism and developing class warfare. Workers soon began forming their own political parties to protect themselves. When elections were close they had some success but the distinction between worker and employer continued to widen.

Large-scale manufacturing was growing with the establishment of large textile mills in Massachusetts and Rhode Island, clock and watch factories in Connecticut and iron foundries in Pennsylvania. The managers who ran these factories sought to hold down wages by hiring young boys and women thus undercutting wage rates for journeymen workers. Many began contracting with prisons for convict labor under agreements that enabled them to produce goods 40% to 60% cheaper than they could by hiring the typical worker.

In response, trade societies proliferated and union officials sought to link local unions to form nation-wide federations, a forerunner to national unions. Strikes increased. Newspaper reported at least 168 strikes between 1833 and 1837 as wages stagnated and the cost of living jumped as much as 66%. There were 44,000 (and perhaps as many as 131,000) unionized workers in the U.S. by the mid-1830s. Two thirds of the workers in New York City were members of unions. The city had some 55 different unions.

> **LESSON: Once again, we see the need for national coordination of grassroots efforts.** It was not until the growth of national unions that the labor movement had any chance of pushing significant legislation through Congress.

Employers fought back by joining to deny employment to anyone who was a member of a union. For example, a group of employers in New York City in the 1830s created a mutual protective association whose member businesses agreed not to employ "any man who is known to be a member [of] any society which has for its object the direction of terms or prices for which workmen shall engage themselves."[222] Employers argued that they and they alone had the right to set the terms of any contract with their workforce. Workers had the right to accept the terms dictated by their employers or seek employment elsewhere without the interference of any type of labor union, society or association.

By late 1840s, women and girls working in the textile mills of New England were making $1.50 a week working up to 13 hours per day. Manufacturers could keep wages low because there was an abundant labor supply not just from young workers anxious to get off the farms but also from an influx of Irish and German immigrants fleeing hard times in Europe and the potato famine of the 1840s. The introduction of power looms in the plants further depressed wages as less skilled workers took the place of skilled weavers.

Unskilled laborers made on the average about one dollar a week in the early 1850s. The *New York Times* at the time estimated that the minimum a typical worker's family required for food, rent, fuel and clothing was about $ 11 per week. The $10 shortfall meant that most workingman families in cities such as New York, Philadelphia or Boston lived in overcrowded, unsanitary, disease-ridden slums with as many as six to sometimes 20 people crammed into "damp, unlighted, ill-ventilated" single rooms.[223]

STATE-BASED EFFORTS TOWARD REFORM

Unions continued to pressure state legislatures for a 10-hour workday. They met with some success in the late 1840s and 1850s. New Hampshire passed a law restricting the workday to 10 hours in 1847 as did Pennsylvania in 1848. In the 1850s, Maine, Connecticut, Rhode Island, Ohio, California, and Georgia adopted similar 10-hour laws. Other states such as Massachusetts resisted fearing that any restriction on the length of the workday would drive manufacturers from their states. Additionally, even when states adopted 10-hour laws they usually included a "special contract" clause that provided an out for most employers. The clause stated that the 10-hour restriction would not apply if a worker signed a contract stipulating that he was willing to work longer hours than the law allowed. This clause was justified by proponents as protecting the right of an individual worker to sell his services as he saw fit. Of course, employers avoided the 10-hour law by simply refusing to hire anyone who refused to agree to the "special contract."[224]

UNIONS GROW IN THE POST CIVIL WAR PERIOD

By the mid 1860's there were an estimated 270 unions, 32 national unions, representing over 200,000 workers. They included the Iron Molders' International Union, Machinists and Blacksmiths Union, The Locomotive Engineers Union, and the American Miner's Association. Labor unions emerged from the Civil War in a strong position to win concessions from employers and to enact legislation guaranteeing worker rights. However, the world was rapidly changing and there were new adversaries committed to crushing the worker.

The country was transformed between the Civil War and 1900. America had it all, abundant natural resources, abundant labor, abundant and insatiable demand for products, and, most of all, a small group of enormously ambitious and totally ruthless men devoted to carving out monopolies for themselves in order to amass great wealth. The country underwent an industrial expansion of a scale and speed unmatched before or since. Giant corporations were created run by such men as Jay Gould, E. H. Harriman, and James J. Hill in railroads, Andrew Carnegie in steel, and John D. Rockefeller in oil. These men built empires where labor was simply another commodity, a raw material for manufacturing to be bought as cheaply as possible, used as efficiently as possible, and discarded whenever possible to be replaced by cheaper human raw material. The replacements were usually immigrants, Italians, Poles, Czechs, Slovaks, Hungarians, Greeks, Russians, and on the west coast, Chinese, Japanese, and Filipinos. They were desperate, ambitious and willing to work for near starvation wages to seize for themselves and their families whatever meager opportunities America might offer. By 1900, the richest 2% of Americans owned a third of the nation's physical wealth. The top 10% owned three-fourths.

WORKLIFE IN THE LATE 1800S

What was it like to be a working man or woman in the America of the late 1800s and early 1900s? Most put in long hours for extremely low pay in often dangerous working conditions. For example, in 1913 alone 25,000 workers died in factory accidents and another 700,000 sustained injuries so serious as to keep them out of work for four weeks are longer, without pay. There was no worker's compensation so every lost hour meant lost pay. American factories had the dubious distinction of having the highest accident rate in the world. Two million of those exposed to workplace hazards were children under the age of twelve. They suffered three times the rate of accidents as adults possibly because they were almost always sleep deprived, so much so that foreman could keep them awake only by dousing them with cold water. Children working in the textile mills suffered from respiratory conditions so serious that they were twice as likely to die before the age of twenty as other children were. The few states that had adopted child labor laws rarely enforced them so employers generally ignored the laws. Anyway, in most cases the only proof of age the laws required employers to obtain was an affidavit from the child's parents who were usually so desperate for the meager wages their children could earn that they would lie.

Labor leaders had little success in creating national unions strong enough to do battle with the national corporations during this period. For example, a group of union leaders created the National Labor Union (NLU) in 1866. The NLU sought to unite local skilled worker trade unions, unskilled workers and farmers in an effort to achieve reform through political action. By 1872, that effort had collapsed. In 1873, the country entered into a prolonged depression during which unions lost membership year after year. Between 1873 and 1877, the number of national unions dropped from 30 to just nine and union membership plummeted from nearly 300,000 to less than 50,000.

Strikes were common in the 1870s and 1880s even with declining membership as workers rose up to protest their working conditions and pay. The strikes often turned violent when police intervened. The Haymarket Affair in Chicago in 1884 was typical. The Knights of Labor, a national union founded in 1869, called for nation-wide demonstrations demanding an eight-hour workday. In Chicago, workers were involved in a strike against the International Harvester plant. The strike turned violent when police intervened and killed one striker. The following night, the leaders of a small anarchist movement in Chicago held a meeting to protest the killing. Anarchists rejected the legitimacy of any government, viewing government as a tool of the rich designed to oppress and exploit workers. They sought to overthrow governments through acts of violence if necessary. On the night in question, the crowd was listening to a series of long speeches on the virtues of socialism and anarchism when police arrived and ordered that the crowd disperse. Someone, it was never determined who, threw a bomb killing seven police officers and wounding several others. In response, the police fired into the crowd killing four. Over sixty police and demonstrators were injured. Although there was no evidence that any of them had thrown the bomb, police arrested eight men, all anarchists with foreign sounding names. The men were tried and quickly convicted of murder. Four were immediately hanged and one committed suicide. The other three eventually had their sentences commuted to life in prison. Although only one of the eight anarchists belonged to the Knights of Labor and there was no evidence that the Knights were an anarchist organization or that many of its members were anarchists, the union was from then on associated in the public mind with anarchists and never recovered. The American Federation of Labor (AFL), which had been founded in 1886 as a national union representing skilled workers, soon replaced the Knights.

INDUSTRIALISTS FIGHT BACK

In spite of the violence and strikes, union membership grew from less than 900,000 at the turn of the century to over 2,000,000 by 1904. As more workers joined unions, employers became increasingly worried and began to fight back. By 1903 Industrial Alliances banded together in an effort to swing public opinion against the unions adopting as their slogan and chief argument the "open shop" Industrialists were united, they said, in their commitment in the name of basic human rights to protect every American's right to work regardless of union affiliation. Of course, the real motive was to make union recognition and collective bargaining difficult, if not impossible, and preserve management's exclusive and unregulated right to determine wages and working conditions. Employers banded together to crush unions and no anti-union measure was considered too extreme.[225]

The introduction of technology in the workplace during the 1920s cut the amount of labor necessary to produce a given amount of output from 25% to 60% depending upon industry. The natural result was increased unemployment for the unskilled where unemployment ran from 10% to 13%. Even in prosperous communities, working people lived in constant fear their employers would lay them off. Yet, union membership did not increase. In fact, it decreased. In 1929 union membership was less than it had been in 1917.

Most businesses in the 1920s were stanchly anti-union and dedicated to the concept of the "open shop," which simply meant the right of the employer to hire anyone he chooses regardless of union membership. In reality application of the open shop meant the employer had the right to refuse to hire union members or union sympathizers, to refuse to recognize unions even when a majority of employees belonged, and to refuse to participate in collective bargaining.

During the 1920s, Businesses banded together to create anti-union open shop associations in New York, Massachusetts, Connecticut, Illinois, Ohio and Michigan. They were supported by local chambers of commerce, the National Association of Manufactures, the National Metal Trade Association, the League for Industrial Rights, local and regional manufacturer's associations, and similar groups. The open shop, argued these organizations, was the American way. Additionally these groups pounced on every instance of suspected union corruption to portray union bosses as engaging in racketeering and promoting revolution. In addition to the propaganda, these anti-union groups did all they could to intimidate anyone who spoke up for the union cause. Many employers forced their employees to sign "yellow dog" contracts agreeing not to support unions. Others placed spies on the factory floor in an effort to identify union sympathizers. Anyone supporting unions was fired. If workers struck, the groups hired strong-arm guards to beat up strikers and recruited the local authorities to protect strikebreakers.

> LESSON: **Conservatives always label any reform, particularly any reform that seeks to alleviate the plight of working Americans as un-American.** You must never let them get away with that argument. Whatever you propose, expect opponents to accuse you of engaging in a conspiracy to destroy the American way of life. You must address that charge directly by turning it on its head with the argument that solving problems and seeking to improve the lives of average Americans is not un-American but indeed the most American thing that anyone can do. Remember this rule. You must counter every charge immediately with a counter-charge. The worst thing you can do is to ignore your opponents' attacks. Counter attack. Respond in kind.

SOME COMPANIES FIGHT UNIONS WITH "KINDNESS"

Some employers used a more benevolent approach to defeat unions. They introduced Scientific Management in their plants. Such programs involved the use of time and motion studies to redesign work and piece rate pay plans "scientifically" to boost productivity. Companies set up shop councils (essentially company-dominated unions) to involve employees in the introduction of these new work practices and pay practices. By 1926, there were more than 400 such company unions. Additionally, the personnel departments of various companies began experimenting with a variety of plans and programs to gain worker loyalty such as profit-sharing plans, group insurance plans, old-age pension programs, and free medical clinics and employee cafeterias. Companies sponsored picnics, glee clubs, dances, sporting events and so on all in an effort to make the company into "one big happy family."

Laborers did benefit from many of these programs and many employees saw their pay increase. Employers increased the wages of working people in the country by about 20% between 1921 and 1928. Simultaneously, companies cut the average hours of work for many, but not all, workers by 15% to as much as 30%. By the end of the decade, a 40-hour workweek was generally accepted. The downside of these improvements was, of course, that working men and women almost never had any voice in which programs would be implemented or how they would be administered. In addition, this so called "welfare capitalism" was entirely at the employer's discretion. These programs and plans could vanish as quickly as they appeared all at the whim of management.

UNIONS STRUGGLE—COURTS TAKE THE SIDE OF BUSINESS

Unions found it difficult to fight back against this coordinated anti-union campaign. The courts routinely sided with employers and supported the right of employers to seek injunctions to end strikes. They recognized business ownership as a property right. Any injury to business (such as physical property damage) and/or the restraint of trade such as would occur with a strike, picketing, or boycott was illegal under most situations. Additionally the Sherman Act of 1890 outlawed combinations or conspiracies that interfered with interstate or foreign commerce and provided for criminal prosecutions, court injunctions and civil suits for triple damages in the case of violations. It is uncertain whether Congress had intended for the courts to apply the Sherman Act to unions but never the less it was. Seeking relief, labor unions lobbied hard for an exemption and thought it got it with the passage of the Clayton Act of 1914. However, the Supreme Court ruled that the Clayton Act exempted unions from the Sherman Act only when they were carrying out lawful activities and strikes, pickets, and boycotts were usually not lawful activities. In its ruling in Adkins v. Children's Hospital in 1923, the Supreme Court even went so far as to strike down minimum wage laws arguing that while workers might have an ethical right to a living wage, employers had no legal obligation to pay them one. Labor was a commodity that was bought and sold just like any other commodity, wrote the court. In principle, said the court, "there can be no difference between the case of selling labor and the case of selling goods."[226] It was just as wrong for the government to compel an employer to pay his workers a living wage, as it would be for the government to use its "naked, arbitrary power" to compel an employer to sell his product for a certain price.

THE STOCK MARKET CRASHS

In October 1929, the stock market crashed. The cause? Speculation. Wild, giddy, euphoric speculation. Everyone wanted to make a fast buck in the stock market and, in the roaring twenties, the market looked like a certain thing. Moreover, there was little regulation. "Smart" investors would form a stock pool where they would buy up a block of stock and trade back and forth among themselves to drive the price of the stock up hoping to draw in suckers looking to reap quick profits. Once the stock reached a certain agreed upon price the insiders who had created the stock pool would all dump their stock, take all the profit and leave the suckers with nothing.

Other "smart" investors who sold short would circulate rumors that a company whose stock was doing well was actually in trouble in order to drive down the price of the stock. They could then buy the stock of the company back at an attractive price and considerable profit.

With the collapse of the stock market, all vestiges of welfare capitalism disappeared, almost overnight as companies fought to survive the depression. Workers found themselves not just without the company pension or profit sharing or access to health care or a free lunch but also without a job. Unemployment soared. Organized labor, demoralized after a decade of losing battle after battle to the business anti-union onslaught, could do little to help workers or pressure government for worker relief.

President Hoover's response to the crisis was to seek to reassure the country that the economy was sound, the stock market crash the result of speculation and that the nation would soon right itself. Unwarranted pessimism and fear had led businessmen to cut back thereby throwing people "temporarily" out of work. Voluntary efforts and a limited expansion of government programs would be sufficient to set things right. They were not.

> By the end of 1929, the entire economy began to snowball downhill. Consumer buying declined sharply and the public, leery of banks, cached currency in safe-deposit boxes and mattresses. Every kind of business suffered and had to discharge employees; they, unable to find other jobs, defaulted on installment payments and exhausted their savings to live...This tailspin of the economy went on until mid-1932 when around 12 million people, about 25 percent of the normal labor force, were unemployed. In the cities, there were soup kitchens and breadlines. Factory payrolls dropped to less than half those of early 1929. Shanty towns, where the jobless gathered to pick over a dump, grew up; bankrupt mills and garment lofts were reopened by unscrupulous promoters who paid a dollar a day to men and half that to girls. Small towns in the farm belt were almost deserted by their inhabitants. Some farmers resisted eviction and foreclosure by force of arms. On the higher

> level, New York apartment houses offered five-year leases for one year's rent, entire Pullman trains rolled along without a single passenger, hotels and resorts like Miami Beach were empty.[227]

In perhaps the understatement of all time, ex-President Coolidge wrote in his syndicated press column on January 20, 1931, "the country is not in good condition." [228]

Not surprisingly, Franklin Roosevelt defeated Herbert Hoover in the 1932 election. New Dealers poured into Washington seeking three common objectives: "first to see that the hungry are fed, but second and more important, to see that men are reemployed and third, to prevent a recurrence of so prolonged a depression." [229] Of course, neither the new President nor anyone else had an overall plan or strategy for how to obtain these objectives. The New Deal would be experimental, improvisational, and would follow no consistent philosophy. The administration chose policies and proposals willy-nilly for their pragmatic value alone. The discernable New Deal "philosophy" would be created by historians and economists after the fact and contain one critical component, collective action by disadvantaged groups such as labor guaranteed by the Federal government as a counterbalance to the big business. The administration routed much of this hodge podge of New Deal legislation through the office of a senator from New York, Robert F. Wagner.

ROBERT FERDINAND WAGNER[230]

Robert Ferdinand Wagner was born on June 8, 1877 in Nastatten, Germany. His family immigrated to the United States in 1885 and settled in a tenement neighborhood in New York City where his father worked as a janitor. Wagner took advantage of a tuition-free education offered by the City College of New York, the "People's University." He graduated in 1898 with the intention of becoming a public-school teacher. During the summer after his graduation, Wagner met a childhood friend, Jeremiah Mahoney, who had just finished law school. Mahoney convinced Wagner that a career in law would better suit his talents. Taking Mahoney's advice,

Wagner entered New York Law School in the fall. He graduated with honors in 1900 and formed a law partnership with Mahoney. Both soon became active in politics. In 1904, with the backing of the Tammany organization, Wagner won election to the New York state legislature at the age of 27. He was a snappy dresser who enjoyed reading Shakespeare and drinking German beers and Rhine wines. No one expected him to last for more than one or two terms in the rough world of Tammany Democratic politics. In fact, he was defeated in 1905 but voters returned him to office in 1906.

Wagner made a name for himself as a liberal crusader by sponsoring such popular legislation as the Five Cent Fare bill, a law that would have required the New York transit authorities to issue transfers that would make it possible for residents of the tenements of Manhattan to travel all the way to Coney Island for a nickel fare. Although the Five Cent Fare bill never became law, it established Wagner's reputation and led to his election to the New York Senate in 1908. In 1910, Wagner became the youngest president pro tem in state's history. Over the next nine years, Wagner became a prominent member of the progressive movement in New York. He sponsored a large number of progressive legislation such as laws regulating insurance, banking, loan sharks, and tenement housing; encouraging the formation of agricultural cooperatives and public markets; providing scholarships to state colleges and universities; creating an old age pension for public workers, limiting the work week to six days for all workers, and requiring workmen's compensation.

Wagner's service on the Triangle Commission that investigated working conditions and fire safety in factories in New York State between 1911 and 1914 strengthened his support for progressive causes. The state legislature established the commission in response to public outrage over a fire at the Triangle Shirtwaist Company in New York City on March 25, 1911. The fire claimed the lives of 146 young immigrant workers who were unable to escape the flames because company managers locked the exit doors. Many of those who died burned to death or jumped to their death from the eighth and ninth floors in order to escape the flames.[231] Initially, the Triangle Commission just investigated the fire but soon the legislature expanded its mission and it began investigating labor and safety practices in factories throughout New York State. The Commission heard testimony from hundreds of witnesses concerning labor and work practices in the state and visited many of these factories to view working conditions for themselves. Wagner service on the Commission profoundly affected him. By 1915, he had become one of the chief advocates of labor reform and had developed close ties with the Consumers' League, the American Association for Labor Legislation, and other liberal groups.

In 1915, Wagner's wife contracted a disease that within two years made her an invalid. Wanting more time with his family, Wagner ran for and won a seat on the New York Supreme Court, the court of original jurisdiction in civil and criminal cases in 1919. He served on the court until 1926 when at the urging of liberal friends he ran for and won a seat in the U.S. Senate from New York.

Wagner arrived in Washington in March of 1927. A widower by then, he was short, rotund, flawlessly groomed with a Phi Beta Kappa key hanging from his watch chain. He smoked cigars, spoke with a New York east side accent, was social, friendly, approachable, and popular with the press. He was humble, unassuming, sincere and demonstrated "neither the desire not the talent for self-exploitation." He had no flair for showmanship and no real or contrived eccentricities. He was a "small, stocky, inconspicuous, gray-haired senator, who [moved] toward his objectives as irresistibly as a glacier." He had a "Teutonic passion for thoroughness." He was "intent, patient, persuasive," never discouraged by opposition. He was tenacious, doggedly determined with "a pragmatic willingness to compromise, to take half a loaf rather than nothing."[232] He developed a network of supporters at the grass-roots level from organizations like the Consumers' League, the League of Women Voters and labor unions who would apply pressure for passage of his progressive legislation. If he introduced a bill and it failed to pass, his supporters would flood the Senate with letters and telegrams. Wagner would then introduce the bill a second time and if needed a third and fourth. He never tired of answering questions and he was always ready with facts to support his position, carefully checked for accuracy. He verified. He focused on one thing, sponsoring legislation to promote economic and social security. He believed that Capitalism must mend its ways and that "business stability, steady employment, and reasonable security [could] be purchased for the price of planning, foresight and preventive action." [233] He believed that "a steadily increasing measure of security, a steadily rising standard of living, a steadily lengthening period of leisure well spent, a never ending increase in the value and nobility of life," was possible for all. Conservative Republicans thought such ideas to be heresy, of course.

When Wagner took his seat in the Senate, the Republicans were still in power and the country was still enjoying Coolidge prosperity; but forces were in motion that would shortly lead to the stock market crash and the beginning of the Great Depression. The progressive junior senator from New York had arrived at just the right time. His first speech to the Senate was entitled "unemployment" and his first legislative efforts involved labor legislation. Within a month of arriving in Washington, he introduced three bills. The first required the Secretary of Labor to compile accurate statistics on the level of unemployment in the country. The second provided for the establishment of public employment agencies to make it easier for those out of work to find jobs. The third called for the federal government to use its purchasing power to stabilize the economy during downturns and reduce unemployment. Others had proposed these ideas in the past but no one had linked the three. With these three proposals, Wagner quickly established himself as a friend of labor and someone who would become a prominent figure in pushing what would come to be called "New Deal" legislation.

In the 1928 election, Wagner supported Al Smith, a close friend he had met in the New York legislature, against Herbert Hoover. The nation was still enjoying Coolidge Prosperity and rural voters were suspicious of the big city, Catholic governor of New York. Smith was soundly defeated. Samuel Morison in his Oxford History of the American People attributed Hoover's victory simply to the fact that in 1928, "the average workingman was contented, the average business man was prosperous, and neither had any desire for change."[234] He quotes Will Rogers: 'You can't lick this Prosperity thing, even the fellow that hasn't got any is all excited over the idea."[235] Of course, prosperity would not last for long. In October 1929, the stock market crashed. In 1932, Roosevelt won and the New Deal began.

> **LESSON: You benefit greatly if the leader or spokesperson for your cause is also a member of congress.** Wagner plays much the same role in as George Washington Wiley did in passing the Pure Food and Drug Act and Wilbur Cohen did in the passage of Medicare. Unions had the added advantage of having a spokesperson who was also and an influential senator. You need a spokesperson who can gain national attention and lend credibility to your cause. It is even better if that person is also an influential member of congress.

THE NEW DEAL

The National Industrial Recovery Act of 1933 (NIRA) was one of the first pieces of New Deal legislation Robert Wagner helped draft. The NIRA freed businesses from antitrust laws and allowed industry groups to write their own codes of fair competition. In return, it granted labor three safeguards:

(1) Employees would have the right to organize and bargain collectively without interference, restraint or coercion by management,

(2) No one seeking employment could be forced to join a company union or prevented from joining any labor organization of his choosing, and

(3) Employees must comply with maximum hours of work and minimum rates of pay as established by the President.

Labor hailed these provisions as a great step forward and for a time industrial unions made significant progress in signing up members.

While some employers voluntarily complied with the wage and hour provisions (most established a forty-hour week with a minimum wage of $12 to $15 per week), many others resisted and found ways to avoid compliance particularly when it came to collective bargaining. For example, while under the provisions of NIRA employers could not force new hires to join the company union they could and did use every form of pressure they could think of to make it obvious to their employees that joining the company union was highly advisable. Additionally, the National Recovery Administration (NRA), that administered the National Industrial Recovery Act, allowed proportional representation in collective bargaining. That meant that even when a union enrolled a majority of workers, it could not speak for the entire workforce but only for that portion of the workforce that belonged to the union. Management could still include any other employee group, such as the company-run union, in the collective bargaining process. Finally, the NRA allowed companies to hire, retain and promote employees "on the basis of merit." While on the surface this seemed reasonable, in reality anti-union companies could use the merit provision to keep employees from joining a union since the company was the judge of "merit." NOTE: Roosevelt eventually ordered the NRA to remove these "merit" provisions from the codes.

> **LESSON: Beware of easy victories**. Occasionally in the wake of a national emergency, legislation Congress passes legislation that appears to contain some real progressive reforms. Do not prematurely celebrate your easy victory. The "reforms" may not be genuine and even if they are, may not be enforce or enforceable.

Employer evasion and the administration's seeming inability to enforce the provisions of the NRA, angered unions and the number of strikes and work stoppages more than doubled from 1932 to 1933 eventually involving more than 7% of the workforce. By 1935, business was generally ignoring the labor provisions of the NRA and labor unions had concluded that the administration had betrayed them.

In March of 1934, Wagner introduced a bill that sought to close the loopholes in the NIRA that allowed companies to avoid compiling with its labor provisions. The president pressured Wagner to withdraw his bill to give the administration time to see if they could make the existing law work. Wagner initially agree, however when it became apparent that the administration was not successful in its efforts, he reintroduced his act in early 1935 and it passed the Senate with strong labor support on May 16.

THE SUPREME COURT PROVIDES A PIVOTAL EVENT

The Wagner Act had passed the Senate but without administration support, it was languishing in the House. Then on May 27, the Supreme Court produced a pivotal event. It ruled in *A.L.A. Schecter v. the United States* that the National Industrial Recovery Act was unconstitutional. That ruling left labor with no protections whatsoever, something that the Administration found unacceptable both for philosophical and political reasons. Although Roosevelt had initially opposed Wagner's bill, he now embraced it and with pressure from the White House, the House of Representative passed the Wagner Bill, officially the National Labor Relations Act and Roosevelt signed it into law on July 5, 1935.

The Wagner Act was a clear victory for unions. It not only reaffirmed labor's right to organize but explicitly forbid all employer interference. It was an unfair labor practice for an employer to restrain or coerce his employees from exercising their rights, to try to dominate or even contribute financially to the support of any labor organization, to encourage or discourage union membership by discrimination in hiring and firing, or to refuse to bargain collectively. Moreover, representatives designated for collective bargaining by a majority of employees in an appropriate unit, whether it was an employer, craft, or plant unit, were to have exclusive bargaining rights for all employees. The Wagner Act also outlawed company unions.

Congress placed administration of the Wagner Act in the hands of a National Labor Relations Board. The Board's three members had sole authority to determine the appropriate bargaining unit and to supervise the elections wherein employees chose their exclusive representatives for dealing with employers. The board could also hear complaints of unfair labor practices, issue 'cease and desist' orders and petition the courts for enforcement of its orders.

Labor was obviously ecstatic. Businesses were just as obviously horrified. Businessmen predicted that the unions would take their newfound rights to excess and that management would lose control. However, for the moment at least, public opinion was on the side of labor.

BUSINESS LAUNCHES EVEN MORE DETERMINED ANTI-UNION EFFORTS

Of course, winning rights and exercising them are two different things. As in the case of the National Industrial Recovery Act, some businesses voluntarily complied with the new law and began bargaining collectively. Many more resisted and more strikes followed. Some businesses, including 2,500 of America's best know companies, took extreme steps to undermine union organizing efforts.

> Labor spies, stool pigeons, and agents provocateurs were hired to ferret out any evidence of union activity, sow seeds of distrust and suspicion among the workers themselves, and furnish the information which would enable the employers to get rid of all those who might be classed as agitators. Strong-arm squads were maintained in some instances to discourage union membership by more forcible methods, and outside organizers were beaten up, run out of town, and threatened with further violence should they ever show up again.[236]

In total, American businesses spent more than $9,000,000 between 1933 and 1936 in such extreme anti-union activities. The National Association of Manufacturers even publicized and promoted an aggressive anti-union strategy called the "Mohawk Valley Formula.

> This formula blueprinted a systematic campaign to denounce all union organizers as dangerous agitators, align the community in support of employers in the name of law and order, intimidate strikers by mobilizing the local police to break up meetings, instigate "back to work" movements by secretly organizing 'loyal employees,' and set up vigilance committees for protection in getting a struck plant again in operation. The underlying purpose behind the Mohawk Valley formula was to win public support by branding union leaders as subversive and threatening to remove

> the affected industry from the community if local business interests stood by and allowed radical agitators to win control over workers otherwise ready and anxious to cooperate with their employers.[237]

Labor fought back with strike after strike after strike, over 4,700 in 1934 alone involving nearly two million workers.

In the mean time, business challenged the Wagner Act in the courts. Business interests were certain the Supreme Court would declare the act unconstitutional just as they had declared the National Industrial Recovery Act to be unconstitutional. They were wrong. On April 12, 1937, in the case of National Labor Relations Board v. Jones & Laughlin Steel Company, the Supreme Court declared that the Wagner Act was constitutional.[238]

The passage of the Wagner Act in 1935 set off an unprecedented growth in union membership. That year only 13.2% of the nonagricultural labor forces were union members. By 1945, 35.5% were union members. Since then unions have been in almost steady decline. The reasons are complex but one thing is certain, a major contributing factor to the de-unionizing of American was the passage of the Taft-Hartley Act in 1947. The story of how the labor movement went from the Wagner Act victory to Taft-Hartley Act legislative defeat is what we will turn to now.

The passage of the Wagner Act reinforces some of the lessons about getting things done in Washington that we learned from the Pure Food story such as the need for grassroots organizing. The story of the Taft-Hartley Act teaches new lessons about maintaining or, in this case, losing hard won legislative victories.

BUSINESS FIGHTS BACK

The National Labor Relations Act and other New Deal measures such as The Fair Labor Standards Act that set a minimum wage and Social Security and so on were not only victories for labor but also a sharp break in the pattern of government involvement in the employer/employee relationship. Foster Dulles and Melvyn Dujbofsky, authors of *Labor in America*, note that the New Deal legislation was not just a victory for working men and women.

> The basic importance of the New Deal program did not lie in immediate gains or losses for labor but in its recognition that this whole matter of working conditions was no longer the concern of employee and employer alone, but of society as a whole. Democratic capitalism could hardly hope to survive unless the great army of workers could obtain, through concerted effort, the freedom and the security which as individuals they were powerless to defend in an industrialized society. The New Deal's policy was pro-labor, but it was pro-labor in order to stabilize an unbalanced economy. It looked to the well-being of workers in the conviction that upon their contentment and security rested the future stability of American capitalism and democracy.[239]

Businessmen, Republicans, and conservatives just saw the New Deal as an evil intrusion into the affairs of the deserving and a threat to free market capitalism, an intrusion they were determined to reverse. It took them twelve years but they ultimately succeeded to an extent no one thought possible.

THE NATIONAL ASSOCIATION OF MANUFACTURERS

The National Association of Manufacturers. (NAM) led the campaign to undo the advances of the Wagner Act. Starting in 1937, shortly after the Supreme Court ruled that the National Labor Relations Act was constitutional, NAM launched a coordinated propaganda campaign.

> Using radio, news, cartoons, editorials, advertising, leaflets, and other devices, often with their source not disclosed, the 'education program' reached every important industrial community...[The NAM] message was directed against 'labor agitators,' against

> governmental measures to alleviate industrial distress, against labor unions, and for the advantages of the status quo in industrial relations, of which company-dominated unions were still a part. Antiunion employers and local employers' association executives used the propaganda material ...to combat the organizational drive of unions in local industrial areas."[240]

The Chamber of Commerce joined with the NAM to argue that the Warner Act "increased strife and created new inequalities in industry," and that action was needed in Congress "to correct unsound legislation so that it [would] operate for the social benefit of the whole people." [241]

The most fundamental charge opponents made was that the Wagner Act was biased in favor of unions. Robert Wagner had this rejoinder to the charge of bias. "If an uninitiated person examined the Act in a vacuum or on the planet Mars, he would be fairly overwhelmed by the obvious justice of these criticisms [of bias]," said Wagner. However, he went on, when one viewed the Act in the total context of the economic, social, and legal restrictions that American law and traditional labor relations placed on workers and unions then one would see that the charges were "absolutely meaningless."[242] By analogy, Wagner noted, no one would criticize traffic laws as biased because they regulated the speed at which cars could travel but not the speed at which pedestrians could walk.

Opponents of the Wagner Act aimed much of their criticism at the National Labor Relations Board that was responsible for administering the act. They made three major charges. First, they said, the NLRB was biased. It acted as prosecutor, judge and jury, prejudged cases, and could not make fair decisions. In addition, subordinates rather than the board itself often made decisions. Second, due process was denied because the NLRB investigators were biased and employers could not get a fair hearing or impartial decision. Finally, they said, the Board did not weigh all the evidence and accepted evidence that would not stand up in court.[243]

None of these charges was true although they gained some credence among the general population simply because opponents of the legislation repeated them so often with such force. In respect to being prosecutor, judge and jury, as Harry Millis and Emily Brown, authors of *From the Wagner Act to Taft-Hartley: A Study of National Labor Policy and Labor Relations*, point out, this is a charge that can be made against all regulatory agencies not just the NLRB. Additionally, as Millis and Brown note the Board itself took steps to separate the investigative and prosecution functions internally from the decision-making functions. In their research, Millis and Brown could find no real evidence of abuse when they examined the Board's decisions. Second, while it was true that the staff or the NLRB believed in the act, such a belief does not necessarily imply bias and prejudice although it is true that in the early years of the act "the enthusiastic staff, operating in an atmosphere of great hostility, some of the criticism had a basis in fact."[244] Millis and Brown admit "the staff…did not achieve the superhuman feat of administering the Act so tactfully that those who came in conflict with it enjoyed the experience."[245] To some extent it was a question of manners, of field examiners and trial attorneys who were young and lacking the polish of professional courtesy. Some of them let their enthusiasm for the purposes of the Act show when cold objectivity in the investigation of a particular set of facts was called for. However, the facts were very human, emotionally charged facts in many cases, and complete objectivity was difficult to achieve. Finally, the charges of mishandling of evidence or using evidence that would not stand up in court were true in respect to a very small number of cases. In fact, of the seven hundred rulings by the courts on the Board's cases by 1947, only four of the Board's decisions were set aside. In many cases, the courts complemented the Board on its fairness, courtesy, and impartiality. For example in the case of NLRB v Weirton Steel Co. in 1943, the court said, "the record does not justify a finding that the Board's decision was reached as a result of bias and prejudice or that the manner in which the hearings were conducted denied the company due process of law. On the contrary we are left with the strong impression that much of the conduct complained of was deliberately provoked by counsel for the Company, possibly to lay a basis for a defense to charges which otherwise could not be met."[246] Of course, critics never mentioned those complements.

LESSON: Opponents of progressive legislation typically make their case for repeal of the legislation by citing so called "abuses" that often have no or very little basis in fact as did the opponents of the Wagner Act. If you fail to mount a swift and strong defense, the opposition will win, not because they are right but because they know that if they repeat an untruth long enough with enough force of certainty and conviction, most Americans eventually will begin to believe that what they are hearing is in fact true. It is doubtful whether the Taft-Hartley Act would ever have been passed accept for the years of a constant drumbeat of false accusations of abuses of the Warner Act that went largely unchallenged. Do not expect Americans to recognize the difference between what is the truth and what is a lie unless you aggressively and repeatedly point out the difference. Lies always have the advantage. Remember Mark Twain's warning: "A lie can travel halfway around the world while the truth is still putting on its shoes."

UNIONS BEGING TO LOSE PUBLIC SUPPORT

The first signs that the false accusations were beginning to sway public opinion away from support of the Wagner Act and unions came at the state level. Initially states adopted "Baby Wagner Acts" which differed little from the federal statute. However, by 1939, first in California and then in many other states, states began enacting "equalizing" laws sponsored by the National Association of Manufacturers, the Chamber of Commerce and other business organizations. These laws placed restrictions on union activities such as:

- prohibiting coercion or intimidation of workers in respect to joining or not joining a union,
- prohibiting picketing or boycotting an employer except when a strike had been called,
- requiring a majority of employees to call a strike, and
- banning mass picketing, sit-down strikes or secondary boycotts.

Texas passed an "antiviolence" law that made it a felony for anyone to use force or violence or threaten to use force or violence to prevent another person from working, as for example, crossing a picket line. Georgia passed a law requiring unions to give a minimum of thirty days notice to employers before calling a strike. Colorado prohibited strikes in any industry with a "public interest." Arkansas passed a law requiring a person to post a $5,000 bond before seeking advertising for union publications. Colorado required union business agents to be registered and required unions to submit regular financial reports to the secretary of state. Many states adopted "right to work" laws and banned closed shops.

Courts found many of these provisions unconstitutional but states continued to enact them. By 1947, only three states, New York, Rhode Island, and Connecticut, had comprehensive labor relations acts like the Wagner Act. Most others had adopted so-called "equalizing" laws that restricted, often severely, union organizing and collective bargaining activities.

The passage of these anti-union statutes at the state level was a clear indication that the propaganda campaign against unions that NAM and others had launched was beginning to turn the tide of public opinion against unions. While these developments worried many union officials, they were not sufficiently worried to launch a united and effective counteroffensive. They allowed business interest free reign. Consequently, Americans heard only one side. Predictably, Americans came to believe that side of the story. Unions were bad. Unions were too powerful. The Wagner Act and Baby Wagner Acts were unfair. Congress should amend or even repeal them.

Opponents hammered home three main arguments for changes in the law:

1. Unions had too much power in the labor/management relationship due to favorable treatment by Wagner Act
2. Unions were not acting in a responsible manner in meeting their obligations to industry, the public or to individual employees.
3. The playing field should be "equalized." Unions should have equivalent responsibilities and restrictions as Wagner Act imposed on employers.

Although the arguments sounded reasonable, they were misleading. The amount of power unions had depended greatly on location and industry. For example, the Teamsters were very powerful and largely bargained with small employers while unions struggled to gain recognition in the textile industry. Unions in the shipping industry in the Pacific Coast were powerful as were unions in mass production but as late as the mid-1940s unions were struggling in their dealings with chain-store companies. In respect to acting responsibly, there were abuses on both sides. Finally, while "equalizing the law" sounded good and garnered much public support, "much of it was [employer] sales talk with little basis in fact [and was] in reality aimed at simply reducing the power of unions. It reflected a struggle over industrial and political power [not a search for fairness or equal treatment.]"[247]

For its part, NAM continued to use newspaper ads and planted stories in the media arguing for a labor policy "that will treat labor and management exactly alike, and above all be fair to the public."[248] While a minority in NAM argued for total repeal of the Wagner Act, NAM leadership opted for a different approach. Rather than repealing the Act, they would seek only "equalizing amendments" along with legislation to outlaw "monopolistic" practices and certain types of strikes.[249]

In 1947, NAM published a pamphlet outlining its "public relations" methods that said its "targets" were "The great, unorganized, inarticulate, so-called 'middle-class'; the younger generation…; and the opinion-makers of the nation." [250] In January of that year, NAM ran a full-page ad in the New York Times, with the headline: "For the Good of all." The ad called for "cooperation," fairness, industrial harmony, equal obligations of unions and employers, the elimination of monopolistic practices whether by unions or employers, freedom to strike except under certain circumstances, freedom from coercion or compulsory union membership, for "impartial administration of improved laws primarily designed to advance the interests of the whole public while still safeguarding the rights of all employees" and for minimum government intervention in labor disputes." [251] Other ads followed with headlines such as:

"How about Some Pro-Public Legislation?"

"Industry-wide Bargaining is No Bargain for You"

"The Road to Freedom for the American Worker"

The ads emphasized "fairness," "equity," and the "right to work." Most were long on sound-good slogans, short on specifics, long on half-truths and deliberate misrepresentations, and short on truth. However, the ads sounded so reasonable. Industry was not anti-union, it was pro-public, pro-American, and even pro-employee, and it wanted to protect employee rights from evil union demands.

Unions responded to what they saw as an anti-union conspiracy on the part of big business with their own ads and public relations efforts but the union efforts were less well organized and well funded than the efforts of anti-union forces. Additionally, the press was generally pro-business and anti-union. According to one study of union treatment in the press at the time, "the viewpoints of organized labor, presented in positive terms, did not appear in any of the major periodicals of wide circulation… [while] the viewpoints of management and related groups that favored the [Wagner] Act appeared frequently." [252]

> **LESSON: Monitor the press and public opinion closely and be prepared to launch an aggressive public relations campaign whenever you notice the first signs of losing support.** Unions paid a big price when they failed to respond to aggressively and in a coordinated manner to the attacks on the Wagner Act and unions in general from the NAM and others.

1943—THE SMITH-CONNALLY, WAR LABOR DISPUTES ACT

At the beginning of World War II, American unions took a no-strike pledge for the duration of the war and in the first two years of the war the number of strikes dropped dramatically. By 1943 however, strikes were increasing. The American public, already turning anti-union due to the success of the NAM propaganda effort, resented unions for undertaking strikes and other work stoppages during the war seeing them as endangering the war effort. That resentment led to the passage of the Smith-Connally or War Labor Disputes Act of 1943 over the President's veto. The Act not only gave the President the power to take over war plants if necessary, as he had requested but added a number of anti-union provisions. These included a provision that made it unlawful for unions to "interfere" with the war effort or make political contributions. Additionally the act required unions in Defense industries to give thirty days notice of a strike and required a majority vote of employees before they could call a strike. Although the act was to terminate six months after the end of hostilities, unions were still angry that Congress had passed such an act largely as a reaction to the strike of John L. Lewis's United Mine Workers when most unions were honoring their no strike pledge.* The President of the Congress of Industrial Organizations (CIO) issued a statement denouncing the law:

> The labor-baiting and Administration-hating forces in Congress enacted this vicious anti-labor measure to wreak vengeance for the acts of one individual (Lewis) who flouted the needs of the nation for continuous production of vital war materials, ignored the machinery established for the adjustment of all labor disputes in order to guarantee continuous production, and recklessly caused a national strike in the coal fields.[253]

Republican Senator Robert Taft responded that the act, rather than causing strikes would prevent them. He was wrong. Unions filed no less than fifty strike notices a month after the act passed.

The number of strikes in 1944 exceeded those in 1943. They were to explode after V.J. Day on August 14, 1945. The next 12 months saw no less than 4,600 work stoppages involving more than 5 million workers about a third of the union workforce. Most of these were over wages and hours. With the end of the war, factories that had been churning out war goods began shifting their focus to peacetime commodities. As they did so they cut hours and resisted demands for wage increases since they did not know how long the conversion from a wartime to peacetime economy

---

* The Act was passed largely in response to a strike by half million mine workers in 1943 that most Americans saw as a disruption of the war effort and that led to President Roosevelt seizing the mines.

would take. Workers saw prices increase while employers cut their wages. Struggling to maintain their income levels, freed from the no-strike pledge and facing an increasingly stubborn management, union after union went out on strike.

THE WAR ENDS AND UNION/MANAGEMENT CONFLICT INTENSIFIES

When World War II ended, the nation faced the task of switching from wartime to peacetime economy. Most workers saw their weekly earnings increase during the war because of longer hours and overtime pay. With the end of the war, workers faced the prospect of shorter hours and less or no overtime pay as the government canceled war orders. Wage issues became a major concern particularly in regard to the relation between wages and prices. Unions had long argued that employers should be required to keep wages in step with the cost of living so that workers' standard of living increased during good economic times and were protected from decline during bad times. The unions insisted that employers make no exception even in times of war so they were certainly unprepared to make an exception in times of peace but that was what was happening. Between April and October 1945, average weekly earnings in manufacturing industries decreased 12.9% while the cost of living began to rise. Unions, particularly in durable goods manufacturing, demanded that wages be increased and that the cost of living be held level through government price controls so that workers' standard of living did not fall during the war to peace time conversion. This came at a time when the War Labor Board, that had mediated labor disputes during the war in areas critical for national defense, was being dissolved and a National Wage Stabilization Board, which was to take over the War Labor Board's functions, was just becoming operational. With the abolishment of the NWLB and the National Stabilization Board not yet fully functioning, there was no government agency with the authority to adjudicate wage-rate disputes between labor and management. So, strikes continued.

In September 1945, 43,000 refinery workers went out on strike demanding that even with a return to a 40-hour week companies pay them at the level they had received for the 52-hour week standard during the war years. The Oil companies refused, even rejecting a proposal for arbitration suggested by the Secretary of Labor. By October, there were gasoline shortages throughout the nation. Eventually, Truman ordered the Navy Department to seize and operate the refineries. The number of strikes continued to increase throughout the remainder of 1945, finally reaching levels considerably above those prior to the war.

TRUMAN CALLS FOR A LABOR-MANAGEMENT CONFERENCE

Truman expressed sympathy for workers and the need for price stability and wage increases "to cushion the shock to …workers, to sustain adequate purchasing power, and to raise the national income."[254] He called for a conference where representatives of labor and management could "discuss their common problems and …settle differences in the public interest."[255]

Truman's labor-management conference got underway on November 5. Representatives of the AFL, CIO, the United Mine Workers, and the Railroad Brotherhoods attended along with representatives from the National Association of Manufacturers and the Chamber of Commerce. President Truman in his opening address to the conference attendees stressed the need for a "broad foundation for industrial peace and progress."[256] He urged the attendees to find a way to resolve their differences without stopping production and warned that if they could not find an answer then the American people would look elsewhere for a solution. Conference attendees were able to reach some consensus on minor issues but there was sharp disagreement between labor and management on the major questions of wages, procedures that should be followed when collective bargaining broke down, and whether any amendments to the Wagner Act would be made (the union opposed any changes to the Act.) The conference closed on November 30 having made little progress. Most attendees left disappointed. Truman reported to Congress that the fact that labor and management met for three weeks indicated some progress and there were some agreements on broad principles, however "on all the important questions of how to avoid work stoppages, the conference arrived at no accord."[257] The unions and business had wasted a last chance to avoid major labor-management conflict.

> **LESSON: Never give the appearance of being unwilling to compromise, even when you are unwilling to compromise.** The unions who had already been losing public and press support for some time took much of the blame for the failure of the Truman conference, particularly when it came to the issue that troubled American voters the most, the work stoppages. While the differences between labor and management were genuine, unions made a tactical error in not giving at least the appearance of making concessions. Remember, while it is important to do what is right, it is even more important for Americans to think that you are not only doing what is right but what is in their best interest.

THE GENERAL MOTORS STRIKE-1945-1946

One of the largest of the post-war strikes, that of the 320,000 United Auto Workers against General Motors, began on November 21st while Truman's labor-management conference was still in session. UAW head Walter Reuther argued that with its profits General Motors could increase wages without raising prices. When the company refused, he demanded that the company open its books to prove that price increases would be necessary if the company were to meet union demands. The company responded that the union had no business meddling with prices, they were a company prerogative and opening the books was totally out of question.

The GM strike lasted 113 days and eventually involved over 200,000 workers at 92 GM plants. The company lost an estimated $600 million in sales and the total cost of the strike was nearly one billion dollars. The strikers lost four month's wages. Those who were fortunate enough to have some savings saw them wiped out. Those without a nest egg relied largely upon the moral and financial support of friends and relatives.

Seven hundred and fifty thousand United Steelworkers struck in January 1946 demanding a two dollar per day increase in base pay. The steel producers refused claiming that price restrictions imposed by the government made any wage increases impossible.

The President appointed fact-finding boards in both instances and appealed to the unions to have their members return to work. While the unions showed some willingness to compromise, particular in the steel workers strike where the union agreed to drop it demand to 18 ½ cents an hour, in both cases the companies refused to give in to union demands and the President's entreaties. The largest steel producer United States Steel offered 15 cents per hour provided price ceilings were increased. As the strike dragged on steel production plummeted from 85% of capacity to just 6% affecting a wide range of industries dependent on steel.

Major strikes followed in key industries, coal, public utilities, electric power, transportation and others. There were strikes at General Electric, and Westinghouse. A coal strike resulted in electrical "dim-outs" and "brownouts" due to lack of fuel to power generators at electrical power plants. A countrywide railway stoppage halted all rail transportation across the country.

Strikes at major companies affected thousands of Americans directly or indirectly. Consumers seeking to purchase goods found the products they wanted to buy were no longer available. Employees of smaller supplier companies found their hours cut and jobs threatened as big company parts orders dried up. The wave of strikes in 1946 and 1947, an election year, caused widespread public interest and concern and swept into office a new Congress with many members dedicated to amending the Wagner Act and exercising greater control over union activities.

ANGRY UNIONS AND ANGRIER AMERICANS

Union members, a quarter of the total workforce, were angry and frustrated with the need to strike repeatedly to get decent wages and working hours. Union leaders charged that big employers were actually inviting strikes in the hopes of building anti-union sentiment. They pointed to a pamphlet written by John W. Scoville, an economist for Chrysler in which Scoville predicted that "as industrial turmoil increases, more and more people will see the evils generated by collective bargaining, and [business] should look forward to the time when all federal labor laws will be repealed."[258] Whether or not big business was actually inviting strikes, he was right about public reaction. While union members were angry at business for constantly forcing them to strike, the other three quarters of non-union working Americans were just as angry with the unions for striking.

> Actions by some unions had made all unions vulnerable to attack and aroused irritation, fear, and resentment; and the labor movement, unfortunately to little sensitive to public opinion about strikes and other union actions, was adamant against any revision of the Wagner Act and failed to propose solutions for problems on which the public was with some justice aroused against labor. The hostile press contributed. The public naturally assumes that the union is responsible for a strike, without inquiring whether management is in some cases equally or even more responsible because of failure to seek a reasonable basis of settlement.[259]

Rather than seeking to find common ground with management on changes to the Wagner Act that were truly needed, unions and supporters of the Act fought a defensive battle seeking to protect the Act from any change what-so-ever. In contrast, those who sought to repeal the Wagner Act had long since shifted their focus to a nationwide propaganda campaign to convince the public that all they were seeking were reasonable measures to amend the Act to reign in union excesses. The disruptive strikes of 1946 and 1947, while justified from the union point of view and perhaps even encouraged by management seeking to undermine the unions, contributed to growing public acceptance of the anti-union, anti-Wagner Act message. They set the stage for passage of the Taft-Hartley act and gutting of the most important pro-union provisions of the Wagner Act.

The labor unions went too far and lost public support. In 1943, when the miners went on strike nearly three-quarters of Americans supported government action to take over the mines in order to force an end to the strike. In 1946, sixty-eight percent of Americans favored Congressional action to limit strikes. Additionally a growing number of Americans were coming to the conclusion that union leaders were calling strikes for trivial reasons or for personal gain and that most strikes could have been avoided if the unions had simply acted reasonably and negotiated in good faith. Congressmen and senators that had supported labor were soundly defeated in the Congressional election in 1946 resulting in an influx of new anti-labor members of Congress.

> **LESSON: Americans, even those who support reforms, rarely want to pay much of a price for change.** One of the most infuriating things for progressives is the inconsistency of the American voter. In general, Americans want their government to take action to make their lives better. On the other hand, Americans do not want government involved in their lives. Americans want governments to provide benefits and services but Americans do not want to pay taxes to fund those benefits and services. In the case of labor unions, Americans thought it was perfectly fine for workers to organize and to even occasionally strike to get better wages and working conditions. That is, it was all right for unions to strike until the strikes became an inconvenience. Keep this quirk of American nature in mind. Whether you are conducting protests, staging image events, or writing policy always consider how you actions might affect the average American. Will your protest unduly disrupt the average American's life? Will your actions overly inconvenience him? Will, God forbid, your proposed reform have to be paid for by a significant increase in taxes? If so, you risk losing public support. You must maintain a delicate balance between doing what is necessary to achieve reform and gain attention without going too far. In the 1940s, the unions overreached. There were too many strikes and too many of the strikes did not seem justified to the average citizen. Unions made a big, big mistake and it cost them dearly.

THE BEGINNING OF THE END

President Truman asked for labor legislation in his 1947 State of the Union message. What he requested was much weaker that what the Congress ultimately passed but the fact that even Truman was asking for amendments to the Warner Act made the passage of some amendments inevitable particularly since Republicans now controlled Congress. By this time, given public sentiment, something like the Taft-Hartley Act was almost inevitable.

Seventeen bills to amend the Wagner Act were introduced in the House in January of 1947 and fifteen similar bills were introduced in the Senate. By the end of February, there were no fewer than sixty-five bills to curb union activity under consideration in Congress. Some of these were mild. For example the "Public Rights in Labor Disputes" bill introduced by five Republicans in the House would have set up a federal system of compulsory arbitration and given the President the power to issue an order, enforceable by court injunction, prohibiting a strike that threatened public health and safety. Union leaders opposed even these moderate efforts, rejecting any revisions to the Wagner Act at all fearing that if they accepted even minor revisions they would open the door for the destruction of the act. They got Taft-Hartley.

> **LESSON: Never draw a line in the sand and stubbornly refuse to compromise.** If you demand it all, you may get nothing or lose what you have already achieved. Progressives do not like to compromise. They particularly do not like backing away from hard won victories. Success takes so long and is so rarely achieved that it is hard to even consider giving up any piece of the achievement. However, sometimes you have to agree to modifications to legislation sought by conservatives or you risk having the legislation completely overturned. Unions could have accepted one of the alternatives to the Taft-Hartley Act and kept most of the gains they had achieved through the passage of the Warner Act. They refused. That was a big mistake.

THE TAFT-HARTLEY ACT

Taft-Hartley actually started out as two bills, one sponsored by Senate Labor Committee Chairman Taft and the other by Fred Hartley of NJ, Chairman of House Committee on Education and Labor.

The House held six weeks of hearings on the Hartley Act amassing over 3,800 pages of testimony from more than 130 witnesses. More than 40% of the witnesses were representatives of employers or employer associations such as NAM or corporate labor lawyers. Only 27 representatives from unions testified. Most of the testimony consisted of coordinated, consistent, and constant set of criticisms of the National Labor Relations Board. The Board itself was given only limited time to answer the charges and then at times of the day when press coverage was limited. The Chairman of the NLRB was given just three hours to testify and much of his prepared remarks, intended to rebut previous testimony, was cut and inserted in the record without comment and therefore never heard by committee members or the press. Supposedly, the House bill was written with employer and industry anti-union assistance. In fact, the final House bill was similar in many respects to legislation NAM had proposed in 1946.

As finally presented to the full House for vote, the Hartley bill was 66 pages. Many sections of the bill were difficult to understand without constant reference back to other sections of the bill. The bill was presented to the house not as an attack on the Wagner Act but rather as a "labor bill of rights," a "boon to labor," an "aid to smoother labor-management relations," and as an improvement to the Wagner Act that awarded "privileges and protections that most working people desired."[260]

Proponents of the Amendments were portrayed as the "real friends of labor, the real champions of the public, for they had considered all the interests involved and not only industry's or labor's alone." "The bill," supporters argued was "a fair bill and would protect the rights of workers. The Hartley Bill," they argued, "was not harsh; it was not restrictive; it was, on the contrary, as fair and unbiased as the Wagner Act had not been in its intent, its interpretation, and its administration." Anyway, proponents went on, the House had a "mandate from the people" to enact major reform legislation.[261]

Supporters of labor countered that "the bill was one-sided, giving all to the interests of business and industry; furthermore, the wishes of employers expressed during the hearings had been given full satisfaction while labor appeals were ignored. "[262] Those favoring the amendments were portraying themselves as friends of labor when, in fact, labor's most bitter enemies were the ones leading the fight for passage of the bill. The Republicans did not, said supporters of labor, win a mandate to reform national labor policy. The voters had been reacting to basic concerns about inflation, housing shortages, and lack of action on a minimum wage and extension of Social Security, none of which were addressed by the Hartley bill. Finally, the changes were being pushed through by the majority without time for an adequate hearing or for the public to develop a clear understanding of how radical these proposed changes were and how much harm they would do to the Wagner Act protections and the labor movement in general. Supporters of labor tried to have portions of the bill reconsidered but it was obvious that they were too late; the bill would pass substantially as reported out of committee.

> **LESSON: Respond immediately and forcefully to knock down conservative claims that the bills they sponsored are "fair and balanced," "a boom to the working man/woman," are based upon a "mandate from the people," and so on.** These claims are usually false and misleading but they sound good. You cannot leave them unchallenged. You must forcefully proclaim that such claims are false and show evidence that you are right. Do not wait. Any delay in attacking conservative claims is dangerous. Unions responded to the conservative claims about the Taft-Hartley Act but, by the time they did, it was too late. The bills had progressed too far.

As in the House, spokespersons from business and industry dominated the Senate hearing on the Taft bill. Out of 97 witnesses the Senate committee heard from, less than a third were representatives or supporters of labor. The bill that emerged was, while better organized than the House version, long, complicated and contained many technical references to labor law that a layperson would have difficulty understanding. As in the case of the House bill, opponents of labor and the Wagner Act had major input in writing the Senate version.

Those in favor of the Taft act argued that it was fair and equitable, simply "equalized" existing law to encourage free collective bargaining, and was neither harsh nor restrictive. Anyway, they argued, the Wagner Act had been experimental, not entirely successful in meeting its objectives and poorly administered by biased officials. Congress needed to change the law to make labor policy more equitable, reduce strikes and bring about peace between management and labor.

Labor supporters countered that the Taft Act would do much damage to the Wagner Act and contained "barriers, traps, and pitfalls" that would make the settlement of disputes more difficult and create misunderstandings and conflict. Additionally, as labor supporters in the House had argued, the Taft act did nothing to address the real problems, particularly the imbalance between wages, prices and profits. The Republican majority was blaming labor for the post-war unrest when the real cause of the strikes and turmoil could be found in the basic social and economic issues the country was facing as it moved from a war to peacetime economy.

The House and Senate versions of the bill passed with more than the two-thirds vote required to override a veto so there was little doubt that a bill severely weakening the Warner Act would become law. The House bill was harsher and more anti-union but union supporters could find little to like in either version. Because of the threat of a veto, the House conferees made more concessions and the final bill as reported out of the conference committee and sent to the House and Senate was closer to the Senate than the House version.

The bill passed the House on June 4, 1947 by a vote of 320 to 79 with 217 Republicans and 103 Democrats voting for the bill and 66 Democrats, 12 Republicans and one American Laborite voting against. The Senate passed the bill by a vote of 54 to 17 with 37 Republicans and 17 Democrats in favor and 15 Democrats and 2 Republicans opposed.

Unions staged huge rallies throughout the country urging the President to veto the Taft-Hartley bill, which he did, as expected, on June 20. In rejecting the bill, Truman wrote:

> The most fundamental test which I have applied to this bill is whether it would strengthen or weaken American democracy in the present critical hour. This bill is perhaps the most serious economic and social legislation of the past decade. Its effects—for good or ill—would be felt for decades to come. I have concluded that the bill is a clear threat to the successful working of our democratic society. [263]

Among other things, the President warned that the bill would:

- increase strikes,
- deprive workers of vital protection,
- discriminate against employees, and
- be unduly burdensome or actually unworkable.

Congress overrode the President's veto. Taft-Hartley became law

THE IMPACT OF TAFT-HARTLEY

The Taft-Hartley Act did some good things. For example, it imposed obligations and restraints on unions similar to those the Wagner Act imposed on employers. On the other hand, Taft-Hartley definitely sided with employers when it came to labor-management relations.

> Highly effective weapons were given to an employer who sought to break a union or to break a strike. Full use of his freedom to carry on campaigns by the spoken or written word, refusal to continue recognition, filing of an employer petition or instigating a decertification petition filed by employees, with strikers not eligible to vote if it had been possible to replace them, the one year rule protecting the employer against further efforts to obtain recognition should an election go against the union, the possibility of charges against the union and even injunctions if the union, harassed and fighting for its life, over stepped the line, or even

> approached it—all these added up to substantial aid and comfort to an employer who undertook to fight a union with all the help he could obtain from the law. And there was no comparable pressure upon him to seek an orderly resolution of the dispute... The weapons were there, available to be used by an employer at his discretion. All this invited conflict rather than reliance upon collective bargaining and peaceable means of settling disputes.[264]

At the end of the war in 1945, one third of the civilian, nonagricultural labor force belonged to a union and union membership and union political influence was expected to increase steadily. In spite of the Taft-Hartley Act, labor continued to have political influence and union support contributed to the passage of legislation to improve health care, education, social security, the minimum wage and other liberal/progressive causes. However, by the late 60's with the election of Nixon and accent of the Republican Party unions began to lose political influence. Reagan's use of the power of the state to end the Air Traffic Controller's strike in 1981 sent a clear signal to business that strike breaking by whatever means was acceptable, even endorsed, by the state. By 2009, only a little more than 12 percent of American workers were members of a union. Nearly a quarter had been union members in 1945.

LESSONS IN WINNING AND LOSING

The passing of the Warner and Taft-Hartley acts provide important lessons in getting things done in Washington and what it takes to protect hard won victories. First, pro-union forces secured passage of the Warner Act because they won grassroots popular support. They won the PR war. Twelve years later, they lost the PR war in the face of a determined propaganda campaign orchestrated by the National Association of Manufacturers (NAM). Additionally, their own overreaching in calling strike after strike angered the very people whose support they most needed, American voters. Once unions lost popular support, their Wagner Act victory quickly unraveled. Second, with Robert Wagner, pro-union forces had a strong advocate and effective vote buyer in Congress who could secure victory. Wagner could not lead the struggle to defeat Taft-Hartley because he was ill and no one stood up to take his place. On the other hand, anti-union forces had strong advocates and vote buyers in Robert Taft and Fred Hartley. Finally, pro-union forces forgot a central principal of politics-compromise. Arthur McClure, author of *The Truman Administration and the Problems of Postwar Labor, 1945-1948* writes this about the chief mistake union leaders made that condemned them to Taft-Hartley:

> Had the unions shown more of a willingness to reform themselves, then perhaps the remedies that were so restrictive would not have been offered or would have at least been of a milder nature. However, as Joel Seidman stated, "while offering no guarantees that they would stamp out offensive behavior on the part of their affiliates, labor leaders attacked every proposed regulatory measure in extreme terms." At the same time, they offered no positive program for righting the evils that even they admitted did exist. Therefore, the unions created a climate of opinion in which they ultimately paid the penalty for their shortsightedness with the passage of the Taft-Hartley Act.[265]

In the next chapter, we will take another look at strategies conservatives employ to kill reform, even reform that is highly popular. This time we will go all the way back to the 1800s and the passage of the Sherman Act, the first effort to rein in big business. The idea about doing something to protect Americans from the excesses of big business was highly popular at the time. Recognizing that it was political unfeasible to defeat proposed reform, conservatives passed a law that was wildly popular but in reality was so vague as to be essentially unenforceable. We will learn new lessons in the saga of the Sherman Act including that progressives should always beware of conservatives who seemingly want to cooperate. They may only want to highjack progress. Additionally, we will learn the importance of implementation. You have accomplished nothing if the reform legislation you struggled so hard to pass is implemented poorly or not implemented at all.

A SUMMARY OF LESSONS FROM THE STRUGGLE FOR WORKER'S RIGHT TO ORGANIZE

Grassroots organizing in essential. Again we see that the effort to right a wrong, in this case the exploitation of workers, begins far away from Washington

Do not expect the courts to be on your side. Regardless of level—state, local federal or even the Supreme Court—courts rarely lead or are even on the side of reform. Voters do not elect nor do politicians appoint people to the bench for challenging conservative keep-things-as-they-are doctrine. Judges are supposed to follow precedent and do nothing to change things. Courts are typically the enemy of progress.

There must be some national coordination of grassroots efforts. Once again, we see the need for national coordination of grassroots efforts. It was not until the growth of national unions that the labor movement had any chance of pushing significant legislation through Congress.

Conservatives always label any reform, particularly any reform that seeks to alleviate the plight of working Americans as un-American. You must never let them get away with that argument. Whatever you propose, expect opponents to accuse you of engaging in a conspiracy to destroy the American way of life. You must address that charge directly by turning it on its head with the argument that solving problems and seeking to improve the lives of average Americans is not un-American but indeed the most American thing that anyone can do. Remember this rule. The worst thing you can do is to ignore your opponents' attacks. Counter attack. Respond in kind.

Respond immediately and forcefully to knock down conservative claims that the bills they sponsored are "fair and balanced," "a boom to the working man/woman," are based upon a "mandate from the people," and so on. These claims are usually false and misleading but they sound good. You can allow them to go unchallenged. You must forcefully proclaim that such claims are false and show evidence that you are right. Do not wait. Any delay in attacking conservative claims is dangerous. Unions responded to the conservative claims about the Taft-Hartley Act but by the time they did it was too late. The bills had progressed too far.

You benefit greatly if the leader or spokesperson for your cause is also a member of congress. Wagner played much the same role in as George Washington Wiley did in passing the Pure Food and Drug Act and Wilbur Cohen did in the passage of Medicare. Unions had the added advantage of having a spokesperson who was also an an influential senator. You need a spokesperson that can gain national attention and lend credibility to your cause. It is even better if that person is also an influential member of congress.

Beware of easy victories. Occasionally in the wake of a national emergency, Congress passes legislation that appears to contain some real progressive reforms. Do not prematurely celebrate your easy victory. The "reforms" may not be genuine and even if they are, may not be enforced or enforceable.

Opponents of progressive legislation typically make their case for repeal of the legislation by citing so called "abuses" that often have no or very little basis in fact as did the opponents of the Wagner Act. If you fail to mount a swift and strong defense, the opposition will win, not because they are right but because they know that if they repeat an untruth long enough with enough force of certainty and conviction, most Americans eventually will begin to believe that what they are hearing is in fact true. It is doubtful whether the Taft-Hartley Act would ever have been passed accept for the years of a constant drumbeat of false accusations of abuses of the Warner Act that went largely unchallenged. Do not expect Americans to recognize the difference between what is the truth and what is a lie unless you aggressively and repeatedly point out the difference. Lies always have the advantage. Remember Mark Twain's warning: "A lie can travel halfway around the world while the truth is still putting on its shoes."

Monitor the press and public opinion closely and be prepared to launch an aggressive public relations campaign whenever you notice the first signs of losing support. Unions paid a big price when they failed to respond aggressively and in a coordinated manner to the attacks on the Wagner Act and unions in general from the NAM and others.

Never give the appearance of being unwilling to compromise, even when you are unwilling to compromise. The unions who had already been losing public and press support for some time took much of the blame for the failure of the Truman conference, particularly when it came to the issue that troubled American voters the most, the work stoppages. While the differences between labor and management were genuine, unions made a tactical error in not giving at least the appearance of making concessions. Remember, while it is important to do what is right, it is even more important for Americans to think that you are not only doing what is right but what is in their best interest. Never draw a line in the sand and stubbornly refuse to compromise. If you demand it all, you may get nothing or lose what you have already achieved. Progressives do not like to compromise. They particularly do not like backing away from hard won victories. Success takes so long and is so rarely achieved that it is hard to even consider giving up any piece of the achievement. However, sometimes you have to agree to modifications to legislation sought by conservatives or you risk having the legislation completely overturned. Unions could have accepted one of the alternatives to the Taft-Hartley Act and kept most of the gains they had achieved through the passage of the Warner Act. They refused. That was a big mistake.

Americans, even those who support reforms, rarely want to pay much of a price for change. One of the most infuriating things for progressives is the inconsistency of the American voter. In general, Americans want their government to take action to make their lives better. On the other hand, Americans do not want government involved in their lives. Americans want governments to provide benefits and services but Americans do not want to pay taxes to fund those benefits and services. In the case of labor unions, Americans thought it was perfectly fine for workers to organize and to even occasionally strike to get better wages and working conditions. That is, it was all right for unions to strike until the strikes became an inconvenience. Keep this quirk of American nature in mind. Whether you are conducting protests, staging image events, or writing policy always consider how you actions might affect the average American. Will your protest unduly disrupt the average American's life? Will your actions overly inconvenience him? Will, God forbid, your proposed reform have to be paid for by a significant increase in taxes? If so, you risk losing public support. You must maintain a delicate balance between doing what is necessary to achieve reform and gain attention without going too far. In the 1940s, the unions overreached. There were too many strikes and too many of the strikes did not seem justified to the average citizen. Unions made a big, big mistake and it cost them dearly.

5

The Struggle to Rein In Big Business

On June 20, 1890, President Benjamin Harrison signed into law the Sherman Anti-Trust Act. Section 1 of the Act read "Every contract, combination, or conspiracy in restraint of trade or commerce among the several States, or with foreign nations, is hereby declared to be illegal." Section 2 read, "Every person who shall monopolize, or attempt to monopolize, or combine or conspire with any other person or persons, to monopolize any part of the trade or commerce among the several States, or with foreign nations shall be deemed guilty of a misdemeanor..." The penalty for violating sections 1 or 2 was a fine, not exceeding five thousand dollars, and, or imprisonment not to exceed one year. [266] The Sherman Act was the first effort by the U.S. government to rein in big business by outlawing monopolistic and other anticompetitive practices large American corporations of the time, most notably by the Standard Oil Company, were adopting. Congress passed the act after a mere two years of debate in the midst of a feverish outpouring of public opposition to big business. Farmers and small business owners, in particular feared the growing concentration of economic power in a few large corporations and trusts that threatened to create a monopoly, control prices and restrain trade.

Reformers who sought to rein in big business were ecstatic with the passage of the Sherman Act. Their joy was short lived. Over the next few decades, the Sherman Act did **not** rein in the abuses of big business. In fact, big business used it as a weapon against the very people who had so forcefully demanded its passage. It would take several additional pieces of legislation and the forceful intervention of at least one U.S. president to finally given meaning to the words of the Sherman Act.

The history of the passage of the Sherman Act is instructive because it teaches one major lesson all progressives should learn.

> **LESSON: A victory is not a victory if the legislation is not enforced or enforceable.** The legislative branch can pass law after law after law. However, they are nothing more than words on paper if the executive and judicial branches do not exert the power of government to require compliance with the law. Quite often, the struggle for change only begins with the president's signature on a piece of legislation. It is what happens the next day and the day after that and the month after that and the next year and next and next, that matters. Meaningful change is the true measure of the success of progressives not the sheer volume of passed legislation alone. Ultimately, success comes from acceptance, a mind change on the part of American citizens in which the departure from the past becomes the norm of today.

I will have more to say about this lesson later. For now, let us look at several mysteries that surround the passage of the Sherman Act. Why did Republicans move so quickly to pass the act? Why would a pro-business Congress rush to enact anti-business legislation? What was wrong with the wording of the Act that made it unenforceable? Finally, was the Act essentially a sham, an intentionally unenforceable and therefore largely meaningless piece of legislation? We will begin looking for answers with a little history concerning enormous changes that occurred in the American economy in the closing decades of the 1800s. Without those changes there would have been no big business, no trusts, no monopolies, no public outrage and, consequently, no Sherman Act.

THE CIVIL WAR CHANGED EVERYTHING

The American Civil War ended in 1865 and everything about the American economy began to change, rapidly. The country was altered in the last three decades of the nineteenth century in ways unimaginable prior to the awful war. America went from being an agrarian nation to the largest manufacturing country in the world. England had taken a century to become an industrial powerhouse. America did it in just three decades. Practically all Americans saw their lives altered in fundamental ways. Some saw their wealth and well being reach dizzying heights. For others the great transformation destroyed a way of life they thought would never end.

Prior to the Civil War men still "worked for a 'livelihood' rather than for 'money.'"[267] Shops and factories were small and interspersed among the farms. Artisans turned out most products and worried about quality more than costs. Many people still wove their own cloth, made their own clothes, built their own furniture and molded their own dishes. Commerce moved at a slow pace by horse drawn wagon, on riverboats or canal barges. Land was the basis of wealth.[268] Prior to the war, America had long been a nation of opportunity. After the war, it still was a land of opportunity but the opportunity was no longer equal.

America's transformation was helped along by a burst of invention, the rapid expansion of the railroads, and the ruthless ambition of a few who sought to make the country literally their own.

AN AGE OF INNOVATION AND INVENTION

The post-Civil War era was the age of American industry and invention. Cyrus Field laid the first transatlantic cable. Alexander Graham Bell created the first commercially viable telephone. Christopher Sholes invented the typewriter. James Ritty invented the cash register. William Burroughs invented the adding machine. Charles Brush invented the arc lamp for street illumination. Thomas Edison invented the incandescent lamp. Factories, offices and even homes began to join the electrical power grid. New and more powerful steam engines began to propel larger and faster ships, some with refrigeration that made it possible to ship meat from North America to Europe. Iron production increased dramatically producing track for a tremendous expansion of the railroads. Abram Hewitt brought the open-hearth process for producing steel from Europe to America making possible a gigantic leap in the tons of steel the country could produce each year for the manufacture of locomotives, girders for the country's first high rise buildings, and rails for the ever expanding railroads. Steel production transformed western Pennsylvania, the upper regions of Michigan, and portions of Alabama and ignited growth in cities such as Birmingham, Cleveland, Detroit, and Chicago. The steel industry's demand for oil for lubrication made drilling for oil commercially viable and oil fields quickly sprouted in Pennsylvania, Ohio and West Virginia. Nicholaus Augus Otto, a German, created a gas engine, the first step toward an engine to power an automobile. By the end of the century, there were four million automobiles on American roads. Wilbur and Orville Wright began work on their first airplane.[269]

AN AGE OF RAILROADS

Nothing changed America more in the decades after the Civil War than the expansion of the railroads. America had 30,000 miles of railroad in 1860. By 1900, it had 193,000.[270] As the railroads gradually extended themselves across the country, they began to link city to town to farmer to consumer. "With the hammering of the Golden Spike at Promontory Point, Utah, in1869, the first transcontinental railroad was completed, and the East and West coasts were united. A cause for celebration by some, the rapid growth of railroads was a mixed blessing to others."[271] The benefits were obvious. Farmers in Minnesota could ship their wheat rapidly to the bakers in New York. A farmer in the San Joaquin valley could order a new threshing machine from its manufacturer in Chicago and receive it in short order.

There were many good things about this progress. Yet, there was a growing sense among the people of the smaller cities and towns that for all they had gained they had also lost something of true importance, control over their lives. The farmer would order the new threshing machine and the railroad would deliver it but only after it passed through his town, on to a central reshipping point and then back with the farmer charged the extra delivery costs. The Minnesota farmer could now easily ship his wheat to market but he soon discovered that when the market for wheat improved the cost of shipping that wheat increased also as the railroads raised prices. The profits the farmer gained from the improved price for his product were suddenly eliminated or even surpassed by the higher freight charges. If the farmer refused to pay the higher rates, the railroad simply told him "fine, let your wheat, corn and oats rot in your granaries."[272] Do not pay and you lose. The farmers knew that. In addition, they knew that if they paid they lost anyway. The railroads were in control.

The people of the country sent their representatives to Washington to complain. The railroad men, they told their representatives, were "blood-sucking vampires" who were engaged in nothing more than "licensed larceny."[273] Their representatives, many of whom were accepting free passes for travel throughout the country and other inducements from the railroads, listened to the complaints of their constituents but did nothing.

Unable to get any relief from Washington, mid-Western farmers began joining an organization called the Grange, which was devoted to fighting the railroads. Eventually the Grange grew to a membership of one and a half million farmers from over 15,000 different communities. The Grange's political power in the states increased as its membership grew and states began creating railroad commissions and to pass Grange laws to rein in abuses by the railroads.

The railroad barons fought back charging that the Grangers were the hated "agrarians" and "communists." The railroads soon packed state railroad commissions with members sympathetic to railroad interests. States like Iowa, Minnesota and Wisconsin that resisted changes to the grange laws sought by the railroads found themselves threatened with lack of access to the railroads and thus the ability to move their goods to market. They had no choice but to abolish their grange laws and neuter their railroad commissions.

Eventually, the Grangers turned to Congress for relief and were successful in 1887 in securing passage of the Interstate Commerce Act that created the first true regulatory agency at the federal level, the Interstate Commerce Commission. Under the act, railroads were required to set shipping rates that were "reasonable and just", had to publish their rates, could not negotiate secret rebates, and could not engage in price discrimination against small markets. The Commission was supposed to investigate abuses and enforce the act but for years Congress never provided the agency with sufficient resources to do its job and presidents frequently appointed pro-railroad men to serve as commissioners. Even with the passage of the Interstate Commerce Act, the railroads had essentially won.

The anger and frustration of the farmers and small business owners only increased. A few men came to symbolize in the minds of most Americans all that was wrong, unjust and immoral about the new economy.

AN AGE OF SCOUNDRELS AND SCALAWAGS

The Civil War brought about a burst of economic activity from the rapid expansion of railroads in the North to the growth of boot and shoe manufacturing in New England, to the launching of meat packing in Chicago, to increased iron and steel production, to gun production, all to feed the demands of the Northern army. This tremendous spurt of economic growth picked up strength at war's end and unleashed greed. As one writer noted, "Booth's bullet released all of the chicanery and cupidity of thirty-five million people."[274] That may be an exaggeration but it clearly released an "era of brass knuckles" during which men of enormous appetite for money and power reigned. As Stewart Holbrook, author of *The Age of the Moguls*, writes these men "have been described variously…as giants and Titans, and more often as rogues, robbers, and rascals. But never as feeble."[275] They were men such as:

Andrew Carnegie in steel,
Jay Cooke and James Fisk in finance,
Henry Flagler in railroads and oil,
J.P. Morgan in banking, finance,
John D. Rockefeller in oil, and
Jay Gould and Cornelius Vanderbilt in railroads.

Most of these men were only in their thirties or forties when the war ended. Cooke was 44. Flagger was 35. Carnegie, Fisk and Gould were just 30. Morgan was 28 and Rockefeller just 26. While they were mostly young, they were determined men, determined to dominate their industries, determined to become very rich, and determined to get their own way regardless of the cost to others.[276]

Cornelius Vanderbilt, by far the oldest, was typical with respect to ambition at least. Commodore Vanderbilt, as he was called, first made his fortune in steamships and then switched to railroads. In less than two decades after the Civil War, he increased his wealth by more than 100 times. The media estimated his fortune to be $100 million or more when he died in 1877, at the age of 82. Vanderbilt was known for getting his way. When he built a house on Washington Place in New York City and moved his family there, his wife refused to move from their Staten Island home saying she did not want to live in the city. Vanderbilt promptly had her confined to a sanitarium where she could contemplate her disobedience. After several months, she was released and "went obediently to her new home in the city."[277] In business dealings, Vanderbilt had no scruple about using "even the most outright trickery to get control of properties he wanted."[278] He considered legislators to be nothing but "holdup men who had to be bribed to keep them from selling out to his opponents."[279]

Andrew Carnegie was much younger than Vanderbilt was, but just as adept at getting his way. He stood just five feet four inches tall, weighed a mere 130 pounds and wore tiny size five shoes but there was nothing small about his drive, ambition or ruthlessness.[280] Carnegie got his start in the iron business first investing in a Pittsburgh company owned by two brothers named Kolman that made railroad-car axles for the rapidly expanding railroads. In 1865, Carnegie joined with his brother and two friends, Tom Miller and Henry Phipps, and the Kolman brothers in founding the Union Iron Mills specializing in producing huge iron beams, which the railroads needed to span the western rivers as they laid their tracks across the country. Two years later, Carnegie began warning Miller that the good days for Union Iron were about to end. Carnegie confided to Miller that he was planning to sell his stock in Union and suggested that

Miller should consider doing the same. After months of such pessimistic talk, Carnegie announced that he had found a person by the name of David A. Stewart who was naïve enough actually to want to buy stock in Union Iron. Carnegie arranged for Stewart to buy all of Tom Miller's shares saying he wanted to help his friend and co-owner. Only later did Miller discover that the real purchaser of Miller's shares was not Stewart, whoever he was, but Carnegie himself. Carnegie's effort to "help" Miller sell his shares in Union had been nothing but a trick to get Miller's stock. A few years later, Carnegie was able to force the Kolman brothers, who had suffered significant losses in the stock market, to sell him their shares of the business for a pittance.

Carnegie was not reluctant to use any means to grow his business. For example, in 1871 a competitor built a new plant producing steel rails using a something called the "direct rolling process" which was a quicker and cheaper process for making steel rails than the process Carnegie used in his plants. This low cost producer threatened Carnegie's mill so Carnegie took action. By then he had gained control of a number of steel mills and was highly regarded by the railroad presidents and purchasing agents who bought his product. Consequently, it was not surprising that these customers took notice when Carnegie sent them a letter warning them that railroad lines built with the direct rolling process were dangerous. The railroads, said Carnegie, risked having their trains derailed and a tremendous loss of life and property if they continued to purchase rails produced with the direct rolling process. Of course, there was nothing to Carnegie's claims. The direct rolling process did not produce a dangerous product. In fact, it produced a better and cheaper product. The only companies endangered by the direct rolling process were Carnegie's companies. Of course, the railroad presidents and purchasing agents did not know that. They trusted Carnegie. Soon Carnegie's direct rolling competitor found itself with piles and piles of unsold rails as it lost customer after customer. Eventually the owners had no choice. They sold the business, to Carnegie. Within two years, all of Carnegie's steel mills were using the same direct rolling process that Carnegie had warned produced such a dangerous product. By 1890, Carnegie controlled two thirds of the steel production in the country.

JOHN D. ROCKEFELLER-THE GREATEST VILLAIN[281]

John D. Rockefeller was not as flamboyant or as openly aggressive as many of his counterparts but he was the most consistently successful in eliminating his competition. Consequently, when the American people turned against the excesses of big business, Rockefeller was the greatest villain. Rockefeller became in the minds of most Americans the symbol of a "grave and startling menace to the social order "a bald-headed, sly-looking and cadaverous figure, dressed in sinister black, grinning like a death's head, and always performing some cruel act. Stealing money from pretty weeping widows appeared to be among his lesser abominations."[282]

John D. Rockefeller was born in 1839 in Richford, NY the son of William and Eliza Rockefeller. His father was frequently absent tending to some mysterious business. During his absence, the family would be impoverished. Upon his return, he filled the pantry and lavished the kids with new clothes. No one in town knew exactly what the elder Rockefeller did for a living. That is, no one knew until one day when a local citizen while traveling in Ohio discovered a poster announcing the eminent arrival of Dr. William Rockefeller who would be in town for only a short period to cure cancer and other ills from which the local citizens suffered. Of course, Rockefeller was not a doctor and his "cures" were not cures. However, the doctor trade was lucrative. Charles Morris in his book *The Tycoons* says there was another reason for William Rockefeller's frequent "long, mysterious, trips." Rockefeller, says Morris, was living a double life "as 'William Livingston' he was married to another woman and more or less supporting two families for much of John's life."[283]

Rockefeller's father may not have been around much but when he was, he spent the time training John D. in the fine art of the con. Rockefeller said of his father, "He himself trained me in practical ways. He was engaged in different enterprises; he used to tell me about these things... and he taught me the principles and methods of business...I knew what a cord of good solid beech and maple wood was. My father told me to select only solid wood...and not to put any limbs in it or any punky wood. That was a good training for me."[284] Rockefeller's father described the training he gave his boys somewhat differently. He is quoted as saying, "I cheat my boys every chance I get, I want to make 'em sharp. I trade with the boys and skin 'em and just beat 'em every time I can. I want to make 'em sharp."[285] He succeeded very well.

Since his father was gone much of the time conning people, Eliza Rockefeller raised John and his five brothers and sisters. Rockefeller recalled that his mother was a strict disciplinarian not reluctant to use a birch switch to "uphold the standard of the family when it showed a tendency to deteriorate."[286] Once while Eliza was applying the birch switch to correct some misbehavior by John at school, she discovered that he was actually innocent. She did not stop. Instead, she told him "never mind, we have started on this whipping and it will do for the next time."[287]

Early on Rockefeller learned the art of making money from money. He recalled working at the age of seven earning 37 cents a day hoeing potatoes for local farmers. Everything he earned went into a blue bowl he kept next to his bed. Eventually, he accumulated the grand sum of $50, which he loaned to a farmer who employed him and needed ready cash. Rockefeller said that transaction taught him a lesson. "I soon learned that I could get as much interest from a $50 loaned at seven per cent—then the legal rate of interest—as I could earn by digging potatoes for ten days." From then on, he said, he resolved to make money be his slave rather be a slave to his money. Rockefeller ultimately came to believe that he was on a mission from God, a mission to make money. He told a reporter:

> I believe the power to make money is a gift from God—just as are the instincts for art, music, literature, the doctor's talent, the nurse's, yours—to be developed and used to the best of our ability for the good of mankind. Having been endowed with the gift I possess, I believe it is my duty to make money and still more money, and to use the money I make for the good of my fellow man according to the dictates of my conscience." [288]

In high school, Rockefeller studied bookkeeping and at the age of sixteen obtained his first job as a bookkeeper. He gained a reputation for conspicuous attention to detail carefully studying every bill prior to payment. His salary grew from $15 a month to $50 in less than three years. He spent almost nothing. He bought few clothes and made no trips to the theatre. He had few friends but attended the Baptist Church regularly. He was pious and worshiped the "lean goddess of Abstinence."[289] He was "pale, bony, small-eyed." He served the Lord while relentlessly pursuing business. "His composed manner, which had a certain languor, hid a feverish calculation, a sleepy strength, cruel, intense, terribly alert."[290] At night, alone in his room, he read his Bible and talked to himself about his business reminding himself to stay his course. Several years later, he married Laura Spelman who reminded him to be silent and say as little as possible. Rockefeller took only moments away from his business day for the marriage ceremony. Earlier when walking home from school with a friend, Rockefeller said as they passed a rich man's house, "When I grow up I want to be worth $100,000. And, I'm going to be too. "[291] Rockefeller rarely smiled and never laughed. In fact, he rarely expressed any emotion except when a business deal went well. Then, he might exclaim, "I'm bound to be rich! Bound to be rich!"[292] He was.

In 1858, Rockefeller used $800 in savings plus a high interest loan from his father, who sought again to cheat him, to open a produce business with a friend. He applied what he had learned about credit. He borrowed against the company receipts, a risky act that he said "gave him great pleasure," and used the proceeds to expand his business by buying produce in wholesale rather than small lots. The business prospered. Rockefeller began to dress in the style of the merchants of his day, high silk hat, frock coat and striped trousers. "His head was handsome, his eyes small, birdlike, on his pale cheeks were the proverbial side-whiskers reddish in color."[293]

Within two years, Rockefeller had impressed a number of Cleveland's prominent business leaders. They selected him as their representative to investigate investment opportunities in the new oil fields of Pennsylvania. Rockefeller looked with distaste on the chaos of the oil fields. "There were continual fires, disasters and miracles; an oil well brought a fortune in a week, with the market price at twenty dollars a barrel; then as more wells came in the price fell to three or even two dollars a barrel before the next season! No one could tell at what price it was safe to buy oil, or oil acreage, and none knew how long the supply would last."[294] Rockefeller returned with a firm recommendation that one should avoid at all costs the uncertain process of oil production. Even an investment in refining would be, he warned, risky at best. The Cleveland businessmen took his advice at least about investing in oil exploration and production. However, they did invest in refineries. Within a couple of years, the Cleveland refineries were going full steam polluting the Cuyahoga River with scum and the Cleveland atmosphere with their noxious odors

In 1862, Samuel Andrews, who was seeking to build a refinery, approached Rockefeller and his partner in the produce business, Clark, for an investment. Andrews had developed a method for extracting kerosene from crude oil that promised much higher yields than traditional methods. Rockefeller and Clark agreed to invest $5,000 in the start up. Rockefeller was soon spending most of his time keeping the books and purchasing crude oil for the new refinery. As kerosene lamps became an increasing popular source of illumination, demand grew and Rockefeller decided to switch career. He bought Clark's shares in the oil refinery, sold his shares in the produce business and joined Andrews as an equal partner in the Rockefeller & Andrews refinery.

Rockefeller now devoted himself to obtaining the best deals in purchases of crude oil for the refinery. His only expression of emotion came when he had negotiated a particularly good bargain in crude oil and then he would explode with shouts of joy before returning to his unrelenting pursuit of profits. Rockefeller had no friends and no interest in anything but the business.

In 1867, Rockefeller and Andrews partnered with Henry Flagler, the son-in-law of a wealthy whiskey dealer and salt-maker, to open a second refinery. By 1869, the firm of Rockefeller, Flagler & Andrews was the biggest refinery operator in Cleveland. Rockefeller and Flagler hatched a scheme to grow their company even bigger. They approached the New York Central railroad that profited greatly from transporting oil to their refineries with a demand for better freight rates. Wanting to keep their business, New York Central agreed. However, the deal was not for a straight and public cut in rates. Rockefeller and Flagler insisted that instead of being granted a lower public rate, they be given a "rebate" on all of their shipments. Rockefeller and Flagler immediately put their competitors, who were not receiving the rebate, at a disadvantage. Consequently, their business grew. By 1870, they had doubled production and were demanding and receiving even higher rebates from the railroads.

Thanks to these rebates, "on crude oil brought from the Oil Regions, Rockefeller paid perhaps 15 cents a barrel less than the open rate of 40 cents; on refined oil moving from Cleveland toward New York, he paid approximately 90 cents against the open rate of $1.30."[295] Rockefeller and his partners kept the rebates in the upmost secrecy. They had to for the simple reason that under common law dating back to the time of Queen Elizabeth such rebates were an illegal "conspiracy" in trade. Rockefeller and Flagler were getting very rich, breaking the law. However, the illegal conspiracy worked. In 1870, Rockefeller and Flagler incorporated, changing the name of their company to the Standard Oil Company of Ohio. At the time of incorporation, Standard Oil was the largest refinery operator in the world, employing over 1,000 workers. Rockefeller, who was only thirty, had become enormously rich. However, he was not satisfied. He wanted more. He had a plan.

In his book, *The Evolution of Modern Capitalism*, J.A. Hobson, an English economist, describes where the best opportunities lie for ruthless capitalists in a modern industrial society.

> Each kind of commodity, as it passes through the many processes from the earth to the consumer, may be looked upon as a stream whose channel is broader at some points and narrow at others. Different streams of commodities narrow at different places. Some are narrowest and in fewest hands at the transport stage, others in one of the processes of manufacture, others in the hands of export merchants…Just as a number of German barons planted their castles along the banks of the Rhine, in order to tax the commerce between East and West which was obliged to make use of this highway, so it is with these 'economic' narrows."[296]

Rockefeller understood that the refining process was the 'narrows' of the oil business and that is where he intended to build his castle.

The plan was simple. Rockefeller and Flagler approached their largest competitors with a proposal. The refiners would ban together as the South Improvement Company (SIC) to demand even larger secret rebates from the railroads than Standard Oil had been able to obtain. They would use the additional rebates to put pressure on the remaining Cleveland refineries to join them. The South Improvement Company would grow to dominate the market, "control output, drive out competitors, and force all foreign countries throughout the world to buy [oil] from them at their own terms. They could finally dictate market prices on crude oil, stabilize the margin of profit at their own process, and do away at last with the dangerously speculative character of their business."[297] It would be so much easier and so much more profitable to do business with no competition. The refiners agreed. They joined with Rockefeller to form the South Improvement Company (SIC). Participants were required to sign a written pledge of secrecy. No one outside the group was to know anything about agreements between the participating companies in South Improvement.

With South Improvement in place, Rockefeller sent representatives of Standard Oil to meet secretly with the railroads. The Standard Oil men informed the railroad representative that Standard Oil had obtained secret control over almost all of the Cleveland refinery capacity through something called the South Improvement Company. South Improvement was demanding rebates and other concessions. In return, the participating refineries in South Improvement would coordinate production to even out shipments and demand for rail cars. The railroads were under pressure from investors who were laying pipelines and threatening to take away large chunks of oil and gas transport. They could not afford to alienate the refiners who might move product to the pipelines. The Standard Oil men came away with a sweet deal.

Refiners who were part of South Improvement would have a rebate of from 40 to 50 percent on the crude oil they ordered shipped to them and from 25 to 50 percent on the refined oil they shipped out. Refiners in the Oil Regions (outside Cleveland and closer to New York) were to pay twice as much to ship their products as the South Improvement companies. In addition, the South Improvement companies were to receive part of this increased rate non-South Improvement companies paid to ship their oil and gas. Further, in order to guarantee that the railroads kept their part of the bargain, the railroads were to turn over detailed information to South Improvement concerning the dates, places, destinations and freight rates South Improvement's competitors paid for their shipments of oil and gas.[298]

Even thought the conspirators made every effort to keep the SIC deal secret, rumors began to circulate that something was about to happen that would cause freight rates to go up, possibly by a substantial margin. Rockefeller was not quite ready to have the new rates published but by accident news of the rate increase got out. A local freight agent for the Lake Shore Railroad was called away suddenly on the news that his son was dying. He left a subordinate in charge who posted the still secret freight rate increases. They had not yet been enacted officially by SIC members and the railroad. Oil Creek residents woke up on the morning of February 26, 1872 to newspaper headlines announcing that rates would double for all refiners but a privileged few led by Standard Oil.

People poured into the streets denouncing Rockefeller and his fellow conspirators as monsters and thieves. The Petroleum Producers Union representing Oil City producers announced that its members would retaliate by selling their crude oil only to Oil City refiners who were not part of SIC. Protests got ugly. Angry mobs threatened Standard employees and vandalized rail cars. Rockefeller turned away reporters demanding an explanation of what SIC was all about announcing that he did not have to explain his actions to anyone. Rockefeller dismissed the protests as just a few hot heads. The Petroleum Producers carried through with their threat and by March, Rockefeller and other refiners in the cabal had to lay off workers.

On March 25, the railroads gave in and canceled their agreement with SIC. In April, the Pennsylvania legislature canceled the SIC charter. Rockefeller finally gave in and notified the oil producers that all of the SIC contracts had been canceled. The whole scheme had blown up. There was never a shipment of oil under the SIC agreement.

SIC was no more but Rockefeller had achieved part of his goal. Faced with threats of being driven out of business by the SIC deal, twenty-two of the twenty-six Cleveland refiners had sold out to Rockefeller between February 17 and March 28. Rockefeller had been blunt during secret meetings with the Cleveland refiners telling them, "You see, this scheme is going to work. It means an absolute control by us of the oil business. There is no chance for anyone on the outside. However, we are going to give everybody a chance to come in. You are to turn over your refinery to my appraisers, and I will give you Standard Oil Company stock or cash, as you prefer, for the value we put upon it. I advise you to take the stock. It will be for your good." [299] They could agree or be crushed. Most agreed. Standard Oil appraisers valued the property and made the offers, which were usually only a third to a half of the actual value. Most refiners gave up and took the offer. Rockefeller mercilessly attacked those who resisted. In his book, *The Tycoons*, Charles Morris writes:

> If a target was especially obdurate, rejecting all reasonable offers, a switch would finally turn and Rockefeller would suddenly unleash total, blazing warfare on every front—price, supplies, access to transportation, land-use permits, whatever created pain. When the target capitulated—they always did—the fair-price offer would still be available, often with an offer to join in the Rockefeller team. It was industrial conquest on the efficiency principle. [300]

Rockefeller told those who resisted they could either sell to him or watch their businesses become worthless. Better to take the little Rockefeller was offering than to end up with nothing at all. The threats were all made in secret. No one questioned that they were real. In three months, Rockefeller gained control of all of the refinery business in Cleveland, which was one fifth of the oil refinery capacity of the country. Rockefeller's response to criticism of his pressure tactics was that selling out to Standard was a "godsend to all of them." [301]

Rockefeller now had a true monopoly on oil in Ohio. Not only did he control the refineries but almost every aspect of production. Standard Oil owned and operated four companies in the state. The Ohio Oil company handled contracts to purchase crude oil. The Buckeye Pipe Line Company, which controlled 85 percent of the pipelines in Ohio, transported the crude oil to the refineries operated by the Standard Oil Company of Ohio and the Solar Refining Company, which together controlled about 80 percent of the refining capacity in the state. In short, Standard Oil controlled the market for purchasing, transporting and refining oil in Ohio and could thus control production and dictate prices for both crude oil and refined products such as kerosene. As one might imagine, such an operation was highly profitable.[302]

Having taken over the refineries in Cleveland, Rockefeller now sought to dominate the refinery business in Pittsburgh and Philadelphia. In secret meeting after secret meeting, Rockefeller sought to convince the refinery owners of these other cities to join his scheme. "Look at what combination has done in one city, Cleveland," he would say.[303] The plan now was for all the chosen ones to become the nucleus of a private company, which would gradually acquire control of all the refineries everywhere, become the only shippers, and have the mastery of the railroads in the matter of freight rates. Those who came in were promised wealth beyond their dreams. The remarkable economies and profits of the Standard were exposed to their eyes. 'We mean to secure the entire refining business of the world,' they were told."[304] Rockefeller had the refiners sign the deals at night and in secret. He allowed them to tell no one, not even their wives, the nature of the deals or the profits. He warned then not to drastically change their lifestyles. They were to do nothing that might reveal the enormous wealth they would soon be amassing. By 1878, Rockefeller had deals with fifteen of the largest refineries in the country and control over four fifths of the country's entire refining capacity. Most of these companies continued to operate under their former names. Having brought the largest refineries under his control, Rockefeller next went after the smaller refineries. He purchased many at 30% to 50% of their true value using the same tactics he had used in Cleveland.

Independent oil dealers who resisted Rockefeller suddenly found railroad freight rates for their product doubled or tripled. Merchants who purchased oil from the independents for resale were threatened. If you do not purchase your oil from Standard Oil, Rockefeller's men told them; we will come into your town, open a competing store, sell at cost, and put you out of business. Competing refineries that could not be bought out were subject to being burned out. In one infamous instance, representatives of the Vacuum Oil Company in Buffalo, NY, a Standard Oil Company operating under its original name, approached the chief mechanic of a competing refinery. The mechanic was promised a lifetime annuity if he would "bust up...or smash up" or otherwise fix the pipes and stills of the competing refinery to interrupt production. The mechanic returned to his company and within a short time a small explosion occurred at the plant. Several years later, the mechanic confessed to the cause of the explosion, and the government brought a criminal suit against several officials of Standard Oil. The officials swore they had no knowledge of the offer to the mechanic and attributed the episode to the "over enthusiasm" of underlings.[305] The court awarded damages to the owners of the refinery but failed to find sufficient evidence of a conspiracy.

Oil well owners rebelled. They announced that they would not do business with Rockefeller or the railroads. They would lay their own pipelines to transport their crude oil to independent refineries. John Archbold, a refiner owner who had made a reputation for himself as one of Rockefeller's ablest and fiercest opponents announced the formation of Acme Oil Company to counter Standard Oil's monopoly. Soon Archbold had signed leases with the remaining twenty or so refineries that had so far maintained their independence from Standard Oil. The independents received stock in Acme only to discover that rather than being independent and a rival of Standard Oil, Acme was actually a subsidiary of Standard Oil. Archbold became a Vice-President of Standard Ohio of Ohio and later President of Standard Oil of New Jersey. People would begin to call him the "arch-corruptionist" of Standard Oil.

In 1877, Rockefeller went after one on his remaining significant rivals, the Empire Transportation Company, a refinery and pipeline company run by Tim Scott, head of the Pennsylvania Railroad. Rockefeller went to Scott and asked him politely to cease competing with Standard Oil. While

Rockefeller was meeting with Scott, he sent an associate to meet with representatives of the Erie and New York Central railroads. The associate explained that a price war was about to break out between Standard Oil and Empire. Standard Oil expected the railroads to lower their freight rates radically on shipments to Standard Oil for the duration of the price war. Faced with a non-negotiable demand from their major customer, the railroads agreed. Standard Oil began aggressively cutting prices in all areas where it directly competed with Empire. Empire had to cut its prices to compete. Soon it essentially had to give away its product to match Standard Oil. Scott gave up and went to Rockefeller to sue for peace. Rockefeller agreed to end the price war on one condition. Standard Oil would buy Empire and all its holding for $3,400,000, which was, of course, a non-negotiable offer. Scott accepted. He had no choice. The remaining independent refineries in Maryland and New York saw what happened to Empire. When asked to join what was now being called the "Rockefeller Alliance" they reluctantly agreed.

Rockefeller was just thirty-eight years old. He grew a mustache and bought himself a new silk hat. He now controlled 95% of the refinery and pipeline capacity in the United States but he was not satisfied. He wanted more but some annoying legal restrictions hampered his efforts to grow his company.

Standard Oil was chartered in Ohio and under Ohio law could not hold stock in other firms or conduct business outside of Ohio.[306] Consequently, when Rockefeller began to expand into other states by purchasing other companies he had to operate these newly acquired companies independent of Standard Oil. They could not become part of Standard Oil of Ohio. As Rockefeller and his associates acquired more and more companies, the management of these separate companies became unwieldy. It was increasingly difficult for Rockefeller to exercise control of his growing empire. What was to be done? Rockefeller's chief legal advisor, Samuel C. T. Dodd, "a wizard at contriving [organizational] forms that obeyed the letter but circumvented the spirit of the law, provided the solution.[307] Dodd suggested that the stockholders of all of the existing Standard corporations place their stock in the hands of a set of trustees that would issue certificates of interest in the Trust. The newly created Standard Oil Trust would "have a common name, a common office, and a common management by means of a common executive committee."[308] The Trust would be legal, argued Dodd, because it would be a union of stockholders, not a union of companies. The latter, of course, would be against the law.

In 1882, Rockefeller implemented Dodd's plan. He placed the stock from all of the existing Standard companies in the trust and investors in the various companies received trust certificates for their stock. The agreement gave full powers to manage all of the companies in the trust to a board of nine trustees, headed by John Rockefeller. The Trust took office space in New York City. As Ron Chernow writes in his Rockefeller biography *Titan*, today we would term the trust a holding company "but at the time it seemed an imaginary entity, lacking real legal existence. It could not make deals, sign contracts, or keep books, though it wielded infinite power. It received the stock of Standard and forty other companies—twenty-six of them partially, fourteen fully—with the power to name their officers and directors. Among the shareholders, the distribution of power and wealth remained lopsided, with Rockefeller holding more than one-third of the trust certificates, a block worth $19 million."[309]

Rockefeller retired in 1896 at the age of 54 and spent the rest of his life avoiding tobacco and alcohol, existing chiefly on milk and graham crackers and playing lots of golf during which biographers said he never cheated on his score.[310] When he retired, he was worth an estimated two hundred million dollars. By 1910, he was worth more than four times that amount thanks to the internal combustion engine and the demand for gasoline to power America's growing fascination with the automobile.

It is impossible to exaggerate the significance of Rockefeller's accomplishment or his impact on American business. The Standard Oil Trust was a $70 million enterprise that controlled 20,000 oil wells, 4,000 miles of pipeline, and 5,000 tanker cars. It employed 100,000 people who oversaw the export of 50,000 barrels of oil to Europe each day. It became "the biggest and richest, most feared and admired business organization in the world."[311] It changed American business in profound ways.

> In many ways, Standard Oil's metamorphosis previewed the trajectory of other major American business organizations in the late nineteenth century as they moved from freewheeling competition to loosely knit cartels to airtight trusts. The 1882 agreement introduced the concept of the trust as something synonymous with industrial monopoly. During the 1880s, industry wide pools sprouted in many industries in America, England, and Germany, but their leaders found it difficult to prevent cheating and secret price-cutting among members. Now, Standard Oil came up with a way to introduce centralized control, backed by enforcement powers and managerial direction. So many companies duplicated the pattern over the years that one can say, with pardonable exaggeration, that the 1882 trust agreement executed by Standard Oil led straight to the Sherman Antitrust Act eight years later.[312]

Standard Oil set the pattern. After Rockefeller led the way, companies formed trusts in industry after industry, sugar, lead, whiskey, cottonseed, linseed oil, and so on. The coal trust was a typical example.

THE COAL TRUST

In the late 1880s, the sellers of coal in Nashville, TN and the mine operators in the Kentucky coalfields that supplied them were distressed. Fierce competition and price wars were depressing prices mine owners and coal distributors could charge for their coal. The mine operators and coal dealers decided that the only practical thing to do to protect their profits was to form a cartel (or trust) where they could fix prices.

At the time, coal was an extremely important commodity since it was the chief source of energy for both industry and individual consumers. Industry used coal to produce the steam to power the factories. Consumers relied upon coal to fire the furnaces and fireplaces to heat their homes. Many used coal to cook their food.

Of the two types of consumers, industrial users had the most options and the most negotiating power. They could purchase coal in large quantities directly from mine operators and have it delivered by rail directly to their factories, which were often located next to rail lines. Additionally, industrial users could switch to cheaper grades of coal whenever the price of coal became a problem.

On the other hand, consumers were locked in. Their only viable options to purchasing coal were to go without heat or use wood that was a less than satisfactory alternative. Consumers were easy prey so the coal dealers and mine operators decided the prices to fix would be the prices consumers paid for coal.

In August 1889, 14 Kentucky coal miners and 14 Nashville wholesale coal dealers formed the Nashville Coal Exchange documenting their price fixing scheme in a small blue-covered conspirator's rulebook. The goals of the Exchange, they said, were simple:

> (a) advance the interest of the coal business at Nashville, (b) treat all parties to the agreement in a fair and equitable manner, and (c) establish prices of coal in Nashville and to change them from time to time as occasion may require. The Exchange declared it was organized to "act in a conservative manner, and to sell coal at a fair and reasonable price so as to allow all parties a fair profit for their product.[313]

Mine operators and coal dealers agreed to set a price for each grade of coal and to split the profits equally. Price changes were subject to a two-thirds vote. The consumer would be taken.

The scheme worked. The price of coal shipped to Nashville from the Kentucky mines was 20% higher than the price of coal shipped to Memphis from the same mines even though rail-shipping costs were virtually the same. The Nashville coal trust eventually got 80% of the market.

AMERICANS BECOME ALARMED AND DEMAND ACTION

Americans were alarmed at what they saw. Prior to 1880, no American company was large enough to impact sizable numbers of people through its actions. Even the largest companies employed just a few hundred people and were worth a million dollars at most. Now, Americans found themselves doing business with railroads that employed a 100,000 workers and companies like Standard Oil that were worth hundreds of millions of dollars. Thomas McGraw in his book *Prophets of Regulation* describes how frightening this change was to most Americans.

> With the rise of big business, the term "private enterprise" acquired a different meaning. Whereas once it had signified liberty, freedom, and individualism, it now meant danger as well—the threat of giant corporations. Suddenly, big business seemed to menace America. Large corporations represented that same centralized power against which the founding fathers had fought their revolution. Perhaps inevitably, American big business evoked a powerful regulatory response.[314]

Small groups of powerful men were creating monopolies or near-monopolies in industry after industry. It was true that in some cases the monopolies actually improved quality, availability and brought down prices. Consumers benefited, for a while. However, it was not the American way. As historian Richard Hostadter says the idea of open and free competition was more than just a theory to most Americans.

> From its colonial beginnings through most of the nineteenth century, [America] was overwhelmingly a nation of farmers and small-town entrepreneurs—ambitious, mobile, optimistic, speculative, anti-authoritarian, egalitarian, and competitive. As time went on, Americans came to take it for granted that property would be widely diffused, that economic and political power would be decentralized. The fury with which they could be mobilized against any institution that even appeared to violate these expectations by posing a threat of monopoly was [great and at times even irrational].[315]

William Jennings Bryan expressed the popular fear of monopolies in a speech at the Chicago Conference on Trusts in 1899:

> I do not divide monopolies in private hands into good monopolies and bad monopolies. There is no good monopoly in private hands. There can be no good monopoly in private hands until the Almighty sends us angels to preside over the monopoly. There may be a despot who is better than another despot, but there is no good despotism.[316]

For some the dangers of monopolies extended far beyond the economic threat to competition to a threat to democracy. Woodrow Wilson worried "if monopoly persists, monopoly will always sit at the helm of the government. I do not expect to see monopoly restrain itself. If there are men in this country big enough to own the government of the United States, they are going to own it."[317]

By the mid-1880s, Americans were demanding action. "The social atmosphere was 'surcharged with an indefinite but almost inexpressible fear of trusts.'"[318] Even those politicians who saw no real need to do anything to rein in big business saw the necessity of appearing to do so for fear of what the masses might do next. Senator John Sherman of Ohio expressed these fears when he warned his fellow senators during the debate on the Sherman Act that "the popular mind is agitated with problems that may disturb the social order." Americans foresaw a future, he said, where there would be "a trust for every production and a master to fix the price for every necessity of life."[319] Something had to be done to placate the disturbed population or the voters would turn to socialists, communists, or nihilists.

> **LESSON: Americans have a visceral fear of the concentration of power and the loss of individual liberty or self-sufficiency.** In an earlier chapter, we learned about the fear Americans have of the power own government and how they instinctive recoil when anyone suggests expanding government control of their lives. They have a similar fear of big business or any entity that seems large and imposing. Coupled with that

fear is a delusion of self-sufficiency. Americans imagine they can go it alone just as they imagine their pioneering forefathers did. Opponents of progressive legislation often tap Americans' fear of power and delusion of self-sufficiency to defeat legislation so be prepared for such attacks. On the other hand, you can tap into that fear when the purpose of proposed change is to rein in powerful entities as in the case of the Sherman Act.

THE STATES GO FIRST

As is typical, the first efforts to respond to the anger of voters toward the trusts came at the state level. Maryland in 1867, Tennessee in 1870, Arkansas and Texas in 1876, and Georgia in 1877 had already passed some form of antitrust law. Twelve states passed antitrust acts in 1889 alone.

The antitrust movement at the state level did not focus on consumer protection but the protection of local business interests. For example, Missouri enacted antitrust legislation in 1889. In the 1880s, Missouri's economy depended upon agriculture particular production of cattle, hogs and wheat. The value of all three was in decline by the late 1880s. For example, the per-head value of cattle declined nearly 29% between 1884 and 1889. The value of hogs declined 19% during the same period and the price of a bushel of wheat was off nearly 27%. Missouri farmers blamed the decline in the price of their products on larger producers from out-of-state who were taking advantage of the expanded railroads and lower transportation costs to ship their goods throughout the country. Larger producers were using their economies of scale to price local farmers out of business. Missouri cattlemen and local butchers were particular threatened by the large Chicago meat packers Swift, Armour, Morris and Hammond who were know as the "big four."

Gustavus Swift had been the first meat packer to find an economically way to ship his beef from his Chicago meat packing plant to other parts of the country by rail. Swift loaded his dressed beef into railroad cars in the winter of 1877, opened the doors to the rail cars, and took advantage of the natural refrigeration to ship his product to the northeast. By 1879, Swift could take advantage of the recently developed refrigerated rail car to ship his meat products to almost anywhere in the country year round. Swift and the other Chicago meat packers found creative ways to utilize the whole hog or cow in innovative new beef and pork by-products making their operations even more efficient thus allowing them to significantly undercut local prices. Local cattlemen who sold to local butchers could not compete with the Chicago "big four." Soon rumors spread that the Chicago packers had formed a "beef trust"

Missouri legislators responded to the voter outcry that followed the beef trust rumors with "An Act for the Punishment of Pools, Trusts, and Conspiracies." The act passed by a margin of 98 to 1 in the Missouri House and 27 to 4 in the Senate. The Act prohibited "restraints of trade" in the form of pooling, forming trust companies, interlocking directorates, and so on, with the intention "to fix or limit the amount or quantity of any article, commodity or merchandise to be manufactured, mined, produced or sold" in Missouri or fix the price of outputs.[320]

Efforts by the states like Missouri to rein in the trusts were largely unsuccessful for several reasons. First, the trusts had become larger and better financed than most states. For example, in 1888 the entire Commonwealth of Massachusetts employed only 6,000 workers and had revenues of just $7,000,000. One Boston railroad company employed three times as many workers and had nearly six times the revenues. Second, the trust could avoid regulation by simply moving out of states with anti-monopoly laws and reincorporating in states like New Jersey that had created, often with the help of attorneys working for the trusts, new incorporation statutes that were much more lenient toward the creation of monopolies. Finally, there was the problem of the courts that ruled against the states in most antitrust cases. For example, in the case of Wabash, St. Louis and Pacific Railroad Company v. Illinois (1886) the Supreme Court ruled that "commerce originating or ending outside of a state could not be regulated by that state, even though the federal government provided no alternative means of regulation." [321]

THE SHERMAN ACT

By 1888, the demand for federal action against the trusts was so strong Congress was forced to act. It did so in extremely short order for legislation that turned out to be so important. The facts of the passage of the Sherman Act are straightforward and the legislative activity stretched over a mere two years. In December 1887, Democratic President Grover Cleveland in a message to Congress warned that "trusts, combinations and monopolies were becoming 'the people's master."[322] In January 1888, Democratic Congressman Henry Bacon of New York introduced a resolution to instruct the House Committee on Manufacturers to investigate the trusts and recommend legislation. 1888 was a presidential election year and both parties include antitrust planks in their platforms. In June 1888, Representative William McKinley (Republican, Ohio) called on Congress "to pass legislation that prevents the execution of schemes to oppress the people by undue charges or rates."[323] In July 1888, Senator John Sherman of Ohio introduced an antitrust bill as did several other Senators. The bills were referred to the Senate Finance Committee that Sherman chaired. Within a month, Sherman's committee reported out a bill for consideration by the full senate that said "all arrangements, contracts, agreements, trusts, or combinations…made with a view, or which tend to prevent full and free competition…or which tend to advance the cost to the consumer… are hereby declared to be against public policy, unlawful, and void."[324] In January 1889, floor debate began on the Sherman bill in the senate. The senate debated the Sherman bill for fifteen months finally referring it to the Committee on the Judiciary. The Judiciary Committee reported out a substitute bill almost immediately that replaced the language in Sherman's bill with vague wording drawn from common law. [325] The substitute bill as passed contained two key provisions:

> *Section 1. Every contract, combination in the form of trust or otherwise, or conspiracy, in restraint of trade or commerce among the several states, or with foreign nations, is hereby declared to be illegal.*

> *Section 2. Every person who shall monopolize, or attempt to monopolize, or combine or conspire with any other person or persons, to monopolize any part of the trade or commerce among the several States or with foreign nations, shall be guilty of a misdemeanor."*

Senator Sherman was not pleased with the wording of the substitute bill arguing that it would be "totally ineffective in dealing with combinations and trusts [who could] ride through it or over it without fear of punishment or detection."[326] The Senate ignored Sherman's concerns and voted on the bill after less than a week of debate. The bill passed by a vote of 52 to 1. Shortly thereafter, the House passed the bill by unanimous vote. There was little significant debate or organized opposition in either chamber. The Sherman Act became law. Interestingly, no one is certain why the Sherman Act was named for Sherman since other senators extensively revised his draft. Some have speculated that it might have had something to do with the name of at least one of the authors, Senator George F. Hoar (Republican, Massachusetts). No one wanted to call the bill the "Hoar Act" for obvious reasons.

THE MYSTERY OF THE SHERMAN ACT

It is a real mystery why the Sherman Act passed so quickly and with such overwhelming support in Congress. True, voters across the country were clamoring for Congress to do something about the trusts. However, the Republican Party that dominated Congress had become increasing close to the trusts and the giant new businesses. The textbook rationale for why Congress passed the Sherman Act was that it sought to protect the consumer. That's the conclusion Yale Law School Professor Robert H. Bork came to in an influential 1966 article in which he examined the Congressional Record in search of Congress's legislative intent with regard to the Sherman Act. Bork wrote:

> My conclusion, drawn from the evidence in the Congressional Record, is that Congress intended the courts to implement (that

> is to take into account in the decision of cases) only that value we would today call consumer welfare. To put it another way, the policy the courts were intended to apply is the maximation of wealth or consumer want satisfaction.[327]

Many researchers today disagree. They argue that the Sherman Act is a classic example of legislation passing for a wide variety of different reasons, few of which have much to do with the welfare of the public. They offer several possibilities for why Congress, after years of ignoring the problem, decided suddenly to move ahead with antitrust legislation.

Some say that the Sherman Act originated as a form of political spite. They argue that Sherman was attempting to get back at the trusts whom he blamed for undermining his bid for the presidential nomination for the Republican Party in 1888. Sherman had gone to the Republican convention as a strong contender for the nomination. However, the trusts were concerned that Sherman might not be as committed to maintaining and increasing tariffs that were particularly important to them. The leaders of the trusts, particularly Russell Alger who was head of the Diamond Match Company trust, worked behind the scenes to deny Sherman the nomination. Being denied the nomination was a big blow to Sherman's political career and something he did not forget. Sherman expressed little interest in anti-trust legislation until after the Republican convention when according to *The New York Times*, he became "suddenly aware to the dangers of monopoly."[328] It is interesting to note along these lines that "in a 382-page volume of [Sherman's] letters (sent between 1837 and 1891) to his renowned brother, General William Tecumseh Sherman, the subject of monopoly (or antitrust, cartels, pools, price-fixing, collusion, or industrial combinations) is raised not once."[329]

Others argue that Congress' real intention in passing the Sherman Act was not to protect consumers, who actually were benefiting often from lower prices but the small business owners like the Grangers, Cattlemen, butchers and small oil refinery operators the trusts were driving out of business. Senator George of Mississippi at the time argued for the bill by citing how the trust threatened small business owners.

> By use of this organized force of wealth and money, the small men engaged in competition with them *[the trusts]* are crushed out, and that is the great evil at which all this legislation ought to be directed.[330]

Another Congressman argued that legislation to rein in the trusts was necessary even if the trust reduced prices to the consumer.

> Some say that the trusts have made products cheaper, have reduced prices; but if the price of oil, for instance, were reduced to one cent a barrel it would not right the wrong done to the people of the country by the 'trusts' which have destroyed legitimate competition and driven honest men from legitimate business enterprises.[331]

Finally, and most likely, Republicans may have passed the act for political cover and the trusts may have allowed them to do so. The Republican Party had become increasingly close to wealthy businessmen and the trusts that were pushing for passage of the McKinley Act that would raise tariffs. However, the public, particularly in Northeast, South and Midwestern states with heavy agricultural interests and labor-intensive industries, were opposed to the trusts and protective tariffs. Many voters saw the Republicans as supporters of tariffs. Consequently, Republicans were losing ground in those parts of the country to Democrats who were publicly taking an anti-tariff stand. The Sherman Act was most likely a sop to the public meant to provide cover to the Republicans so they could vote for the McKinley Act. Voting patterns on the Sherman and McKinley acts tend to suggest a linkage. Of the 62 House Democrats who voted "No" on the Sherman Act, none voted "Yes" on the McKinley Tariff Act. Of the 117 Republican congressmen who voted "Yes" on the Sherman Act, none voted "No" on the tariff act. Those who supported the Sherman Act supported the McKinley Act and those who opposed the Sherman Act opposed both acts. Only 17 of 142 House members changed their vote when it came to the two acts—voting "Yes" on one and "No" on the other. A similar pattern can be found among Republicans in the Senate but not among

Democrats. Further evidence comes from comments by Democrats at the time. Congressman William Elliot (Democrat, S.C.) while debating the McKinley Tariff Act of 1890 questioned the motives of the Republicans in passing the Sherman Antitrust act:

> Lately, with great shout and flourish of trumpets, you passed a bill against trusts. When your actions in this [the McKinley tariff] bill are considered it is impossible to believe you were in earnest in passing that measure. You now give the trusts everything they want. [332]

Of course, the trusts could have exercised political power to prevent passage of the Sherman Act. They did not. Instead, they went along with passage of the act on the condition that it contain vague wording, which they assumed, would make the act largely unenforceable. In other words, the trusts were willing to accept weak anti-trust legislation, in order to provide lawmakers cover so they could vote for the tariff increases. An attorney by the name of Jame Withrow claims to have evidence that Rockefeller actually bribed Senator Sherman to keep the language of the Sherman Act vague. Withrow recalled a conversation with a former employee of Rockefeller:

> It fell to my lot to have as a friend and client an elderly but active financial man who often reminisced about his first job. In the 1880's and 1890's he was a special messenger/office boy for John D. Rockefeller at 26 Broadway in New York City. Among his duties was to ride down in the elevator eavesdropping on persons who had just left an important meeting with J. D. Rockefeller. Having performed this service, he was given other sensitive jobs. He told me that on one occasion he was given an envelope that he was to deliver to Senator Sherman. John D. told him that it contained $10,000 and that the Senator had assured him that the antitrust law to be passed would be quite mild and without real teeth.[333]

> **Lesson: A frequent tactic used by the conservative opposition faced with a loud public outcry for some legislative action is to propose legislation that appears to address the issue angering voters but has little practical effect or is so vague as to be largely unenforceable.** Such situations present Progressives with a dilemma. Should they oppose the weak remedy conservatives are offering and hold out for tougher legislation or should they take what they can get and hope to strengthen the legislation later on. If they hold out, they risk being charged with resisting reform. If they agree to the conservative proposal, they may be stuck for years with an ineffective remedy allowing the problem to worsen or opponents time to placate the public and build opposition to further reform.

Whether because of bribes or simply because Republicans had little interest in truly reining in the trusts, the Sherman Act was extremely vague. Democratic Senator George Vest described the Sherman Act as "vox et praeteria nihil; sound and fury signifying nothing." [334] Sherman himself said the bill as rewritten by the Republican leadership was so weak that he predicted it would be "ineffective in dealing with combinations and trusts."[335] Reflecting on the accomplishments of the session of Congress that passed the Sherman and McKinley acts, Sherman left no doubt to which he found most significant. He wrote:

> The most important measure adopted during this [51st] Congress was what was popularly known as the McKinley Tariff Law. Passed on October 1, 1890, the tariffs were a 'matter of constant debate in both houses' between 1882 and 1890..., as opposed to the monopoly law, which came and went with little discussion.[336]

Why did the Sherman Act pass? Like most acts, the Sherman Act was not passed for one reason but many. It did not serve one interest but many interests some of which were in strong opposition to each other. The act was the product of a mult-faceted political compromise benefiting a variety of interest the most important of which was definitely NOT the consumer.

> **LESSON: There are many reasons why legislators decide to support legislation but they usually have little to do with concern for the public welfare or what is good for the country.** Appeals to their sense of patriotic duty are rarely as good as appeals to their self-interest, particularly their self-interest in being reelected or in punishing a political enemy.

ENFORCEMENT MATTERS

It does little good to pass legislation if there is no effort or interest on the part of the government to implement it. In the case of the Sherman Act the government pursued what historian Arthur Johnson called a "policy of drift" in the decades after enactment.[337] It was clear as soon as the act was passed that the Senate and House had zero interest in its enforcement. Sherman never proposed any amendments to the act even when it became obvious that the vague wording was making it unenforceable on the courts. Additionally, Congress was indifferent. It provided no additional funding or staff for the Department of Justice to enable it to take aggressive enforcement actions.

President Harrison, then President Cleveland and finally President McKinley demonstrated by their inaction that they were not only uninterested but also actually hostile toward enforcing anti-trust laws. With the except of moving against a few truly blatant abuses, each succeeding administration took a decidedly business-friendly posture of inaction when it came to enforcing the ACT. The Harrison administration filed no suits to enforce the Sherman Act. Cleveland and McKinley together filed just seven. In fact, Cleveland's Attorney General had defended the whiskey trust just the year before he was sworn into office, hardly a sign that the Department of Justice under his stewardship was going to move aggressively against the trusts. In fact, he filed only three anti-trust suits, the least of any of the three administrations.

Of course, each political party included the gospel of anti-trust as a plank in each succeeding election year platform. However, both parties rapidly forgot those planks after each election.

The Supreme Court was indifferent if not outright hostile to the act. In case after case, it narrowly construed antitrust and other business regulation. The Court was consistent in harnessing the doctrines of freedom of contract and due process to protect business from its customers. In 1895, in the Knight case, the court went so far as to the absurd pro-business ruling that the manufacture of sugar was not commerce and therefore sugar manufacturers were out of reach of anti-trust laws. Additionally, the government often used the act against unions rather than against large corporations. During the Pullman Strike in 1894, the Attorney General cited the Sherman Act in seeking an injunction to stop strikers from interfering with the operation of trains because the strike constituted a "restraint of trade." A few years later, the Supreme Court ruled in the Danbury Hatters Case that a boycott of Loewe's hats organized by the AFL in order to force the company to recognize the hatters' union was a "restraint of trade" and thus illegal under the Sherman Act.

There were a number of enforcement problems when the government attempted to use the act to rein in large corporations. First, prosecutors had to conduct lengthy investigations into the business practices of large and complex organizations to gather the evidence necessary to build a case. Corporations simply refused to cooperate. "Corporate officials frequently refused to testify or provide material, delayed investigations by continuous consultations with their attorneys, or claimed that the required witness was out of town or that the relevant books had been lost or destroyed. In the end, the company under investigation might provide a mountain of material, much of it irrelevant, that required a great deal of effort to analyze. Whatever the form of resistance, the result was an incredibly time-consuming investigation" before a case could even be brought to trial.[338]

Once a case came to trial, prosecutors faced additional problems. First, they encountered teams of highly skilled and well-paid corporate lawyers who used every legal tactic they could devise to delay the trials and complicate the issues under consideration. Second, judges who tried the cases and determined guilt or innocence typically had little, if any knowledge of economic matters but had a high regard for protecting property rights they worried might threaten by a too strict an interpretation of the antitrust laws. Finally, if a company lost at one level it immediately appealed to a higher court, thus dragging out the process for years.

Enforcement difficulties did not end with a conviction at the highest appellate level. Court decrees dealt with prior practices that the courts usually defined narrowly. Corporations were free to pursue new opportunities for consolidation and control not prohibited by the decree that declared its previous actions to be illegal. Additionally, the courts had no power to enforce their decrees. That was up to law enforcement agencies that would have to conduct lengthy investigations to uncover violations of the court's decree and bring a new suit, a process that could be as expensive and time-consuming as the initial case.

Additionally, large businesses fought back in more direct ways. "The trusts hired leading regional and national politicians, ostensibly as legal advisers, to help cool the zeal of antimonopolists or mitigate the effects of antitrust litigation," hired lobbyists to discourage lawsuits, employed public relations firms to defuse antitrust sentiment, and bought leverage with massive campaign contributions to key legislators.[339] If that didn't work the large trusts would remind local politicians that their companies provided large numbers of jobs and paid substantial taxes that supported the local economy. Antitrust prosecutions might, they warned, mean that the trust had to close factories, lay off workers, and move out of state.

> **Lesson: Enforcement matters, a lot. In drafting legislation, pay careful attention to the issue of enforcement**. What tactics might those who are the target of the legislation and/or those opposed to the legislation use to resist or delay enforcement? How can you draft the legislation to make anti-enforcement efforts more difficult? A victory is not a victory if the legislation you get passed is not enforced or enforceable. The legislative branch can pass law after law after law. However, they are nothing more than words on paper if the executive and judicial branches do not exert the power of government to require compliance with the law. Quite often, the struggle for change only begins with the signature on a piece of legislation. It is what happens the

> next day, the day after that, the month after that, and the next year and next and next, that matters. Define success by meaningful change, not by the volume of legislation you pass. Ultimately, success comes from acceptance, a mind change on the part of American citizens in which the departure from the past becomes the norm of today.

The Sherman Act did nothing to stop business consolidations. In fact, many of America's giant firms were created in the 1890s. The multi-unit national industrial corporation that had been the exception prior to the 1890s became the "standard instrument for managing the production and distribution of goods in America."[340] Two great waves of trust building took place, the first from 1890 to 1893 and a second from 1895 to 1904. In 1899 alone, 1,208 companies disappeared, gobbled up larger corporations. The number of industrial companies with more than $50 million in assets went from eight in 1897 to 40 in 1903. By 1904 a mere 318 companies controlled 40% of all manufacturing in the United States.[341]

During the presidential election of 1900, the antitrust issue once again became a subject of intense debate. Both parties responded with antitrust planks in their platforms. The Republican Party took a modest and cautionary approach to antitrust. It announce that it understood "the necessity and propriety for honest cooperation of capital [trusts] to meet new business conditions, and especially to extend [the country's] rapidly increasing foreign trade; but [that it condemned] all conspiracies and combinations intended to restrict business, to create monopolies, to limit production, or to control prices.[342]

The Democratic Party took a much tougher line. It "denounced the trusts for robbing producers and consumers, reducing employment, arbitrarily dictating the terms of jobs, and, in general, benefiting a few at the expense of many." The Democrats pledged that if elected they would wage "an unceasing warfare in nation, state, and city against private monopoly in every form."[343]

The Democrats lost and McKinley, with his new Vice-President Theodore Roosevelt, was elected to a second term. [Note: Vice President

Garett Hobart had died on heart failure in 1899.] No one expected antitrust enforcement to be any more of a priority during McKinley's second term than it had been during his first. That was until September 6, 1901. McKinley was attending the Pan-American Exposition in Buffalo. He was shot twice by Leon Czolgosz, an anarchist. Six days later McKinley died of his wounds and Roosevelt became president.

An astute politician, Theodore Roosevelt latched on to antitrust as an issue he could use for political advantage. Roosevelt conveniently distinguished between "bad trusts" and "good trusts." "Good" trusts made great material development possible and increased the nation's international prestige." They were good for the country and "an unavoidable characteristics of the new economy.' Roosevelt said good trusts should be left alone.

On the other hand, "bad" trusts should be broken up. "Bad" trusts were the result of unconscionable business practices." They should and must be controlled. The key in distinguishing between good and bad trusts, said Roosevelt, was not size, wealth, or even the degree of market control but intention.[344]

UNINTENDED CONSEQUENCES

The Sherman Act outlawed anti-competitive practices and made the restraint of trade unlawful. What it did not do was to define with any precision what was unlawful. Moreover there is little in the legislative history to suggest what Congress meant by "restraint of trade" or "monopolization." In fact, the authors of the legislation avoided precise definition.

The vagueness of the act had totally unexpected and unintended consequences. The authors of the bill assumed that it would be and remain unenforceable because of its vagueness. They were right during the first few decades. However that changed in 1911 when Chief Justice Edward D. White wrote in the opinion in the Standard Oil case that Sherman Act "was a confirmation of the common law…to which a rule of reason, befitting the context of the times, could be applied, and this was the intent of the legislators and the act."[345] The courts in subsequent cases turned to the debates in the Congressional Record to justify their right to interpret and reinterpret the law. In the case of Apex Hosiery Co. vs. Leader, et. al. in 1940, Chief Justice Harlan F. Stone wrote:

> The prohibitions of the Sherman Act were not stated in terms of precision or of crystal clarity and the Act itself does not define them. In consequence of the vagueness of its language, perhaps not uncalculated, the courts have been left to give content to the statute, and in the performance of that function, it is appropriate that courts should interpret its words in the light of its legislative history and of the particular evils at which the legislation was aimed. [346]

The Rule of Reason was adopted by the courts as a means for determining whether a restraint of trade was prohibited by the Sherman Act. Essentially the rule meant that the courts would decide on a case-by-case basis taking into consideration several factors:

1. specific information about the nature of the business involved,
2. the history, nature, and effect of the restraint, and
3. the applicable market power of the parties involved, and the reasons for the restraint.

In 1914, Congress sought to remedy some of the problems associated with the Sherman Antitrust Act and the way courts had interpreted and applied it by passing the Clayton Act. Among other things, the Clayton Act focused antitrust policy on preventing actions such as price discrimination between different purchasers of commodities that would substantially lessen competition. It excluded human labor and therefore union as well as agricultural, and horticultural organizations from antitrust enforcement. In addition, it made the acquisition of stock of a competitor illegal if it would result in a substantial lessening of competition. Finally, the act placed enforcement authority in the Interstate Commerce Commission (for common carriers), the Federal Reserve Board (for banks), and the Federal

Trade Commission (for all other forms of commerce.). What the Clayton Act did not do is change the Rule of Reason.

As authors Peter Dickson and Philippa Wells point out, legislation can have unintended consequences. In the case of the Sherman Act, the trusts and Republicans outsmarted themselves. They codified into U.S. commercial law the common law rule of reason principle that the courts used later to apply the act in ways the drafters of the legislation never imagined. "Freed from the restrictions imposed by initial intent," write Dickson and Wells, "the courts and judges have extraordinary latitude under the rule of reason to take competitive policy and antitrust laws in new directions."[347] If the authors had written the act more precisely it is doubtful that the Sherman Anti-trust Act would have had anywhere near the impact on the economy. In fact, the act may have become quickly obsolete and forgotten.

> **LESSON: All legislation has the potential for unintended consequences, some good and some bad.** It is not enough to pass legislation with an eye to how it fits the current time. You must think of the future. How might the legislation be interpreted by the courts? How will it be implemented? Will it be implemented at all? Who might pervert the legislation to their own advantage and how can such perversion be prevented or made more difficult? You must consider not just how the legislation will impact the nation in the days and weeks after passage but also how it might impact the nation years in the future.

THE LEGACY OF THE SHERMAN ACT

As one leading authority on American capitalism put it, the Sherman Act declared "the rules of the game for the American economy...[and] is one of the great foundations of American civilization...If not the most powerful instrument of economic policy in the United States, the Sherman Act is the most characteristic."[348] No one in Congress at the time would have imagined that the vague little act they were passing would have such impact, least of all those reformers who so desperately wanted to rein in big business. But then, stranger things have happened. In our final chapter dealing with legislative accomplishments, we will look at the passage of a piece of legislation that few people think about today but that had an enormous impact on the country not for what it did but for the pattern of future legislation it set in motion. It was the opening shot in the struggle for 20^{Th} century civil rights and it pitted a determined southern future president against an equally determined southern senator and close friend who was threatening to employ the ultimate senate rule to block progress.

A SUMMARY OF LESSONS FROM THE STRUGGLE TO REIN IN BIG BUSINESS

A victory is not a victory if the legislation is not enforced or enforceable. The legislative branch can pass law after law after law. However, they are nothing more than words on paper if the executive and judicial branches do not exert the power of government to require compliance with the law. Quite often, the struggle for change only begins with the president's signature on a piece of legislation. It is what happens the next day and the day after that and the month after that and he next year and next and next, that matters. Meaningful change is the true measure of the success of progressives not the sheer volume of passed legislation alone. Ultimately, success comes from acceptance, a mind change on the part of American citizens in which the departure from the past becomes the norm of today.

Americans have a visceral fear of the concentration of power and the loss of individual liberty or self-sufficiency. In an earlier chapter, we learned about the fear Americans have of the power own government and how they instinctive recoil when anyone suggests expanding government control of their lives. They have a similar fear of big business or any entity that seems large and imposing. Coupled with that fear is a delusion of self-sufficiency. Americans imagine they can go it alone just as they imagine their pioneering forefathers did. Opponents of progressive legislation often tap into Americans' fear of power and delusion of self-sufficiency to defeat legislation so be prepared for such attacks. On the other hand, you can tap into that fear when the purpose of proposed change is to rein in powerful entities as in the case of the Sherman Act.

A frequent tactic used by the conservative opposition faced with a loud public outcry for some legislative action is to propose legislation that appears to address the issue angering voters but has little practical effect or is so vague as to be largely unenforceable. Such situations present Progressives with a dilemma. Should they oppose the weak remedy conservatives are offering and hold out for tougher legislation or should they take what they can get and hope to strengthen the legislation later on. If they hold out, they risk being charged with resisting reform. If they agree to the conservative proposal, they may be stuck for years with an ineffective remedy allowing the problem to worsen or opponents time to placate the public and build opposition to further reform.

There are many reasons why legislators decide to support legislation but they usually have little to do with concern for the public welfare or what is good for the country. Appeals to their sense of patriotic duty are rarely as good as appeals to their self-interest, particularly their self-interest in being reelected or in punishing a political enemy.

Enforcement matters, a lot. In drafting legislation, pay careful attention to the issue of enforcement. What tactics might those who are the target of the legislation and/or those opposed to the legislation use to resist or delay enforcement? How can you draft the legislation to make anti-enforcement efforts more difficult? A victory is not a victory if the legislation you get passed is not enforced or enforceable. The legislative branch can pass law after law after law. However, they are nothing more than words on paper if the executive and judicial branches do not exert the power of government to require compliance with the law. Quite often, the struggle for change only begins with the signature on a piece of legislation. It is what happens the next day, the day after that, the month after that, and the next year and next and next, that matters. Define success by meaningful change, not by the volume of legislation you pass. Ultimately, success comes from acceptance, a mind change on the part of American citizens in which the departure from the past becomes the norm of today.

All legislation has the potential for unintended consequences, some good and some bad. It is not enough to pass legislation with an eye to how it fits the current time. You must think of the future. How might the legislation be interpreted by the courts? How will it be implemented? Will it be implemented at all? Who might pervert the legislation to their own advantage and how can such perversion be prevented or made more difficult? You must consider not just how the legislation will impact the nation in the days and weeks after passage but also how it might impact the nation years in the future.

6
The Struggle for Civil Rights

I'm going to conclude this book, at least the part of this book dealing with specific legislative accomplishments, by discussing an accomplishment involving the struggle for rights affecting only a small percentage of Americans and even then largely affecting only a small percentage of Americans living in certain states in our nation. This struggle can teach us many things but foremost it teaches us that the violation of any individual's rights or any group's rights no matter how large or small affects all of us. If we do not protect the rights of the least powerful, we can never truly secure the rights we seek for ourselves. Ultimately, that is the progressive goal. We do not seek power, privilege, or fortune for the few or even the many but only the opportunity to secure the benefits of life, liberty, property and freedom for all. We strive for basic civil rights for every single human being. Ultimately, nothing else is worth pursuing. I will begin this chapter with a story of something that happened in 1957. In truth, the story began more than a hundred years before.

MRS. MARGARET FROST

On August 2, 1957, Ms. Margaret Frost stood before a waist-high wooden counter in the office of the Barbour County Registrars in Eufaula, Alabama along with two other residents of the county.[349] Ms. Frost and the other two applicants had come to register to vote. Ms. Frost had tried to register before in January of that year so she understood how the process worked. The registrar would ask a series of questions such as the names of local, state and federal officials. You had to answer all of the questions correctly or you could not register. In January, William (Beel) Stokes, the Chairman of the Board of Registrars, questioned Ms. Frost. She had studied hard to prepare for the questioning and thought she answered Stokes' questions correctly. She was surprised when, after just a few questions, he stopped and with an amused expression told she should go home and study some more. Ms. Frost did as instructed, studying even harder this time.

One of the registrars explained the rules to the applicants standing before him on that August day. He would ask them twelve questions and they had to answer all twelve questions correctly or they could not register. The registrar then asked two questions of each of the applicants in turn. Ms. Frost answered both correctly as did the second applicant. The third applicant answered his first question correctly but missed the second. The registrar stopped the questioning. "You've all failed," he said, "You all go on home and study a little more."

Ms. Frost and her two fellow applicants were African Americans. The registrar was White. It was not surprising that the registrar denied Ms. Frost and her colleagues the right to register to vote. Most Black people were at that time. What was surprising is that Ms. Frost and the other applicants would even try to register. Everyone knew what could happen to Black people who tried to register to vote in Barbour County or anywhere in South for that matter in the 1950s. Black men who tried to register would lose their jobs. Black farmers who tried to register would lose their farms because they could no longer get loans from the local bank to buy seed for their crops. Ms. Frost's husband, David Frost, recalled that when he had successfully registered several years before a White man reminded him "the White folks are the nigger's friend as long as the nigger stays in his place" and that by registering Frost had gotten out of his place. Frost the White man did not call him "David" or "boy," as was his custom for months after. Instead, he called David "nigger" or "nigra," terms Frost said he "hated, hated, hated." When word got out that Frost actually planned to vote, he received a visit one night. A car filled with men pulled up outside his house and someone shot out the porch lights. At first, Frost thought of calling the police. Then, he noticed that the car the men who were shooting at his home were in was a local police car.

Ms. Frost knew all of this. She recalled that when she visited the Barbour County registrars' office that hot August day, she was so nervous she was shaking. "I was scared," she recalled, "I was scared I would do something wrong…Scared that the White people would do something to me." Nevertheless, she went on, "I wanted to be a citizen…I figure all citizens, you know, should be able to vote."

White people did not allow Ms. Frost to be a citizen that day. She would not be allowed to be one for some time to come. Neither would most other Black people in Alabama and the rest of the South. Additionally, Ms. Frost had no legal recourse. She could not sue in court to force the Board of Registrars to allow her to vote. No lawyer would take her case. Even if one did, Ms. Frost had no chance of winning. Just that year, the U.S. Justice Department had completed a study examining that very issue. It concluded that Black people had "no adequate legal remedy" for being refused the right to register even though they were theoretically guaranteed the right to vote by the 15th Amendment to the Constitution,. There was no federal law enforcing the provisions of the 15th Amendment. Liberals and progressives introduced hundreds of such bills over the years but none passed. That would change in a little over a month.

On September 9, 1957, Congress passed Public Law 85-315 or The Civil Rights Act of 1957. The Act would not bring an end to discrimination in voter registration or any other activity. However, it would bring a beginning to the end. The Civil Rights Act of 1957 is not notable for what it accomplished in advancing the rights of Black people because in that regard it accomplished very little. However, at the time the 1957 act was the first act dealing with civil rights passed in 82 years. The 1957 act broke the log jam when it came to civil rights legislation and made the better known civil rights acts of 1964 and 1965 all possible. In that regard, it was a great progressive legislative accomplishment. Ironically, it was the almost single-handed political accomplishment of a southern senator with questionable motives

The passage of the 1957 Civil Rights act teaches important lessons about getting things done in Washington. We will get to those in this chapter. First, we will go back, all the way back to the end of the America's bloody Civil War.

THE STRUGGLE FOR CIVIL RIGHTS BEGINS

America's civil war ended in the spring of 1865. In total, 620,000 Americans died so that 4 million slaves could be free. In December the 13th amendment was ratified abolishing slavery. Black people were now free but what should happen to the former slaves? Should they be allowed to vote? Should they be treated as equals? The former slave was free but as Frederick Douglas said his condition had barely changed. "He had neither money, property, nor friends. He was free from the old plantation, but he had nothing but the dusty road under his free...He was turned loose, naked, hungry, and destitute to the open sky." [350]

The 14th and 15th amendments were quickly added to the Constitution to provide Black people and everyone equal protection under the law, guarantee citizenship for all those born in the U.S. regardless of race, and protect American citizens from being denied the right to vote based upon their "race, color, or previous condition of servitude (i.e., slavery).[351] Congress quickly passed five major pieces of legislation to enforce provisions of the three amendments. Perhaps the most significant of these was The Civil Rights Act of 1875. It declared that "all persons within the jurisdiction of the United States shall be entitled to the full and equal enjoyment of the accommodations, advantages, facilities, and privileges of inns, public conveyances on land or water, theaters, and other places of public amusement; subject only to the conditions and limitations established by law, and applicable alike to citizens of every race and color, regardless of any previous condition of servitude."[352] That should have been the end of it. The civil rights of all Americans should have been protected. They were not.

LESSON: There is no guarantee that a victory, even one won at the cost of thousands of lives, will endure. Opposition continues. Those who are defeated rarely accept their defeat gracefully. They do not change their minds just because others hearts were won and legislation to remedy awful wrongs was passed. Memories of wrongs fade over time. Ultimately, we lose if we do not constantly remind our fellow citizens of what evil was vanquished, why legislation was needed, and the consequences of returning to what Conservatives like to call the "good old days."

THE RISE OF JIM CROWE

Almost as soon as the war ended, the reconstituted southern state legislatures enacted "Black Codes" designed to keep Black people in as close a state of slavery as possible without actually returning then to slavery. As one White southern put it, "the ex-slave was not a free man; he was a free Negro."[353]

The content of the Black Codes varied from state to state but the following features were common:

> Existing marriages, including common-law marriages, were recognized (although interracial marriages were prohibited), and testimony of Black people was accepted in legal cases involving Black people-and in six states, in all cases. Black people could own property. They could sue and be sued in the courts. On the other hand, Black people could not own farm lands in Mississippi or city lots in South Carolina; they were required to buy special licenses to practice certain trades in Mississippi; and in some states they could not carry firearms without a license. Black people were required to enter into annual labor contracts. Dependent children were subject to compulsory apprenticeship and corporal punishment by masters. Unemployed (vagrant) Black people were punished with severe fines, and, if unable to pay, they were forced to labor in the fields for those who paid the courts for this source of cheap labor. To many people it indeed seemed that slavery was on the way back in another guise.

> The new Mississippi penal code virtually said so: "All penal and criminal laws now in force describing the mode of punishment of crimes and misdemeanors committed by slaves, free negroes, or mulattoes are hereby reenacted, and decreed to be in full force." [354]

In 1883, the Supreme Court ruled that the Civil Rights Act of 1875 was unconstitutional because, said the court, the 14th Amendment upon which it relied applied only to discrimination by states, not by private individuals or businesses. After that, states began enacting so-called "Jim Crowe" laws specifically designed to enforce second-class citizenship on African Americans and the courts generally backed these efforts.[355] In 1890, Louisiana passed a law requiring that Black people ride in separate railroad cars. Black people challenged the law by having a light-skinned African American by the name of Homer Plessy attempt to sit in a rail car reserved for White people. Local authorities arrested Plessy and a local judge ruled against him. The Supreme Court upheld the decision in Plessy v Ferguson, arguing that the state did not violate Plessy's rights because the accommodations were "separate but equal." A long series of court cases followed in which courts used the "separate but equal" doctrine to deny Black people their civil rights.

In 1899, the court applied the doctrine of separate but equal for the first time to education. In the case of Cumming v. Richmond County Board of Education, the court ruled that the Board could operate White-only schools even when the county provided no schools for Black people. In this and other similar cases, the court made it clear that it was much more interested in enforcing the separate part of the "separate but equal" doctrine than the equal part.

States responded to such decisions by enacting laws segregating all forms of public areas, accommodations, transportation and other facilities. Signs went up throughout the south designating "White people Only" and "Colored" water fountains, restrooms, waiting rooms, and entrances, exits, and seating areas in libraries, public building, and theaters.

By 1877, the federal government had essentially abandoned any effort to enforce the Black voting rights guaranteed by the Fifteenth

Amendment. States like Mississippi first used violence and intimidation to stop Black people from voting. In some instances, White people boasted of shooting down Black voters "just like birds." The scare tactics worked. By the time of the 1880 presidential elections, less than a third of Black people dared vote.

Beginning in the 1890s, Southern states began changing their constitutions and statutes to disenfranchise Black people systematically. Many adopted a plan developed first in Mississippi that placed a heavy burden on Black people who might try to register to vote. Among other things, the Mississippi Plan required that those wishing to register had to pay a poll tax and pass a literacy test. The poll tax was a significant burden for freed slaves who lived in poverty as well as poor White people. The literacy test made it possible for White registrars to refuse to register Black people by simply declaring that they had failed to pass the test regardless of how they actually performed.

Thereafter, the Black vote practically disappeared from State politics. Supporters of the constitutional disfranchisement provisions argued that such measures did not violate the 14th and 15th amendments because the provisions applied to all potential voters without regard to race. In fact, however, the test fell most heavily on Black people because of the way White registrars administered the tests. Other supporters reasoned that legal disfranchisement would lessen the level of violence in the Southern states, because law would replace force. Mississippi's plan was so successful in keeping Black people from voting that other Southern states quickly adopted similar laws and Constitutional amendments.

LIVING BEHIND THE VEIL

Few of us today can imagine what it was like to be a Black person living in the South or almost anywhere in the country for that matter, in the period before Congress passed meaningful civil rights legislation in the 1960s. Civil Rights activists and scholar W.E.B. Dubois wrote that it was like living "behind a veil."

> It is a peculiar sensation, this double-consciousness, this sense of always looking at one's self through the eyes of others, of measuring one's soul by the tape of a world that looks on in amused contempt and pity. One feels his two-ness, -- an American, a Negro; two souls, two thoughts, two unreconciled strivings; two warring ideals in one dark body, whose dogged strength alone keeps it from being torn asunder.[356]

Black Americans confronted racists' institutions and racial stereotypes daily. Survival required masking one's true feelings, acting a part scripted by White people, not responding to White insults. To do otherwise was to risk death. If you were a Black person, White people expected that you would avoid looking them in their eyes. If you were a young, Black male, you dared not look directly at a White woman and certainly not ever touch her even by accident. Dubois said he learned that lesson early on.

> I quite accidentally jostled a White woman as I passed. She was not hurt in the slightest, nor even particularly inconvenienced. Immediately in accord with my New England training, I raised my hat and begged her pardon. I acted quite instinctively and with genuine regret for a little mistake. The woman was furious; why I never knew; somehow, I cannot say how, I had transgressed the interracial mores of the South. Was it because I showed no submissiveness? Did I fail to debase myself utterly and eat spiritual dirt? Did I act as equal among equals? I do not know. I only sensed scorn and hate: the kind of despising which a dog might incur.[357]

If you were a Black American in the South, White people expected you to stare at the ground when speaking to them. Even if you were an adult, White people called you "boy," or "girl," or "auntie," or "uncle" or worse. They never addressed you by your last name or as "Mister" or "Mrs." or "Miss." If you were a Black American in the South, White people expected you to wait until they were served before you could transact your business in a store even if you were there first. You never spoke first or asked for assistance. You were expected to wait quietly for as long as it took for someone to get around to asking you what you wanted. People of your race were portrayed as lazy, silly, incompetent, ignorant fools in all of the circuses, shows, and films that came to town and all the radio programs on the air. As a Black parent, you tried to protect your children from the degrading images but rarely succeeded for long. If you were a Black American in the South, White people expected you to put on a mask of servitude whenever you were around them. Behind that mask, you seethed in anger but there was little you could do to address the wrongs and humiliation. The African American poet Paul Laurence Dubar wrote of the mask and the yearning of African Americans to be free in his poem entitled "We Wear the Mask."

> We wear the mask that grins and lies,
> It hides our cheeks and shades our eyes,
> This debt we pay to human guile;
> With torn and bleeding hearts we smile,
> And mouth with myriad subtleties.
>
> Why should the world be over-wise,
> In counting all our tears and sighs?
> Nay, let them only see us, while
> We wear the mask.
>
> We smile, but, O great Christ, our cries
> To thee from tortured souls arise.
> We sing, but oh the clay is vile
> Beneath our feet, and long the mile;
> But let the world dream other-wise,
> We wear the mask![358]

In 1929, American author Scott Nearing described the living conditions of most Black people in the South at that time this way:

> The Negro shanties, built of logs in a few cases and of wood in most instances, are usually unpainted, old, out of repair, 'squalid, lacking modern conveniences, unsupplied with the simplest necessaries such as running water, adequate toilet facilities, heating facilities, and the like.[359]

The schools Black children were forced to attend, which were supposed to be 'separate but equal,' were definitely separate and just as definitely unequal. Nearing wrote:

> The churches and lodge rooms which are used for Negro schools are chiefly old, dilapidated buildings, unfit for teaching purposes. In some cases, they have no means of getting light; often there are no desks. In most of the churches' and lodge halls, the children sit on plank benches which sometimes have no backs to them. In some counties there is not a single school building for colored children.[360]

If you were Black in the South, life was intolerable but you dared not complain and you certainly dared not violate the social etiquette White people imposed upon you. If you did, White people might lynch you.

LYNCHINGS

Between 1882 and 1968, mobs lynched 4,863 people in the United States. Black people represented ninety seven percent of those who died. Often White people made a kind of sporting event out of lynching an uppity Black.

> After 1890, [White] mobs usually subjected their Black victims to sadistic tortures that included burnings, dismemberment, being dragged to death behind carts and autos, and horribly prolonged suffering. [R]ailroad companies sold tickets to attend lynchings...White people hawked body parts of dead victims as

> souvenirs...White families brought their children to watch the torture and death of Black people by lynching,...[N]ewspapers carried advance notices, and ...White participants proudly posed for pictures of themselves with the burned corpses of lynched men and women-- and then allowed the images to be reproduced on picture postcards.[361]

In his book, *The Walls of Jericho*, Robert Mann tells the following grisly tale of what happened to one Black woman in Georgia whom White people accused of breaking the social rules governing proper behavior.

> In Georgia in 1918, a White mob hanged a pregnant Black woman from a tree, soaked her with gasoline and motor oil, and then set her afire. As her charred body dangled from the limb, a White man stepped forward with a pocketknife and slashed open her abdomen. When a screaming baby tumbled out of her lifeless body, the man promptly stomped the child to death.[362]

Such atrocities should have outraged all Americans regardless of region or race. Some were outraged and demanded federal action to stop the murders. Liberals in Congress passed anti-lynching legislation in the House in 1922, 1937 and 1940. Southern senators killed the legislation each time in the Senate by filibuster or the threat of filibuster.

The Southern Senators had an explanation for their opposition to federal anti-lynching legislation. They said they were not condoning the killing. No, they certainly were not. Their opposition was not a defense of lynching. It was a defense of the Constitution and a way of life. Typical was the explanation Senator Richard Russell of Georgia offered for his opposition to an anti-lynching law that came before the Senate in 1938. Russell consistently opposed anti-lynching bills and other Civil Rights measures but not because he was prejudiced, he said. Indeed he proclaimed on the floor of the Senate in 1938 that "there are no members of the Negro race in my state tonight...who would say that any official or personal act of mine had resulted in any unfairness to the Negroes...I was brought up with them. I love them."[363] No, argued Russell, his opposition to civil rights was not racist, it only reflected a concern for the Constitution and protecting the rights of individual states and "the rights of private property and the rights of American citizens to choose their associates" and/or whom they would hire to work in their businesses. The Southern way of life that would be destroyed by federal intervention, even intervention to stop lynching, said Russell, had "been evolved painfully through seventy years of trial and error, suffering and sacrifice, on the part of both races." Segregation was the Southern way of life but he argued, it was " necessary to preserve peace and harmony between the races." Black people and White people both benefited from segregation, said Russell. Segregation promoted "the welfare and progress of both races." The system, in fact, said Russell had done much for the Black person. "In a short space of time the race that had only known savagery and slavery had been brought into a new day of civilization, where education and opportunity had been provided for them…The White people and Black people alike in our section have learned that it is better for the races to live apart socially."[364] Amazingly, Russell apparently believed this nonsense. Regardless, no Federal anti-lynching law was ever passed until the 1960s when Congress empowered the executive branch to prosecute anyone hurting or killing a person trying to exercise their federally guaranteed civil rights.

THE POST WORLD WAR II PERIOD

Little happened to address the plight of Black people in the country, and in the South in particular, until near the end of World War II. Then, in 1944, a more liberal Supreme Court ruled that the Texas Democratic Party's "White only" primary was unconstitutional. That ruling opened the door somewhat for Black people to register to vote. By 1948, an estimated 15 percent of eligible Black people in the South had registered to vote.

White people did all they could to keep Black people from voting. Some resorted to violence. Black people who tried to register were intimidated both physically and economically. Some White people shot and killed Black people who tried to vote. Some other White people were "kinder."

They just maimed Black people who tried to vote. Black people who were able to register in spite of the threats of violence found it difficult and even dangerous to attempt to vote. In the 1948 elections, less than one in ten Black people of voting age were able to cast ballots. After 1948, state after Southern state implemented "literacy" tests requiring those seeking to register to demonstrate their "understanding" and "interpretation" of state laws or the U.S. Constitution to the satisfaction of White registrars whose decisions were not subject to appeal. Liberals introduced thirteen separate bills in Congress to strengthen voting rights for Black people between 1946 and 1954. Southern senators blocked every one.

BLACK SOLDIERS RETURN HOME FOR WORLD WAR II

If you were among the million Black Americans who fought in World War II, particularly if you were from the South, you found upon your return that in spite of the medals and other decorations for valor and defense of liberty you and your fellow Black soldiers had earned, little had changed. You could legally do a few things. You could not do many more things just because of your race. You could ride the train or bus home but only if you sat in prescribed and less desirable seats. At the bus or train station you could get a drink of water or use the bathroom but only if a "colored" water fountain or bathroom was available. If you wanted something to eat, you could purchase it but only if you went around to the back of the restaurant or sandwich stand and had your meal handed to you through a window. Only White people could go in the front door and sit at a table. When you got home, you could apply for a job but not a good one even if you were the best qualified. Those were reserved for White people only. You could walk the streets of your hometown but the only paved streets were in the White areas of town. You could rent or, if were lucky, purchase a home but only in a designated area of town and that area would most likely not have a water or sewer system like of those in White neighborhoods. You could take your wife or girl friend to a movie but you had to sit in the balcony and when a Black character appeared in the movie, you would cringe because the role he/she played would demean your race. Your children and younger brothers and sisters could attend schools but the schools they attended would not be as good as White schools. The typical Southern state spent only a quarter as much on schools for Black children as it did on schools for White children. Your children's teachers would be paid 30 percent less than their White counterparts would. Unlike White children, your kids would have no school bus to take them to and from school. You could attend college on the G.I. Bill but only if you could find an opening in the overcrowded Black colleges since you could not attend a White college or university regardless of how smart you were.

During the war, you had been required most likely to serve in a segregated unit but, chances are for the first time in your life you had day to day contact with White people who actually treated you with a degree of decency. Some may have even called you "Mister." They might even have been willing to shake hands with you. If you were from the South, you noticed something significantly different about the way Black people lived outside the South. Their lives were not perfect but, their lives were better, much better.

When you returned home, you wanted something better for yourself, your family and your race. George Crockett, a Black columnist, wrote at the time about the Black soldiers in WW II and the impact he said it had upon them and their new expectations:

> Negro men literally saw the world. And they began to associate English imperialism in India, Chiang Kai-shek's autocracy in China, and Dutch despotism in Java, as part and parcel of the same brand of fascism they thought existed only here at home. I do not believe that Negroes will stand idly by and see these newly opened doors of economic opportunity closed in their faces. Negro women will not be content to toil in other people's kitchens again for $3, $4, or $5 per week and a bag of left-over food scraps to take home to their poorly fed young ones.
>
> Nor will Negro GIs permit our propaganda machine to forget that it did the world's best job when it sought to convince these same

> Negro GIs that this was really a war for democracy and against fascism.[365]

A returning Black soldier from Alabama expressed the determination of many a Black soldier returning to the South after the war when he told the Pittsburgh *Courier*...

> I spent four years in the army to free a bunch of Frenchman and Dutchmen, and I'm hanged if I'm going to let the Alabama version of the Germans kick me around when I get back home. No sirreee-bob! I went into the army a nigger; I'm coming out a man."[366]

The Southern reaction to the returning Black people who saw themselves as men was frequently violent as it was in the case of Isaac Woodard, a returning Black soldier. Recently honorably discharged and still in uniform, Woodard boarded a bus in Atlanta in February 1946 for the trip back to his home in South Carolina. At a bus stop, Woodard sought to use the bathroom. The bus driver refused. Woodward argued with the driver instead of lowering his head and remaining silent as the Jim Crowe code said he should. At the next stop, the driver called a police officer, Lynwood Shull, to complain about Woodward's behavior. Shull dragged Woodard off the bus, beat him and hauled him off to jail. There Shull proceeded to beat Woodard some more and then used his nightstick to ground out Woodard's eyes. After local authorities refused to charge Shull with any crime, the U.S. Justice Department charged Shull with violating Woodard's civil rights. Shull pleaded self-defense and a local jury acquitted him after less than a half hour deliberation. Shull went free. Woodard was blinded for life.

THINGS BEGIN TO CHANGE

As the forties gave way to the fifties, the South was as determined as ever to maintain things as they had been for decades. Many southern White people were willing to condone or, at a minimum, look the other way when atrocities were committed against Black people like they were against Woodard. However, things were beginning to change on the national level at least. In 1948, President Truman issued Executive Order 9981 desegregating the armed forces.

Then, in 1954, the Supreme Court took up the case of Brown v. Board of Education of Topeka, Kansas. Oliver Brown, a Black welder from Topeka, filed a suit against the Topeka Board of Education, challenging its decision that Brown's eight-year old daughter had to attend an inferior Black school twenty-two blocks from her home rather than a much better White school fifteen blocks closer. The Brown case was just one of a number of similar cases that Black people from Kansas, South Carolina, Virginia and Delaware had filed challenging the Plessy vs. Ferguerson ruling condoning "separate but equal." In May 1954, Chief Justice Warren wrote the unanimous opinion of the court. "We conclude," said the court, "that in the field of public education the doctrine of 'separate but equal' has no place. Separate educational facilities are inherently unequal." Thurgood Marshall was the NAACP attorney who argued and won the case. He would later become the first Black Supreme Court justice.

A year later in a separate case, the court decreed that the dismantling of separate school systems for Black people and White people could proceed with "all deliberate speed." Opponents of civil rights were angered at the court's haste. Supporters worried that the South would use the court's use of the word "could" instead of "should" to delay the inevitable. They were right.

White people in the South formed White Citizens Councils to oppose the court's ruling. One of the councils published a book by Tom P. Brady, a Mississippi circuit court judge who had become the intellectual leader of their cause. Brady argued that the court had failed to take into account the "fact" that Negroes, as he called Black people, were incapable of learning. He wrote:

> The Supreme Court refuses to recognize that it cannot by a mandate shrink the size of a Negro's skull which is one-eighth of an inch thicker than a White man's...The American Negro was

> divorced from Africa and saved from savagery. In spite of his basic inferiority, he was forced to do that which he would not do for himself. He was compelled to lay aside cannibalism, his barbaric savage custom. He was transported from aboriginal ignorance and superstition. He was given a language ...His soul was quickened. He was introduced to God! The veneer had been rubbed on, but the inside is fundamentally the same .... You can dress a chimpanzee, housebreak him and teach him to use a knife and fork, but it will take countless generations of evolutionary development, if ever, before you can convince him that a caterpillar or a cockroach is not a delicacy"[367]

Many Southern White people agreed with Brady's assessment. They created hundreds of White Citizens Councils throughout the South within months of the *Brown* decision. The South's most prominent citizens joined the Councils and pressed their state legislatures to take action to counter the court's orders. Southern state legislatures obliged by passing laws authorizing local school boards to transfer Black students back to their former schools should any court order the integration of a school. States authorized school boards to withdraw funding from any White-only school that accepted Black students even under a court order. South Carolina went further. There the legislature authorized local school boards to close any school ordered integrated by the courts. Local school boards could even go so far as to close all schools in their district and allow White people to send their children to segregated schools in a different district. That would force Civil rights advocates to file suits in district after district if they wanted to integrate the schools. If all else failed and South Carolina's public schools were forced to integrate, then the legislature said all schools in the state would be closed. White people could then set up their own private schools. Of course, Black people would not be able to afford to do the same so Black kids would just go unschooled. Georgia went so far as to amend its Constitution to remove the requirement that the state even provide for a public school system. These laws largely succeeded. Only three Southern states—Tennessee, Arkansas, and Texas—had any desegregated schools when the school year began in 1955. Even in those states only a few hundred Black people attended schools with White people. It was obvious that the South would never change without the passage of Civil Rights legislation to demand change. The prospects of that happening remained dim. However, two events that occurred in the South in 1955 brought national attention to the plight of Black people in the south and ignited popular support for some form of civil rights legislation. The first event occurred during the summer of 1955 and involved a fourteen-year-old boy.

THE EMMETT TILL MURDER

In August of 1955, Mrs. Mamie Bradley of Chicago agreed to allow her fourteen year old son, Emmett (Bobo) Till to accompany his uncle, Reverend Moses Wright of Mississippi and his cousin Wheeler Parker for a visit to the Reverend's farm near Money, Mississippi in the Mississippi Delta. Emmett, Wheeler and the Reverend Wright arrived in Money on Sunday, August 21st. The following Wednesday evening around 7:30 PM, Emmett accompanied seven of his cousins, ranging in age from 13 to 19 years old and all Black, on a trip to a local store to buy some treats. The store, which was really a ramshackle shack with living quarters in the back, was owned and operated by a White man, Roy Bryant, then twenty, and his wife Carolyn, then twenty-one. Carolyn was five feet tall and weighed around 100 pounds. That evening she was tending the store alone since Roy, who drove a truck to supplement their income, was away on a job hauling shrimp from New Orleans to San Antonio and Brownsville, Texas. Carolyn's sister-in-law had come to stay with Carolyn until the normal 9:00 PM closing time since Carolyn did not like to be alone in the store at night. The sister-in-law was with her two small sons in the living quarters at the rear of the store. Carolyn was tending the store alone.

Emmett was a stocky, muscular teenager around five feet five inches tall and weighing about 160 pounds. Reverend Wright later testified that even at his age, Emmett "looked like a man." According to various accounts, since arriving in Money, Emmett had been showing off, exciting his cousins by daring to say "Yeah" and "Naw" to White people in the community when even adult Black people dared say nothing more than "Yassuh" and "Nawshuh." He bragged that he had a White girlfriend back in Chicago and even circulated a picture of her that he carried in his wallet in support of his claim. That Wednesday evening the eight Black teenagers spent some time laughing and horsing around in front of the Bryant store. Emmett eventually left the group and went into the store to buy some candy. There are a number of different versions of what happened next.

Some say Emmett, who had a speech impediment that caused him to stammer, went into the store, bought his candy from Carolyn and as he was leaving, said "G-g-g-g-goodbye." One of Emmett's cousins who was from the area laughed at his stuttering and as they walked away said" "Bobo, don't you know you're not supposed to say goodbye to a white woman?" Another cousin said, "She was good lookin', wasn't she." At that point, Emmett either attempted to give or actually gave out with a "wolf whistle." According to this version that was all that occurred.

A different version of the story has Emmett entering the store to purchase the candy and speaking to Carolyn. According to this version when Carolyn started to hand him his change, Emmett touched her hand said: "How about a date, baby?" and possibly "Don't be afraid o' me, baby. I ain't gonna hurt you. I been with white girls before."

No one really knows what Emmett may have said to Carolyn and whether or at what point he gave a "wolf whistle," if he did so at all. Carolyn later said that she told no one about the incident. Never the less, somehow the story got around the White community that a Black kid by the name of Emmett who was visiting Reverend Wright from Chicago had insulted Carolyn, scared her, or done something even worse.

On Friday afternoon, Roy Bryant returned home and quickly learned of the incident. He was incensed. On Saturday, Bryant told his half-brother, J. W. Milam, about the insult. Milam was thirty-six, six foot two and weighed 235 pounds. He had served under Patton in WW II where he earned a reputation as an expert street fighter and accomplished close-range killer. Like Bryant, he was angry about what Emmett had supposedly done to Carolyn. He was determined to teach the boy a lesson.

Around 2 AM on Sunday, August 28, Milam picked up Bryant and they drove to Reverend Wright's home. Milam carried his favorite gun, a .45 Colt automatic pistol. Bryant pounded on the door, waking the Reverend up, and asked to see the boy visiting from Chicago. Wright showed Bryant and Milam to the back bedroom where Emmett was sleeping in the bed with the Reverend's youngest son, Simeon. Bryant and Milam demanded that Emmett get out of bed, get dressed and accompany them. The Reverend apologized for anything the boy had done, asked them not to take him, and even offered to pay for the damages. He pleaded for the boy, "He ain't got good sense," said the Reverend, "He was raised Up Yonder. He didn't know what he was doing." Of course, that was true. It did not matter. Bryant and Milam ordered Emmett to get in the back of their pickup and left. No one other than Bryant and Milam would see Emmett alive again.

We know what happened next because Bryant and Milam later confessed to what they had done in an interview with a *LOOK* magazine reporter.[368] Of course, that was after an all-White local jury had found them innocent of murder. According to Milam, he and Bryant did not intend to kill Emmett but to "just whip him…and scare some sense into him." Milam's idea was to take Emmett to "the scariest place in the Delta," a bluff overlooking a nearby river that Milam had found while hunting. He wanted to stand Emmett up right on the edge of the bluff, "whip" him with the .45, shine their flashlights down the 100-foot sheer drop, and make him think they were going to throw him in. The problem was Bryant and Milam could not find the road leading to the bluff. Bryant and Milam drove around for nearly three hours. Emmett never tried to escape even though he was riding in the open bed of the pickup all the time. It was obvious that he was not afraid of Bryant and Milam. As Milam put it: "We were never able to scare him. They had just filled him so full of that poison that he was hopeless."

Eventually, Bryant and Milam gave up looking for the bluff and drove to Milam's house. They took Emmett into the tool shed behind the house and began "whipping" him. Milam pistol-whipped Emmett with his .45, employing techniques he had used in the service to get information from

German prisoners. Emmett took the blows. He would not yield to the White men. Milam recalled at one point Emmett said: "You bastards, I'm not afraid of you. I'm as good as you are. I've 'had' white women. My grandmother was a white woman." It was too much for Bryant and Milam. A Black teenager was defying them. Milam justified what they did next this way:

> Well, what else could we do? He was hopeless. I'm no bully; I never hurt a nigger in my life. I like niggers -- in their place --I know how to work 'em. But I just decided it was time a few people got put on notice. As long as I live and can do anything about it, niggers are gonna stay in their place. Niggers ain't gonna vote where I live. If they did, they'd control the govemment. They ain't gonna go to school with my kids. And when a nigger gets close to mentioning sex with a white woman, he's tired 0' livin'. I'm likely to kill him. Me and my folks fought for this country, and we've got some rights. I stood there in that shed and listened to that nigger throw that poison at me, and I just made up my mind. 'Chicago boy,' I said, 'I'm tired of 'em sending your kind down here to stir up trouble. Goddam you, I'm going to make an example of you -- just so everybody can know how me and my folks stand.'[369]

Later that night, Bryant and Milam took Emmett Till to the nearby Tallahatchie River. Milam raised his big .45 and shot, hitting Emmett in the head just at his right ear. The two murderers then tied a three-foot wide, metal gin fan around Emmett's neck with barbwire and dumped his body in the river.

At daylight, the morning after Bryant and Milam took Emmett, Reverend Wright and his wife drove to the home of her brother, Crosby Smith and told him what had happened. Wright and Smith then reported the abduction of Emmett to the local Leflore County sheriff. In the mean time, one of Emmett's cousins borrowed a phone and called Mamie Bradley in Chicago to tell her Emmett was missing. Mrs. Bradley reported the abduction to the Chicago police. The Chicago police phoned the Sheriff's office in Leflore County to inquire about what was being done to find the missing boy. Eventually, after numerous calls from the Chicago police, the Leflore County sheriff arrested Milam and Bryant. Milam and Bryant admitted abducting Emmett but claimed they had just "whipped his ass a little" and let him go. The last time they saw Emmett, said Milam and Bryant, he was walking down the railroad tracks getting the "hell back to Chicago" where he belonged.

A young White boy who had gone fishing discovered Emmett's body the next day. The body had snagged in shallow water. Emmett was horribly mutilated. Most of the left side of his head was gone. An eye dangled from one socket. Injuries to his head indicated he had suffered "torture, [and a] horrible beating." The local sheriff wanted to bury the body immediately. Mamie Bradley refused, insisting that the sheriff return her son's body to Chicago. Then, Mrs. Bradley did an extraordinary thing. She insisted that Emmett's body be displayed in a open casket so all could see what Milam and Bryant had done to her boy.

Thousands of Black people in Chicago lined up to move pass Emmett's open casket and view the body. "Men's faces changed as they saw what was inside, women fainted, some women flnging up their arms in horror, covering their faces as if to shield themselves from the sight."[370] *The Nation* reported on the case and the anger it generated in Chicago's Black community. Then, the magazine *Jet* ran a story about Emmett's murder and included a photograph of his horribly mutilated body. Black newspapers and then White newspapers began picking up the story. Thousands attended rallies in Black communities in Chicago, New York, Youngstown, Baltimore, Cleveland, Detroit and Los Angeles. White people in the South had committed many atrocities against Black people before but this time a body and photograph that once people saw they could not forget vividly documented the extent of the raw brutality.

On September 19, 1955, Roy Bryant and J.W. "Big" Milam stood trial for Emmett's murder. The trial lasted just five days. The all-White, all-male jury took just a little over an hour to find the defendants not guilt in spite of all of the evidence and testimony from Black eye witnesses who were brave enough to come forward. Members of the jury said they could have completed their deliberations faster if they had not taken a Coke break. In January 1956, Bryant and Milam agreed to an interview with *Look* magazine during which they confessed to the murder. Bryant and Milam could not be tried again for the murder of Emmett since they could not be subjected to double jeopardy. They were never even tried for violating Emmett's civil rights. They just went free. J. W. Milam died on December 31, 1980. Roy Bryant died on September 1, 1994. Both were still unrepentant for what they had done to Emmett.

The murder of Emmett Till sent shock waves through the country. As Robert Caro says, it produced a tidal wave of support for civil rights even in the South.

> By the 1950s, millions of American Negroes had never lived in the South, and while they may have been intellectually aware of conditions there, of what segregation was like, they did not really know those conditions… [N]ow reporters [for Black newspapers who covered the murder] made northern Black people see it. And they responded. A new wave of mass meetings swept across black communities in the North, and the response came not only in cheers but in cash. Before the Till trial, the NAACP had been deeply in debt because of its legal expenses in the Brown trials. Now contributions to its "fight fund," the war chest to help victims of racial attack, soared to record levels.
>
> Nor was the tide rising only among Black people. Large, influential newspapers like the *New York Times* and the *Washington Post* and *Times-Herald* had sent reporters to cover the trial, but while it was still going on, coverage was mostly on inside pages… When justice failed, however, the story wasn't inside anymore, but on the front page…
>
> White indignation rose, and with it, a white sense of responsibility. There had really been two verdicts, not one, rendered at [the Bryant/Milam trial, journalist] I. F. Stone wrote. One was the

> "not guilty" against Bryant and Milam. "The other, unspoken, unintended, unconscious but indelible, was a verdict against the rest of us and our country.[371]

Black people had been truly aroused; they needed a Gandhi to lead them. They would soon get one because of a second incident that happened in 1955. The victim this time was a Black tailor's seamstress in Montgomery, Alabama, who after a long day of work refused to give up her seat in the Black section of the bus to a White man as she was ordered to do by the bus driver. Her name was Mrs. Rosa Parks.

MARTIN LUTHER KING AND THE MONTGOMERY BUS BOYCOTT

On December 1, 1955, Mrs. Rosa Parks, a seamstress working for the Montgomery Fair Department Store in Montgomery, AL, finished work just before 5:00 PM. She walked a half-block to the bus stop on the corner of Court Street and Dexter Avenue to catch the bus to her home. Mrs. Parks was tired from a long day of sewing and anxious to get off her feet but she decided not to board the 5:00 bus since it was already crowded and there was no place to sit. When the next bus arrived, Mrs. Parks boarded, paid her dime fare, and walked toward the back of the bus past several rows of empty seats, as Black passengers were required to do by law. In Montgomery, a bus segregation law reserved the first 10 rows of seats on public buses for White passengers. The law designated the remaining 23 rows to the rear as the "Colored" section.

Mrs. Parks took a seat in the first row of the "Colored" section. Three other Black passengers took seats in the same row. Mrs. Parks sat quietly, balancing some packages on her lap and thinking about the upcoming holidays. At the next two stops, the bus began to fill up with passengers. At the third stop, several White passengers boarded the bus and took their seats. One White man was left standing since there were no more seats available in the White section. The bus driver, James L. Blake, turned, looked at Mrs. Parks and the other three Black people seated in the first row of the "Colored" section and said, "Now, y'all move. I've got to have those seats." Everyone on the bus knew what Blake meant. He intended to expand the White section to accommodate the single White passenger. The bus segregation law required all of the Black passengers in Mrs. Parks' row to get up and move to the rear of the bus even though only one White person needed a seat. The law did not allow White people to sit in the same row with Black people even if they chose to do so.

At first, none of the Black people moved. Then, Blake said, "You had better make it light on yourself and let me have those seats." Reluctantly, three of the Black people got up and moved to the back of the bus where they would have to remain standing for the rest of their trip. Mrs. Parks remained seated. Blake got up and walked back to where Mrs. Parks was seated. He glared down at her and said, "Look woman, I told you I wanted the seat. Are you going to stand up?" Mrs. Parks took a deep breath and calmly said, "No." Now angry that this Black woman was defying him, Blake warned, "If you don't stand up, I'm going to have you arrested." "You may do that" said Mrs. Parks. She had decided, she was not going to move. At that point, Blake got off the bus and went to call the police.

Years later in an interview with Donnie Williams, author of *The Thunder of Angels: The Montgomery Bus Boycott and the People Who Broke the Back of Jim Crow*, Mrs. Parks had this to say about her actions on the chilly December day:

> When I got on the bus that evening I wasn't thinking about causing a revolution or anything of the kind. I was thinking about my husband, how he'd spent his day at the barber shop at Maxwell Air Force Base, where he worked. I was hoping he'd had a good day. I was thinking about my back aching and about the pretty sights and sounds of Christmas. I was thinking about how we were going to have a good time this Christmas, and everybody was going to be happy.
>
> But when that white driver stepped back toward us, when he waved his hand and ordered us up and out of our seats, I felt a

> determination cover my body like a quilt on a winter night. I felt all the meanness of every white driver I'd seen who'd been ugly to me and other black people through the years I'd known on the buses in Montgomery. I felt a light suddenly shine through the darkness.[372]

Blake returned shortly with two police officers who arrested Mrs. Parks for violating the segregation law. They hauled her off to jail.

Later that evening, Arlet Nixon, the wife of Ed Nixon who was the head of the local NAACP, received a phone call from Mrs. Bertha Butler informing her that the police had arrested Mrs. Parks. Nixon and Butler were both friends of Mrs. Parks. Mrs. Butler had just happened to have been on the bus and witnessed Mrs. Parks' arrest. Arlet Nixon called her husband. Nixon knew Mrs. Parks well since she had worked with the NAACP in Montgomery for more than a decade as a volunteer. He immediately called the city jail, told the desk sergeant who he was and asked why Mrs. Parks had been arrested. The desk sergeant recognized Nixon immediately as a long time civil rights activists who had led a number of voter registration drives in the Black community. He abruptly told Nixon that Mrs. Parks' arrest was none of his business.

Recognizing he needed help, Nixon picked up the phone and dialed the number of a local White attorney by the name of Clifford Durr. Durr had tried a number of NAACP cases and was a close friend of Nixon. Durr and his wife, Virginia, were both liberal activists. They had developed a close friendship with Rosa Parks during a time when Mrs. Parks had undertaking various sewing jobs for Virginia. Durr immediately agreed to accompany Nixon to the city jail to get Parks out on bond.

That night Nixon and the Durrs gathered around the kitchen table in Parks' home with Parks, her mother and her husband, Raymond. Nixon began pressing Parks to agree to serve as a test case for a legal challenge to overturn the bus segregation law. He had been trying to put together such as case for some time but had never found the right person and situation for a test case. He was confident he had found that person in Parks.

David Halberstam in his book *The Fifties*, says the most interesting thing about Parks was how ordinary she was, at least on the surface.

> [She was] almost the prototype of the black woman who toiled so hard and had so little to show for it….she was a person of unusual dignity and uncommon strength of character…Rosa was a serious reader, a quiet, strong woman much admired in the local community...Parks had attended the integrated Highlander Folk School, in Monteagle, Tennessee, a school loathed by segregationists because it held workshops on how to promote integration. At Highlander she not only studied the techniques of passive resistance employed by Gandhi against the British, she also met White people who treated her with respect. The experience reinforced her sense of self-esteem.[373]

Segregationist would later argue that the local NAACP orchestrated Parks refusal to relinquish her seat. Parks denied that saying when she boarded the bus that December evening she had no thoughts of challenging the law or anyone. Parks was familiar with previous incidences earlier in the year when Black people had challenged the bus segregation law. For example, in March, Claudette Clovin, a fifteen-year-old student at Booker T. Washington High School, had refused to give up her seat. Another Black teenager, Mary Louise Smith, had done the same in October. Police arrested both Clovin and Smith. A judge had placed Clovin on indefinite, unsupervised probation. Smith pleaded guilty and her father paid her $5.00 fine. Initially, Nixon had thought Clovin might make a good case subject but he later changed his mind. However, Parks maintained she had not been thinking about the Clovin or Smith cases that December evening.

> I'd been happy early in the year when Claudette Colvin had been arrested for refusing to give up her seat on the bus. I'd been with Mr. Nixon when he'd declared it was exactly what the black community needed. I'd seen the light in his eyes at the thought of being able to fight against the oppression of the laws that were

> keeping us down. I'd called my white lady friend Virginia Durr and we started calling folks to alert them to what was going to happen. We knew we were going to have to have help for a long struggle. Then I saw the hurt in Mr. Nixon's eyes when he found out the Claudette Colvin case wasn't the one we could use. I saw the silent hurt take over. But I wasn't thinking about all of that while I sat there and waited for the police to come. All I could think about, really and truly, was the Lord would help me through all of this. I told myself I wouldn't put up no fuss against them arresting me. I'd go along with whatever they said. But I also knew I wasn't gonna give up my seat just because a white driver told me to; I'd already done that too many times.[374]

Nixon very much wanted Parks to agree to participate in a test case. He paced back and forth. "Mrs. Parks, your case is a case that we can use to break down segregation on the bus," he said. "I gonna ask you...I want to ask you: let us use your case for a test case. I'll tell you this: it won't be easy. It'll be long and hard. We might have to take it all the way to the Supreme Court, and that'll be a struggle."[375] Clifford Durr assured Rosa that he could probably get her off with a small fine if she did not want to take the case any further.

Parks was reluctant. Her husband, Raymond, was afraid for her safety if she were to agree. "Oh, the white folks will kill you, Rosa. Don't do anything to make trouble, Rosa," he said over and over, "Don't bring a suit. The White people will kill you."[376]

Nixon kept talking and answering questions from Rosa and Raymond. Finally, Raymond agreed. "I think Nixon is right," he said. Rosa's mother said she agreed also. Finally, Rosa said, "Well, in that case, we'll go along with you."[377]

The next day, Nixon began planning what to do next. He called Jo Ann Gibson Robinson, an English professor at Alabama State College for Women, to ask her advice. Nixon respected Robinson's ideas. She had given him good advice concerning the Colvin case earlier in the year. As a young college student, Robinson had her on run in with a Montgomery bus driver when she accidently sat in the fifth row of a nearly empty bus when she was supposed to sit in the tenth row. The driver kicked her off the bus. The incident angered and embarrassed her. When she had returned to Montgomery to accept a teaching job at all Black Alabama State in 1949, Robinson decided that she would do whatever she could to get bus segregation abolished. Consequently, she was more than willing to help Nixon in any way she could. At one point as they were discussing Rosa Parks' case, Robinson suddenly said she had an interesting idea. They should do something more than just file a lawsuit. Nixon asked what she meant. Robinson replied that a month earlier she had attended a speech by New York Congressman Adam Clayton Powell. Powell had described a successful bus boycott in New York. Robinson suggested, why not try the same thing in Montgomery. The majority of bus riders in the city were Black, primarily Black women domestics taking the bus across town to work in the affluent White suburbs. The city bus company could not survive without Black passengers. Nixon agreed. A boycott might be just the thing to convince the city to changes its policies.

Someone had to organize and lead the effort. Nixon was not overly concerned about the organizing part. He knew how to do that as he recalled some years later:

> There's one thing I know. I know how to organize. I ain't gonna argue with you about doing paperwork. I ain't never been a newspaperman. I ain't gonna argue with no schoolteacher about teaching school. I never taught school. I ain't gonna argue with no minister about preaching. I ain't never preached. But when it comes to civil rights and organizing, I know how to do it.[378]

Nixon was not so sure about being the leader. He was nearly sixty. He thought the leader of the boycott should be a younger man. Additionally, he had to be gone from Montgomery frequently on business. The boycott leader need to be someone who could be in town most of the time. Additionally, the boycott leader needed to be someone who was persuasive, articulate, and who would give the movement a positive image. Nixon thought he knew just the right man for the job—Martin Luther King.

King was only twenty-six years old. He and his young wife Coretta had arrived in Montgomery just the year before. King had accepted an offer to become the new pastor of Dexter Avenue Baptist Church with its affluent Black congregation. He had a PhD from Boston University where he had been exposed to the teachings of Mahatma Gandhi. He enjoyed classical music and had a habit of sprinkling his sermons with quotations from Socrates, Aristotle, Shakespeare, and Galileo. As Halberstam notes, as a speaker, King was nothing short of brilliant.

> He had the ability to make complex ideas simple: By repeating phrases, he could expand an idea, blending the rational with the emotional. That gave him the great ability to move others, Black people at first and soon, remarkably enough, White people as well. He could reach people of all classes and backgrounds; he could inspire men and women with nothing but his words.[379]

When Nixon approached King about leading the boycott, King was not sure he wanted the job. Nixon recalled:

> When he heard me talk about how long it'd take and how hard the struggle would be, he wasn't sure. He was a young man just getting started in the ministry. His family was young. His wife had given birth to their first child, a little girl, less than a month ago. He said, 'Let me think about it a while and call me back.' After some more calls, I went to see him at the parsonage on South Jackson Street, and I told him straight out that I thought he was the man who should lead this thing. He paced the floor a time or two, then he turned to me and said in that strong and powerful voice of his, he said, 'Brother Nixon, if you think I'm the one, I'll do it.' I nodded and clasped his hand and held it, and I swear there was something stronger than ever in that handshake. I knew we'd all be one together.[380]

The Montgomery bus boycott began on Monday, December 5, 1955, just four days after the police arrested Rosa Parks. King and his wife woke early. Organizers had distributed leaflets to the Black community announcing the boycott. Pastors in Black churches throughout the city had encouraged their Sunday congregations to join in the boycott. King and other leaders of the boycott, who had organized themselves as the Montgomery Improvement Association (MIA) with King as president and chief spokesperson, felt if they could get participation from just 60 percent of the Black community, the boycott would be a success.

King recalled that the house he and Corretta lived in was just a short distance from a bus stop. They could see the buses passing by from their front window. Around six o'clock in the morning, the first bus pulled up to the bus stop. King was in the kitchen having a cup of coffee when Coretta rushed into the room. "Martin, Martin, come quickly!" she said. King put down his cup and rushed to the front window. The first bus was still sitting at the bus stop—empty. King knew that the South Jackson bus line that ran by his house was one the busiest in the city. He and Corretta remained at the window waiting. Finally, the second bus came—empty. Then the third bus came. It was also empty except for two White passengers.

King rushed out and jumped in his car. He drove up and down the Montgomery streets closely examining every bus he passed. Most were empty or carried only White riders. King said he counted no more than eight Black people on all the buses he passed that morning. All day long, the buses remained largely empty. Black people walked or thumbed rides or car-pooled. The boycott organizers had hoped for sixty percent participation. They got nearly 100 percent.

The boycott dragged on day after day and month after month. The city refused to make any changes to the bus segregation law and protesters refused to give in and start using the busses again. Ironically, at first, boycotters weren't asking that the busses be desegregated. They were only asking that the bus company eliminate the arbitrary and moveable dividing line between Black and White sections. They wanted an arrangement in which Black people would fill the bus from back to front and White people from front to back and that no one would have to give up their seat once they were seated. It was a perfectly reasonable request but the White city administration refused so the boycott went on and on. Black leaders were surprised at the city administration's position since they felt their demands were sufficiently limited such that even the most conservative White should be able to accept.

When it became obvious that the city leaders were not willing to settle, MIA filed a suit in the U.S. Federal District Court. The suit asked for more than a change in the seating arrangement. It asked that the court declare bus segregation itself unconstitutional because it violated the Fourteenth Amendment. The court ruled in favor of the plaintiffs. The city immediately appealed the case to the Supreme Court.

Months passed and there was no end to the boycott in sight. Eventually, some affluent White people got so desperate to have their domestic help back cleaning their houses that they began driving them to and from work. The Mayor of Montgomery remarked, "The Negroes are laughing at white people behind their backs. They think it's very funny that White people who are opposed to the Negro boycott will act as chauffeurs to Negroes who are boycotting the buses."[381]

Some White people reacted to the boycott with violence. King and his family began receiving threatening phone calls. One night while King was away at a meeting, someone set off a bomb on the porch of King's home. Fortunately, no one was hurt. Two nights later, someone tossed a stick of dynamite onto Nixon's lawn. The dynamite exploded but again the bomb harmed no one.

Three months into the boycott, the Montgomery city attorney announced that he had found a way to put an end to the nonsense. He cited a 1921 state anti-labor law that made it illegal for anyone to engage in restraint of trade. Police arrested King and 114 Black leaders of the boycott. They fingerprinted them and released them on a $300 bond each. In late March, King case came to trial. The charge was conspiracy "without a just cause or legal excuse" to engage in activities designed to hinder a company in its conduct of business.

A number of Black witnesses testified to the numerous abuses they had suffered on the bus lines over the years that provided just cause. A woman testified that a bus driver had once shut the door on her blind husband's leg and then drove off dragging him along beside the bus. A Black man testified that a bus driver had forced him off a bus at pistol point once because he could not produce exact change. Another said a driver had forced his pregnant wife to surrender her seat and stand simply because a White woman needed a seat. Others told of drivers verbally abusing them. One Black woman recalled that a bus a driver had once called her an "ugly black ape." The judge listened to the testimony and was unmoved. He declared King guilty as charged, ordered him to pay a fine of $1,000 plus court costs, and released him on bail pending appeal. City officials thought they had won. They had not. In fact, they made matters worse for themselves. Black people rallied on the courthouse lawn after hearing the verdict against King shouting their determination to keep the boycott going. They did.

Spring turned into summer. Summer turned into fall. The boycott continued with no end in sight. Black people walked to work, bicycled, shared rides, and did anything to get around the city but ride the busses. The bus company sank into debt. It had to lay off drivers. City officials could not believe it. They thought the first rainy day would drive Black people back to the buses. It did not. City police began stopping Black cabdrivers who were carrying groups of five or six passengers at a time for ten cents a ride. The drivers were charged for violating an old city ordinance requiring cabbies to charge a minimum of 45 cents per passenger. Police started arresting Black carpool drivers for any minor traffic violation. Police stopped King for driving 30 miles per hour in a 25-mile-per-hour zone and jailed him for his "crime." When Black people heard of his arrest and stormed the police station, King was let go on his own recognizance.

Black people in Montgomery did not give up. They had never shown such determination to defy a Jim Crowe law before. Black people in Montgomery were making history and the news media took notice.

MEDIA COVERAGE

On Christmas Day, 1954, Montgomery obtained its second TV channel when WSFA-TV went on the air. Two months later the Oklahoma Publishing Company purchased it. The new owners of WSFA were former newspapermen and had a strong commitment to local news coverage. They promised their audience a full 15 minutes of news and 15 minutes of weather coverage each night. Such local coverage of the news and weather was almost unheard of at the time. The other TV channel in Montgomery, in fact, offered no local programming at all, news or otherwise.

WSFA hired as its first news director a young man named Frank McGee. McGee was just 30 years old and had only a high-school equivalence. He grew up in northern Louisiana and Oklahoma, the son of oil rig worker. He was not ideological but he sympathized with the plight of Black people. He recognized immediately that the bus boycott was a very big news story so he pursued it with vigor. McGee later said the owners of the station gave him pretty much a free hand to put on the air whatever he wanted. He speculated that the owners primarily saw the boycott as an exciting story that would help the station compete with the local newspapers. The story got even more exciting as White people continued to resist any change. The fact that WSFA happened to be one of the few stations outside major markets to have its own film processing equipment helped McGee tell his story and gain national attention. WSFA was a key source of film feeds to the national networks including NBC for stories from the Deep South. McGee's ongoing Montgomery boycott coverage was included in those feeds and NBC network news picked up the story. Soon the national press corps that had only recently been involved in covering the Emmett Till trial, began arriving in Montgomery. The national reporters had little sympathy for the Montgomery officials when they arrived. They had even less after they met Martin Luther King and Rosa Parks.

THE BOYCOTT ENDS

In October, the city of Montgomery sought a court injunction to end the car pools and other means of transportation MIA had put in place as alternatives to the bus system. The city alleged that the car pools were a "public nuisance" and a "private enterprise" operating without a business license. It sought compensation for damages the "illegal enterprise" had caused the city due to lost revenue from bus company revenues and an end to the car pools. MIA asked for a restraining order from the federal courts but the courts denied their request. King and other leaders of the MIA received subpoenas to appear at a hearing on Tuesday, November 13.

As the chief defendant, King was seated at the front table along with the prosecuting and defense attorneys on the day of the hearing. It was around noon and the court was taking a brief recess. Suddenly, King saw the Mayor and other city officials called to a back room along with the city attorneys. Excited reporters were streaming in an out of the courtroom. King turned to the attorneys sitting next to him and said, "Something is wrong." At that point, Rex Thomas, an Associated Press reporter, walked up to King and handed him a sheet of paper. "Read this," he said. King opened the paper. It was a news flash.

> The United States Supreme Court today affirmed a decision of a three-judge U.S. District Court in declaring Alabama's state and local laws requiring segregation on buses unconstitutional. The Supreme Court acted without listening to any argument; it simply said 'the motion to affirm is granted and the Judgment is affirmed.

The Montgomery bus boycott was over and because the City of Montgomery had been unwilling to compromise bus segregation was now illegal not just in Montgomery but throughout the South.[382] More importantly, advocates for civil rights had found their Gandhi in King. Thanks to the Montgomery boycott and the Till case, Americans had discovered civil rights or, more accurately civil wrongs that needed a remedy.

> **LESSON: Image events that garner national media attention are essential. In almost every instance of legislative accomplishment, something must happen that is so shocking or scary that the average American cannot resist noticing.** These events sometimes just happen as in the case of the Till murder and the Montgomery bus boycott. At other times, progressives have to create the events. Never the less they are necessary whether by accident or design.

EISENHOWER ATTEMPTS TO HIGH-JACK CIVIL RIGHTS

In early 1956, as Robert Mann puts it, President Dwight David Eisenhower emerged from three and one half years of civil rights "legislative hibernation" to call for the creation of a bipartisan Commission on Civil Rights to investigate voting fraud and racial discrimination. Eisenhower admitted in his memoirs that he was never fully committed to the cause of civil rights. He wrote, "I did not agree with those who believed that legislation alone could institute instant morality [or that] coercion could cure all civil rights problems."[383] Eisenhower's biographer, Stephen Ambrose, says Eisenhower "had many southern friends and he shared most of their prejudices against Negroes."[384] Reportedly, Eisenhower pulled Chief Justice Earl Warren aside after one White House dinner before the ruling in the Brown case and urged him not to move too fast on school desegregation. "These [southerners] aren't bad people," said Ike. "All they are concerned about is to see that their sweet little girls are not required to set in school alongside some big overgrown Negroes."[385]

Although he was aware of the president's lack of enthusiasm for enacting any meaningful civil rights legislation, Eisenhower's attorney general, Herbert Brownell, urged the president to do more than just propose a commission. Brownell cited data on the increasing importance of the urban Black vote. From the end of the Civil War until the 1930s, Black people who could vote almost always voted for the party of Lincoln. Large numbers switched party allegiance to the Democrats in response to Roosevelt's New Deal. Black people suffered greatly during the Depression and were grateful for the work and relief programs enacted by the New Deal Democrats. William Dawson, one of the few Black members of Congress in the 1940s expressed the opinion of most Black people who lived through the Depression when he said that without the New Deal, "Negroes would have died like flies."[386]

Black people had been migrating to the North for some years. In 1910, only 10% of Black people lived outside the South. In the 1940s, the Black migration increased dramatically as Black people deserted the agricultural South for the industrial North and Mid-West. By 1950s, a third of Black people no longer called the South their home. Black ghettos sprang up in many northern and mid-western cities. Black people in these states began to vote in larger numbers. They became a pivotal voting bloc in at least nine states—Illinois, Pennsylvania, New York, Michigan, Ohio, Indiana, Missouri, New Jersey and California. These states accounted for 223 of the 266 electoral votes needed to elect a President. Even politicians in these states who had no ambition to run for President began to discern that the Black vote was becoming as significant as that of big labor, big business or other interest groups. If Republicans could pass some form of comprehensive civil rights legislation when Democrats had consistently failed to do so, said Brownell, the Republican Party might garner enough Black votes in urban areas to pick up dozens of Congressional seats. In fact, Republicans might gain some political mileage among Black voters just for proposing civil rights legislation even if it failed to pass. It would not hurt Eisenhower's reelection campaign either. Eisenhower was reluctant at first since he did not like meddling in state affairs. However, Brownell persisted and Ike eventually agreed to let Brownell proceed to draft legislation.

> **Lesson: The support you receive from politicians will seldom be a function of ideology.** Usually it will be a function of politics. While a few Congressman, Senators or presidents may support progressive legislation because they believe it is in the best interest of the country, most will support such legislation only if they feel it is in their best interest or, at a minimum, can do them no harm at the next election. Washington does not operate on logic, compassion or any of those things. It operates on greed, avarice, hatred, personal whim, the naked pursuit of power and money for their own sake, and all those other nasty drivers of human behavior and ambition to which we are all subject. A few in Washington pursue a mission to serve or solve the nation's problems or to correct injustice but they are the exception. Most politicians have baser goals. You are not going to get very far in gaining support for your cause by appealing to a politician's sense of what is right. What is right has a different meaning for a politician than for most people. What is right is gaining power.

> What is right is being elected and staying in office. What is right is moving up to higher office. What is right is gaining a prominent position. What is right is being alternately feared by and courted by those in need or those in power. What is right is collecting money to support the next campaign and the next and the next. What is right is finding a fact, issue or knowledge of a character flaw whether true or false that one can use to gain advantage over an existing or possible future political opponent. You must appeal to the politician's sense of right, not your own, if you wish his support. That is what Brownell did to get the southern sympathizer's permission to pursue civil rights legislation.

In April, Brownell came forward with his proposal. The Eisenhower plan would:

- create a bipartisan civil rights commission to investigate civil rights grievances; establish a civil rights division in the Justice Department,
- expand federal laws to prohibit the intimidation of voters in federal elections,
- authorize the attorney general to file civil injunctions for civil rights plaintiffs, and
- permit individuals to take their civil rights complaints directly to federal courts; and allow the Justice Department to sue in cases of attempted jury or witness intimidation.

By late April, the House was moving forward rapidly toward a vote on a slightly scaled-down version of the Brownell plan.

Senate Democratic leaders were furious. They saw the administration's civil rights proposal as nothing more than a transparent attempt to highjack the civil rights issue to gain Black votes in the upcoming election. Additionally, they feared that a long drawn out debate over civil rights could splinter the party.

The Senate had among its Democratic membership a small band of mostly first term senators united in their determination to see some form of civil rights legislation passed. They were:

Hubert Horatio Humphrey of Minnesota,
Paul Douglas of Illinois,
Estes Kefkauver of Tennessee,
Wayne Morris of Oregon,
Stuart Symington of Missouri,
Frank Church of Idaho, and
Henry (Scoop) Jackson of Washington.

These men were courageous, determined and honorable. Humphrey had delivered an address to the 1948 Democratic National Convention so powerful that it inspired the convention to reject their leaders and adopt a strong civil rights plank in the platform. These senators wanted to see a civil rights bill passed. "Yet," writes Caro, "eloquent though they were, courageous and determined through they were, honorable as their motives may have been, these men had been eloquent, courageous, determined and honorable in many previous fights for civil rights legislation, and each time they had lost."[387] Each time a civil rights bill passed the House, it was defeated in the Senate by a determined "Southern Bloc." The last thing the Democratic leadership wanted in 1956 was a messy, public battle between the southerners and the highly vocal young liberals. The leadership had to find a way to bury the Eisenhower civil rights bill before it could do damage. That job fell primarily to one man—Senator Lyndon Baines Johnson of Texas, the Democratic Party majority leader. As I will explain, Johnson found a way to kill the Republican civil rights bill. Then, just the next year, Johnson rammed through the Senate the first civil rights bill to be passed in 82 years. It seemed a total contradiction, but those who knew Johnson well were not surprised. He had a good reason for changing his opinion about passing a civil rights bill, a personal reason.

LYNDON BAINES JOHNSON—MASTER OF THE SENATE

Born August 27, 1908, the son of "failed and ridiculed parents," Lyndon Baines Johnson grew up in a "land of humiliation and fear, even the fear of having his home taken away by the bank."[388] Johnson attended a little teachers college, a "poor boys' school" but while there at twenty-one he was already heavily involved in politics running campaigns for a state legislator and candidate for lieutenant governor in the Texas Hill Country where he had been raised. His goal from the beginning never changed. Johnson wanted to be President.

Johnson's political career advanced rapidly at first. At twenty-three, he was a congressman's aide and boss of the "Little Congress," an influential club of congressional aides. At twenty-six, he became the youngest person ever appointed to take charge of a statewide New Deal program, in this case as Director of the National Youth Administration for the State of Texas. At twenty-eight, he ran against seven better-known opponents for a seat in Congress and won. By the time he was thirty-two, Congressman Johnson was funneling Texas oil money into the Democratic Congressional Campaign Committee, thereby gaining influence and power among his fellow Democratic Congressmen.

In 1941, he got his chance to try for the Senate when one of the Senators from Texas died forcing a special election. Johnson was favored to win and become the youngest Senator in history. Then, he made a mistake. It was not like the Johnson people had come to know. Johnson did not make mistakes. This time he did.

Johnson had plotted and planned his run for the Senate carefully. He had even lined up some extra votes from some of the state's more corrupt counties just in case. He was relaxed on Election Day, certain of victory. That is when he made his mistake. Johnson's principal opponent, Governor W. Lee (Pappy) O'Daniel somehow learned the number of corrupt votes Johnson had in reserve. That was all O'Daniel needed to know. He merely lined up more votes from the corrupt counties he controlled. Johnson lost the election. He wanted to try again for the Senate in 1942 but the war made that impossible. He would be stuck in the House for eleven more years.

Johnson "had to be *somebody*," he just had to. He could not just be one of the crowd. He had to stand out if he was to become president someday. However, that was impossible in the House. Only a few of the 435 Congressmen stood out or had authority. Only those who had been in the House for decades had any real influence. As a junior congressman, Johnson was just one of the crowd. He hated it. In eleven years, he only introduced four bills that did not deal with matters affecting his congressional district. He only introduced three bills affecting his district and only two of these passed. Eleven years, seven bills—no other member of his Congressional class introduce as few bills as Johnson. He made few speeches. He participated in few debates. Others fought for issues, liberal or conservative causes. Johnson did not. No one was sure whether Johnson was a liberal or conservative.

Johnson was in despair much of the time between 1941 and 1948. He was forced to wait but felt he could not wait. He was convinced that his time was limited. Johnson men had weak hearts. Johnson men—his father, his uncles—died early, in their fifties or sixties. He told his friends he did not expect to live pass sixty. The path to power in the House was, he said, "Too slow. Too slow."[389] He sought a way out. Perhaps as Secretary of the Navy, he could make a name for himself in the war effort. He campaigned for the job. He did not get it. After that he lost interest in the war. He had already lost interest in the House and his district. His efficient staff handled district matters. Before the war he had earned a reputation as the best Congressman a district could have, bringing scores of New Deal programs to his constituents. That was over now. "Without the prospect of new, greater power, the power he possessed was meaningless to him."[390]

Not able to achieve greater power, Johnson turned his attention to amassing wealth. From 1941 to 1948, Johnson used his political influence to build a small fortune. He "grabbed for money as greedily as he had grabbed for power." By 1948, he was a millionaire.

In 1948, he made a second try for the Senate. It was a huge gamble. First, he had to give up his Congressional seat to run. More importantly, his opponent in the Democratic primary was Coke Robert Stevenson.

Stevenson was well known and universally liked in Texas. He had served as Lieutenant Governor and Governor. In the last Democratic primary, Stevenson had taken every county in the state, something no one else had ever accomplished. Most people considered Stevenson, the "Cowboy Governor," unbeatable. Unbeatable that is, unless someone was prepared to steal the election. Johnson was. Johnson's biographer, Robert Caro, says Johnson stole not just thousands but tens of thousands of votes.[391] When those didn't prove to be enough, writes Caro, Johnson stole even more including 202 decisive "votes" cast in alphabetical order six days *after* the polls closed. The media suspected voter fraud. Authorities launched an investigation. Fortunately, Johnson's Attorney Abe Fortas was able to get the investigation canceled before the judge could rule. The judge later said that he would very likely have ruled that Johnson stole the election. It did not matter. Johnson was now in the Senate.

Johnson realized if he was to gain power in the Senate and advance toward his goal of becoming president, then he had to learn how things got done, which were the best committee assignments and, most importantly, who possessed the true power in the Senate. He heard of a young Senate page by the name of Bobby Baker who had a reputation among the other pages for knowing "where the bodies were buried in the Senate." Johnson called Baker in for a conversation. Baker recalled that Johnson "came directly to the point…

> For two hours, he peppered me with keen questions. I was impressed. No senator ever had approached me with such a display of determination to learn, to achieve, to attain, to belong, to get ahead. He was coming into the Senate with his neck bowed, running full tilt, impatient to reach some distant goal I then could not even imagine.[392]

When Johnson asked where the power lay in the Senate, Baker had one answer, the only answer—Senator Richard Russell of Georgia. Baker said, Johnson immediately recognized something about Russell: "that Russell, who was no longer so young, was a bachelor and lonely."[393] Johnson had learned a lesson early on, "the way to get ahead is to get close to the one man at the top."

Throughout his life, Johnson had cultivated a father/son relationship with older men who could help him get ahead. In college, it had been the college president. In his early political career in Texas, it had been the powerful Texas Senator Alvin Wirtz. In Washington, it had been the powerful Speaker of the House Sam Rayburn and President Roosevelt. In each case, Johnson had succeeded in endearing himself like a son to both of them. Wirtz had given a photograph of himself to Johnson with the inscription: "To Lyndon Johnson, whom I admire and love with the same affection as if he were in fact my own son."[394] When Roosevelt died, Johnson told a reporter, "He was just like a Daddy to me; he always talked to me just that way."[395] Jim Rowe, a Roosevelt aide, had often observed Roosevelt and Johnson together and recalled that they exhibited a special, almost father-son feeling for each other. In each case, these older father figures had helped Johnson get ahead. He had now found the "father" that would help him gain power and influence in the Senate, Richard B. Russell.

RICHARD B. RUSSELL

Richard Russell's grandparents had been wealthy owners of a cotton mill near Marietta, GA prior to the Civil War. When Sherman marched through Georgia toward the end of the war, he burned the Russell mill to the ground and the family never recovered financially. Russell's father was born into poverty but was determined to restore the Russell family to its former prominence. Richard B. Russell, Sr. was at the top of his class at the University of Georgia, mastering five languages by the time he was eighteen. He graduated from law school at nineteen and by the age of twenty-one was the youngest member of the Georgia House of Representation. At twenty-seven, he was elected prosecuting attorney of a seven-county judicial circuit and then to a series of judgeships, finally joining the Georgia Supreme Court where he served as Chief Justice for sixteen years. Russell, Sr. was dissatisfied with his progress and sought higher office, running for Governor of Georgia twice, Congress twice and for Senator once. Each time he was defeated. His salary as a judge was meager, so the family continued to live in near poverty.

Unable to return the Russell family to its former glory, Russell, Sr. began to shift his ambition from himself to his son. In a series of letters to Richard, Jr when he was away at school, Richard, Sr. reminded his son of his destiny. "You are my oldest son and you carry my full name...You can have—and you must have—a future of usefulness and distinction in Georgia or it will break my heart...My son—my namesake—never let this thought leave your mind and may it influence your every act....Son I swear you to carry on my work and fulfill what I leave undone...[You] can make the name of R.B. Russell live long after I die and thus you will help to keep me alive."[396] After one of his many political defeats, Russell, Sr. wrote his son: "You bear my name...and I want you to carry it higher than I have ever done or can do in my few remaining days."[397]

Russell, Jr. took his father's words seriously. After graduating from the University of Georgia law school, he. joined his father in a law practice—Russell & Russell. At twenty-three, Richard B. Russell, Jr. entered politics, running for and winning a seat in the Legislature.

Russell was six feet tall with an aristocratic bearing. His mouth was usually set in a soft pleasant smile beneath a large, sharp, hawk-like, "Roman" nose. When he gave a speech, which he seldom did, he stood firmly erect with the fingers of one hand resting on the podium and spoke in a deep, rich, booming voice. In private, he spoke in a soft, pleasant southern drawl. He rarely offered an opinion until asked. When he was, he would respond with a careful analysis of both sides of the issue at hand before stating his opinion. He was judicious, fair, friendly, and always dignified, if a bit reserved. He was familiar with many but truly friends with few.

Russell's family connections and personality enabled him to rise rapidly in Georgia politics. At twenty-nine, his fellow legislators elected him Speaker of the Georgia House of Representatives. He gained a reputation for honesty and for an uncanny ability to get people to cooperate and follow his lead. One legislator said, Russell "leads without one's consciousness of his leadership."[398]

In 1930, Russell entered the race for governor. Opponents, political pundits and the press dismissed his candidacy. Russell was "the schoolboy candidate" who, they said, was just seeking to get himself known so he could later run seriously for statewide office. Everyone expected him to run poorly and drop out. He refused. Russell did not have much money to run a campaign but he had the full backing of his family, his younger brother handled PR and his other brothers and sisters typed and mailed letters and staffed the phones, and Russell had the legislature. Ninety percent of the state legislators were supporting Russell so he had at least one politically powerful friend and supporter in just about every county in the state. Russell was not the traditional firebrand southern campaigner, popping red suspenders and entertaining small town crowds with his folksy tirades against the far-away evil oppressors of the working man and farmer. Instead, Russell toured the state, sleeping in his beat up Oldsmobile to save money and giving as many as fifteen speeches a day to anyone who would show up to his rallies. Dignified in his suit and tie on even the hottest day, Russell spoke calmly, praising farming as the superior way of life. He supported farmers and emphasized their importance to the Georgia economy but he refused to make the farmers promises he could not keep. He had integrity and it showed. He was young, clean-cut, serious, and honest. People liked him. They liked him so much that on June 27, 1931, at the age of thirty-three, Russell became the youngest Governor in the history of the state.

Russell's governing style was unconventional and he served only eighteen months as Governor. While in office, he worked only until four in the afternoon before he retired to his private office where he would spend the rest of the day reading letters to the Governor. He personally answered all but routine correspondence. That done, he spent the rest of the day and well into the night reading novels, biographies, history, and anything about the Civil War. He read *War and Peace* so many times he became a near expert on the battles Tolstoy describes. He read what the Roman, Greek, and English historians had to say about successes and failures of kings, emperors and prime ministers. Russell dated frequently but never seriously. Many nights he just stayed in and read.

Immediately upon taking office, Russell pushed a government reorganization plan through the legislature. His plan cut the number of state agencies from 102 to 18, placed strict budget controls on state agency heads, and created the state's first central purchasing department. Within eighteen months, the state which had been behind on payments to public schools and pension payments to veterans, had not only caught up with its obligations but had cut its debt by a third. Russell began a highway construction program and, convinced that the state had to move away from reliance on cotton as its major crop, funded agricultural and forestry research.

Russell accomplished all of this quietly. He would "flatter, cajole, encourage and support others to get out in front to achieve a desired goal," writes Russell biographer Gilbert Fite, "Russell had a knack for making other people feel important;…he led without people realizing that the action was his rather than their own."[399]

In 1932, Georgia's senior U.S. Senator, William J. Harris, died of a heart attack. Russell called for a special election in September and announced that he would be running for the office. His opponent was Charles Crisp, the senior member of Georgia's Congressional delegation, Acting Chairman of the House Ways and Means Committee, and a member of a prominent political family. Everyone expected Crisp to win. Again, they underestimated the "boy wonder of Georgia politics." Russell ran a highly aggressive campaign. The final vote was 162,745 votes for Russell, 119,193 for Crisp. Russell, who had become the youngest Governor in Georgia history, now became the youngest member of the United States Senate. He was just thirty-five.

Arriving in the Senate, Russell immediately asked the Senate Majority Leader, Joseph Robinson, for an appointment to the Appropriations Committee. In any other year, such an appointment would have been out of reach for a freshman senator. However, Russell lucked out. That year there were five open slots on the Appropriations Committee. Additionally, Robinson was already having trouble with one rebellious, southern firebrand, Huey Long of Louisiana, who was making wild speeches on the floor and embarrassing the Democrats. He did not want trouble from another southern politician. Robinson mistakenly thought Russell might be another Huey Long because of what he had heard about Russell's aggressive campaigning and stunning victory. He decided to give Russell one the five open Appropriations seats in order to, as Russell put it, buy his peace with the young senator. Russell quickly made friends with the Appropriations Committee Chairman, Carter Glass, who unexpectedly passed over a more senior senator whom he disliked and appointed Russell Chairman of the Subcommittee on Agricultural Appropriations.

The Subcommittee on Agricultural Appropriations was one of the most powerful subcommittees in the Senate. One third of American families still made their living farming in the 1930s and the flow of federal dollars to these families at any time but particularly during the Depression was important to every senator. Funding for big New Deal agricultural programs such as the Agricultural Adjustment Act (AAA) which controlled the supply of seven "basic crops"—corn, wheat, cotton, rice, peanuts, tobacco and milk—by offering payments to farmers in return for not planting a crop were important to every Senator. They had to pass through the Subcommittee on Agricultural Appropriations before the Agricultural Committee could approve them so they could reach the floor of the Senate. So did funding for smaller programs for such things as research on crop diseases, agricultural experimental stations, and soil conservation. Russell became a powerful senator almost immediately.

There were three reasons for the young bachelor senator's rapid rise to power. First, he mastered the Senate rulebook. He learned quickly that the Senate operated according to precedent and formal rules. The Senate rulebook was 1,326 pages long. Most senators never even attempt to read it. Not Russell, he sat up at night in his small hotel reading every word. There were twenty-two key rules. Russell memorized each one. During the day, Russell found time to visit the Senate Parliamentarian's office to discuss the origins and rationale for various precedents. Most importantly, Russell wanted to learn how to circumvent the rules when necessary. Rapidly Russell gained a reputation for expertise in Senate parliamentary procedure, so much so that senators would come to him with questions rather than asking the Parliamentarian.

> **LESSON: The U.S. Senate operates according to complicated rules and precedents to a greater extent that almost any other governing body.** Most senators do not understand or poorly understand them because they do not take the time to learn them as Russell did. For that reason, any senator with a command of the Senate rulebook can be your best ally or worst enemy. You want to cultivate a relationship with at least one senator who has taken the time and/or been in office long enough to have truly mastered the Senate rules.

The second reason Russell gained power is that he read newspapers and not just newspapers from Georgia. The Senate maintained a complete set of newspapers from all over the county in the Marble Room just off the Senate floor. Russell spent hours in the Marble Room reading papers from all over the country. Gradually, he became conversant with the political landscape in just about every state. He understood the rationale and political significance of legislation other senators were introducing and how the legislation affected their states.

Finally, the more people got to know Russell the better they liked him. He ate most of his meals in the Senate's private dining room and most of his fellow senators looked forward to his arrival. Many senators timed their lunch to be in the dining room when Russell arrived. People liked Russell's soft, southern drawl and pleasant self-depreciating humor. Russell never offered advice to a fellow senator unless asked to do so. Then, he would offer a well-thought out opinion. It was as if he had thought through the issue well in advance, prepared to make a suggestion if asked to do so. Of course, that was exactly what he had done. The entire Senate grew to both like and respect Richard Russell.

> **LESSON: The Senate has operated much like an exclusive gentleman's club throughout much of its history even though women have served in the Senate since 1931 when Hattie Wyatt Caraway of Arkansas was elected.** (Rebecca Latimer Felton of Georgia did serve for 24 hours in 1922 but that was more of a symbolic gesture toward a person who was ending a long career in Georgia politics and journalism.)

> There are only 100 members in the Senate gentleman's club but they are by no means all equal members. A small group of highly powerful and skilled legislators runs much of the business of the Senate. Russell became one of these. Like the senator who masters the rules, the most liked and/or most respected senator can be a valuable ally or formable enemy. It is not enough just to know who the senators are; you must know who are THE senators.

When Lyndon Johnson arrived in the Senate in 1949, Russell was more powerful than ever. He still chaired the powerful Appropriations Agricultural Subcommittee. He was one of the most influential members of the Armed Services Committee, important to every Senator in any state with a military base. He led the Southern Caucus, sat on both the Democratic Policy Committee, which determined what legislation would go to the floor of the Senate and in what order, and the Democratic Steering Committee that determined committee assignments. Finally, and most importantly for the issue I am addressing in this chapter, Russell was the "general" leading the southern blog in fighting civil rights legislation.

JOHNSON AND RUSSELL

After his conversation with Bobby Baker, Johnson set his sights on getting to know Richard Russell and he knew exactly how he could make that happen. He sought membership on Russell's Armed Forces Committee. Johnson explained later that he knew there was only one way to see Russell every day, and that was to get a seat on his committee. Otherwise, they would be passing acquaintances and nothing more

The Democratic leadership granted Johnson's request and he threw himself into work on the committee. Most especially, he threw himself into getting to know Russell. At the end of each day, he would drop by Russell's office in the late afternoon seeking a moment of the senator's time to discuss some aspect of the committee's work. Bill Jordan, who was an aide to Senator Russell at the time, recalled later that Johnson was careful to treat Russell greatest of deference.

> Johnson learned to observe amenities with Senator Russell. With other senators, [Johnson] would just walk right into their offices, wouldn't even say how d'ya do. He would just barge in single-mindedly. Amenities were not part of his relationships. [But such "old World" courtesies were important to Russell] so Johnson learned. He always referred to him as 'Senator Russell' and always sent in a note from the outer office to say he would like to come in.[400]

Johnson's requests for a audience with the "old master," as Johnson began referring to Russell, were usually granted. John Connally, who had the opportunity to observe many of these meetings, said, "If you saw them together, you would not see Johnson walking back and forth, and talking, like he usually did...Russell would be doing the talking. He [Johnson] would be sitting quietly, listening, absorbing wisdom, very much the younger man sitting at the knees of the older man."[401] Soon, Johnson was working closely on committee business with Russell drafting committee reports for Russell to review or developing a line of questioning for witnesses scheduled to appear before the committee.

Johnson began getting up much earlier than usually and rushing to the senators' private dining room for breakfast. He would arrive at about the same time as Russell, who typically had his breakfast there. Soon Johnson and Russell were meeting for breakfast each morning to discuss committee business. Johnson later said:

> Richard Russell found in the Senate what for him was a home. With no one to cook for him [Russell] at home, he would arrive early enough in the morning to eat breakfast at the Capitol and stay late enough at night to eat dinner across the street [at O'Donnell's]. And in these early mornings and late evenings I made sure that there was always one companion, one Senator, who worked as hard and as long as he, and that was me, Lyndon Johnson. On Sundays the House and Senate were empty, quiet and still, the streets outside were bare. It's a tough day for a politician, especially if, like Russell, he's all alone. I knew how he felt for I, too, counted

> the hours till Monday would come again and knowing that, I made sure to invite Russell over for breakfast, lunch, brunch or just to read the Sunday papers. He was my mentor and I would take care of him.[402]

Johnson started suggesting that Russell join him and Lady Bird for dinner at their home so he and Russell could continue their work into the evening. Russell soon began accepting these invitations. The Johnson children, Lynda Bird and Lucy Baines, soon began calling Russell "Uncle Dick." They were encouraged to do so by their parents. Johnson discovered that Russell enjoyed baseball so in the spring as the season started he began inviting Russell to night games. Johnson had never shown an interest in baseball before.

JOHNSON BECOMES DEMOCRATIC WHIP

By December of 1950, Johnson was depressed. Committee Chairman wielded the real power in the Senate. It would take years for Johnson to gain enough seniority to earn chairmanship of any significant committee. He could not wait. He told Russell he just had to get a leadership position, even if Senate leaders had no formal authority.

The Democratic Majority Leader in the previous session of Congress had been defeated in the November election. Consequently, the position was vacant. Russell could have had the position for the asking but he did not want it. Additionally, Russell thought that the position should not go to a Southerner. When Senator John Sparkman of Alabama, urged him to take the position, Russell replied that a southern Majority Leader would only invite more criticism of the South whenever someone did not like what the Majority Leader did. Russell threw his support behind Senator McFarland of Arizona, a non-southerner who was never-the-less a friend of the South. Russell decided Johnson could be the Assistant Majority Leader, or Whip. As one historian noted, Johnson had no claim to the position, except that Dick Russell wanted him to have it. That is all it took. The Southern bloc backed Russell as expected. McFarland became Majority Leader. Johnson became Assistant Democratic Leader or Democratic Whip. He was just forty-two and he had served only two years in the Senate. However, he had obtained something no other ambitious young junior senator had at the time, the backing of Richard B. Russell.

As Democratic Whip, Johnson had little power. The job was considered to be a "nothing job." However, Johnson quietly began to make himself indispensible. He started collecting information about such things as the status of bills in committees, the timing of roll call votes, when various bills would come to the floor, what amendments might be proposed, time allotted for discussion, and so on. Senators began to learn that Johnson was the person to ask if you needed information about the what, when and where of Senate business. Most importantly, Johnson was good at the art of voting counting, predicting the outcome of votes for and against legislation. Johnson was a master at identifying those senators that might be encouraged to change their vote and what might persuade them to do so. Part of what made Johnson such a good vote counter is that he never engaged in wishful thinking. He never counted a vote as a vote unless he was sure. In short, he was reliable. If Johnson said you had the votes for a particular piece of legislation, then you could be confident it would pass. If Johnson was uncertain, then you knew you had a lot of work left to do. Johnson carried around long tally sheets containing a list of members of the Senate on which he recorded his vote counts. Often the counts were incomplete with blank spaces next to names of senators concerning whose likely vote Johnson was still unsure. However, other senators and the White House came to understand that Johnson's tally sheets contained the best vote count available on any bill.

Senators learned that Johnson could have influence on the House also. The House of Representatives has a constitutional officer, the Speaker of the House. Speakers have frequently wielded significant power and have been able to tame the House with strong rules and regulations. In regard to the Senate, the Constitution provides that the Vice President shall preside over the Senate but not have a vote accept in the case of a tie. In the Vice President's absence, a president pro tempore is to preside.

The way the founders designed the government, the House was to have a leader, the Speaker. The Senate was to function as a leaderless body. The only leaders in the Senate were the Majority Leader and Minority Leader, but they were leaders of their parties, not leaders of the Senate and positions of Majority and Minority Leader did not exist until the early 1990s. Under the Constitution, Senators were to be like ambassadors representing their respective sovereign states. Committee chairmen might exercise power over legislation that passed through their committee and party leaders and members of "policy committees" might exercise power over the flow of legislation to the floor. However, no official had formal authority over the Senate in any way close to the authority the Speaker exercised in the House. No one could tell a Senator what to do or not do, particularly how long a Senator could talk on the floor or what he could talk about or when he could express himself. Lyndon Johnson once asked the Legislative Reference Service of the Library of Congress to provide him with a list of the powers of party floor leaders in the Senate. The Reference Service researched the question and responded with a list containing just one item: "priority in recognition." Dissatisfied, Johnson had a member of his staff research the question. The answer he got was the same. The reality was that leaders in the Senate had no formal authority over other Senators.

The contrast between the powers of the House Speaker vs the lack of power of Senate leaders is stark. Sam Rayburn was the powerful Speaker of the House when Johnson was in the House and continued as Speaker after Johnson moved on the Senate. During the early 1950s, Rayburn was angered when a bill he favored was defeated. He responded by calling for a second vote and summoned twenty freshmen Congressmen for a chat during which he ordered them to vote for the bill. They did and the bill passed. Once just before a controversial resolution was scheduled for a vote, Rayburn announced that he did not want to hear one word of opposition. He did not. If a member of House rose to make a point of order Rayburn did not like, he would just announce that "the Chair does not desire to hear the gentleman on the point of order" and the gentleman would not be heard. No leader in the Senate had anything approaching such power.

The fact that Johnson long ago had developed a relationship with Sam Rayburn akin to the relationship he had developed with Richard Russell did not hurt Johnson's influence in the Senate. All senators knew that just getting their bills passed in the Senate was not enough. Their bills had to pass in the House also. That meant the bills had to get by Sam Rayburn and Johnson had the ability to influence Rayburn.

Finally, Johnson gained power in the Senate by developing the reputation of being a master fund raiser. If you needed money for your campaign, Johnson could tap some rich Texan to help you out. When Stuart Symington ran for the Senate for the first time in 1952, he had the backing of rich Missourians but their contribution to his campaign fell far short of what Johnson was able to raise for him from Texas millionaires. Symington never admitted to just how much money he received from Texas although reportedly one oil man gave him $10,000 alone. Arthur Stehling, one of Johnson's lawyers, remembered sitting in a room in the early 50s listening to Johnson talk on the phone to someone about fund raising. He would say, "Well, I got twenty for him, and twenty for him, and thirty for him [meaning, of course, twenty or thirty thousand dollars.][403] Today, twenty or thirty thousand dollars would not seem that much for a Senate campaign but in the early 1950s, it was huge.

As Robert Caro says, by the early 1950s, Johnson was the go-to guy in the Senate. Need information on the status of a pending bill in some committee, go to Lyndon. Need an accurate vote count, go to Lyndon. Need help gettin a bill passed in the House, go to Lyndon. Need money for your campaign, go to Lyndon. Johnson became the go-to guy for senators. He next sought to become the go-to guy for the press.

JOHNSON AND THE PRESS

At the beginning of his second term, Harry Truman had made a name for himself when he secured chairmanship of a special committee to investigate military preparedness at the outset of World War II. Publicity from the operation of the Truman Committee propelled Truman from obscurity to national prominence and the Vice Presidency. When America entered the Korean War in 1951, Johnson saw the opportunity to repeat Truman's feat. With the help of Richard Russell, Johnson secured the chairmanship of a Preparedness Investigating Subcommittee to investigate and report on military preparedness to meet the challenges of fighting a new war. In the first two years, Johnson's subcommittee issued forty-four reports. Most lacked any real substance but all were filled with catch phrases designed to capture the eye of reporters hungry for news about the war effort. Soon reporters were writing about the activities of the New Truman Committee. It was just the publicity Johnson wanted.

Johnson avoided public hearings, instead focused on closed-door sessions, and published reports where he could control not only the content but also the presentation to insure that they garnered the widest possible favorable coverage. Johnson kept committee reports secret prior to release to enhance the appearance that they were truly important. Reporters fought to get the earliest pre-release look at each report helped along by well-orchestrated leaks.

Johnson worked the press with selective leaks. Once he personally gave an advance copy of one of his committee's secret reports to a Time magazine reporter. It was on a Friday afternoon. Johnson reminded the reporter that he could only let her see the report because no one would notice it gone over the weekend. She had to get it back to him before Monday so he could return it to the subcommittee safe and keep the leak a secret. The reporter was happy to be part of the intrigue. When reporters complained about another reporter getting the scoop on a story because they got a leak, Johnson soothed their feelings assuring them that he had no idea who had leaked the information but that he promised he would make it up to them in the future. Reporters came to see Johnson as their friend, their go-to guy.

JOHNSON BECOMES MAJORITY LEADER

Richard Russell tried for the Democratic Party nomination for president in 1952 only to be rejected by all but southern Democrats. Northern

Democrats told him to his face that they could not vote for him for the simple fact that he was a southerner and the country would never elect a southern president. It was a gut wrenching blow to Russell. He loved, even idolized the south. Bitterly disappointed, Russell came to accept that he would never be president. However, he would not, could not, accept that no southern could be president. He was determined that the south would not be denied their man in the White House. He wanted Johnson to be that man. From then on, Russell was committed to electing Johnson president.

After Russell's 1952 campaign, Johnson became convinced that he could never secure his party's nomination for the presidency unless he could somehow get members of his own party and the nation as a whole to stop thinking of him as a Southerner. He needed to move up in the party to have that chance. He wanted to be Majority Leader. That position would put him one-step closer to running for president, provided he could be a powerful majority leader. He could not become a powerful majority leader unless he could find a way to bring together or at least moderate the ideological dispute within the Democratic Party between Southern Conservatives and Northern Liberals. Johnson could appeal to the Southern Conservatives and had the support of the most influential southern conservative—Richard Russell. He needed the support, or at least cooperation, of a northern liberal, a Senator like Hubert H. Humphrey to appeal for moderation on the other side.

As I mentioned earlier, Humphrey was one of the new liberal senators devoted to the passage of some kind of civil rights bill. Humphrey had gained a reputation from an impassioned pro-civil rights speech he given at the 1948 Democratic convention. Humphrey had presidential ambitions like Johnson. Johnson saw those ambitions as an opportunity.

No one knows exactly what Johnson said to Humphrey or exactly how he courted him but we have a general idea based upon comments Humphrey made later. Johnson knew that Humphrey knew that he wanted to be president. There was no point in trying to convince Humphrey otherwise so he did not try. Johnson admitted that he and Humphrey had the same ambition. The difference between the two ambitious men argued Johnson was that the party would never nominate a southerner. Russell's experience had demonstrated that. Johnson was a southern. Therefore, the party would not nominate him. He could get support from the south with Russell's help, solid support, support he could swing behind another candidate when it became obvious that Johnson could not win. Humphrey could be that candidate if he helped Johnson become Majority Leader and then become a powerful majority leader who could mediate between the liberal and southern factions of the party. Humphrey knew Johnson was trying to use him. Humphrey was convinced also that Johnson was right about the party never nominating a southern. Fine, thought Humphrey, Johnson wanted to use him. He would go along. He would use Johnson. Johnson could become Majority Leader. Humphrey would settle for president.

Democratic senators elected Johnson Majority Leader in January of 1953. At forty-four, he was the youngest senator ever elected majority or minority leader. He was only the second senator to become majority leader while still in his first term. Three years later, Johnson was facing just the kind of intra-party fight he had sought Humphrey's help to avoid—a nasty, public battle between southern senators led by Richard Russell and the block of northern liberals of which Humphrey was a part over the question of civil rights.

GAMES SENATORS PLAY

There are time limits on Capitol Hill. If you introduce a bill during one session of Congress but you cannot get it passed during that session, then it dies. You have to reintroduced your bill in the next session and start over from scratch. Each session of Congress lasts just two years. If you can keep a bill bottled up for two years then that bill is dead. If you want to prevent something from being done, delay is on your side. Russell and Johnson understood the advantages of delay when it came to killing the Republican-sponsored civil rights bill at least for the current session of Congress.

> **LESSON: If you are not sure you have the votes to kill a bill, your best bet is to find a way to delay having the bill ever come to the floor for a vote.** Delay is not just a means of putting off the inevitable. It can be a path to victory. It can be a path to defeat if your goal is to pass legislation rather than kill it. Your opponents will use delaying tactics that you will have to counter if you are to pass meaningful reform.

THE FIGHT FOR CIVIL RIGHTS IN 1956

In early 1956, liberals and civil rights advocates were hopeful. A version of the administration's civil rights bill was making it through the House and likely to pass. Several members had introduced civil rights bills in the Senate. The traditional path to the floor for such a bill was through the Senate Judiciary Committee. There liberals were in luck because Judiciary was one of just three major committees chaired by a liberal, in this case Senator Harley Kilgore of West Virginia, a reliable New Deal Democrat. Liberals expected Kilgore to help smooth the way for some kind of civil rights bill to make it through Judiciary and to the floor. Russell's southern block would then be forced to filibuster to stop a bill from passing. Johnson would be in a bind. If he supported passage of a civil rights bill, he would lose the support of his southern base. A filibuster would tear the Senate apart and ruin his chances of ever getting the Democratic presidential nomination. Chances looked good for a vote on civil rights or at least a floor fight. Then, something unexpected happened.

On February 28, 1956, Senator Kilgore had a stroke and died. There would be a new Chairman of the Judiciary Committee. The next person in line according to seniority was Senator James Eastland of Mississippi. Eastland was the most outspoken of the southern bloc when it came to opposing all civil rights legislation. A Chairman Eastland would never allow a civil rights bill to reach the Senate floor. The NAACP and other liberal groups supporting civil rights were outraged. Liberal publications called upon Johnson to block Eastland's ascent to the position of Chairman. Johnson demurred. It was not he but the Democratic Steering Committee that made committee assignments. He was just one member of the committee. The Steering Committee met and on March 2nd, the Senate in an unrecorded voice vote elevated James Eastland to the Chairmanship of the Judiciary Committee. Clarence Mitchell of the NAACP declared, "a mad dog is loose in the streets of justice."[404] Senator Eastland was just fifty-one years old and occupied a secure southern seat. This "mad dog" could be around for a very long time.

> **LESSON: Committee chairpersons have enormous power.** Consequently, it makes a great deal of difference which committee or committees have jurisdiction over your bill. You obviously want to exercise as much influence as possible in determining committee assignment to the point of writing the bill in matter to give it a chance of a favorable committee assignment.

The liberals had to find a way of keeping Chairman Eastland from getting his hands on the civil rights bill. Senator Paul Douglas had an idea. The House was about to adopt a civil rights bill. The process was straightforward once that happened. The bill would be "engrossed," in other words typed in final form with any amendments inserted. The Government Printing Office would print copies of the engrossed bill and the Clerk of the House would sign them attesting that all was in order. One of the clerks of the House would carry a copy by hand to the Senate. The House clerk would stand at the back of the Senate chamber until acknowledged by the presiding officer. The House clerk would then bow deeply and say, "Mr. President, I am directed by the House to deliver to the Senate H.R. 627, a Bill to provide a means of further securing and protecting the civil rights of persons within the jurisdiction of the United States, in which the concurrence of the Senate is requested." The House clerk would bow deeply again and hand the bill to a Senate clerk who would bring it to the presiding officer who would ask for unanimous consent to have the bill referred to the Judiciary Committee. It was at that point that Douglas proposed the liberals spring a trap to prevent the House civil rights bill from ever getting to the Judiciary Committee where Eastland could bury it.

Typically, the presiding officer's request for unanimous consent to refer a bill to a committee is pro forma. No one objects. Not this time. Douglas proposed that a liberal senator, most likely Douglas himself, take the opportunity to object, which under the rules he was entitled to do. At that point, the presiding officer would have to place the bill on the Senate Calendar, bypassing the Judiciary Committee entirely. Douglas knew other senators could try to keep him from objecting. Johnson could try to block his objection by exercising the majority leader's right to control the order in which senators were recognized. However, eventually Douglas or some other liberal senator would have to be recognized. Johnson would not indefinitely be able to prevent a senator from speaking who desired to do so.

Of course, liberals had to know exactly when the House bill might arrive in the Senate in order to insure that one of them was there to object when the opportunity came. Otherwise, Johnson could just sneak the bill pass them on the pro forma vote and that would be it. The Judiciary Committee would get the bill and Eastland would lock it away. Douglas proposed that instead of waiting for the House clerk to deliver the bill to the Senate, he would go to the House as soon as the civil rights bill passed. He would wait there until the bill was engrossed and signed and then accompany the House clerk back to the Senate where he could raise his objection. It sounded like a good plan but Johnson found out and developed his own plan with the help of his friend House Speaker Rayburn.

Johnson proposed that Speaker Rayburn use a seldom-used procedure called "hand engrossing" instead of having the civil rights bill follow normal procedure. The bill would be typed in final form, signed and sent directly to the Senate as soon as it was passed, thereby bypassing the Government Printing Office. Rayburn agreed.

Douglas rushed to the House as soon as he heard that the civil rights bill had passed. He asked about the status of the bill. The clerk told him it had already been sent to the Senate. Douglas rushed back but was too late. Johnson had already had the presiding officer call for unanimous consent. The House civil rights bill was already on its way to the Judiciary Committee.

Douglas and the liberals tried one more time to get the House civil rights bill to the floor. Toward the closing days of the session, Douglas decided to make a motion to discharge, or remove the civil rights bill from the Judiciary Committee and bring it to the floor. Douglas reasoned even if his motion were defeated, he would still force a debate on civil rights. Johnson and Russell learned of Douglas' plan. Russell suggested a tactic. Make sure Douglas could not get the floor until late in the day or morning. When he rose to make his motion, have the presiding officer inform him than under Senate rules without unanimous consent a motion to remove was out of order accept during the morning hour at the beginning of each day. Douglas would have no choice but to wait until the next morning to present his motion. How would that help? Well, said Russell, there was one additional thing. At the end of the day, Johnson would rise to make a motion that the Senate adjourn until the next day, the normal way the Senate ended its work for the day. This time, said Russell, make a motion to *recess* rather than *adjourn*. Johnson agreed. None of the liberals, including Douglas, noticed the change in words. The next morning, Douglas rose to make his motion. The presiding officer informed him that he was out of order. Senators could present Motions to discharge during the morning hour only. Douglas objected. This was the morning hour. No, Johnson responded, the Senate had not adjourned. It had only been in recess. The morning hour had nothing to do with the time of day. It was just the first part of the day after the Senate reconvened. Since the Senate had never adjourned, it was not the morning hour. Douglas was not only defeated, he was humiliated. The southerners were laughing. The liberals did not know proper Senate procedure.

These seem like silly games but they are not. They were just examples of the games politicians play to get legislation passed or, as in this case, keep it from passing. Johnson and Russell had won. There would be no civil rights bill in 1956. Then there was an election and everything changed.

JOHNSON CHANGES HIS MIND

The 1956 presidential election pitted Eisenhower in a rematch with Democrat Adlai Stevenson. Eisenhower was very popular. He won by 57% to 42% bettering his margin of victory from 1952. Democratic politicians in the know were not that surprised at the outcome. However, as they poured over the results to see what they could learn, they found something truly disturbing. The percentage of Black voters casting their ballot for the Democratic candidate had dropped from 68% in 1952 to 61% in 1956. Digging deeper Democratic strategists found even more troubling trends. Voters in heavily Black districts were trending Republican in presidential elections. For example, 34% of voters in the heavily Black Harlem district in New York where Republicans historically could rarely get 10% of the vote had voted for Ike up from 17% in 1952. Black voters in the Chicago's South Side First Congressional District had increased their support for the Republican candidate from 25% in 1952 to 34% in 1956. Democratic strategists warned party leaders. Republicans were making major erodes into a voting bloc that was becoming increasingly important in key northern states with large electoral votes at the very time when the size of the Black vote in those states was increasing dramatically due to Black migration to the north from the south. The Black vote could comprise the margin of victory in future presidential election. They were trending Republican. The strategists pointed out that the eleven solidly Democratic southern states accounted for only 128 electoral votes and only 104 if you discounted Texas that had gone for Ike in both elections and was trending Republican. Nine key northern states where the Black vote was becoming more important accounted for 223 electoral votes more than twice the number of the non-Texas southern states.

Any Democrat wanting to become president had to be concerned. No one could be sure just how much the fight over civil rights during 1956 had affected the Black vote but it clearly did not help. Lyndon Johnson immediately saw the significance of all of this. If he got tagged as the one preventing passage of civil rights legislation, he might keep southern support but he could never win sufficient northern support to win the Democratic nomination in 1960, as was his goal, much less the presidency itself. He changed his mind about civil rights. Some kind of civil rights bill had to be passed, and soon. But, how could he get any civil rights bill through the Senate as long as the southern senators led by Russell were prepared to filibuster just as they had always done?

JOHNSON PLEADS WITH THE SOUTH NOT TO FILIBUSTER

In early January, Johnson went to Russell and the other southern senators and presented his case. They were going to have to allow some kind of civil rights bill to pass. He reviewed the results of the election. Blacks in key northern states were trending Republican and Republicans were using civil rights as a leverage to get even more of their votes. The violence in the south that had continued all during 1956 and was still going on was disturbing to northern and western white voters. There was growing support in the country outside of the south among White and Black voters alike for civil rights legislation. Increasingly, voters were beginning to see the Senate, and in particular Democrats in the Senate, as the stumbling block when it came to civil rights legislation. Democrats could lose the Senate. After all, they only had a two-vote majority. Republicans would use the civil rights issue to steal the Black vote from Democrats along with control of Congress and the White House. Democrats could not afford to let that happen.

There was something else. Southerners had used the filibuster successfully to block civil rights legislation in the past. That could change. Southern senators by themselves could not assemble the thirty-three votes to prevent cloture (cutting off debate). They had to count on help from sympathetic Republicans and Democrats from western states. They could no longer count on those votes. Southern influence and power had long depended upon the threat of filibuster. What would happen if they went to those Democrats and Republicans they had depended upon in the past for the extra votes they needed and the votes were not there? They might never be able to use the threat of filibuster again successfully.

There was one more argument. Johnson did not have to make this one. Everyone understood. Russell and the rest knew Johnson wanted to run for president. They supported his ambition. They wanted a southerner in the White House. They knew the the rest of the country would force the south to change eventually. A southern president might be able to easy or delay the most grievous changes. The southerners would have preferred Russell as president but knew that could not happen. Johnson was their best chance of getting a southerner in the White House.

Johnson pleaded with the southern senators not to filibuster a civil rights bill in 1957 and allow some kind of civil rights bill to pass. He assured them that if he could get their agreement, he would make sure that any civil rights bill that passed was a weak one they could accept even if they did not particularly like it.

JOHNSON MAKES A DEAL WITH THE SOUTH

The 1956 civil rights bill that had passed the House and been buried in the Judiciary Committee contained four sections. The first created a bi-partisan commission to investigate civil rights violations and make recommendations to Congress. The second, created a Civil Rights Division in the Department of Justice to direct government legal activities when it came to the field of civil rights. The third, authorized the Attorney General of the United States to file a civil action or seek an injunction (a court order for the defendant to stop a practice or behavior) when there was evidence that a person's constitutional or civil rights were in danger. Finally, section four, made it illegal to interfere with a person's voting rights in federal elections and empowered the Attorney General to file civil actions to prevent such interference. A defendant could be tried before a judge for criminal contempt for ignoring a court order.[405] The majority report from the House Committee on the Judiciary described the bill as the "necessary minimum." Supporters argued the bill did not encroach upon or diminish the respective powers of a State or the Federal Government nor did it increase the areas of civil rights in which the Federal Government could act. It merely allowed the Attorney General to substitute civil proceedings for criminal proceedings to enforce the law.

The southern senators were not overly concerned about sections one and two. They were totally opposed to sections three and four, in particular section three. Johnson suggested that he might be able to get an amendment to section four so that anyone charged with violating the act would be entitled to a jury trial. No all White southern jury would ever convict a White man for violating a Black man or woman's civil rights. The southern senators said they might be able to go along with section four if

Johnson could add the trial amendment provided, of course, that he had section three removed completely.

Johnson struck a deal. Russell and the southern senators would agree not to filibuster the civil rights bill and allow it to come to the floor of the Senate provided the bill contained no section three and included an amendment to section four providing for jury trials. It was not going to be easy. Northern liberal Democrats and Republicans who were pushing for civil rights legislation considered section three to be the entire guts of the bill. They would never agree to its removal. Additionally, these supporters of civil rights would recognize the trial amendment for what it was, just a trick to make the bill essentially unenforceable against Whites in the south.

> **LESSON: Deal making is part of bill making.** If you are serious about getting things done in Washington, you cannot remain above the dirt and grime of politics. And, as we learned from other battles sometimes the deal you have to make is to take less, perhaps much less, than you would like in order to move forward toward your ultimately goal. When it is necessary, make the deal. Then, go wash your hands.

VOTE BUYING

On January 21, the administration reintroduced the Brownell bill. It began making its way through the House all over again. The Senate bill was assigned to the Judiciary Committee in the Senate. Chairman Eastland was as determined as ever to block it regardless of any deal Johnson might have struck with the other southern senators. Johnson began negotiating for votes to strike section three and insert the jury trial amendment in section four. Things did not go well. By late May, he thought he might not be able to get the votes he needed.

The southern senators had multiple points in the legislative process where they could mount a filibuster. They could filibuster on the motion to put the bill on the Senate calendar, on the motion to discharge the bill from the Judiciary Committee, and on the motion to call the bill off the calendar and bring it to the floor for a vote. Of course, they could filibuster on any motion to bring a House passed bill to the floor for a vote without sending it first to the Judiciary Committee. Russell and the southern senators were smart enough to know that their best chance of killing a bill was to start filibustering at the first opportunity unless they were sure they had the votes to avoid cloture on a filibuster on the final vote. Even if the liberals were able to get cloture on a filibuster on the first stage in the process, the south could just mount another filibuster at the next stage, the next, and the next. Johnson had to find a way to reassure the southern senators that they could still filibuster successfully at the final stage should he not be able to hold up his end of the bargain to delete section three and add the jury trial amendment. Otherwise, the south would start filibustering at the first opportunity. The question was how to line up enough votes to make the southerners comfortable with delaying their filibuster. The southern senators needed thirty-three votes to block cloture. They had twenty-two votes. Johnson had to find them an additional eleven senators who would vote with them at the final stage to avoid cloture if needed or there would be no deal.

Johnson started looking for the votes he needed. He could not count on getting any from the twenty-seven non-southern liberal Democrats or from most of the Republicans. He turned his attention to the Mountain States. He had an idea.

There were twelve senators in nine western states-Idaho, Montana, Wyoming, Colorado, Utah, New Mexico, Nevada, Washington and Oregon—who had a common interest. They wanted dams on the great western rivers to provide a source of cheap water for their farmers and to generate electricity to attract industry to their states. They wanted the federal government to develop the rivers, build the dams, and generally protect the environment. They saw public ownership as the best way to keep costs down. Republicans and the Eisenhower administration opposed such public investment. They considered it socialism and an unwarranted public expenditure since there were plenty of private investors and utility companies that were more than willing to develop the rivers in return for control of the product and profits.

The struggle between the public and private power advocates had been centered around one major project for ten years—the Hells Canyon dam project. Hells Canyon is an 8,000-foot deep gorge carved by the Snake River in a remote area along the border between Oregon and Idaho. Public power advocates wanted authorization and financing from the federal government to build a dam at Hells Canyon. Private power advocates, including the Eisenhower administration wanted to let the Idaho Power Company build the dam on public property and sell the electricity for a profit. The administration had sweetened the deal for Idaho Power by agreeing to give it a accelerated tax write-off estimated to be worth some $239 million to the company. Public power advocates were outraged at what they considered a give-away of an invaluable piece of the nation's natural resources but they did not have the votes in the Senate. Johnson proposed to give them the votes.

Johnson decided to link the Hells Canyon project to civil rights. The twelve public power senators from the western states would agree to vote against cloture thus protecting the southern senator's filibuster option. In return, the southern senators would provide the pubic power senators the votes they needed to get their Hells Canyon project passed. Johnson reasoned that the southerners did not care about the Hells Canyon issue and the western senators, even the liberal western senators, were more interested in Hells Canyon than civil rights since there were very few Black people in their states.

Johnson did get some resistance. Liberal western senators did not particularly want to be seen as opposing civil rights. Johnson understood and agreed to keep the deal a private gentleman's agreement. No one would have to know. Additionally, Johnson promised he would only ask for the minimum extra votes he needed at any point. He might not need all of their votes at any one time. Some of the southerners said they were uncomfortable with going along with something that some people might consider socialism. Johnson assured them that they did not have to worry. Eisenhower was never going to sign a bill authorizing a public dam anyway. The western senators were reassured when Richard Russell came to them and said he had changed his mind about the Hells Canyon bill. He would support it. The westerners relaxed. If Russell were giving his word, the southerners would honor the deal. It was sealed.

On June 18, the House passed the civil rights bill and sent it to the Senate. A liberal senator made a motion to bypass the Judiciary Committee and bring the bill to the floor of the Senate. Russell took the floor with an angry protest but there was no southern filibuster. The motion to bypass Judiciary passed 45 to 39. Five western senators who normally supported civil rights voted with the south to block the bill from being brought to the floor. Their votes were not enough to defeat the motion. They did not need to be. Russell did not really want to block the motion. He just wanted a demonstration that he could count on the westerners if he needed them later on. Johnson voted with the south then he brought up the Hells Canyon bill. It passed 45 to 38. Five southern senators voted for Hells Canyon, including Russell. Liberals immediately charged vote buying which everyone involved with the vote buying denied, of course. Senator Paul Douglas had the last word. He approached the western senators and reminded them that the House, much less the administration, would never go along with the Hells Canyon bill. He suggested Johnson and the southerners had given the public power folks nothing but counterfeit money.

Johnson was one-step closer. He still had to deal with the problem of how to get rid of section three. The Hells Canyon western senators gave him enough votes to block cloture if needed but they did not given him enough votes to amend the bill to remove section three. He would need the vote of liberals and Republicans. It did not look good. Then, Ike gave him a gift.

IKE CAVES

On July 2, 1957, Richard Russell took to the floor of the Senate to speak in opposition to the House civil rights bill. He opened his remarks with a special request. "Mr. President," he said, "for the first time since I have been a member of the Senate, I respectfully request that I not be interrupted in the course of my prepared discussion." The Senate grew silent. Senators who had been standing around and chatting returned to their desks.

This was going to be an important speech from one of the most powerful members of the Senate. Russell did not disappoint his audience.

Standing ramrod straight at his desk and speaking in a soft voice, Russell began to dissect the bill and explain its implications. The House, said Russell, sent this bill to the Senate under the false colors of a moderate voting rights bill. Proponents obscured the larger purposes of the bill. It was not a modest bill. They cunningly designed it to vest the Attorney General with enormous new power.

Russell said he had carefully examined the House bill, particular section three of the bill. That section included a provision that authorized the Attorney General to file a civil action seeking preventive relief, including injunctive relief to stop acts or practices that would give rise to a cause of action pursuit to Section 1985 of Title 42 of the United States Code. Well, said Russell, he examined Section 1985 and it was very broad. It dealt not only with voting rights but also with civil rights in general. Furthermore, said Russell, Section 1985 referred to another section of the code, Section 1993. That section was leftover from reconstruction and authorized the President or his designee to use military force to enforce court orders throughout the conquered South. Finally, section three would allow the Attorney General to sue in cases involving a conflict between individuals, civil suits in which one party was seeking damages. That provision was a great expansion of the powers of the Attorney General whose primary duty was to enforce criminal law.

Section three, said Russell, made the House civil rights law much more than some modest effort to guarantee voting rights. If the Supreme Court determined that segregated eating-places, hotels, amusement parks, swimming pools and so on constituted a denial of equal privileges and immunities, as it might do, then the Attorney General would have the authority to use the full powers of the federal government including military force to enforce the court's order. "This great power [of the federal government] can be applied throughout the South… Under this bill, if the Attorney General should contend that separate places of amusement… constituted a denial of equal privileges and immunities, he could move in…even if the person denied admission did not request him to do so and was opposed to his taking action. The white people who operated the place of amusement could be jailed without benefit of jury trial and kept in jail until they either rotted or until they conformed to the edict to integrate their place of business." [406] Russell suggested that authors of the bill had hidden the full implications of the bill from the Senate and from the president himself.

Then, he issued a warning.

> What I say now is in no sense a threat. I speak in a spirit of great sadness. If Congress is driven to pass this bill in its present form, it will cause unspeakable confusion, bitterness and bloodshed... If it is proposed to move in this fashion, the concentration camps may as well be prepared now, because there will not be enough jails to hold the people of the South who will oppose the use of raw federal power to forcibly commingle white and Negro children in the same schools and in places of public entertainment.[407]

Russell said he doubted very much whether anyone had fully explained the implications of the bill to President Eisenhower or the American people. He promised to correct that through a "lengthy educational campaign." Listeners heard "filibuster."

> **LESSON: Legislation can contain surprises, particularly when it amends previous legislation that may reference or amend still previous legislation**. The result can be good or bad for progressives. Most congressmen do not read legislation in depth before casting their vote, if they read it at all. They rely upon summaries prepared by their staff or testimony at hearings. Reading legislation is an awful task. It can be long, perhaps hundreds or thousands of pages, and, even if short, is always boring accept to the very few. Still, it is a major part of getting things done in Washington.

Members of the Senate were stunned. Eisenhower began backing away from his own bill the next day. Reporters asked Ike about the civil rights bill at a news conference. Eisenhower replied he wanted to examine some of the provisions in detail. It was obvious that Russell had been right. Ike really did not know the full implications of his own bill. He said he had intended the bill to deal with voting rights only. The president continued to back away from the bill over the next couple of weeks. Republican support for the bill and section three in particular began to fade particularly among Midwestern conservative Republicans. Johnson's vote count for eliminating section three went up but not by enough. Russell's remarks made a southern filibuster even more likely if Johnson did not remove section three. Additionally, Russell might now have the votes to avoid cloture. Johnson needed something dramatic to get rid of section three. He got it.

THE ANDERSON IDEA

It was during the afternoon of July 11. Southerners and northern liberals were engaged in what the *New York Post* called an "increasingly bitter" debate about the civil rights bill. Members of the Senate were jumping up, gesticulating wildly, and almost yelling at each other. As he looked around the room, Johnson's eye settled on one senator sitting quietly in the far back corner on the Democratic side. It was Senator Clinton Anderson of New Mexico, a member of the pro-civil rights liberal group. Johnson got up and walked over.

Anderson had been sitting at his desk for several days listening to the debate. Although he was a member of the group of liberal, Democratic senators supporting civil rights, Anderson later admitted his real interest was not so much civil rights as defeating any attempt by the southern senators to successfully filibuster the bill. Anderson knew that a southern filibuster was likely if section three was not changed. He tinkered with the wording of the section hoping to find some wording that might be acceptable to the southern bloc. Nothing seemed to work. That day he concluded that the part of section three that the southerners so disliked simply had to go. He took his pen and marked an "X" through those sections on his copy of the bill. About that time, Johnson walked over and asked Anderson what he was doing. Anderson showed Johnson the marked up bill and suggested that Johnson have a southerner or conservative introduce it as an amendment. Johnson thought for a second and said, "No, *you* do it. " Anderson's immediate reply was that he was a civil rights man. People would think he was betraying the cause. Then, said Johnson, get a Republican to co-sponsor the amendment, someone with strong civil rights credentials. People could not accuse Anderson of betraying the cause if a strong advocate of civil rights joined him. It could be another liberal Democrat but a Republican would be even better particularly if he was someone whose opinion carried weight with Republican moderates. Anderson agreed and said he knew just the person. He walked over to Republican Senator George Aiken of Vermont. Aiken was a well-respected liberal. Anderson showed Aiken his marked up bill and asked if Aiken would join him as co-sponsor. Aiken took only a second to agree. Several other Republicans volunteered to join Aiken and Anderson as co-sponsors. Now, Johnson knew he had the votes to delete section three. It was gone in a few days. The issue of trial by jury in section four remained to be resolved. Johnson still did not have the votes to amend section four. Then someone, no one remembers who, made a suggestion to link civil rights to union rights.

LINKING CIVIL RIGHTS AND UNION RIGHTS

The Taft-Hartley Act (see a previous chapter) had limited strikers' rights to a jury trial in labor disputes. Unions had fought for some time to get these jury trial rights restored with little success. Liberals in the Senate who were passionately committed to civil rights would never agree to the civil rights jury trial amendment. However, there were a number of liberal senators with more moderate civil rights views and the labor vote was critical for many of them. Johnson had previously secured the cooperation of western senators by linking the Hells Canyon issue to civil rights. Pro-union liberals would find it easier to vote to amend section four if it was amended to add the right of a jury trial for *all* criminal contempt proceedings, including those involving labor disputes. Johnson told union leaders about his idea. They resisted supporting such a deal initially arguing that Johnson could not buy their commitment to civil rights. Johnson responded by reminding labor leaders that a number of bills were under consideration in the Senate that labor unions wanted passed. For example, there was a bill dealing with union retirement benefits, a pay raise for postal workers, and a bill that would provide tax exemptions for retirement contributions. There were no direct threats but the union leaders soon came to a better understanding concerning how the Senate worked. Union lobbyists were soon flooding Senate offices urging passage of the jury trial amendment. Johnson's vote count for the amendment improved but he still did not have the votes. He needed two more, three at the most.

> **LESSON: Voting buying often degenerates to hostage taking and threats.** It starts out nice, the offer of a simple trade. However, at some point if things are not going well, you have to get tough. Johnson did not directly threaten the union leaders with withdrawal of support for legislation they wanted if they refused to go along with his scheme to get the votes he needed to add the jury trial amendment. He didn't need to. The union leaders understood.

CHURCH'S CLINCHER

In January of that year, the freshman Democratic senator from Idaho, Frank Church, had done something no young senator wanted to do. He had angered the Majority Leader. Church had not intended to anger Johnson. Johnson had been under the impression that Church had committed to vote with him on a certain motion. He had checked Church's name off on his vote count. Church had given his word as far as Johnson was concerned. Actually, Church had not given the matter much thought. He voted against Johnson. It was months later and Johnson still had not forgiven Church. Church was looking for a way to get back in the good graces of the Majority Leader. He knew Johnson needed a few more votes on the jury trial amendment. He had an idea.

Southern states barred Blacks from serving on juries. Church proposed to add a new civil right to the voting rights discussed in section four. It would provide that any citizen over the age of twenty-one would be deemed qualified to serve on a jury unless he was illiterate, mentally incompetent or a convicted criminal. Church recognized that the jury service right would be mostly symbolic. Whites would still serve on juries in the South. They could still block convictions. However, Johnson might be able to persuade a few additional moderate senators to vote for the jury trial amendment if jury service was included. Johnson agreed to Church's proposal and a few days later orchestrated a dramatic moment for the young senator from Idaho to submit his amendment to the amendment. Church was back. There would be no more hard feelings between him and the Majority Leader.

On August 2, 1957, shortly after mid-night the Senate approved the jury trial amendment with Church's addition by a vote of 51 to 42. Johnson had kept his word to the southerners. There would be no Russell-led filibuster. On Wednesday, August 7, the civil rights bill passed the Senate by a vote of 72 to 18.

The bill went back to the House. The House passed the Senate version by a vote of 279 to 97 with one minor change. The bill returned to the Senate for a final vote to approve the House's minor change. On August 29, 1957, the Senate passed the final bill by a vote of 60 to 15. There was a filibuster but by only one southern senator. Strom Thurmond of South Carolina broke with the other southern senators and angered Russell by engaging in the longest filibuster in the Senate's history, 24 hours and 18 minutes. It did not matter. On September 9, 1957, President Eisenhower signed into law the first civil rights bill in 82 years. Southerners had been able to use the filibuster to lock the door to civil rights legislation tight all that time. It was open now.

WHAT DID THE BILL ACCOMPLISH?

Paul Douglas, the liberal senator from Illinois, said the final bill was "like a soup made from the shadow of a crow which had starved to death." Civil

Rights leaders immediately dismissed the bill as "half a loaf." President Eisenhower declared that the bill was "largely ineffective." Today, the bill is largely forgotten. Those who even recall its existence treat it as nothing compared to the Civil Rights Act of 1964 and Voting Rights Act of 1965. In truth, the law is noteworthy not so much for what it did than for the fact that Congress passed it at all. Lyndon Johnson said:

> Maybe I voted wrong on some civil rights bills in the past, but I'm learning all the time. I got all I could on civil rights in 1957. Next year I'll get a little more, and the year after that I'll get a little more. The difference between me and some of my northern friends is that I believe you can't force these things on the South overnight. You advance a little and consolidate; then you advance again. I think in the long run my way may prove to be faster than theirs.[408]

> **LESSON: Do not assume that legislation that falls short of your goal is a wasted effort**. As we have seen in other chapters and reinforced here, what appears to be a sellout or excessive compromise may be a wise move. Half a loaf may turn out to be just what you need to start assembling a meal.

The struggle for civil rights teaches us many additional lessons about getting things done in Washington. In the next chapter, I am going to bring together the lessons we have learned from this and all of the previous chapters. Ultimately, what can we as progressives learn from these stories? What do our parents and grandparents and great grandparents have to teach us about getting things done in Washington? Moreover, are the lessons they have to teach still relevant today? I address those questions in the next and final chapter.

A SUMMARY OF LESSONS FROM THE STRUGGLE FOR CIVIL RIGHTS

LESSON: There is no guarantee that a victory, even one won at the cost of thousands of lives, will endure. Opposition continues. Those who are defeated rarely accept their defeat gracefully. They do not change their minds just because others hearts were won and legislation to remedy awful wrongs was passed. Memories of wrongs fade over time. Ultimately, we lose if we do not constantly remind our fellow citizens of what evil was vanquished, why legislation was needed, and the consequences of returning to what Conservatives like to call the "good old days."

Lesson: Image events that garner national media attention are essential. In almost every instance of legislative accomplishment, something must happen that is so shocking or scary that the average American cannot resist noticing. These events sometimes just happen as in the case of the Till murder and the Montgomery bus boycott. At other times, progressives have to create the events. Never the less they are necessary whether by accident or design.

Lesson: The support you receive from politicians will seldom be a function of ideology. Usually it will be a function of politics. While a few Congressman, Senators or presidents may support progressive legislation because they believe it is in the best interest of the country, most will support such legislation only if they feel it is in their best interest or, at a minimum, can do them no harm at the next election. Washington does not operate on logic, compassion or any of those things. It operates on greed, avarice, hatred, personal whim, the naked pursuit of power and money for their own sake, and all those other nasty drivers of human behavior and ambition to which we are all subject. A few in Washington pursue a mission to serve or solve the nation's problems or to correct injustice but they are the exception. Most politicians have baser goals. You are not going to get very far in gaining support for your cause by appealing to a politician's sense of what is right. What is right has a different meaning for a politician than for most people. What is right is gaining power. What is right is being elected and staying in office. What is right is moving up to higher office. What is right is gaining a prominent position. What is right is being alternately feared by and courted by those in need or in power. What is right is collecting money to support the next campaign and the next and the next. What is right is finding a fact, issue or knowledge of a character flaw whether true or false that one can use to gain advantage over an existing or possible future political opponent. You must appeal to the politician's sense of right, not your own, if you wish his support. That is what Brownell did to get the southern sympathizer's permission to pursue civil rights legislation.

LESSON: The U.S. Senate operates according to complicated rules and precedents to a greater extent that almost any other governing body. Most senators do not understand or poorly understand the Senate rules because they do not take the time to learn them as Russell did. For that reason, any senator with a command of the Senate rulebook can be your best ally or worst enemy. You want to cultivate a relationship with at least one senator who has taken the time and/or been in office long enough to have truly mastered the Senate rules.

LESSON: The Senate has operated much like an exclusive gentleman's club throughout much of its history even though women have served in the Senate since 1931 when Hattie Wyatt Caraway of Arkansas was elected. There are only 100 members in the Senate gentleman's club but they are by no means all equal members. A small group of highly powerful and skilled legislators runs much of the business of the Senate. Russell became one of these. Like the senator who masters the rules, the most liked and/or most respected senator can be a valuable ally or formable enemy. It is not enough just to know who the senators are; you must know who are THE Senators.

LESSON: If you are not sure you have the votes to kill a bill, your best bet is to find a way to delay having the bill ever come to the floor for a vote. Delay is not just a means of putting off the inevitable. It can be a path to victory. It can be a path to defeat if your goal is to pass legislation rather than kill it. Your opponents will use delaying tactics that you will have to counter if you are to pass meaningful reform

LESSON: Committee chairpersons have enormous power. Consequently, it makes a great deal of difference which committee or committees have jurisdiction over your bill. You obviously want to exercise as much influence as possible in determining committee assignment to the point of writing the bill to give it a chance of a favorable committee assignment.

LESSON: Deal making is part of bill making. If you are serious about getting things done in Washington, you cannot remain above the dirt and grime of politics. And, as we learned from other battles sometimes the deal you have to make is to take less, perhaps much less, than you would like in order to move forward toward your ultimately goal. When it is necessary, make the deal. Then, go wash your hands.

LESSON: Legislation can contain surprises, particularly when it amends previous legislation that may reference or amend still previous legislation. The result can be good or bad for progressives. Most congressmen do not read legislation in depth before casting their vote, if they read it at all. They rely upon summaries prepared by their staff or testimony at hearings. Reading legislation is an awful task. Bills can be long, perhaps hundreds or thousands of pages, and, even if short, are always boring. Still, it is a major part of getting things done in Washington.

LESSON: Voting buying often degenerates to hostage taking and threats. It starts out nice, the offer of a simple trade. However, at some point if things are not going well, you have to get tough. Johnson did not directly threaten the union leaders with withdrawal of support for legislation they wanted if they refused to go along with his scheme to get the votes he needed to add the jury trial amendment. He didn't need to. The union leaders understood.

LESSON: Do not assume that legislation that falls short of your goal is a wasted effort. As we have seen in other chapters and reinforced here, what appears to be a sellout or excessive compromise may be a wise move. Half a loaf may turn out to be just what you need to start assembling a meal.

7

A Way Forward

Congress has changed and not for the better. It is less civil, more populated with genuine nut cases, and its members are less concerned with the nation's welfare and more influenced by special interests and money. Those changes make the lessons of this book more relevant, not less. Navigating a path to legislative accomplishment is more challenging than ever. The lessons of this book show a way to go forward. That is what I want to address now.

I assume since you are reading this book that you are a progressive, liberal, or social democrat. Whatever you call yourself, I assume that you believe that we can and should harness the great power of the federal government to improve the lives of all Americans, in particular the poor, powerless and struggling of which there are too many. I assume that like me you are frustrated. You see so much we need to do, so many problems we need to fix. Yet, it seems we can barely move forward. Those who resist any and every idea for change, out of either ignorance or greed or hate or spite, seem to have such success in slowing progress to a crawl when they do not defeat it outright. Is there anything we can do to defeat these enemies of the future? I believe there is. In this final chapter, I am going to draw upon the lessons from all of the previous chapters to sketch out a way forward. I am going to suggest things we should start doing or doing better to fight back against those who always say "No, you can't" whenever we say "Yes, we can!"

WE MUST PICK THE RIGHT PROBLEMS TO TACKLE

As progressives, we see so many problems facing our nation in education, healthcare, immigration, women's rights, gay rights, consumer protection... the list goes on and on. Unlike conservatives, we believe the federal government can and should play an important role in solving these problems. In our zeal to harness the power of government to achieve meaningful change however, we sometimes end up scaring many Americans. We pick the wrong issue or issues to address and prematurely propose solutions that many Americans are not prepared to accept. We need to be more realistic about what is possible.

Get the timing right

We need to get the timing right when choosing the reform to pursue. Timing may not be everything, but it is extremely important. Madison and the Federalists probably would have had little luck in getting their constitution ratified in 1781. As weak as they were, the Articles of Confederation were probably all that the country was ready for then. The American people or at least the powerful business and political leaders needed to experience the defects of the Articles first hand before they were prepared to adopt a stronger form of government. Sadly, the country was probably not ready for any civil rights law until the mid-fifties. Blacks from the south had to get out of the south and experience life out from under the Jim Crowe laws to gain hope for a better life. It is hard to launch a revolution when you live under an iron fist and can see no viable path to success. Politicians were not prepared to challenge the power of the southern bloc in the senate until they began to see the growing political power of Blacks in the urban north. Whites found it too easy to ignore the embarrassing contradiction of segregation until stark and unavoidable reminders of the wrongs committed against Blacks flashed across their TV screens and appeared in the headlines of their morning papers.

Focus on national issues the states cannot solve

We need to focus on problems that are national in scope that states cannot solve on their own. When pressured by an aroused public to do something about an issue at the national level conservatives usually take political cover by arguing that if something must be done the best approach is for the federal government to simply provide funding and let the states actually administer the program. In some cases, they are correct when they say state and local governments should take the lead. State and local governments sometimes can do a better job of solving problems, but not always. State and local governments tried to solve the food and drug problem but they could not. It was the same when it came to reigning in big business and insuring the poor and elderly. Some problems such as those dealing with the big business trusts extend across state boundaries. In other cases, states simply lack the resources to fund meaningful programs to address a problem on their own. The problem with the federal government providing funding and allowing the states to administer the programs is that often these state-run programs never get implemented because the state legislatures will not or cannot provide matching funding. Our best counter-argument to state-based approaches is to support state efforts in the beginning. If the states succeed, then we have succeeded in our goal to improve the lives of our fellow Americans. If the states fail, as they often will, we can point to these failures as evidence that conservative state-based remedies do not work.

Focus on problems that affect most Americans

We must focus on problems that affect the majority of Americans or have the potential for doing so. We must accept the fact that most Americans will not support substantive policy changes for altruistic reasons. Americans are selfish when it comes to what their government does. They may contribute to private charities and support limited government intervention in times of disaster when confronted with vivid, emotion-arousing, heart-rending images of suffering, but American support for such efforts quickly fades. If we want to gain the support of the majority of Americans for reform legislation, then we must construct a rational or better yet highly emotional argument that the problem affects or potentially could affect nearly every American personally in some way. Americans only support public policy from which they believe they or their family will benefit directly and concretely or that they believe will cost them little or nothing. The majority of Americans were not elderly but most had relatives who were and everyone if they lived long enough would become elderly. It was not hard to convince Americans, even young Americans that they could personally benefit from the government caring for their aging parents or grandparents so they would not have to do so. In addition, it was confronting to know that when one became old, that the government through Medicare would be protecting one from the financial harm that an extended serious illness might cause. Most Americans did not suffer from the Jim Crowe laws but they had no reason to believe that the abolishment of those laws would cost them anything of real value. They might even gain. Maybe the violence would stop. Maybe there would be fewer uncomfortable images of southern brutality on TV and in the papers. We must give the majority of Americans, and ideally a super-majority, something to gain personally from passage of the legislation we propose even if the gain we promise is only partially real.

WE MUST PROPOSE SOLUTIONS AMERICANS CAN ACCEPT

Even when we get the timing right, often we propose solutions to problems that seem reasonable to us but scare many Americans. When we do that, we give conservatives a big gift. All they have to do is play on American's fears to build opposition to our proposals.

We must be sensitive to redistribution issues

We frequently fail to give sufficient attention to redistribution issues. Most Americans are not rich but most Americans love rich people. We love to watch movies and TV shows about them, read about them, listen to stories about them and gossip about them. Deep down, most Americans not only want to be rich but fantasize that they will become rich tomorrow, next month, next year…someday, somehow. Otherwise, why would so many people with limited means invest money in state lotteries where their chance of winning anything, much less anything of consequence, is almost zero. Of course, most Americans do not become rich. Far from it. Most Americans just get by. Some get financially comfortable but usually not before they are too old or nearly too old to enjoy their financial comfort. Never the less, the love of the rich, the rich love, remains. It is real.

The other reality is the Americans accumulate. It is part of the American character to seek out, assemble and hoard possessions, our stuff as the comedian George Carlin put it. Americans live in constant fear of losing their stuff or having their stuff taken away. They are ever watchful that something or someone, particular some government official, might come along and take their stuff. Conservatives prey on these fears.

If the funding for our proposal involves what appears to be or what conservatives can claim to be taking from the rich, then Americans get nervous. Remember, most Americans are convinced they will be rich one day. When that happens, they will have even more stuff or the opportunity to get even more stuff. We have to accept the reality that most Americans feel any attack on the rich is, if not an attack on them as they are now, an attack on them as they envision themselves becoming. We do not need to create enemies. There are too many conservatives as it is.

We must frame our proposals as definitely NOT an attack on the rich but rather an effort to reward initiative and good old American enterprise. We must reassure Americans that no one will lose because of the changes we propose. We must make the case that the result of our proposal will not involve taking from anyone but rather creating opportunity for all. We must reassure the voters that no American, rich or poor, will lose because of the changes we propose. We intend to raise all boats whether canoes or yachts. All futures must be positive. There will be only gains.

We must keep our proposals simple

Whatever we propose, we should present our proposals in the simplest possible terms. Americans are uncomfortable with complexity and never understand nuance. We must provide unambiguous options. The path forward must be clear. We must appear confident in the direction we want to take the country and certain of the steps necessary to achieve success. We must convey the sense that we have thought out the implications and details surrounding our proposal. We must be ready to offer details on how we would implement our proposal. We must be prepared with evidence to counter the rumors, wild charges and dire warnings of impending disaster that our opponents will use to defeat legislation we propose.

We must not ask Americans for much of a sacrifice

We must face the reality that most Americans, even those who support our reforms, rarely will want to pay much of a price for change. One of the most infuriating things for progressives is the inconsistency of the American voter. In general, Americans want their government to take action to make their lives better. On the other hand, Americans do not want government involved in their lives. Americans want government agencies to provide benefits and services but Americans do not want to pay taxes to fund those benefits and services. In the case of labor unions, Americans thought it was perfectly fine for workers to organize and to even occasionally strike to get better wages and working conditions. That is, it was all right for unions to strike until the strikes became an inconvenience.

We must keep this quirk of American nature in mind. Whether we are conducting protests, staging image events, or writing policy, we must always consider how our actions might affect the average American. Will our protest unduly disrupt the average American's life? Will our actions overly inconvenience him? Will, God forbid, our proposed reform have to be paid for by a significant increase in taxes or any increase at all? If so, we risk losing public support. We must maintain a delicate balance between doing what is necessary to achieve reform and gain attention without going too far. In the 1940s, the unions overreached. There were too many strikes and too many of the strikes did not seem justified to the average citizen. Unions made a big, big mistake and it cost them dearly. We should avoid such a mistake.

We must minimize big government solutions

Although the Federalists won the struggle for the constitution, most Americans have never gotten over their visceral fear of big government. Anything we do or propose that suggests a growth of big government, the concentration of power in Washington or a threat to state or local government sovereignty is a gift to conservatives. We cannot totally avoid the big government charge. After all many of the problems we wish to address can be addressed through big government only. However, we should do all we can to make it difficult for conservatives to make a credible big government charge. We must reassure Americans that they have little to fear from our proposals. One way to do that is to avoid creating new government agencies whenever possible. We should merely propose expanding existing programs and/or the functions of existing government departments or agencies. Medicare was sold as a merely an expansion of Social Security, which was a popular program familiar to most Americans.

We must never overreach

We work hard and long to gain voter support for our proposals. Once we obtain that support, particularly if the voters also give us control of both houses of Congress and the presidency, it is tempting to expand our legislative agenda to accomplish more. We must not do that. If we overreach, we give ammunition to our opponents. They will use it to scare the public. Public support for any legislative effort is a fragile thing. We must not abuse it. We are better off taking what we can get today and returning tomorrow for more. After the 1964 election, the Johnson administration could have sought to use its Democratic majorities in Congress to expand Medicare coverage. It did not. That was a smart decision and likely saved Medicare. Americans were ready to support Medicare. They were not ready yet to support national health insurance that extended much beyond coverage of just the elderly.

Remember what Wilbur Cohen had to say about salami slicing He advocated an incremental approach to passing legislation in which he got one piece of political salami at a time until he could get enough to build a whole policy sandwich. Salami slicing is an important tool for all who want to achieve policy revolutions. Policy revolutions are rarely built all at once but rather slowly, bit-by-bit and step-by-step. The real trick is not to lose sight of the ultimate goal. We must take advantage of any opportunities to move our proposal forward. Mason saw the meeting between Maryland and Virginia to discuss navigation rights on the Potomac and Chesapeake as an opportunity to call for another conference with a wider agenda. The Maryland/Virginia discussions led to the Annapolis Convention that led to Philadelphia. We must make sure that each piece of political salami adds to the ultimate policy sandwich and that we keep adding pieces. We must stay focused on the main objective and make compromises to expand the base of our support without alienating those who are truly committed to our cause. We must focus on the big picture.

We should not expect our fellow citizens to react positively to our proposal when we first present it to them. We must accept initial defeat and rejection whether in the legislative arena or arena of public opinion as a building block. Each failure is a step forward if for no other reason than that our ideas for reform become less foreign and less strange. Progressive accomplishments are rarely won by miles crossed but by inches gained. Getting things done in Washington usually results from a thousand little advances rather than one great victory.

WE MUST WIN THE BATTLE FOR GRASS ROOTS SUPPORT

We must tap into the needs of widely diverse interest groups. We must find common advantage in moving ahead by marshaling the facts and structuring the argument for change to appeal to the greatest number. However, we must not alienate those in who support our movement that are most devoted to change. We need to build and sustain grassroots support if we are to keep adding those pieces.

One of the very first lessons we learned in this book was that real change must start out far away from Washington in the villages, towns and cities across America. Ordinary citizens in ordinary towns far away from Washington started the struggle for food and drug safety, the right of labor to organize, access to healthcare, regulation of big business and civil rights, all of the struggles I covered in this book. That is where we should start in building support for our reforms. We fail too often to build the level of grassroots support we need to get legislation passed.

As progressives, we see wrong and want to use the power of government to right those wrongs. We fail to realized that most Americans not only do not see the wrongs, even when they are themselves being wronged, but they do not see how big government can be their savior. We must never allow the logic of our ideas or rightness of our causes to seduce us. We must never assume that what is obvious to us is obvious to our fellow Americans.

We must talk to those who are not already on our side. We must make those who are not yet convinced comfortable with our ideas. We need leaders and the more charismatic the better. It helps to have a Martin Luther King. It feels good to have enthusiastic, adoring crowds roaring their support for our charismatic leader but we should never lose sight of the fact that those fans of our ideas are not the ones we need to convince. The people we need to reach are the show-me skeptics that frown and twitch as we lay out our ideas. Our task is not just to rally the already convinced, to cater to the faithful. Our task is to turn the frown and nervous ticks of the skeptics into relaxed nods and smiles. We have to make Americans comfortable with our ideas.

We must play offense, not defense

We must never shy away from a fight, debate, or allow an accusation to go unchallenged. We must engage in the battle for public opinion. We must make the case for the need for change. We must assemble and present the data supporting legislative action. We must provide a well-reasoned response to the objections of our opposition. Madison's extensive preparations prior to the Philadelphia convention, particularly his extensive research on the problems with confederate forms of government made him by far the most knowledgeable delegate. He was able to discredit alternative proposals and at the Virginia Convention systematically and persuasively counter the Anti-Federalist arguments.

We must respond immediately and forcefully to knock down conservative claims that the bills they sponsor are "fair and balanced," "a boom to the working man/woman," are based upon a "mandate from the people," and so on. These claims are misleading but they sound good. We cannot leave them unchallenged. We must forcefully proclaim that such claims are false and show evidence that we are right. We must not wait. Any delay in attacking conservative claims is dangerous. Unions responded to the conservative claims about the Taft-Hartley Act but by the time they did it was too late. The bills had progressed too far.

Remember this rule. We must counter every immediately charge with a counter-charge. The worst thing we can do is to ignore our opponents' attacks. We must counter attack. Respond in kind. We must play offense;

not defense. The Federalists countered the Anti-Federalists by going on the offense, not playing defense. Instead of defending the Constitution against the Anti-Federalists arguments that it gave too much power to the Federal government thereby threatening individual rights and freedoms, the Federalists changed the base of the argument and counter attacked on a new flank—national defense and foreign policy. Later when the Ant-federalists argued that prior amendments were necessary to correct deficiencies in the Constitution, Madison and the Federalists countered by shifting the debate to the continuation of the union, a debate they knew they would win.

We must never let conservatives label our reforms as un-American

Conservatives always label any reform, particularly any reform that seeks to alleviate the plight of working Americans as un-American. We must never let them get away with that argument. Whatever we propose, expect opponents to accuse us of engaging in a conspiracy to destroy the American way of life. We must address that charge directly with the argument that solving problems and seeking to improve the lives of average Americans is not un-American but indeed the most American thing that anyone can do. We should never make the case for our policy change by citing what other countries have done, particularly European countries, even if these countries have been highly successful and we are basing our proposal on lessons learned from their efforts. Opponents of reform champion the uniqueness of America and the American people that make any system developed and implemented in a foreign country, particular Europe, entirely unworkable in the United States. The un-American argument is a standard conservative opposition tactic and one we should be prepared to counter. In particular, they will claim that what we are proposing is European and point to any weakness; failing or flaw in the "European" approach, no matter how minor, as evidence that such a reform is not anything Americans would want for their country. Failure immediately to counter such attacks from the opposition can lead to certain disaster for the reform effort particularly if the opposition is engaging in fear tactics that it usual will be.

We must show how the change we propose, rather than being un-American, is indeed, what America is all about. We must turn the un-American argument on its head. We must argue that the opponents are the ones who are being un-American since they are setting out to destroy the country by ignoring a wrong and not fixing it, wishing a cancer away rather than treating it aggressively with the healing power of change. We must argue that the truly un-American thing to do would be to do nothing. Americans are not "do nothings," they are doers and that is what we are proposing

We must mount an immediate and strong defense to any charge of abuse

Opponents of progressive legislation typically make their case for repeal of the legislation by citing so called "abuses" that often have no or very little basis in fact as did the opponents of the Wagner Act. If we fail to mount a swift and strong defense, the opposition will win, not because they are right but because they know that if they repeat an untruth long enough with enough force of certainty and conviction, most Americans eventually will begin to believe that what they are hearing is in fact true. It is doubtful whether the Taft-Hartley Act would ever have been passed accept for the years of a constant drumbeat of false accusations of abuses of the Warner Act that went largely unchallenged.

We must turn our opponents' arguments in on themselves

We should placate our opposition by carefully constructing a response that appears to meet their objections without actually doing so. We should appear to be accommodating while simultaneously advancing our own position. We must turn our opponent's arguments in on themselves. We must find a way to show that what our opponents argue is a vice is in reality a virtue; they can accomplish their goal only by doing that which they argue one must not do. We must use a form of logical judo in which we leverage the power of our opponents' arguments against them. Madison did this with his argument that contrary to what the Anti-Federalists thought, the best way to preserve individual freedom and liberty was through a strong central government that could prevent the excesses from factions and tyranny of the majority. Consider what Madison did with the Bill of Rights. Madison had been opposed to a Bill of Rights. However, he came to realize that they were necessary to win Anti-Federalist support, or at least minimize, their opposition to the new form of government. The Anti-Federalists sought much broader amendments to the Constitution than Madison was prepared to accept. His challenge was to design a set of amendments that would reassure his opponents without weakening the new government. Madison omitted most of the changes that the Anti-Federalists wanted. However, he included amendments that offered sufficient assurance to the people that the new government would respect and protect their rights. That was enough.

We must never assume that facts alone will be enough to sell our ideas

We must never assume that the average American will accept the facts we present in support of our cause or the logic of our reasoning more readily than he or she will accept arguments based upon speculation, superstition, outright fabrication, exaggerations, misrepresentations and outright lies offered by conservatives. We cannot expect Americans to recognize the difference between truth and lies unless we specifically, repeatedly, and aggressively point out the difference. We must never rely simply on our facts and logic. We must keep in mind that American think with their hearts and not with their heads. Lies always have the advantage. Remember Mark Twain's warning: "A lie can travel halfway around the world while the truth is still putting on its shoes."

We cannot assume Americans will know about or understand the problem we seek to address even when it affects them directly. We must put the topic on the national agenda. Often that means staging events or taking advantage of a crisis or tragedy to garner attention. The Montgomery bus boycott and the murder of Emmett Till attracted the kind of media attention and public outrage that were necessary to move Congress to action on civil rights.

We must court the press

Even in an age of expanded outlets for opinion, we must court the press and feed the press our story. We must monitor the press and public opinion closely and be prepared to launch an aggressive public relations campaign whenever we notice the first signs of losing support. Unions paid a big price when they failed to respond aggressively and in a coordinated manner to the attacks on the Wagner Act and unions in general from the

National Association of Manufacturers and others. We must frame the national discussion in a way that is favorable to our cause. We need one or more spoke persons to do that. Our cause must have a human face and voice, an attractive, articulate and empathetic symbol.

We must be prepared to be outspent

We must anticipate well-funded opposition and be prepared to counter it. It is the nature of change that one or more groups, often well financed and influential, will be threatened by the changes we propose just doctors in the AMA were threatened by proposals for universal health care. Some people and groups will see the changes we propose as a threat to their power, position, prestige, and even financial well-being. Our challenge is to identify such individuals and groups early on, understand how our proposed changes affects them, anticipate the form their opposition might take, and prepare to defend our effort. We should try to structure the change we propose to minimize the threat or make it less apparent. Ideally, we should try to co-opt the opposition.

WE MUST PLAY THE POLITICAL GAME

We must be prepared to work with a broken government and with politicians who frequently behave badly. Policy change is not something for ideologues.

We must be willing to compromise

Our purpose is to achieve passage of something that moves our agenda forward even if that means we do not get everything we want. Madison had to back off some of his extreme ideas. He learned to lose. He favored proportional representation for both houses and lost. He favored giving the national legislature the power to negate state laws and lost. He favored the popular election of the executive and lost. One Constitutional scholar has estimated that during the Philadelphia Convention, of seventy-one specific proposals that Madison moved, seconded, or spoke unequivocally about, he was on the losing side forty times. Moreover, recall that Madison saw his favorite amendment to hold the states accountable for personal freedoms go down to defeat. Still, Madison won in the long term on the major issue. He got a new and much stronger constitution. Madison himself said that the compromise over proportional representation that gave the small states equal representation in the Senate was critical to the success of the convention.

We must court the powerful

We must court the powerful even if we find the task distasteful. Most frequently, proposed legislation in the House and Senate moves ahead, is stalled, or disappears because of what a few powerful individuals do or fail to do. We must know who these individuals are. We must know their personal criteria for supporting or opposing legislation that usually has nothing whatsoever to do with what is best for the country, their party, or even necessarily their constituents. It frequently has much more to do with personal power, privilege, position and sometimes just the desire for attention. Wilbur Mills shifting role in Medicare had more to do with status and power than it had to do with policy. Similarly, Russell Long's efforts to amend, and perhaps destroy, Medicare during the final debate over its provisions had as much to do with attention-seeking and just play cussedness, as it had to do with concern for the long term care of the elderly. Regardless of why or how we feel about why powerful individuals support policy proposals, we must obtain their support. That means catering to their eccentricity, even those we find unwarranted and/or even distasteful.

Inevitably, the support of a few powerful figures in Congress is critical to success. We must cater to their needs whatever they are. Each of these figures have their own personal criteria for what they will and will not support and until we draft our legislation to at least appear to meet the requirements of these powerful men and women, no change is possible. We must focus on winning the support of key opinion leaders. If Washington and Franklin were involved in the drafting of the Constitution and supported its ratification, that was enough for many people. At the Virginia Convention, Randolph's change of sides and stirring final argument in favor of ratification undoubtedly had a significant impact on swaying delegates who were still wavering.

We must show politicians how they can benefit from supporting our cause

The support we receive from politicians will seldom be a function of ideology. Usually it will be a function of politics. While a few congressman, senators or presidents may support progressive legislation because they believe it is in the best interest of the country, most will support such legislation only if they feel it is in their best interest or, at a minimum, can do them no harm at the next election. Washington does not operate on logic, compassion or any of those things. It operates on greed, avarice, hatred, personal whim, the naked pursuit of power and money for their own sake, and all those other nasty drivers of human behavior and ambition to which we are all subject. A few in Washington pursue a mission to serve or solve the nation's problems or to correct injustice but they are the exception. Most politicians have baser goals. Senators and congressmen may proclaim that they work for their constituents and "the good of the country," but they actually work for themselves. We must show them how they can get personal political mileage out of supporting our proposals to get their support. We should not expect them to get behind our cause just because our cause is right and does a lot of good for the country. They could care less. They want to know, "what's in it for me?" We must provide a good answer to that question. In the case of Kennedy and McNamara with regard to Medicare, they knew that getting to go around the country holding hearings on the plight of old people would be good for their political careers. They had a lot to gain and little to lose. We are not going to get very far in gaining support for our cause by appealing to a politician's sense of what is right. What is right has a different meaning for a politician than for most people. What is right is gaining power. What is right is being elected and staying in office. What is right is moving up to higher office. What is right is gaining a prominent position. What is right is being alternately feared by and courted by those in need or in power. What is right is collecting money to support the next campaign and the next and the next. What is right is finding a fact, issue or knowledge of a character flaw whether true or false that one can use to gain advantage over an existing or possible future political opponent. Congressmen and senators must be pushed into joining the fight. Senator Weldon Heyburn of Idaho became interested in and a supporter of the pure food and drug cause only after women's groups in Idaho announced that they would work to defeat any candidate who did not support pure food and drug legislation. We must appeal to the politician's sense of right, not our own, if we wish his support. That is what Brownell did to get the southern sympathizer's permission to pursue civil rights legislation.

We must engage in vote buying

Vote buying in the final push for legislation often degenerates to hostage taking and threats. It starts out nice, the offer of a simple trade. However, at some point if things are not going well, we have to get tough. Johnson did not directly threaten the union leaders with withdrawal of support for legislation they wanted if they refused to go along with his scheme to get the votes he needed to add the jury trial amendment. He did not need to. The union leaders understood. Deal making is part of bill making. If we are serious about getting things done in Washington, we cannot remain above the dirt and grime of politics. And, as we learned from other battles sometimes the deals we have to make are to take less, perhaps much less, than we would like in order to move forward toward our ultimately goal. When it is necessary, we make the deal. Then, we can go wash our hands. We must remember that politics is the art of the possible. We have to take what we can get. That is hard for us. Progressives do not want to make things just a little bit better. They want to right wrongs. Unfortunately, it is hard to get a lot done in one piece of legislation. The framers did not construct our government that way.

We must not accept delays to 'study the problem further"

Whenever the opposition proposes to study the problem, we should respond by pushing harder to get something done right away. Any offer to study the problem is a standard delaying tactic opponents will resort to when they discover that public pressure is building to get something done. It is a sign that our efforts to educate the public and garner support from politicians are paying off. It is a signal that we should redouble our efforts to move legislation forward. We should not back off or agree to slow down. We should push harder.

We must not count on any president, even a sympathetic one

Just because a presidential candidate or a sitting president, even a popular one, expresses support for a change effort, we should not assume that achieving that change will be easy. It might be easier to have the president behind our cause but that does not make the passing legislation easy or guaranteed. We often get over confident when we are finally able to elect a popular president who shares our agenda. We expect him to expend his considerable political capital on our behalf. We forget that presidents are not all powerful even if they are extremely popular and they are never pursuing a single agenda item. There are no single-issue presidents. Progressive legislation has to compete with all the other legislation, conservative, moderate, liberal, domestic and foreign that presidents have to juggle. At least four presidents or presidential candidates, including Kennedy who was very popular, supported some form of health insurance reform but only one was successful in passing Medicare and then, as we will see, it was less than proponents of change had originally sought.

WE MUST NEVER GIVE UP

Finally, we must never give up. The battle for progressive American ideas never ends. We cannot afford to pause long to celebrate a victory. Even when we achieve enormous breakthroughs in legislation, we should be prepared for the opposition to seek vigorously to undo all we have accomplished. Enforcement will be problematic usually. Conservatives will seek to starve our legislative accomplishments with inadequate funding when they cannot reverse the legislation outright. They will seek to have the legislation declared unconstitutional by the courts that will be almost never entirely or even remotely on our side. Ours will be a constant battle to protect our gains as much as it will be to extend them. Still, we can and will succeed if we heed the lessons progressives of the past can teach us. They won and so can we.

Those progressives who say today that we can accomplish nothing in Washington because Conservatives will just use the filibuster or threat of filibuster or something else forget how the solid southern bloc of senators held the civil rights issue hostage for more than 80 years. Those who say we cannot pass legislation because corporations will use money against us forget the efforts the richest men in America at the time made to prevent us from reigning in big business.

We must reject the idea that simply because our opponents have formable weapons at their disposal that we need not try. Yes, the opponents of progress have plenty of practice but we have a record of accomplishment also. In addition, we have won, not all the time and not without effort and not without a struggle that often lasted decades, but we won. We can and will win again if we learn the lessons our past successes can teach us.

More importantly, we can win again if we remain true to our purpose. Our enemies will lose because in the end they are out to serve their own narrow interest. We will win because the effort we make is not just for ourselves but also for every American who asks nothing for themselves or their family but the opportunity to compete for the riches this great country has to offer on a level playing field.

Our struggle has taken centuries. It will take many more, but why should we worry about the years? How long is too long to struggle to protect the right of workers to organize? How long is too long to struggle for the civil rights of minorities? How long is too long to fight so that mothers and fathers can be assured that the food and drugs they feed their children and themselves will not kill them? How long should we fight for those rights? Should it be one year, one election, one session of Congress, or one term of the presidency? When should we give up? At what point can we tell those who suffer wrongs that we no longer will seek to use the power of government to remedy those wrongs, to alleviate their suffering? Was it wrong for those who fought for the civil rights of Black Americans to spend 80 years before achieving a small success? Moreover, what about all of the other struggles I have documented in this book? Was it wrong to spend decades to achieve those victories even when they sometimes fell short of solving the problem?

I ask of you these final questions. Are you willing to undertake the type of challenges your parents and grandparents undertook? Are you willing to commit your time, effort, and money to a cause or many causes that you cannot win today, tomorrow, or next year or in decades or perhaps even in your lifetime? Are you willing to fight for a cause simple because the cause is right and that because it is right somewhere, somehow, someone fighting just like you for the same cause will have a brief moment to celebrate victory before starting all over to defend what they have achieved? That is the challenge. That is the struggle. That is the task before us. Join in the cause or give it up. Give me a hundred determined to never given up in the pursuit of what is right and we will defeat hundreds of thousands seeking short-term greed. That is the battle if we are willing to wage it. I am. Are you?

ABOUT THE AUTHOR

Joseph H. Boyett (Ph.D) is the author of 16 previous books including *Won't Get Fooled Again: A Voter's Guide to Seeing Through the Lies, Getting Past the Propaganda, and Choosing the Best Leaders, Workplace 2000: The Revolution Reshaping American Business,* and the five volume *Guru Guide* series. Dr. Boyett is a member of the Author's Guild, the American Society of Journalists and Authors, and the American Political Science Association. He holds a Ph.D. in Political Science from the University of Georgia. Dr. Boyett lives in Alpharetta, Georgia near Atlanta.

SELECTED BIBLIOGRAPHY

Aaron, Daniel. *Men of Good Hope: A Story of American Progressives.* New York: Oxford University Press, 1951.

Arthur, Anthony. *Radical Innocent: Upton Sinclair.* New York: Random House, 2006.

Barbash, Fred. *The Founding: A Dramatic Account of the Writing of the Constitution.* New York: Simon and Schuster, 1987.

Bausum, Ann. *Muckrakers: How Ida Tarbell, Upton Sinclair, and Lincoln Steffens Helped Expose Scandal, Inspire Reform, and Invent Investigative Journalism.* Washington,D.C.: National Geographic, 2007

Bellamy, Edward. *Looking Back.* New York: The Modern Library, 1951.

Berman, Edward. *Labor and the Sherman Act.* New York: Russell & Russell, 1969.

Boardman, Fon Wyman. *America and the Progressive Era, 1900-1917.* New York: H.Z. Walck, 1970.

Bowen, Catherine Drinker. *Miracle at Philadelphia: The Story of the Constitutional Convention, May to September 1787.* Boston: Little Brown, 1986.

Bringhurst, Bruce. *Antitrust and the Oil Monopoly: The Standard Oil Cases, 1890-1911.* Westport, CT: Greenwood Press, 1979. p. 11.

Caro, Robert A. *Master of the Senate: The Years of Lyndon Johnson*. New York: Alfred A. Knopf, 2002.

Cashman, Sean Dennis. *America in the Age of Titans: The Progressive Era and World War I.* New York: New York University Press, 1988.

Cerami, Charles. *Young Patriots: The Remarkable Story of Two Men, Their Impossible Plan and the Revolution that Created the Constitution.* Naperville, IL: Sourcebooks, 2005.

Chamberlain, John. *The Enterprising Americans.* New York: Harper and Row, 1974.

Chambers, John Whiteclay. *The Tyranny of Change: America in the Progressive Era, 1900-1917.* New York: St. Martin's Press, 1992.

Collier, Christopher and James Lincoln Collier. *Decision in Philadelphia: The Constitutional Convention of 1787.* New York: Random House, 1986.

Copin, Clayton A. and Jack High. *The Politics of Purity: Harvey Washington Wiley and the Origins of Federal Food Policy.* Ann Arbor, MI: The University of Michigan Press, 1999.

Corning, Peter. *The Evolution of Medicare: From Idea to Law.* Washington, D.C.: Government Printing Office, 1969.

David, Sheri I. *With Dignity: The Search for Medicare and Medicaid.* Westport, CT: Greenwood, 1985.

Donald, Aida DiPace. *Lion in the White House: A Life of Theodore Roosevelt.* New York: Basic Books, 2007.

Dubofsky, Melvyn. *The State and Labor in Modern America.* Chapel Hill, NC: The University of North Carolina Press, 1994.

Dulles, Foster Rhea and Melvyn Dubofsky. *Labor in America: A History, 4th Edition.* Arlington Heights, ILL 60004, 1984. p 256.

Evans, Rowland and Robert Novak. *Lyndon Johnson: The Exercise of Power.* New York: New American Library, 1966.

Fein, Rashi. *Medical Care, Medical Costs.* Cambridge, Mass.: Harvard University Press, 1989.

Feinberg, Barbara Silberdick. *The Articles of Confederation: The First Constitution of the United States.* Brookfield, CT: Twenty-First Century Books, 2002

Feingold, Eugene. *Medicare: Policy and Politics: A Case Study and Policy Analysis.* San Francisco: Chandler, 1966.

Fite, Gilbert C. *Richard B. Russell, Jr: Senator from Georgia.* Chapel Hill: University of North Carolina Press, 1991.

Garraty, John Arthur. *Theodore Roosevelt: American Rough Rider.* New York: Sterling Publishing Company, 2007.

Gillespie, Michael Allen and Michael Lienesch. *Ratifying the Constitution.* Lawrence, Kansas: University Press of Kansas, 1989.

Gilmore, Glenda Elizabeth. *Who Were the Progressives?* New York: Palgrave Macmillan, 2002.

Goodwin, Lorine Swainston. *The Pure Food, Drink, and Drug Crusaders, 1879-1914.* Jefferson, N.C.: McFarland, 1999.

Gould, Lewis L. *The Most Exclusive Club: A History of the Modern U.S. Senate,.* New York: Basic Books, 2005.

Goulden, Joseph C. *The Best Years: 1945-1950.* New York: Atheneum, 1976.

Halberstam, David. *The Fifties.* New York: Villard Books, 1993.

Harness, Cheryl. *The Remarkable, Rough-Riding Life of Theodore Roosevelt and the Rise of Empire America.* Washington, D.C.: National Geographic, 2007.

Harris, Leon A. *Upton Sinclair, American Rebel.* New York: Crowell, 1975.

Harris, Richard. *A Sacred Trust.* New York: New American Library, 1966.

Harrison, Robert. *Congress, Progressive Reform, and the New American State.* 2004

Hirshfield, Daniel S. *The Lost Reform: The Campaign for Compulsory Health Insurance in the United States from 1932 to 1943.* Cambridge, Mass.: Harvard University Press, 1970.

Hoffman, Beatrix. *The Wages of Sickness: The Politics of Health Insurance in Progressive America.* Chapel Hill: University of North Carolina Press, 2001.

Holbrook, Stewart H. *The Age of the Moguls.* Garden City, NY: Doubleday, 1953.

Huthmacher, J. Joseph. *Senator Robert F. Wagner and the Rise of Urban Liberalism.* New York: Atheneum, 1968.

Jacobs, Lawrence R. *The Health of Nations: Public Opinion and the Making of American and British Health Policy.* Ithaca, N.Y.: Cornell University Press, 1993.

Josephson, Matthew Josephson. *The Robber Barons.* New York: Harcourt, 1934.

Kennedy, David M. Editor. *Progressivism: The Critical Issues.* Boston: Little Brown, 1971.

Ketcham, Ralph Louis. James Madison: A Biography. Charlottesville: University Press of Virginia, 1990.

Kovaleff, Theodore P., Ed. *The Antitrust Impulse: Volume I: An Economic, Historical, and Legal Analysis.* Armonk, NY: M.E. Sharpe, 1994.

Lubove, Roy. *The Struggle for Social Security, 1900—1935*. Cambridge, Mass.: Harvard University Press, 1968.

Main, Jackson Turner. *The Antifederalists: Critics of the Constitution, 1781-1788*. Chapel Hill, NC: The University of North Carolina Press, 1961.

Manchester, William Manchester. *The Glory and the Dream: A Narrative History of America, 1932-1972*. New York: Little Brown, 1973.

Mann, Robert Mann. *The Walls of Jericho: Lyndon Johnson, Hubert Humphrey, Richard Russell and the Struggle of Civil Rights*. New York: Harcourt, Brace and Company, 1996.

Marmor, Theodore R. *The Politics of Medicare*, Chicago: Aldine Publishing Company, 1973.

Marmor, Theodore. *Understanding Health Care Reform*. New Haven, CT: Yale University Press, 1994.

Martin Luther King, Jr. *Stride Toward Freedom: The Montgomery Story*. Boston: Beacon Press, 1958.

McChesney, Fred S. and William F. Shughart II, Eds. *The Causes and Consequences of Antitrust: The Public-Choice Perspective*. Chicago: University of Chicago Press, 1995.

McClure, Arthur F. *The Truman Administration and the Problems of Postwar Labor, 1945-1948*. Crnbury, NJ: Associated University Presses, 1969.

McShane, Clay and Joel Arthur Tarr. *The Horse in the City*, Baltimore, MD: John Hopkins University Press, 2007.

Millis, Harry A. and Emily Clark Brown. *From the Wagner Act to Taft-Hartley: A Study of National Labor Policy and Labor Relations*. Chicago: University of Chicago Press, 1950.

Morison, Samuel. *Oxford History of the American People*. New York: Oxford University Press, 1965.

Morris, Charles. *The Tycoons: How Andrew Carnegie, John D. Rockefeller, Jay Gould, and J.P. Morgan Invented the American Supereconomy*, New York: Henry Holt, 2005.

Oberlander, Jonathan. *The Political Life of Medicare*. Chicago: University of Chicago Press, 2003.

Okun, Mitchell. *Fair Play in the Marketplace: The First Battle for Pure Food and Drugs*. Dekalb, IL: Northern Illinois University Press, 1986.

Olson, Nathan. *Theodore Roosevelt: Bear of a President*. Makato, Minn: Capstone Press, 2007.

Page, Smith, Page. *America Enters the World: A People's History of the Progressive Era and World War I*. New York: McGraw-Hill, 1985.

Peritz, Rudolph J. R. *Competition Policy in America, 1888-1992*. New York: Oxford University Press, 1996.

Poen, Monte M. *Harry S. Truman versus the Medical Lobby*. Columbia: University of Missouri Press, 1979.

Ron Chernow. *Titan: The Life of John D. Rockefeller, Sr.* New York: Random House, 1998.

Rossiter, Clinton. *1787: The Grand Convention, The Year that Made a Nation*. New York: The Macmillan Company, 1966.

Rutland, Robert Allan. *James Madison: The Founding Father*. New York: McMillan, 1987.

Sinclair, Upton. *The Jungle*. New York: Robert Bentley, Inc., 1946.

Star, Paul. *The Social Transformation of American Medicine*. New York: Basic Books, 1982.

Stewart, David O. *The Summer of 1787: The Men Who Invented the Constitution*. New York: Simon & Schuster, 2007.

Sullivan, E. Thomas, Ed. *The Political Economy of the Sherman Act: The First One Hundred Years.* New York: Oxford University Press, 1991.

Sundquist, James. *Politics and Policy: The Eisenhower, Kennedy, and Johnson Years.* Washington, D.C.: Brookings Institution Press, 1968.

Tindall, George Brown and David E. Shi. *America: A Narrative History, 6th Edition.* New York: W.W. Norton, 2004. p.717

Unger, Irwin and Debi Unger. *LBJ: A Life.* New York: John Wiley, 1999.

Van Doren, Carl. *The Great Rehearsal: The Story of the Making and Ratifying of the Constitution of the United States.* Westport, CT: Greenwood Press, 1948.

Wiley, Harvey W. *Harvey W. Wiley: An Autobiography.* Indianapolis, IN: The Bobbs-Merrill Company, 1930.

Wiley, Harvey Washington. *The History of a Crime Against the Food Law: The Amazing Story of the National Food and Drug Law Intended to Protect the Health of the People, Perverted to Protect Adulteration of Foods and Drugs.* Washington, D.C.: H.W. Wiley, 1929.

Williams, Donnie. *The Thunder of Angels: The Montgomery Bus Boycott and the People who Broke the Back of Jim Crow.* Chicago: Lawrence Hill Books, 2006.

Wills, Garry. *James Madison.* New York: Henry Holt and Company, 2002.

Wood, Donna J. *Strategic Uses of Public Policy: Business and Government in the Progressive Era.* Marshfield, MA: Pitman, 1986.

Young, James Harvey. *Pure Food: Securing the Federal Food and Drugs Act of 1906.* Princeton, NJ: Princeton University Press, 1989.

NOTES

1. Clinton Rossiter, *1787: The Grand Convention* (New York: The Macmillan Company, 1966), pp. 24-25.
2. Ibid, p. 25
3. Christopher Collier and James Lincoln Collier, *Decision in Philadelphia: The Constitutional Convention of 1787* (New York: Random House, 1986), p. 15.
4. Clinton Rossiter, *1787: The Grand Convention* (New York: The Macmillan Company, 1966), p34
5. Ibid, p. 31.
6. Clinton Rossiter, *1787: The Grand Convention* (New York: The Macmillan Company, 1966), p. 31.
7. For more on Shay's rebellion see David P. Szatmary, *Shay's Rebellion: The Making of an Agrarian Insurrection* (Amherst, MASS: University of Massachusetts Press, 1980).
8. David O. Stewart, *The Summer of 1787: The Men Who Invented the Constitution.* (New York: Simon & Schuster, 2007), pp. 15-16.
9. Fred Barbash, The *Founding: A Dramatic Account of the Writing of the Constitution.* (New York: Simon and Schuster, 1987), p. 33.
10. Christopher Collier and James Lincoln Collier. *Decision in Philadelphia: The Constitutional Convention of 1787* (New York: Random House, 1986),p. 15
11. Ibid, p. 3.
12. Ibid, p 3.

13. Ibid, p. 47.
14. Barbara Silberdick Feinberg, *The Articles of Confederation: The First Constitution of the United States* (Brookfield, CT: Twenty-First Century Books, 2002), P. 56.
15. Catherine Drinker Bowen, *Miracle at Philadelphia: The Story of the Constitutional Convention, May to September 1787* (Boston: Little Brown, 1986), p. 5.
16. Ralph Louis Ketcham, *James Madison: A Biography*, (Charlottesville: University Press of Virginia, 1990), pp. 116-117
17. Ibid, p. 115.
18. Clinton Rossiter, *1787: The Grand Convention* (New York: The Macmillan Company, 1966), p 38.
19. This description is drawn from Garry Wills, *James Madison* (New York: Henry Holt and Company, 2002), pp 3-7 and Robert Allan Rutland, *James Madison: The Founding Father* (New York: McMillan, 1987), pp 4, 10, 18, and 25.
20. Garry Wills, *James Madison* (New York: Henry Holt and Company, 2002), p 6.
21. Ibid, p 6.
22. Christopher Collier and James Lincoln Collier, *Decision in Philadelphia: The Constitutional Convention of 1787* (New York: Random House, 1986), pp 26-27.
23. Garry Wills, *James Madison* (New York: Henry Holt and Company, 2002), p 4.
24. Ibid
25. Ibid, pp. 4-5.
26. Ibid, p 5.
27. Robert Allan Rutland, *James Madison: The Founding Father* (New York: McMillan, 1987), p 15.
28. Ralph Louis Ketcham, *James Madison: A Biography*, (Charlottesville: University Press of Virginia, 1990), pp 183-185.
29. Ibid, p 184.

30. Douglas Adair, *Fame and the Founding Fathers*, edited by Trevor Colbourn (New York: Norton, 1974), p. 134 cited in Garry Wills, *James Madison* (New York: Henry Holt and Company, 2002), p 27.
31. David O. Stewart, *The Summer of 1787: The Men Who Invented the Constitution.* (New York: Simon & Schuster, 2007), p. 10.
32. Garry Wills, *James Madison* (New York: Henry Holt and Company, 2002), pp. 25-26.
33. To read a transcript of the Virginia Plan go to http://www.ourdocuments.gov/doc.php?flash=true&doc=7&page=transcript accessed February 18, 2008.
34. Catherine Drinker Bowen, *Miracle at Philadelphia: The Story of the Constitutional Convention, May to September 1787* (Boston: Little Brown, 1986), p 18.
35. Garry Wills, James Madison (New York: Henry Holt and Company, 2002), pp 25-26.
36. Catherine Drinker Bowen, *Miracle at Philadelphia: The Story of the Constitutional Convention, May to September 1787* (Boston: Little Brown, 1986), p 4.
37. Ibid, p 4.
38. Carl Van Doren, *The Great Rehearsal: The Story of the Making and Ratifying of the Constitution of the United States* (Westport, CT: Greenwood Press, 1948), p 18.
39. To read a transcript of the Virginia Plan go to http://www.ourdocuments.gov/doc.php?flash=true&doc=7&page=transcript accessed February 18, 2008.
40. David O. Stewart, *The Summer of 1787: The Men Who Invented the Constitution.* (New York: Simon & Schuster, 2007), p. 65.
41. Ibid, p. 66.
42. Ralph Louis Ketcham, *James Madison: A Biography*, (Charlottesville: University Press of Virginia, 1990), p 215.
43. Ibid, p 215.
44. David O. Stewart, *The Summer of 1787: The Men Who Invented the Constitution.* (New York: Simon & Schuster, 2007), p. 105.

45. Clinton Rossiter, *1787: The Grand Convention* (New York: The Macmillan Company, 1966), p 261.
46. Ibid, p 297.
47. Ibid, pp. 258-260.
48. Ibid, pp 262-263.
49. Ibid, p 264.
50. Ibid, p 265.
51. Robert Allan Rutland, *James Madison: The Founding Father* (New York: McMillan, 1987), p 19.
52. Jackson Turner Main, *The Antifederalists: Critics of the Constitution, 1781-1788* (Chapel Hill, NC: The University of North Carolina Press, 1961), pp xi-xii.
53. Ralph Louis Ketcham, *James Madison: A Biography*, (Charlottesville: University Press of Virginia, 1990), p 236.
54. Thomas L. Pangle, *The Great Debate: Advocates and Opponents of the American Constitution Lecture Transcript and Course Guidebook.* (Chantilly, VA: The Teaching Company, 2007), pp 36-37.
55. Ibid, pp 55.
56. Catherine Drinker Bowen, *Miracle at Philadelphia: The Story of the Constitutional Convention, May to September 1787* (Boston: Little Brown, 1986), p 245.
57. Ibid, pp 245-246.
58. Cited in Catherine Drinker Bowen, *Miracle at Philadelphia: The Story of the Constitutional Convention, May to September 1787* (Boston: Little Brown, 1986), p 246.
59. Clinton Rossiter, *1787: The Grand Convention* (New York: The Macmillan Company, 1966), p 278.
60. Ibid, p 280.
61. Lance Banning, "Virginia: Sectionalism and the General Good." In *Ratifying the Constitution*, by Michael Allen Gillespie and Michael Lienesch, 261-299 (Lawrence, Kansas: University Press of Kansas, 1989) p.262.
62. Garry Wills, *James Madison* (New York: Henry Holt and Company, 2002), p 36.

63. Catherine Drinker Bowen, *Miracle at Philadelphia: The Story of the Constitutional Convention, May to September 1787* (Boston: Little Brown, 1986), pp 297-299. You can read a transcript of Patrick Henry's oratory by visiting http://teachingamericanhistory.org/ratification/elliot/vol3/ accessed February 18, 2008 and clicking on June 5, 1788.
64. Ralph Louis Ketcham, *James Madison: A Biography*, (Charlottesville: University Press of Virginia, 1990), pp 255-256. Ketcham is paraphrasing here.
65. Charles Cerami, *Young Patriots: The Remarkable Story of Two Men, Their Impossible Plan and the Revolution that Created the Constitution* (Naperville, IL: Sourcebooks, 2005), p 61.
66. Ibid, p 63.
67. Catherine Drinker Bowen, *Miracle at Philadelphia: The Story of the Constitutional Convention, May to September 1787* (Boston: Little Brown, 1986), p 296.
68. Ralph Louis Ketcham, *James Madison: A Biography*, (Charlottesville: University Press of Virginia, 1990), p 206.
69. Ibid, p 177.
70. Ibid, p 177.
71. See http://www.teachingamericanhistory.org/ratification/elliot/vol3/june13.html accessed February 18, 2008 for James Monroe's remarks on June 13, 1788.
72. http://www.teachingamericanhistory.org/ratification/elliot/vol3/june13.html accessed February 18, 2008.
73. Ibid
74. Ibid
75. Ibid,
76. Quoted in Lance Banning, "Virginia: Sectionalism and the General Good." In *Ratifying the Constitution*, by Michael Allen Gillespie and Michael Lienesch, 261-299 (Lawrence, Kansas: University Press of Kansas, 1989) p 284.

77. Lance Banning, "Virginia: Sectionalism and the General Good." In Ratifying the Constitution, by Michael Allen Gillespie and Michael Lienesch, 261-299 (Lawrence, Kansas: University Press of Kansas, 1989) p 284.
78. Ibid, p 285.
79. http://www.teachingamericanhistory.org/ratification/elliot/vol3/june24.html accessed February 18, 2008.
80. Robert Allan Rutland, *James Madison: The Founding Father* (New York: McMillan, 1987), p 61.
81. Ibid, p 62.
82. Ralph Louis Ketcham, *James Madison: A Biography*, (Charlottesville: University Press of Virginia, 1990), p 311.
83. Ibid, p 312.
84. Ibid, p 313.
85. Clinton Rossiter, *1787: The Grand Convention* (New York: The Macmillan Company, 1966), p 38.
86. David O. Stewart, *The Summer of 1787: The Men Who Invented the Constitution*. (New York: Simon & Schuster, 2007), p. 105.
87. Clinton Rossiter, *1787: The Grand Convention* (New York: The Macmillan Company, 1966), p 261.
88. Ibid, p 297.
89. The Beekman Hill story is told in Lorine Swainston Goodwin, *The Pure Food, Drink, and Drug Crusaders, 1879-1914*, (Jefferson, N.C.: McFarland & Company, 1999), pp 7-21. Manure discussion and statistics on number of horses in the city is based on Clay McShane and Joel Arthur Tarr, *The Horse in the City*, (Baltimore, MD: John Hopkins University Press, 2007), pp124-125.
90. Mrs. Ralph Trautman, "Twelve Years' Work of the Ladies Health Protective Association," *New York Medical Times*, 24, no. 9 (September 1896), pp. 257-261.
91. Ibid, p 257.
92. Ibid, p. 258.

93. Lorine Swainston Goodwin, *The Pure Food, Drink, and Drug Crusaders, 1879-1914*, (Jefferson, N.C.: McFarland & Company, 1999), p. 89.
94. Ibid, p. 132.
95. Ibid, 152-166.
96. James Harvey Young, *Pure Food: Securing the Federal Food and Drugs Act of 1906* (Princeton, NJ: Princeton University Press, 1989), pp 35-39
97. In 1879, Germany blamed an outbreak of trichinosis on American pork. In response, Germany, Spain, France, Austria-Hungary, Turkey, Rumania and Denmark banned American pork. American livestock producers convinced Congress to pass a bill to reassure the Europeans and convince them to lift the ban. Interestingly, packers and exporters opposed the bill calling it an unnecessary expense. Europeans, they said, just needed to cook the meat thoroughly as Americans did. Additionally, said the opponents, such a bill would be an unacceptable intrusion into their operations. They preferred tariff retaliation to get the ban lifted.
98. Harvey W. Wiley, *Harvey W. Wiley: An Autobiography*, (Indianapolis, IN: The Bobbs-Merrill Company, 1930) pp. 202-203.
99. Ibid, p. 202.
100. James Harvey Young, *Pure Food: Securing the Federal Food and Drugs Act of 1906* (Princeton, NJ: Princeton University Press, 1989), p. 99
101. Copin, Clayton A. and Jack High, *The Politics of Purity: Harvey Washington Wiley and the Origins of Federal Food Policy,* (Ann Arbor, MI: The University of Michigan Press, 1999) p. 31.
102. James Harvey Young, *Pure Food: Securing the Federal Food and Drugs Act of 1906* (Princeton, NJ: Princeton University Press, 1989), pp. 101-102.
103. Ibid, p. 106.
104. Lorine Swainston Goodwin, *The Pure Food, Drink, and Drug Cursaders, 1879-1914*, (Jeffeson, N.C.: McFarland & Company, 1999) p. 222.
105. Ibid, pp 229-232.

106. Ibid, pp. 218.
107. Ibid, pp. 220.
108. Ibid,) pp 227.
109. Ibid, pp 228.
110. Ibid, p. 162.
111. James Harvey Young, *Pure Food: Securing the Federal Food and Drugs Act of 1906* (Princeton, NJ: Princeton University Press, 1989), pp. 190-191.
112. Lorine Swainston Goodwin, *The Pure Food, Drink, and Drug Cursaders, 1879-1914*, (Jeffeson, N.C.: McFarland & Company, 1999), pp. 162.
113. See Gabriel Kolko, *The Triumph of Conservatism: A Reinterpretation of American History, 1900-1916* (New York: Macmillan, 1963), 285, 305
114. Upton Sinclair's son cited in Anthony Arthur, *Radical Innocent: Upton Sinclair* (New York: Random House, 2006), p. 4.
115. Ibid, p. 7.
116. Sinclair quoted in Anthony Arthur, *Radical Innocent: Upton Sinclair* (New York: Random House, 2006), p. 11.
117. Anthony Arthur, *Radical Innocent: Upton Sinclair* (New York: Random House, 2006), pp3.
118. Ibid, p. 14.
119. Ibid, p. 23.
120. Ibid, p. 42.
121. Upton Sinclair, *The Jungle*, (New York: Robert Bentley, Inc., 1946), p. v.
122. Ibid, p. vi.
123. Ibid, pp. 34-36
124. Ibid, p.135-136.
125. James Harvey Young, *Pure Food: Securing the Federal Food and Drugs Act of 1906* (Princeton, NJ: Princeton University Press, 1989), pp. 232-233.

126. This section is based upon a lengthy discussion of the debate in Congress over the Meat Inspection Act and Pure Food and Drug Act found in James Harvey Young, *Pure Food: Securing the Federal Food and Drugs Act of 1906* (Princeton, NJ: Princeton University Press, 1989), pp. 230-262.
127. James Harvey Young, *Pure Food: Securing the Federal Food and Drugs Act of 1906* (Princeton, NJ: Princeton University Press, 1989), pp. 236-237.
128. Quoted in James Harvey Young, *Pure Food: Securing the Federal Food and Drugs Act of 1906* (Princeton, NJ: Princeton University Press, 1989), p. 239.
129. Ibid, pp. 242.
130. Ibid, p.244.
131. Ibid, p. 245
132. Harvey W. Wiley, *Harvey W. Wiley: An Autobiography*, (Indianapolis, IN: Bobbs-Merrill, 1930), p. 238-239.
133. http://www.walletpop.com/tag/FDA+Food+Safety+Modernization+Act/ Accessed 01/10/11
134. Quoted in Sheri I. David, *With Dignity: The Search for Medicare and Medicaid*, (Westport, CT: Greenwood Press, 1985), P. 142
135. Marmor, Theodore R., *The Politics of Medicare*, (Chicago: Aldine Publishing Company, 1973), p. 5.
136. Beatrix Hoffman, *The Wages of Sickness: The Politics of Health Insurance in Progressive America* (Chapel Hill: University of North Carolina Press, 2001), p.6
137. Ibid, p.10.
138. Ibid, p.20.
139. Ibid, p.22.
140. Marmor, Theodore R., *The Politics of Medicare*, (Chicago: Aldine Publishing Company, 1973), p. 7.
141. The quotes that follow are from Beatrix Hoffman, *The Wages of Sickness: The Politics of Health Insurance in Progressive America* (Chapel Hill: University of North Carolina Press, 2001), p.85-106..

142. Beatrix Hoffman, *The Wages of Sickness: The Politics of Health Insurance in Progressive America* (Chapel Hill: University of North Carolina Press, 2001), p. 3.
143. Ibid, p.84.
144. Quotes from Beatrix Hoffman, *The Wages of Sickness: The Politics of Health Insurance in Progressive America* (Chapel Hill: University of North Carolina Press, 2001), p. 86..
145. Ibid, p.53,
146. Ibid, p.53.
147. Rashi Fein, *Medical Care, Medical Costs: The Search for a Health Insurance Policy*, (Cambridge, MASS: Harvard University Press, 1986), p.36-37.
148. Beatrix Hoffman, *The Wages of Sickness: The Politics of Health Insurance in Progressive America* (Chapel Hill: University of North Carolina Press, 2001), p.83.
149. Ibid, p.83.
150. Rashi Fein, *Medical Care, Medical Costs: The Search for a Health Insurance Policy*, (Cambridge, MASS: Harvard University Press, 1986), p. 35-36.
151. Marmor, Theodore R., *The Politics of Medicare*, (Chicago: Aldine Publishing Company, 1973), p. p. 8-9.
152. Feingold, Eugene, *Medicare: Policy and Politics, A Case Study and Policy Analysis*, (San Francisco: Chandler Publishing Co., 1966), p. 6-12.
153. Marmor, Theodore R., *The Politics of Medicare*, (Chicago: Aldine Publishing Company, 1973), pp. 11-12.
154. Feingold, Eugene, *Medicare: Policy and Politics, A Case Study and Policy Analysis*, (San Francisco: Chandler Publishing Co., 1966), p. 97-100.
155. Oberlander, Jonathan. *The Political Live of Medicare*, (Chicago: University of Chicago Press, 2003), p. 22
156. Feingold, Eugene, *Medicare: Policy and Politics, A Case Study and Policy Analysis*, (San Francisco: Chandler Publishing Co., 1966), p. 100.

157. Sheri I. David, *With Dignity: The Search for Medicare and Medicaid*, (Westport, CT: Greenwood Press, 1985), p. 13.
158. This discussion draws largely from Sheri I. David, *With Dignity: The Search for Medicare and Medicaid*, (Westport, CT: Greenwood Press, 1985), P. 4-5.
159. Rashi Fein, *Medical Care, Medical Costs: The Search for a Health Insurance Policy*, (Cambridge, MASS: Harvard University Press, 1986), p. p. 54-55.
160. Marmor, Theodore R., *The Politics of Medicare*, (Chicago: Aldine Publishing Company, 1973), p. 20
161. Rashi Fein makes this point in *Medical Care, Medical Costs: The Search for a Health Insurance Policy*, (Cambridge, MASS: Harvard University Press, 1986), p. 64.
162. Oberlander, Jonathan. *The Political Live of Medicare,* (Chicago: University of Chicago Press, 2003), p. 25.
163. Sheri I. David, *With Dignity: The Search for Medicare and Medicaid*, (Westport, CT: Greenwood Press, 1985), p. 5.
164. Ibid, p. 5.
165. Rashi Fein, *Medical Care, Medical Costs: The Search for a Health Insurance Policy*, (Cambridge, MASS: Harvard University Press, 1986), p. 34.
166. Ibid, p. 34.
167. Ibid, p. 58-59.
168. Oberlander, Jonathan. *The Political Live of Medicare*, (Chicago: University of Chicago Press, 2003), p. 26.
169. Feingold, Eugene, *Medicare: Policy and Politics, A Case Study and Policy Analysis*, (San Francisco: Chandler Publishing Co., 1966), p. 159.
170. Oberlander, Jonathan. *The Political Live of Medicare*, (Chicago: University of Chicago Press, 2003), p. 27.
171. Sundquist, James L. *Politics and Policy: The Eisenhower, Kennedy and Johnson Years*, (Washington, D.C.: The Brookings Institution, 1968), p. 300.

172. Feingold, Eugene, *Medicare: Policy and Politics, A Case Study and Policy Analysis*, (San Francisco: Chandler Publishing Co., 1966), p. 159-160.
173. Quoted in Oberlander, Jonathan. *The Political Live of Medicare*, (Chicago: University of Chicago Press, 2003), p. 27.
174. Sheri I. David, *With Dignity: The Search for Medicare and Medicaid*, (Westport, CT: Greenwood Press, 1985), p. 14.
175. Ibid, p. 19.
176. Ibid, p. 21-22.
177. Sundquist, James L. *Politics and Policy: The Eisenhower, Kennedy and Johnson Years*, (Washington, D.C.: The Brookings Institution, 1968), pp. 298-299.
178. Ibid, p298-299.
179. Sheri I. David, *With Dignity: The Search for Medicare and Medicaid*, (Westport, CT: Greenwood Press, 1985), p. 27 makes this argument.
180. Ibid, pp. 28-29.
181. Ibid, p. 28.
182. Ibid, p. 28.
183. Ibid, p. 28.
184. Ibid, p. 24.
185. Ibid, p. 13
186. Ibid, p. 81.
187. Ibid, p. 29.
188. Ibid, p. 30.
189. Rashi Fein, *Medical Care, Medical Costs: The Search for a Health Insurance Policy*, (Cambridge, MASS: Harvard University Press, 1986), pp. 57-58.
190. Sheri I. David, *With Dignity: The Search for Medicare and Medicaid*, (Westport, CT: Greenwood Press, 1985), p. 37.
191. Ibid, p. 39.
192. Ibid, p. 39.
193. Ibid. p. 39
194. Ibid, p. 39.
195. Ibid, p. 42.
196. Ibid, p. 42-44

197. Ibid, p. 38-39.
198. Sandquist, James L. *Politics and Policy: The Eisenhower, Kennedy and Johnson Years.* (Washington, D.C.: The Brookings Institution, 1968), p. 310.
199. Rashi Fein, *Medical Care, Medical Costs: The Search for a Health Insurance Policy*, (Cambridge, MASS: Harvard University Press, 1986), p. 61.
200. The 10 percent limit on Social Security taxes wasn't a legal limit it was just something that had been surggested by Abraham Ribicoff in 1960 as a psychological limit. The 10 percent figure stuck and became known as the "Rubicon" that could not be crossed.
201. Marmor, Theodore R., *The Politics of Medicare*, (Chicago: Aldine Publishing Company, 1973), p. 55.
202. Ibid, p. 55.
203. Sheri I. David, *With Dignity: The Search for Medicare and Medicaid*, (Westport, CT: Greenwood Press, 1985), P. 131
204. From AMA publication cited in Marmor, Theodore R., *The Politics of Medicare*, (Chicago: Aldine Publishing Company, 1973), p. 61.
205. Sheri I. David, *With Dignity: The Search for Medicare and Medicaid*, (Westport, CT: Greenwood Press, 1985), p. 126.
206. Ibid, p. 129.
207. Marmor, Theodore R., *The Politics of Medicare*, (Chicago: Aldine Publishing Company, 1973), p. 64.
208. Sheri I. David, *With Dignity: The Search for Medicare and Medicaid*, (Westport, CT: Greenwood Press, 1985), p. 129.
209. Oberlander, Jonathan, *The Political Live of Medicare*, (Chicago: University of Chicago Press, 2003), pp, 30-31
210. Sheri I. David, *With Dignity: The Search for Medicare and Medicaid*, (Westport, CT: Greenwood Press, 1985), p. 131.
211. Marmor, Theodore R., *The Politics of Medicare*, (Chicago: Aldine Publishing Company, 1973), p. 66.
212. Sheri I. David, *With Dignity: The Search for Medicare and Medicaid*, (Westport, CT: Greenwood Press, 1985), p. 132 tells this story of the Johnson meeting.

213. Ibid, p. 132.
214. Ibid, p. 136.
215. Oberlander, Jonathan. *The Political Live of Medicare,* (Chicago: University of Chicago Press, 2003), p. 31.
216. Dulles, Foster Rhea and Melvyn Dubofsky, *Labor in America: A History, 4th Edition.* (Arlington Heights, ILL 60004, 1984), p 256.
217. Ibid, p. 12.
218. Ibid, p. 13
219. Ibid, p. 62.
220. Millis, Harry A. and Emily Clark Brown, From the Wagner Act to Taft-Hartley: A Study of National Labor Policy and Labor Relations. (Chicago: University of Chicago Press, 1950), p. 6.
221. Dulles, Foster Rhea and Melvyn Dubofsky, *Labor in America: A History, 4th Edition.* (Arlington Heights, ILL 60004, 1984), p 58-59.
222. Ibid, p. 61.
223. Ibid, p. 75.
224. Ibid, p. 82.
225. Ibid, pp. 184-189.
226. Ibid, p. 241.
227. Samuel Morison, *Oxford History of the American People*, (New York: Oxford University Press, 1965), p. 944.
228. Ibid, p. 944.
229. Huthmacher, J. Joseph, *Senator Robert F. Wagner and the Rise of Urban Liberalism*, (New York: Atheneum, 1968), p 130.
230. This section is based upon Huthmacher, J. Joseph, *Senator Robert F. Wagner and the Rise of Urban Liberalism*, (New York: Atheneum, 1968).
231. For more information on the Triangle fire including eye witness accounts visit http://www.ilr.cornell.edu/trianglefire/texts/ Accessed 06/30/2009.
232. Huthmacher, J. Joseph, *Senator Robert F. Wagner and the Rise of Urban Liberalism*, (New York: Atheneum, 1968), pp. 109-113.
233. Ibid, p. 116.
234. Samuel Morison, *Oxford History of the American People*, (New York: Oxford University Press, 1965), p. 936.

235. Ibid, p. 936.

236. Dulles, Foster Rhea and Melvyn Dubofsky, *Labor in America: A History, 4th Edition*. (Arlington Heights, ILL 60004, 1984), p. 268.

237. Ibid, p. 269.

238. See: http://supreme.justia.com/us/301/1/case.html Accessed 5/20/2009.

239. Dulles, Foster Rhea and Melvyn Dubofsky, *Labor in America: A History, 4th Edition*. (Arlington Heights, ILL 60004, 1984), p. 277.

240. Millis, Harry A. and Emily Clark Brown, *From the Wagner Act to Taft-Hartley: A Study of National Labor Policy and Labor Relations.* (Chicago: University of Chicago Press, 1950), pp. 283-284.

241. Ibid, pp. 283-284.

242. Huthmacher, J. Joseph, *Senator Robert F. Wagner and the Rise of Urban Liberalism*, (New York: Atheneum, 1968), p 234.

243. Millis, Harry A. and Emily Clark Brown, *From the Wagner Act to Taft-Hartley: A Study of National Labor Policy and Labor Relations.* (Chicago: University of Chicago Press, 1950), p. 66.

244. Ibid, p.67.

245. Ibid, p. 67.

246. Ibid, p. 71.

247. Ibid, pp. 273-274.

248. Ibid, 1950), p. 287.

249. Ibid, 1950), p. 288.

250. Ibid, p. 288.

251. Ibid, p. 289.

252. See footnote 53, Millis, Harry A. and Emily Clark Brown, *From the Wagner Act to Taft-Hartley: A Study of National Labor Policy and Labor Relations.* (Chicago: University of Chicago Press, 1950), p. 295.

253. Cited in McClure, Arthur F., *The Truman Administration and the Problems of Postwar Labor, 1945-1948*, (Crnbury, NJ: Associated University Presses, 1969), P. 31

254. McClure, Arthur F., *The Truman Administration and the Problems of Postwar Labor, 1945-1948.* (Crnbury, NJ: Associated University Presses, 1969), p. 50.

255. Ibid, p. 54.
256. Ibid, p. 307.
257. Ibid, p. 60.
258. Millis, Harry A. and Emily Clark Brown, *From the Wagner Act to Taft-Hartley: A Study of National Labor Policy and Labor Relations.* (Chicago: University of Chicago Press, 1950), p. 287.
259. Ibid, p. 315.
260. Ibid, p. 371.
261. Quotes in this paragraph are from Millis, Harry A. and Emily Clark Brown, *From the Wagner Act to Taft-Hartley: A Study of National Labor Policy and Labor Relations.* (Chicago: University of Chicago Press, 1950), pp. 371-372
262. Millis, Harry A. and Emily Clark Brown, *From the Wagner Act to Taft-Hartley: A Study of National Labor Policy and Labor Relations.* (Chicago: University of Chicago Press, 1950), p. 372.
263. Ibid, p. 390.
264. Ibid, pp. 663-664.
265. McClure, Arthur F., *The Truman Administration and the Problems of Postwar Labor, 1945-1948.* (Crnbury, NJ: Associated University Presses, 1969), P. 102.
266. See http://www.ourdocuments.gov/doc.php?flash=old&doc=51 for a copy of the act. Accessed 05-05-2010.
267. Matthew Josephson, *The Robber Barons*, (New York: Harcourt, 1934, 1962 edition), p 5
268. Ibid, p. 5
269. See Jerold G. Van Cise, "Past-Present-Future," in Theodore Kovaleff, "Historical Perspective: An Introduction," in Theodore P. Kovaleff, Ed., *The Antitrust Impulse: Volume I: An Economic, Historical, and Legal Analysis*, (Armonk, NY: M.E. Sharpe, 1994), p. 22-25 for more on American's transformation during this period.
270. "Past-Present-Future," in Theodore Kovaleff, "Historical Perspective: An Introduction," in Theodore P. Kovaleff, Ed., *The Antitrust Impulse: Volume I: An Economic, Historical, and Legal Analysis*, (Armonk, NY: M.E. Sharpe, 1994), p. 22-25.

271. Theodore Kovaleff, "Historical Perspective: An Introduction," in Theodore P. Kovaleff, Ed., *The Antitrust Impulse: Volume I: An Economic, Historical, and Legal Analysis,* (Armonk, NY: M.E. Sharpe, 1994), p. 7-12.
272. Matthew Josephson, *The Robber Barons*, (New York: Harcourt, 1934, 1962 edition), p. 250.
273. Ibid, p. 250.
274. Stewart H. Holbrook, *The Age of the Moguls*, (Garden City, NY: Doubleday, 1953), p.20
275. Ibid, p. viii
276. In the foreword to the 1962 edition of his book *The Robber Barons,* Matthew Josephson notes that revisionist historians have attempted to paint the barons in a more favorable light. The revisionists, writes Josephson, "reject the idea that our nineteenth century barons-of-the-bags may have been inspired by the same motives animating the ancient barons-of-the-crags—who, by force of arms, instead of corporate combinations, monopolized strategic valley roads or mountain passes through which commerce flowed. To the revisionists or our history, our old-time money lords 'were not robber barons but architects of material progress,' and in some ways 'saviors' of our country. They have proposed rewriting parts of American history so that the image of the old-school capitalists should be retouched and restored, like rare pieces of antique furniture." Matthew Josephson, The Robber Barons, (New York: Harcourt, 1934, 1962 edition), p.vi. Well, there will be no revisionism here. My purpose is not to rehabilitate the titans of big business but rather to illustrate through a few examples why by 1890 there was a public outcry for Congress to do something to rein in their activities. Justly or unjustly, many Americans viewed the big business capitalists of the late 1800s as a threat to the country, if not outright evil men. You should understand the passage of the Sherman Act in the context of that public outrage against big business.
277. Stewart H. Holbrook, The Age of the Moguls, (Garden City, NY: Doubleday, 1953), p.14.
278. John Chamberlain, *The Enterprising Americans,* (New York: Harper and Row, 1974), pp185.

279. Ibid, p143.
280. Stewart H. Holbrook, *The Age of the Moguls,* (Garden City, NY: Doubleday, 1953), p 75.
281. This discussion of the life of John D. Rockefellers is based upon a number of sources, primarily Stewart H. Holbrook, *The Age of the Moguls,* (Garden City, NY: Doubleday, 1953), Charles R. Morris, *The Tycoons: How Andrew Carnegie, John D. Rockefeller, Jay Gould, and J.P. Morgan Invented the American Supereconomy*, (New York: Henry Holt, 2005), Matthew Josephson, *The Robber Barons,* (New York: Harcourt, 1934, 1962 edition), Bruce Bringhurst, *Antitrust and the Oil Monopoly: The Standard Oil Cases, 1890-1911,* (Westport, CT: Greenwood Press, 1979), and Ron Chernow, *Titan: The Life of John D. Rockefeller, Sr.*k (New York: Random House, 1998).
282. Stewart H. Holbrook, *The Age of the Moguls,* (Garden City, NY: Doubleday, 1953), p 134.
283. Charles R. Morris, The Tycoons: How Andrew Carnegie, John D. Rockefeller, Jay Gould, and J.P. Morgan Invented the American Supereconomy, (New York: Henry Holt, 2005), p. 17.
284. Matthew Josephson, *The Robber Barons,* (New York: Harcourt, 1934, 1962 edition), p.46
285. Ibid, p.46.
286. Ibid, p.46.
287. Ibid, p.46
288. Ron Chernow, *Titan: The Life of John D. Rockefeller, Sr.*k (New York: Random House, 1998), p. 153.
289. Matthew Josephson, *The Robber Barons* , (New York: Harcourt, 1934, 1962 edition), p47
290. Ibid, p.47
291. Ibid, p.49
292. Ibid, p.49
293. Ibid, p.48
294. Ibid, p. 110.
295. Ibid, p. 115.
296. Ibid, p. 115.

297. Ibid, p. 116.

298. Ibid, pp. 117-118.

299. See Ron Chernow, *Titan: The Life of John D. Rockefeller, Sr.*k (New York: Random House, 1998), p. 144-145 and Matthew Josephson, *The Robber Barons*, (New York: Harcourt, 1934, 1962 edition), pp. 118-119.

300. Charles R. Morris, *The Tycoons: How Andrew Carnegie, John D. Rockefeller, Jay Gould, and J.P. Morgan Invented the American Supereconomy*, (New York: Henry Holt, 2005), p. 20. Note: Morris maintains that Rockefeller's offers for the purchase of the competing refineries were always fair. Many other writers disagree.

301. Ron Chernow, *Titan: The Life of John D. Rockefeller, Sr.*k (New York: Random House, 1998), p. 145.

302. Bruce Bringhurst, *Antitrust and the Oil Monopoly: The Standard Oil Cases, 1890-1911*, (Westport, CT: Greenwood Press, 1979), p. 11.

303. Matthew Josephson, *The Robber Barons* , (New York: Harcourt, 1934, 1962 edition), p. 266

304. Ibid, p. 266.

305. Ibid, p. 269.

306. This was true of many states at the time.

307. Ron Chernow, *Titan: The Life of John D. Rockefeller, Sr.*k (New York: Random House, 1998) p. 226.

308. Ibid, p. 226

309. Ibid, p. 227.

310. Stewart H. Holbrook, *The Age of the Moguls*, (Garden City, NY: Doubleday, 1953), p. 134.

311. Ron Chernow, *Titan: The Life of John D. Rockefeller, Sr.*k (New York: Random House, 1998), p. 249.

312. Ibid, p. 227.

313. John J. Siegfried and Michelle Mahony, "The First Sherman Act Case: Jellico Mountain Coal, 1891, " in Theodore Kovaleff, "Historical Perspective: An Introduction," in Theodore P. Kovaleff, Ed., *The Antitrust Impulse: Volume I: An Economic, Historical, and Legal Analysis*, (Armonk, NY: M.E. Sharpe, 1994), p. 54

314. Thomas K. McCraw, *The Prophets of Regulation: Charles Francis Adams, Louis D. Brandeis, James M. Landis, Alfred E. Kahn*, (Cambridge, MASS: Harvard University Press, 1984), p. 64-65.
315. Richard Hofstadter, "What Happened to the Antitrust Movement?" in E. Thomas Sullivan, Ed. *The Political Economy of the Sherman Act: The First One Hundred Years.* (New York: Oxford University Press, 1991), p. 20-21.
316. Ibid, p. 29
317. Ibid, p. 30.
318. Ibid, p. 22.
319. Ibid, p. 22.
320. For more on the act see Donald J. Boudreaux, Thomas J. DiLorenzo, and Steven Parker, "Antitrust Before the Sherman Act," in Fred S. McChesney and William F. Shughart II, Eds., *The Causes and Consequences of Antitrust: The Public-Choice Perspective*, (Chicago: University of Chicago Press, 1995), p. 257-266
321. Thomas K. McCraw, *The Prophets of Regulation: Charles Francis Adams, Louis D. Brandeis, James M. Landis, Alfred E. Kahn*, (Cambridge, MASS: Harvard University Press, 1984), p. 61
322. Jerrold G. Van Cise, "Past-Present-Future," in Theodore Kovaleff, "Historical Perspective: An Introduction," in Theodore P. Kovaleff, Ed., *The Antitrust Impulse: Volume I: An Economic, Historical, and Legal Analysis*, (Armonk, NY: M.E. Sharpe, 1994), p. 22
323. Peter R. Dickson and Philippa K. Wells, "The Dubious Origins of the Sherman Antitrust Act: The Mouse that Roared," 20, No. 1 (Spring, 2001), p. 8.
324. Rudolph J. R. Peritz, *Competition Policy in America, 1888-1992.* (New York: Oxford University Press, 1996), p. 13
325. Ibid, p 14.
326. Ibid, p 14.
327. Robert H. Bork, "Legislative Intent and the Policy of the Sherman Act," *Journal of Law and Economics*, 9, (October 1966), pp. 7-48., p. 7.

328. Peter R. Dickson and Philippa K. Wells, "The Dubious Origins of the Sherman Antitrust Act: The Mouse that Roared," 20, No. 1 (Spring, 2001), p. 8
329. Thomas W. Hazlett, "The Legislative History of the Sherman Act Re-examined," *Economic Inquiry,* 30, (April 1992), p. 266.
330. Ibid, p. 266.
331. Quoted in Ibid, p. 266.
332. Thomas W. Hazlett, "The Legislative History of the Sherman Act Re-Examined," *Economic Inquiry,* 30, (April 1992), p. 269
333. Theodore P. Kovaleff, Ed. *The Antitrust Impulse, Vol. 1.* (Armonk, NY: M.E. Sharpe, 1994), p 19...
334. Peter R. Dickson and Philippa K. Wells, "The Dubious Origins of the Sherman Antitrust Act: The Mouse that Roared," 20, No. 1 (Spring, 2001), p. 10.
335. Ibid, p.11.
336. Thomas W. Hazlett, "The Legislative History of the Sherman Act Re-Examined," *Economic Inquiry,* 30, (April 1992), p. 267.
337. Eleanor M. Fox and Lawrence A Sullivan, "The Good and Bad Trust Dichotomy: A Short History of a Legal Idea," in Theodore Kovaleff, "Historical Perspective: An Introduction," in Theodore P. Kovaleff, Ed., *The Antitrust Impulse: Volume I: An Economic, Historical, and Legal Analysis,* (Armonk, NY: M.E. Sharpe, 1994), p. 93.
338. Bruce Bringhurst, *Antitrust and the Oil Monopoly: The Standard Oil Cases, 1890-1911,* (Westport, CT: Greenwood Press, 1979), p. 5.
339. Ibid, p. 6.
340. Eleanor M. Fox and Lawrence A Sullivan, "The Good and Bad Trust Dichotomy: A Short History of a Legal Idea," in Theodore Kovaleff, "Historical Perspective: An Introduction," in Theodore P. Kovaleff, Ed., *The Antitrust Impulse: Volume I: An Economic, Historical, and Legal Analysis,* (Armonk, NY: M.E. Sharpe, 1994), p91.
341. Ibid, pp. 91-92.

342. Eleanor M. Fox and Lawrence A Sullivan, "The Good and Bad Trust Dichotomy: A Short History of a Legal Idea," in Theodore Kovaleff, "Historical Perspective: An Introduction," in Theodore P. Kovaleff, Ed., *The Antitrust Impulse: Volume I: An Economic, Historical, and Legal Analysis*, (Armonk, NY: M.E. Sharpe, 1994), p. 95.
343. Ibid, p. 95.
344. Quotes from Eleanor M. Fox and Lawrence A Sullivan, "The Good and Bad Trust Dichotomy: A Short History of a Legal Idea," in Theodore Kovaleff, "Historical Perspective: An Introduction," in Theodore P. Kovaleff, Ed., *The Antitrust Impulse: Volume I: An Economic, Historical, and Legal Analysis*, (Armonk, NY: M.E. Sharpe, 1994), p. 96.
345. Peter R. Dickson and Philippa K. Wells, "The Dubious Origins of the Sherman Antitrust Act: The Mouse that Roared," *Journal of Public Policy and Marketing*, 20, No. 1 (Spring, 2001), p. 12.
346. Ibid, p. 12.
347. Ibid, p. 13.
348. Annie Mayhew, "The Sherman Act as Protective Reaction," *Journal of Economic Issues*, 24, No. 2 (June 1990), pp. 389-396, p. 389.
349. Based upon a story told by Robert A. Caro in *Master of the Senate: The Years of Lyndon Johnson*, (New York: Alfred A. Knopf, 2002), pp. ix-xii.
350. George Brown Tindall ad David E. Shi, America: A Narrative History, 6th edition, (New York: W.W. Norton, 2004), p.717
351. See http://topics.law.cornell.edu/constitution/amendmentxiv and http://caselaw.lp.findlaw.com/data/constitution/amendment15/ for copies of the 14th and 15th amendments.
352. See http://chnm.gmu.edu/courses/122/recon/civilrightsact.html for a copy of the 1875 act.
353. George Brown Tindall and David E. Shi, *America: A Narrative History, 6th edition*, (New York: W.W. Norton, 2004), p 724.
354. Ibid, pp. 724-725

355. Ronald L. F. Davis in "Creating Jim Crow: In-Depth Essay" traces the term "Jim Crowe" to a White, minstrel show performer, Thomas "Daddy" Rice who performed around 1830. "Rice created this character after seeing (while traveling in the South) a crippled, elderly Black man (or some say a young Black boy) dancing and singing a song ending with these chorus words: Weel about and turn about and do jis so, Eb'ry time I weel about I jump Jim Crowe... On the eve of the Civil War, the Jim Crow idea was one of many stereotypical images of Black inferiority in the popular culture of the day--along with Sambos, Coons, and Zip Dandies. The word Jim Crow became a racial slur synonymous with colored, or Negro in the vocabulary of many White people; and by the end of the century acts of racial discrimination toward Black people were often referred to as Jim Crow laws and practices." See http://jimcrowhistory.org/history/creating2.htm. Accessed 1/10/2010.

356. See Dubois' essay at http://www.theatlantic.com/past/docs/unbound/flashbks/Black/dubstriv.htm Accessed 08-19-10.

357. Quoted in Ronald L. F. Davis, "Surviving Jim Crow: In-Depth Essay," at http://jimcrowhistory.org/history/surviving1.htm and http://jimcrowhistory.org/history/surviving2.htm Accessed 06/03/2010

358. Read other poems by Dubar and read about his life at http://www.dunbarsite.org/default.asp

359. Quoted in Thomas E. Mann and Norman J. Ornstein, *The Broken Branch: How Congress is Failing America and How to Get it Back on Track,* (New York: Oxford Unversity Press, 2006), p. 225.

360. Ibid., p. 225.

361. Source; Ronald L. F. Davis, "Creating Jim Crow: In-Depth Essay," http://jimcrowhistory.org/history/creating2.htm and http://jimcrowhistory.org/history/resisting2.htm

362. Robert Mann, *The Walls of Jericho: Lyndon Johnson, Hubert Humphrey, Richard Russell and the Struggle of Civil Rights*, (New York: Harcourt, Brace and Company, 1996), p. 152.

363. Robert A. Caro, *Master of the Senate: The Years of Lyndon Johnson,* (New York: Alfred A. Knopf, 2002), p. 182
364. These quotes from Russell's 1938 speech are taken from Robert A. Caro, *Master of the Senate: The Years of Lyndon Johnson,* (New York: Alfred A. Knopf, 2002), pp 183-186.
365. Joseph C. Goulden, *The Best Years: 1945-1950,* (New York: Atheneum, 1976), pp. 353-354.
366. Ibid, p. 353.
367. Quoted in Robert A. Caro, *Master of the Senate: The Years of Lyndon Johnson*, (New York: Alfred A. Knopf, 2002), p. 697
368. You can read the entire article at http://www.emmetttillmurder.com/Look%201956.htm. Accessed 08-26-2010. Quotes in this story are from the text of the Look interview with Bryant and Milam.
369. Quoted in http://www.emmetttillmurder.com/Look%201956.htm
370. Robert A. Caro, *Master of the Senate: The Years of Lyndon Johnson*, (New York: Alfred A. Knopf, 2002), p. 702.
371. Ibid, pp. 707-708.
372. Quoted in Donnie Williams, *The Thunder of Angels: The Montgomery Bus Boycott and the People who Broke the Back of Jim Crow*, (Chicago: Lawrence Hill Books, 2006), pp. 47-48.
373. David Halberstam, *The Fifties*, (New York: Villard Books, 1993), pp. 541-542.
374. Quoted in Donnie Williams, *The Thunder of Angels: The Montgomery Bus Boycott and the People who Broke the Back of Jim Crow*, (Chicago: Lawrence Hill Books, 2006), p. 48
375. Donnie Williams, *The Thunder of Angels: The Montgomery Bus Boycott and the People who Broke the Back of Jim Crow,* (Chicago: Lawrence Hill Books, 2006), p. 51
376. David Halberstam, *The Fifties*, (New York: Villard Books, 1993), p. 543.
377. Donnie Williams, *The Thunder of Angels: The Montgomery Bus Boycott and the People who Broke the Back of Jim Crow*, (Chicago: Lawrence Hill Books, 2006), p. 52.
378. Ibid, p. 59.

379. David Halberstam, *The Fifties*, (New York: Villard Books, 1993), pp. 547-548.
380. Donnie Williams, *The Thunder of Angels: The Montgomery Bus Boycott and the People who Broke the Back of Jim Crow*, (Chicago: Lawrence Hill Books, 2006), p. 60.
381. William Manchester, *The Glory and the Dream: A Narrative History of America, 1932-1972*, (New York: Little Brown, 1973), p. 909.
382. The following are excellent sources for additional information about the Montgomery boycott. Donnie Williams, *The Thunder of Angels: The Montgomery Bus Boycott and the People who Broke the Back of Jim Crow*, (Chicago: Lawrence Hill Books, 2006),; David Halberstam, *The Fifties*, (New York: Villard Books, 1993), Chapter 36; Martin Luther King, Jr., *Stride Toward Freedom: The Montgomery Story*, (Boston: Beacon Press, 1958), and Robert Mann, *The Walls of Jericho: Lyndon Johnson, Hubert Humphrey, Richard Russell and the Struggle of Civil Rights*, (New York: Harcourt, Brace and Company, 1996), Chapter 8.
383. Quoted in Robert A. Caro, *Master of the Senate: The Years of Lyndon Johnson*, (New York: Alfred A. Knopf, 2002), p. 777.
384. Ibid, p. 777.
385. Ibid, p. 778.
386. Ibid, p. 774.
387. Ibid, p.xiii.
388. Ibid, p.109.
389. Ibid, p. 114.
390. Ibid, p. 114.
391. Ibid, p. 116.
392. Ibid, p. 161.
393. Ibid, p. 161.
394. Ibid, p. 162.
395. Ibid, p. 163.
396. Ibid, pp. 168.
397. Ibid, p. 168.
398. Ibid, p. 171.

399. Gilbert C. Fite, *Richard B. Russell, Jr: Senator from Georgia*, (Chapel Hill: University of North Carolina Press, 1991), p. 87.
400. Robert Mann, *The Walls of Jericho: Lyndon Johnson, Hubert Humphrey, Richard Russell and the Struggle of Civil Rights*, (New York: Harcourt, Brace and Company, 1996), p. 108.
401. Robert A. Caro, *Master of the Senate: The Years of Lyndon Johnson*, (New York: Alfred A. Knopf, 2002), pp 208.
402. Robert Mann, *The Walls of Jericho: Lyndon Johnson, Hubert Humphrey, Richard Russell and the Struggle of Civil Rights*, (New York: Harcourt, Brace and Company, 1996), p. 108.
403. Robert A. Caro, *Master of the Senate: The Years of Lyndon Johnson*, (New York: Alfred A. Knopf, 2002), p. 412.
404. Ibid, p. 784.
405. For a copy of the bill along with the majority and minority report, see 85th Congress, 1st Session, January-August 30, 1957, House Reports, Vol. 1: Miscellaneous Reports on Public Bills, I, Report No. 291, 23009—58 H. Rept. 85-1, vol. 1—88, (Washington, U.S. Government Printing Office, 1957).
406. See U.S. Congressional Record, Vol. 103, Part 8, June 21, 1957 to July 10, 1957, pp. 10771-10775 (Washington, D.C.: Government Printing Office, 1957) for the text of Russell's speech.
407. Ibid, p. 1074.
408. Quoted in Irwin Unger and Debi Unger, *LBJ: A Life*, (New York: John Wiley, 1999), p. 216.

INDEX